The Color of Guilt and Innocence is perhaps the most comprehensive and readable book on the topic of racial profiling by police. Steve Holbert and Lisa Rose have written a common sense, understandable, and down to earth criticism of race-based law enforcement. In even-measured tones, this book analyzes the legal and policy problems caused by racial profiling. This book should be read by all persons interested in this controversial issue.

—Kevin R. Johnson
Associate Dean for Academic Affairs
and Professor of Law and Chicana/o Studies
University of California at Davis

As a retired law enforcement officer with over twenty-three years of experience in policing and an equal amount of time in the struggle for the humane and decent treatment of People of Color, this book does what so many have missed. It is plain, clear, and to the point, which provides us with an understanding of how race is used in America's policing philosophy and practice.

—Ronald E. Hampton
Executive Director
National Black Police Association, Inc.

Racial profiling is a controversial and difficult issue challenging police agencies and minority communities in America today. Rose and Holbert's balanced and thoughtful presentation recognizes the legitimate concerns of all who are involved with or are affected by this practice. By dispelling myths and presenting factual data, this book assists the reader in comprehending the true nature of the problem. Additionally, Rose and Holbert's discussion of practical ideas for resolving this complicated predicament demands that both law enforcement agencies and civil rights advocates critically examine their current practices and, perhaps most importantly, work together to find solutions.

For anyone interested in this issue, this book is a comprehensive examination of racial profiling, giving credence to all who have a stake in making our society safe and free of bias and discrimination.

— Sue Stengel
Western States Counsel
Anti-Defamation League

I felt as though I should have paid someone tuition to learn what I did in this book, which speaks to its academic potential as a classroom manual. This book is exceptionally dense with technical information that probes behind the public debate of racial profiling and its relationship to law enforcement.

Very impressive, this book. Every sentence is a testament to the authors' hard work. Lisa Rose and Steve Holbert did incredible legal research to bring the world this piece of work. For years, I have always said that as an author on the subject I didn't have the resources nor were there enough days in a year's time to write "The Encyclopedia of Racial Profiling: Everything You Needed to Know." While my book provided a snap shot of racial profiling in a variety of social situations for young people to know what to do should they become a victim of it, Rose and Holbert provide a look at racial profiling from a technical point of view, diving into in-depth case law that shows why racial profiling exists on a social—and sometimes legal—manner. While my narratives were anecdotal evidence supported by documents that I was able to unearth in my research, Rose and Holbert have made use of a whole universe of documents that suggests that there was a pattern of legal maneuvering that allowed racial profiling to exist as it did in such notorious places as the New Jersey State Highways.

The Color of Guilt and Innocence is a must-read for getting a complete argument from both sides of the national debate. And while racial profiling was scrutinized in one context prior to September 11, 2001, the authors have effectively examined how it has changed to focus on people of Middle Eastern decent. Regardless of the context law enforcement personnel—or the world in general—view the practice of racial profiling, the authors do acknowledge the difference between rogue cops with racist attitudes and professional agents who understand the science of criminal psychology. A great book for law students and people studying in the police academy, this book examines racial profiling from every possible angle as it relates to law enforcement. From a technical point of view, Rose and Holbert managed to simplify this complicated issue and process it into a comprehensive reading manual for rank-and-file men and women on the front line of law enforcement. This book helps agency personnel understand both sides of the debate, and why it's such an important topic of the decade.

Considering that racial profiling has been an intricate part of American culture since its founding, I have to compliment Rose and Holbert for tackling this subject from yet a more clear and focused perspective. I have always said there are many books to be written on the subject of racial profiling. While I provided everyday students with ways to protect themselves against becoming a victim of it, and what to do if they become a victim, Rose and Holbert provide the professional student who works in law enforcement with ideas and points of discussion so that they are aware of the problem. I salute Rose and Holbert on their comprehensive work in providing a public manual guide for law enforcement officers in an effort to end racial profiling from within our national police departments.

—Kenneth Meeks
Author, *Driving While Black*
New York, New York

Rose and Holbert's study is a valuable step in resolving the debate over racial profiling that has polarized law enforcement and civil rights groups. Rather than seeking to place blame, as is so often the case, the authors defend both civil liberties and the position of the many police who are simply trying to enforce the law. There is a crucial difference, they remind us, between unlawful racial profiling and legitimate criminal profiling, notwithstanding the tendency of media and special interest groups to conflate these two distinct practices. Also important to recognize, they tell us, are the profound social forces that have caused the cycle of racism to periodically replay itself in one form or another from the days of slavery through the aftermath of September 11.

Law enforcement is just one of the many groups that have been caught up in these repeated surges of prejudice. Because of its visibility, however, law enforcement is well placed to lead a broader social crusade against prejudice and inequity. Rose and Holbert address this important goal through a number of recommendations that cut through the ideological impasse over racial profiling by effectively responding to the interests of both law enforcement and the public. History, they acknowledge, has shown the difficulty of regulating individual prejudices and opinions, which are often intractable to external pressures. Their useful counsel regarding education, training, data collection, and hiring provides a roadmap for curtailing outward demonstrations of racism by police agencies.

—Hubert Williams
President, Police Foundation
Washington, D.C.

the color of
GUILT &
INNOCENCE

RACIAL PROFILING AND POLICE PRACTICES IN AMERICA

STEVE HOLBERT & LISA ROSE

PAGE MARQUE PRESS
San Ramon, California

Published by Page Marque Press
P.O. Box 1672
San Ramon, CA 94583

Publisher's Cataloguing-in-Publication Data
Holbert, Steve.

    The color of guilt and innocence: racial profiling and police practices in America / Steve Holbert and Lisa Rose. –San Ramon, CA : Page Marque Press, 2004.

    p. ; cm.
    Includes index.
    ISBN: 0-9746640-0-6

       1. Racial profiling in law enforcement–United States. 2. Police–Complaints against–United States. 3. Police–United States–Attitudes. 4. Police administration–United States. I. Rose, Lisa. II. Title. III. Racial profiling and police practices in America.

HV7936.R3 H65 2004   2003113959
363.2/3/089/0973–dc22   0403

Book production and coordination by Jenkins Group, Inc.
Interior design by Royce Deans
Cover design by Chris Rhoads

Printed in the United States of America
08 07 06 05 04 • 5 4 3 2 1

We dedicate this book first, to our children, that they may always treasure the diversity and uniqueness found in all human beings.

Next, to our family and friends, for their love and support throughout this important project.

And finally, to our many colleagues around the country who continue to work tirelessly for the causes of equality and justice for all people.

Contents

⎯•◆•⎯

Preface

———◦•◦———

Racial profiling has emerged as undoubtedly one of the most controversial challenges facing America in the new millennium. Though the practice takes on many forms, it is most commonly associated with the act of directing law enforcement activities toward particular racial and ethnic groups based on the belief that these groups are more likely than others to commit certain crimes. It has been depicted by its critics as discriminatory, unconstitutional, and rampant and has been dubbed by many Americans as "DWB" or "Driving while Black or Brown." In law enforcement circles, the practice of pursuing a person on the basis of skin color is sometimes referred to as a "Black in Progress." These acronyms have also been applied to people of color who are flying, hailing a cab, or shopping. Despite its negative publicity, there are those who defend the practice of racial profiling, touting it as a necessary, legal means of eradicating crime and keeping America safe from its enemies. There are also those who believe the practice of racial profiling doesn't exist.

In an effort to understand better these often contentious and divergent views, we have openly challenged those on all sides of the issue to put their cards on the table. While navigating this rough and uncharted territory, we take an extensive look at the taboos surrounding racism and civil rights and the mounting challenges posed by the complex and private world of law enforcement. The result is a book unlike any other on the subject of racial profiling. This extensive work candidly uncovers the controversial views held by those on each side of the problem. It outlines current case law and legislation at the local, state, and federal levels and presents a new, viable approach that can serve as a springboard for new legislation, community education, and police officer training. Most important, it reveals how racial profiling's reach extends far beyond the precincts of law enforcement.

In order for the ideas in this book to facilitate effective change, they had to be challenged. Only through careful scrutiny of the variety of views on the topic and a balanced analysis of current information could we identify gaps and suggest viable solutions that could be acceptable to all sides. Anything less would merely perpetuate the distrust and stereotyping that have been inhibiting real progress.

It should be noted that by taking such a candid approach, we realize we risk including information and presenting arguments that may not be palatable to all sides. In fact, some of the arguments may incense you. We hope that they do. These emotions will spark action and change.

For measurable progress to result, all sides must be willing to initiate change, whether it is in the fundamental way we view race and racism or in the manner in which we interact with those who are different from us. Either way, this book will serve as a guide. This comprehensive publication is designed as a handbook for victims, a training manual for law enforcement, a reference for politicians and communities, and a source of valuable information for those who have yet to take a stand on the issue of racial profiling. It explores why the practice of racial profiling developed thousands of years ago and why it is still occurring today. It enables you to walk in the shoes of the victim and make life-and-death decisions behind the badge of a cop.

In addition to an in-depth look at the many sides of the issue, we have included references to several organizations and resources on this important topic. We hope these will serve as tools for all citizens to become involved in the fight to end racial profiling.

This approach will permit each group to take a step back in order to understand the underlying issues and come together to engage in constructive dialogue, strategize, and perhaps compromise so that one day, all sides will be able to claim victory.

Lisa Rose, Esq.[1]
Steve Holbert, J.D.[2]

(Endnotes)

1. Lisa Rose is a San Francisco Bay Area attorney whose work is presently exclusive to research in the areas of police and consumer racial profiling, civil rights, and police practices. She earned her JD degree from Lincoln Law School of San José. She resides in San Ramon, California.

2. Steve Holbert is a 30-year veteran of law enforcement and works at a San Francisco Bay Area Police Agency. In his law enforcement tenure, Steve has held positions in detectives, crime prevention, traffic, and SWAT. He is a court-recognized expert in traffic investigation and accident reconstruction. In addition to his diverse law enforcement background, Steve is a California POST-certified racial profiling instructor. Steve holds a bachelor's degree from Loma Linda University and a JD degree from Lincoln Law School of San José. Upon retirement from law enforcement, Steve will pursue a career as an attorney, legal consultant, and instructor in the areas of racial profiling and law enforcement reform. He resides in San Ramon, California.

PART I: How Did We Get Here?

CHAPTER ONE

———•••———

Racial Profiling and the Pretext Traffic Stop

Racial profiling, the practice of drawing conclusions about a person based upon factors such as race, ethnicity, or other characteristics, is illegal, immoral, and unconstitutional. Though it may be possible to regulate an outward deed that is illegal, it is much more difficult when a person's racially motivated thoughts are camouflaged by legitimate actions. Between these inequitable thoughts and outward acts lies a gray area that is most difficult, if not impossible, to regulate externally. As such, it is only when our society becomes so ethnically intermixed that racial profiling will meet its natural demise.

—Steve Holbert and Lisa Rose

Feeling a sense of relief, Officer Ken Swanson pushed open the heavy door at the back of the patrol division annex that led out into the secured compound where his black and white mobile observation platform, more commonly known as his police cruiser, was awaiting his arrival. He briefly closed his eyes and let the late afternoon breeze cool his face. He was now entering his domain: the freedom of movement, the excitement of the hunt, closing in for the capture, and the resulting trophy to reward his endeavors.

As Ken swung "One David Sixteen" out of the lot onto the dark asphalt roadway, the summer sun had nearly set. Lingering sunrays appeared as orange fingers weaving in and out of the darkening sky and obscured objects that only hours before had been clearly visible. This visual spectacle reminded Ken of the sensation he often experienced when scuba diving in an underwater lagoon, and resurrected a picture his training officer had painted for him years before: "Imagine yourself as a killer whale, the great black and white body of Orca, slicing through the cold Alaskan waters searching for prey. A creature whose cunning use of senses keenly and swiftly identifies those to be captured. Its decisive yet innocent means of approach leave even the most vigilant target unsuspecting and, finally, the strategic positioning to prevent escape."

Even though Ken had been with the department for 15 years, he still vividly remembered his first days as an officer. Despite his seniority, he never tired of the challenges and the dangers inherent in police work. His office was the street, where the independent nature of his work enabled him to use his experience and expertise to identify and capture the wrongdoer.

As night fell, Ken almost instinctively drove toward his favorite "fishing hole" as he alertly eyed other vehicles and pedestrians and negotiated his black and white in and around traffic. Chuckling to himself, he vividly recalled the locker room banter of a rookie officer complaining of making numerous stops with nothing to show for it except a couple of complaints to the sergeant. Ken knew all too well that merely chasing down mechanical violations would not yield a catch. Years of experience directed him to look for more subtle clues to identify those who might be engaging in criminal activity. Where the vehicle was coming from, for example, or the significance of the area it was in were often better indicators than randomly targeted, minor mechanical violations.

A suspicious-looking vehicle caught Ken's attention and interrupted his thoughts. "Bingo! I got one!" he shouted to himself. It had been the ole "dirt pile" look—that far-away gaze with which the driver intentionally focuses his attention on everything but the shiny black and white police cruiser. The driver's backward-facing baseball cap and the Hispanic radio station sticker displayed prominently in the rear window of the vehicle only helped to solidify Ken's determination that this car was a "keeper." With a rush of adrenalin and a keen alertness, he slipped his patrol car into the left turn lane and swung directly behind his target. The result was certain. Only the mechanics of the stop were yet to be determined.

"Ah, there it is," he thought. "Some illegal rearview mirror décor." Today, it was the air freshener on a string. As his patrol car neared, the driver changed lanes and exaggerated the use of his turn signal. In doing so, the red Christmas tree–shaped spice strip swung from side to side and resulted in a marked interference with the driver's view of the road. As trivial as it seemed, this was all Ken needed to make the stop.

The red and blue strobes of flashing light served as a menacing backdrop as Ken pulled the vehicle over and activated his bright white spotlight to illuminate the car's interior. He cautiously calculated his approach. Just slow enough to shake the calm of the violator but not slow enough to risk the destruction of evidence he was sure he would find.

As Ken positioned himself just to the rear of the driver's door, he instinctively illuminated the driver's hands with a direct stream of brilliant white light from the black metal flashlight he held tightly in his left hand. With a firm and decisive grasp, he pushed the switch forward just far enough to cause the light to come on but not enough to lock the switch in the "on" position. Officer safety was constantly on his mind. If the driver intended to harm him, it would more than likely involve the use of his hands.

With speed and precision, Ken illuminated the passenger and back seats, the floorboards, and then the rear compartment of the car. The edge of a brown paper bag just barely visible from under the front seat instinctively caught his glare. As the beam of his light slowly moved up the torso of the male seated behind the steering wheel, the face emerging from the darkness showed the distinctive characteristics of a Hispanic manual laborer. The rugged, weathered, and worn dark brown face, the jet black hair with matching untrimmed mustache, and the partially filled gold front tooth confirmed his suspicion that he was probably dealing with an unlicensed illegal. The driver's eyes, the very passageway to his soul, had been the final giveaway.

Ken edged closer to the driver's door as his distinctive, low voice rang out with a friendly "Good evening, sir. May I see your driver's license?" There was no immediate response or acknowledgement of any kind, no turn of the head, no release of the hands from the tightly gripped steering wheel, and no verbal response to the simple question. This was going to be an easy arrest. Ken repositioned himself slightly and directed the beam of his flashlight toward the lower portion of the driver's nonresponsive face. As the driver's head rotated toward him, he strategically lowered the beam of light to illuminate the eyes of this person who was only beginning to acknowledge his presence.

As their eyes met, any doubt in Ken's mind was quickly laid to rest. All was not right with the world; in fact, something was drastically wrong. The deep black of the pupils and their high-gloss, watery appearance accentuated by a backdrop of tiny rivers of red offered him the confirmation he needed. There was only one piece of the puzzle missing, concealed by the breeze that was preventing any distinguishable odor from escaping the confines of the car.

Ken's right hand momentarily left its position near his holstered Barretta 92F to depress the transmit key on his lapel mic to summon the assistance of a backup unit. As he relayed his request, there was hardly a discernable pause between his call to dispatch and his second request for a driver's license.

Ken recognized that all that remained were the formalities. Further detention had been justified. Entry into the court-protected, inner sanctuary of the vehicle was imminent. Closure was near.

"I don't have one" muttered in better-than-expected English caught him slightly off guard. He was more accustomed to the response "No comprende," which was usually a predictable response by most illegals, even those who spoke fluent English.

"No license, huh? Is that because it's suspended or because you're here illegally and can't get one?" Before the driver could respond, Ken continued. "By the way, why don't you hand me that bottle of beer in the brown paper bag." Analogous to the strategy of an experienced poker player, he had transformed some of his best tactics into tried-and-true methods for luring others into believing he knew more than he actually did. As the driver began to lean forward to reach for the bag, Ken instinctively extended his arm through the open window and placed his hand on the driver's shoulder. Simultaneously, Ken assured the driver: "No, I'll get it. How about you just hopping out of the car, partner." There was no way he was going to let this person reach under the seat for anything. He didn't need to. The driver's mere movement toward the bag provided him with the admission of guilt he had hoped for.

The driver, still unidentified, slowly exited the vehicle. Ken stepped back slightly and allowed him room to extend his body to a full standing position. Safety wasn't the only reason he was making detailed observations as the driver exited the car. Any loss of balance, disorientation, or even the slightest use of the car door for support would nicely translate into probable cause for an arrest. He was making his case for a "duce driver," a term in use long before Ken entered police work. It had been the last number in the vehicle code section for drunk driving, probably back before radio cars, even before his grandfather had been a deputy sheriff in Arizona. He liked to believe cop work was still cop work, but deep down, he knew it was nothing like the stories his grandfather had told him as a child or even the ones his field training officer had often embellished as he became indoctrinated into the brotherhood.

Out of the corner of his eye, Ken saw the headlights of a vehicle approaching. The white lights abruptly went out and were replaced by the softer yellow glow of parking lights. As the vehicle glided silently to the curb, he felt a sense of added confidence as he saw the driver's door open to reveal the reflective silver shield of the police department. Backup had arrived in the form of John Anderson, 6' 2", 280 pounds, and an ex-varsity football player. John and Ken went way back. They were the best of friends. They made it a habit to cover each other as often as possible. There were no two other officers anywhere who worked as well together. It took only a nod or a glance for one to communicate his desires to the other. But what Ken liked most about John was his wonderful sense of humor. This quality made the rigors of the job a little more tolerable.

As the three met on the sidewalk, the breeze had shifted slightly and allowed the distinctive and fermented odor of beer and the stale, smoky stench of a tobacco to permeate the air. Ken's third request for identification was met once again with a confused stare. John moved closer and positioned himself just to the right rear of the driver as he patted with his open left hand the buttocks area of the driver's faded blue jeans, up to the tooled brown leather belt held together by a large silver cowboy buckle. His black, gloved fingers invaded the right rear pocket, one passing on each side of a rectangular flat object easily recognizable as a wallet.

"Imagine that! The feller does have a wallet!" said John. "How much do you want to bet he has no license, a fake immigration card, and 22 names all beginning with José or Juan?" As Ken took the wallet from John's grasp, he knew John was probably right. This person met the stereotypical profile of most unlicensed and illegal Hispanics. Even without completing the required tests, Ken knew the outcome.

The black wallet was nearly empty, except for a couple of pieces of off-white paper that had obviously been torn from a much larger sheet. The printing was in pencil, scrawled in an early elementary school fashion with street names spelled incorrectly. The papers had been folded many times, as was evident by the fragile condition of each. As Ken unfolded the wallet fully, he found that it was absent any money. Deep in an inner crevice, however, he found the flea market immigration card, pressed tightly to its counterpart, the off-colored social security card. Without even adjusting his gaze, Ken muttered: "Bet these aren't real. Maybe 10 bucks each, huh?"

As Ken raised the immigration card with his left hand so that it intercepted the beam from his flashlight, he could read the name of Juan Hernandez Garcia. This was going to be the fifth Hispanic drunk driver he had arrested this week. Not that race had anything to do with it. It meant something only to those ticket counters who believed profiling could be determined by the number of stops and the race of the person detained.

"Sure would make it a lot easier if this guy was white," Ken muttered as he prepared to administer a series of balancing tests.

Ken had never considered himself a racist or, for that matter, one who even cared what color a person's skin was. The only colors that mattered to him were "black and white"—those who commit crimes and those who don't. Like any successful hunter, he knew and used the weaknesses of his prey to determine his strategy for capture. Social and economic factors coupled with addictions and customs merely helped him determine which people he wished to pursue. As any sportsman knows, the difference between the legitimate and the protected often cannot be determined until a personal observation is made. As with this stop, experience coupled with "gut instincts" may not always result in an accurate, prophetic prediction of things to come, but they sure helped to improve the odds.

Though the ultimate arrest and conviction of Mr. Garcia, an illegal alien, were consistent with Ken's suspicions, the lessons we can learn from this encounter go far beyond Mr. Garcia's guilt or innocence.

As this account clearly illustrates, racial profiling is a complicated phenomenon. Not only is it difficult to define but it's also difficult to detect when shrouded behind a traffic stop that is legitimate in every other way. Some would argue that Officer Swanson was using the race of the suspect as his sole motivation for the vehicle stop. Others might disagree. As with most racial profiling allegations, we will never know for sure. Absent the ability to delve into Officer Swanson's thought process at the point he decided to stop the vehicle, any subsequent allegation of racial profiling will remain just that. Unless a clear link can be established between the officer's mental mindset (racial bias) and the resulting act, racial profiling, as it presently stands under the law, has not occurred.

The ability to establish this clear link often hinges on that which can be proven by direct evidence and that which is merely circumstantial. When direct evidence is available that clearly reveals the officer's true motives, identifying whether racial profiling has occurred is an easy task. Absent a confession or statement revealing the officer's true mindset, however, proof of racial profiling is elusive, even though the individual circumstances may suggest a racial motivation. As long as the resulting act is legal, no amount of circumstantial evidence will definitively establish whether the legal act was motivated by the illegal use of a race-based profile. As most prosecutors will tell you, this kind of smoking gun is rare when allegations of racial profiling surface, yet it is this unknown linchpin that often draws the dividing line between law enforcement and the community.

Regardless of how you view the above example, it undoubtedly poses some important questions about the practice of racial profiling and how society can work toward eradicating so elusive a problem. It also illustrates how difficult it is for one to define and identify an act of racial profiling when in many cases, it may fall into a gray area and be defended as good, proactive police work.

As we attempt to balance some of these conflicting variables, let's look back to the above example. Were the tactics Officer Swanson used to identify the potential suspect legitimate? Were his observations of the Hispanic radio station sticker, the location the vehicle was coming from, and the rearview mirror décor good police work or racial profiling? Did the end justify the means? In other words, did the confirmation of Officer Swanson's instincts about the suspect driving while intoxicated tip the scales in the direction of making Officer Swanson's stop legitimate and lawful? If, in fact, Mr. Garcia was an illegal alien, should he have been entitled to the same constitutional safeguards as a U.S. citizen?

Many of Officer Swanson's observations were related to the vehicle the suspect was driving. In fact, there was no indication the officer was aware of the suspect's race prior to the stop. If an officer's suspicion is based on the mere *appearance* of a vehicle, has some form of racial profiling occurred? What if the officer's suspicions are heightened by the socioeconomic class of the suspect? Is it appropriate or lawful for an officer to consider a person's class when determining whether to initiate a citizen contact? What about when race becomes an inadvertent by-product of these enforcement tactics?

Officers Swanson and Anderson were both veteran officers who, in this instance, had many of their stereotypes confirmed in their encounter with Mr. Garcia. During the encounter, many of these stereotypes were vocalized in the presence of the suspect. Did any portion of their exchange raise a code of silence dilemma, or, in other words, should either officer have reported the comments made by their fellow officer to a superior? These are just a few of the questions we will explore as we examine the complicated practice of racial profiling and its effects on both law enforcement and the community.

Though some instances of racial profiling may be clear cut, the majority are not. As such, racial profiling, the practice of drawing conclusions about a person on the basis of skin color, has become one of the most emotionally charged topics of this decade. The basic premise is not new; rather, it has historically evolved under the guise of many other labels: prejudice, discrimination, racial bias, and segregation. Racial profiling takes on many forms in our society and is inevitable given the tremendous racial, ethnic, and cultural diversity in our country. Regardless of its widespread practice, one of its most publicized applications is its use in the profession of law enforcement. In fact, a 1999 Gallup Poll study neutrally defined racial profiling as the practice by which police officers target "certain racial or ethnic groups because the officers believe that these groups are more likely than others to commit certain types of crimes."[1] Though some defend this practice as a legitimate crime-fighting tactic, others disagree. For many minorities, racial profiling remains nothing short of unjustified discrimination by law enforcement aimed at violating numerous rights guaranteed them under the U.S. Constitution.

When we talk about racial profiling, it is important to remember that its use in the context of law enforcement is only one small part of the larger picture. Though its significance as it relates to the field of law enforcement cannot be underestimated, it is important to note that racial profiling and its pernicious counterparts were in force long before the invention of the automobile.

History has taught us that this practice is not limited to the color of a person's skin nor his or her activities on the roadways. Racial profiling occurs in all facets of life, from seeking an education to securing employment. It can encompass physical, psychological, and behavioral characteristics. It can happen while hailing a cab, applying for a job, shopping in a mall, or traveling on an airplane. It is not confined to those of African American heritage. If you are Asian, Hispanic, Middle Eastern, Russian, or any other race that has ever been labeled a "minority," you probably believe you have been the victim of racial profiling at one time or another.

In some instances, the victimization is obvious and easily detectable. Whether manifested through open bigotry directed toward a particular group or, in the more extreme cases, through violent hate crimes, society generally does not tolerate these blatant forms of racism. But because we are a culture that prides itself on the freedom to speak uncensored, we are more willing to tolerate—and even sometimes to participate in—the more subtle forms of racism. We often do not stand up to seemingly harmless comments or racial jokes and slurs, particularly when they are directed at someone else. But when racial profiling occurs in one of the most visible professions in the nation, we demand an instant solution and look to law enforcement to eradicate a problem that society has been unable to solve for more than 200 years.

The past several decades have brought an acute awareness of the issues surrounding racial injustice, with police power remaining fertile ground for discrimination to occur. Racial profiling has been criticized by some as part of a national trend toward biased policing. Others have defined its scope more narrowly as it relates to the pretext traffic stop—the practice of stopping a driver for a minor traffic violation in order for the officer to carry out his or her primary objective, searching for evidence of a greater offense for which the officer lacked probable cause to conduct the stop. Some have even suggested that racial profiling may be nothing more than a natural byproduct of ticket and arrest quotas, which may have the unintended effect of encouraging such practices. Whichever the true motive, one thing remains certain: when racial profiling and pretext traffic stops are unjustifiably used as the sole crime-fighting tactic by law enforcement, officers have a motive (skin color) and a means (police officer discretion) to stop and detain a citizen on the hope that criminal activity will be uncovered. Regardless of whether the officer's hunch is confirmed, both sides walk away losers.

The adversarial relationship between the police and the community that these sorts of enforcement tactics promote is almost inevitable given the enormous amount of discretion given to each individual officer to stop, detain, frisk, and interview, on the basis of an officer's own interpretation—or misinterpretation—of a set of observations. If the suspect is a minority, race becomes an unavoidable factor, and racial profiling is immediately suspected.

Before the terror attacks of September 11, 2001, on the Pentagon and the World Trade Center, the attention to this problem was primarily focused on pretext traffic stops directed toward young African American and Hispanic men. But as Arabs and Middle Easterners were detained for questioning about potential terrorist affiliations or pertinent intelligence information, the larger counterpart of racial profiling resurfaced in the national headlines and forever changed the definition of "us" versus "them." Tensions between the United States and Middle Easterners further escalated during the U.S.-led invasion into Iraq in 2003.

In the course of these events, law enforcement was once again thrown into the forefront of this civil rights debate and was forced to choose between racial profiling and national security. While some minorities complained of being unjustifiably detained and questioned because of skin color, race, or religious affiliations, those not affected openly criticized law enforcement's unwillingness to engage in racial profiling prior to the deadly attacks.

Likewise, the expansion of these investigatory practices prompted both citizens and scholars to question the validity of the constitutional safeguards guaranteed to American citizens and foreigners alike, as well as to examine further the legal and political ramifications of racial profiling in a free society. These debates quickly gained political fervor, with some questioning whether law enforcement's fear of racial profiling accusations circumvented national security and caused government agencies to miss or ignore warning signs that ultimately allowed would-be hijackers to live in America undetected while training to carry out the largest and most deadly terrorist attack ever perpetrated on American soil. Any doubts about whether racial profiling was occurring quickly disappeared when law enforcement at all levels joined forces in a frantic search for foreign terrorists living among us.

Throughout the aftermath of this tragedy, reports of racial profiling continued to make national headlines and linked such practices to police corruption and scandal. Images deluged the media and often ran side by side with stories of heroic law enforcement and fire department personnel working selflessly at Ground Zero to rescue human beings of every race and creed. The only colors of any significance to these dedicated heroes were red, white, and blue. This new war left many Americans wondering why our country was singled out and attacked simply because of our way of life and what we represent. It also posed the question of whether this very public campaign to stop and detain those with certain ethnic or religious affiliations was legal under the Constitution.

Whether it's hidden under the guise of crime prevention or national security, one need not look far to discover that racial profiling in law enforcement is illegal and has been for a long time. Many states have outlawed this practice by statute, and most police agencies have policies in place that prohibit such activity. Even the federal government has issued guidelines that bar federal law enforcement agents from using race or ethnicity in routine investigations.

On a national level, the Fourth and Fourteenth Amendments of the U.S. Constitution impose specific obligations on law enforcement concerning detentions, searches and seizures, and the equal treatment of its citizens.

Specifically, the Fourth Amendment[2] requires that police officers have probable cause or, at the very least, reasonable suspicion to stop an individual they believe may be involved in criminal activity, a premise that has been reaffirmed by courts in landmark cases such as *Terry v. Ohio*.[3] The U.S. Supreme Court has also ruled that as long as the traffic stop is for a legitimate traffic violation, no matter how minor, it is not unconstitutional just because the real motive for the stop is to investigate evidence of criminal activity.[4] The Fourth Amendment also describes unreasonable searches and seizures and requires that law enforcement have reasonable suspicion or probable cause to search either a person or a vehicle.

Likewise, the Fourteenth Amendment[5] sets forth specific guidelines designed to protect citizens from unjust treatment by the government. These guidelines require that all government officials and law enforcement personnel conduct their business without regard to race or any other protected class. In other words, it would be deemed unconstitutional for law enforcement to use race as the primary factor for pursuing a suspect unless the person's race was one part of a description provided to aid in the identification of a potential suspect. In this same regard, the amendment provides that it is unconstitutional for the government and law enforcement personnel to direct enforcement efforts on a particular ethnic group while disregarding similar unlawful conduct by other groups.

Though enforcement practices motivated by skin color have been deemed unconstitutional for a long time, in reality, some government and law enforcement agencies still use such practices. Perhaps this is due in part to case law in the area empowering law enforcement to engage in pretext stops as long as the officer can articulate some legitimate reason for the stop, usually a vehicle code violation. Many view these parameters set forth by the courts as a means for framing the scope of police officer discretion. Some legal scholars, however, voice concern that the unintended effects of these constitutional interpretations have left these public safeguards with little bite to prevent and deter misdirected law enforcement tactics.

Consistent with 1999 Gallup Poll statistics,[6] public perception is that these pretext traffic stops, criticized by some as encouraging racial profiling, are commonly targeted at minority drivers. This practice leads many to wonder whether skin color is now considered evidence of a crime or, more recently, evidence of terrorist activities or affiliations.

Particularly during these vulnerable times, the enormity of the underlying problem of racism becomes painfully apparent and shakes the very foundation upon which our nation is built. We are reminded that America is a complex place to live. We want freedoms, but we don't want people to come here and use these freedoms to harm us. We want law enforcement to protect us from harm without stepping over the line, but we quickly see that the line is often different for each one of us depending on our race, color, or religion.

This difficult balancing act has positioned citizens and law enforcement at two extremes as far apart as the labels they supposedly represent: law enforcement as "racists" and civil rights organizations as "radicals." Although some progress has been made toward mending the differences between these two groups, it is more often a case of one step forward, two steps back as current events unfold. Unfortunately, many of the proposals to date are not designed to bring about change; instead, they focus on establishing blame in order to assert that racial profiling is or is not occurring. Naturally, the blame brings defensiveness and results in further polarization of the two groups. This concept is probably best illustrated in the following race-neutral scenario. A statement is made: "You're a bad driver because you're a woman." Not many women would be eager to engage in a discussion about their driving ability after hearing this accusation. The immediate reaction is to defend the "...because you're a woman." This is all that is heard, and polarization will prevent either side from addressing the real issue, whether this person really is a bad driver. The same can be said for racial labels. Often, the vigorous fight to defend racist accusations masks the real issues.

In order for any long-term solution to result, we must consider some fundamental principles. First, citizens must be able to trust law enforcement and have an effective remedy when their rights are violated. In order for this to occur, law enforcement officers must receive the requisite training and equipment to do their jobs safely and effectively. These officers must also have an appropriate forum for defending their rights when falsely accused of misconduct while acting in the course and scope of their duties.

Although these basic premises should remain at the forefront of any path toward change, they are far from all encompassing. It would be remiss to move forward without first understanding and repairing the damage that has historically fostered the distrust and hate between law enforcement and society. In order to do this, we recognized the need to develop a new approach that would maximize the chances of creating an effective solution. To end the polarization between civil rights groups and law enforcement, the discussion must first be moved out of the racism arena and analyzed from a broader perspective. This step will open the lines of productive communication by refocusing the dialogue away from the idea that it's wrong for a person to be unjustifiably stopped or judged because they are *black* or *brown* and toward the notion of why it is wrong that they are stopped because they are a *person*. When racism is discussed as one component of the broader problem, both parties can begin negotiating on neutral ground absent the need for defensive stances that inevitably inhibit real progress.

Once this nonadversarial forum is established, both sides can come together as equal partners to engage in a candid discussion about racism. It is easy to point the finger at another person and label him or her a racist. The fact is that we all have racist tendencies regardless of whether our skin is white, black, or brown. Whether an officer on the street or an outspoken civil rights leader, all of us have the *human* tendency to fear those who are different from ourselves.

To control this fear, we must each understand its source within ourselves. We can begin this process by expressing a willingness to walk in the other person's shoes, specifically, by looking back through our own nation's history to uncover the events that have shaped our modern attitudes about race. By exploring why we feel the way we do about other ethnicities, we can uncover the truth about racial labels and stereotypes and how they correlate with the diverse socioeconomic patterns and beliefs within America. This process will empower the *human* race to conquer its fears of those who are different and enhance appreciation of these differences as valuable qualities that make us all unique.

Throughout this process, we must also understand law enforcement's role in society as both a paramilitary organization and a crime-fighting entity. With the unprecedented challenges facing the nation, is it realistic, or even wise, to expect that these agencies protect us from crime, drugs, violence, and terrorism while at the same time work scrupulously to preserve the constitutional safeguards guaranteed to all Americans more than 200 years ago? With the unique and complex challenges facing our world, is it possible for these objectives to exist simultaneously?

Regardless of how we answer these questions, the fact remains that charges of racial profiling are difficult to prove. One key reason is that the acts suspected of being the result of racial profiling and complained about by alleged victims do not usually result in a ticket or arrest. The person is stopped, detained, questioned, and then let go. Though these investigatory stops are commonplace and legal, they fail both the victim and the officer in that they do not generate any kind of official report. Whether the stop is legitimate or suspect, it becomes difficult to quantify or investigate when the sole record of the detention revolves around an individual's account of what happened. Likewise, the lack of documentation makes it nearly impossible to identify which officers may be conducting questionable stops, particularly in larger police organizations. With this kind of system in place, even the most lawful stops become the target of racial profiling accusations and prompt officers to do less to avoid being labeled racist.

Surprisingly, accusations of racism are directed not only at Caucasian officers. Though one might suspect that minority officers are less likely to engage in race-based crime enforcement, surveys indicate that an officer's race does not have a lot to do with his or her tendency to engage in illegal stops and searches. With this being the case, it becomes apparent that for the mutual protection of both the citizens and the officers, law enforcement must start by keeping better records on who is being stopped and why.

Though the concept of data collection will be discussed later in more detail, it is important to note here that although this idea may seem good in theory, many remain skeptical. Despite its critics, voluntary and mandatory data collection have served as the basis for state and national legislation and have often prompted heated debates about whether these efforts would be effective in eradicating racial profiling. Departments that are already engaged in voluntary data collection are often looked upon with distrust when racial profiling statistics are released to the public. Some communities have found the distrust well placed when reports generated by some organizations under these data collection plans have been deemed untrustworthy, as they were in New Jersey, where officers were indicted for falsifying activity logs in an effort to conceal their racially motivated activities. Some in law enforcement have also criticized these efforts and doubt whether collecting data will be an effective tool to identify the very small percentage of officers who may be engaging in biased police work.

Whether or not data collection is implemented, measurable change will be impossible to achieve without making modifications throughout the entire system. One of the most recent examples of a failed system occurred in a mid-sized California city where a video surfaced of a young black man being punched in the face and thrown up against a police car during a routine investigatory stop. What followed was public outcry, a grand jury investigation, indictments, and heightened animosity between the citizens and the police. The jury deliberating the case ultimately could not reach a verdict, and the judge declared a hung jury.

Understandably, such high-profile incidents cause the police, prosecutors, and the public to focus a majority of their attention on the act itself rather than to look to the racism within both the community and justice system that has permitted this kind of practice to flourish. Regardless of where these incidents take place, one can often point to several commonalities among them. Other police officers and citizens stand by while these very public acts are occurring. There are dispatchers, supervisors, lieutenants, and captains that know this kind of activity has occurred before. The suspicions of judges, prosecutors, defense attorneys, and jurors may have been aroused in similar incidents. At the end of the day, however, the problem becomes someone else's. Even after such incidents are caught on videotape, some officers may choose to falsify reports and give false testimony about the suspect's actions in attempts to justify the violence rather than come forward to reveal the real criminals. These subversive acts expand the scope of victims in these incidents from the individual who is allegedly mistreated by the police to the thousands of officers across the country who work hard to do their jobs within the confines of the law.

The fact remains that without incontrovertible evidence, these kinds of crimes continue to go unreported and unpunished. Similar occurrences generally do not seem to pose a problem before videotape evidence surfaces. Whether future civil rights violations will be a problem within these communities rests largely on the system itself.

Much of this uncertainty depends on whether the racism within these communities is allowed to flourish. If all we take away from these incidents is an opinion on who is to blame, they will happen again. The system of racism is dependent on many things, two of which are silence and ignorance. As a society, we often choose to ignore racist slurs and practices unless they pose a direct personal threat. Instead, the taboo topic of race must be addressed in our homes, schools, businesses, churches, and community groups in a format conducive to discussion among people of all ages and ethnicities.

In this vein, it is essential that race discussions become a primary objective in the law enforcement community, specifically in police officer training. Cultural sensitivity and diversity training must be implemented for all police personnel, including the command staff, throughout their years of service. The importance of comprehensive training for administrators and line officers cannot be underestimated. It is theorized that if the misuse of stereotypes and prejudices is dealt with at the academy level and reinforced throughout an officer's career, it will set a new standard within the law enforcement profession. Likewise, by acknowledging and exploring our underlying fears of those who are different, we can work to eradicate the stereotypes and prejudices that hold us hostage in our day-to-day endeavors. Above all, this new standard within law enforcement may ultimately prove to be a first step toward a new standard within humanity.

(Endnotes)

1. "The Gallup Poll. Gallup Poll Social Audit on Black/White Relations in the U.S.," (December 9, 1999), Gallup Organization, Princeton.

2. Fourth Amendment of the United States Constitution: "The right of the people to be secure in their persons, houses, papers and affects against unreasonable searches and seizures, shall not be violated and no warrant shall issue but upon probable cause supported by oath or affirmation and particularly describing the place to be searched and the persons or things to be seized."

3. *Terry v. Ohio*, 392 U.S. 1 (1968).

4. *Whren v. United States*, 116 S.Ct. 1769 (1996).

5. Fourteenth Amendment of the United States Constitution: "All persons born or naturalized in the United States, and subject to the jurisdiction thereof, are citizens of the United States and of the state wherein they reside. No state shall make or enforce any law which shall abridge the privileges or immunities of citizens of the United States; nor shall any state deprive any person of life, liberty, or property, without due process of law; nor deny to any person within its jurisdiction the equal protection of the laws."

6. "The Gallup Poll. Gallup Poll Social Audit on Black/White Relations in the U.S.," Gallup Organization, Princeton (December 9, 1999).

CHAPTER TWO

————◆·◆————

Monsters in the Closet

"I have had a great many troubles, but most of them never happened."

> —Mark Twain,
> nineteenth and early twentieth century
> American author

Lisa had a very uneasy feeling the moment she and her family stepped off the cable car into a dark and unfamiliar San Francisco neighborhood. The dimly lit streetlights illuminated the slow movement of fog and mist enveloping the street. Despite her husband's reassurances that they were just a few blocks from where they should be, she could not ignore the anxious feeling she had as she grabbed her daughter's hand tighter and pulled her coat over her purse. Her feelings of anxiety turned to unrelenting terror one block later when they passed three homeless men sitting in front of a closed storefront in a virtually empty, industrial part of town. Out of the corner of her eye, she saw one of the men stand up. He started to yell something in their direction, but the wild and angry tone of his voice compelled them to walk faster rather than turn around to acknowledge him. When she was sure they had escaped his view, she turned her head to the side for a brief respite from the cold night air and the icy mist that was stinging her face. As her eyes glanced back over their trail of footprints on the wet street, she noticed a dark figure rapidly following them about a block and a half away. Their focus immediately shifted from that of holiday shoppers and tourists to prey as they searched for every possible avenue of escape from imminent danger.

In that brief moment, time seemed to stop, and her mind replayed a recent news report warning of a man in his 20s with a dark complexion who had been robbing tourists. She simultaneously flashed back to a newspaper article recounting the same story warning tourists that this man was becoming more and more aggressive and reminding them to be wary of their surroundings at night.

She looked back again at this man who was quickly gaining ground. As he approached closer, she began to hear the splash of his shoes on the wet sidewalk. He wore a dark-hooded, heavy coat and dark gloves, similar to that of many homeless men on the San Francisco streets. The shadows cast from the dim lights overhead made it difficult to see whether he fit the description of the man wanted by the police. She tried to discern whether this man looked familiar, but the jacket hood pulled around his face made it impossible to tell whether it was the same person who had been yelling at them a few blocks earlier.

As she looked over her shoulder again, she could see the darkness of his skin and the detail of something in his right hand. She began to feel as though time had stopped. She instantly became keenly aware of every building and every street sign they passed. Despite the icy air, her skin began to tingle from the clammy sweat on her neck and back. She could hear her heart beat faster with every step they took. They looked around for a safe refuge, but the streets were dark and deserted, and they were still a few blocks from their destination.

She did not break from this state of paralyzing fear until her daughter began pulling her in the opposite direction, pointing to the wet sidewalk—toward the man who was now less than a block behind them. Their hurried pace had caused their daughter to drop the candy cane she had been given by the cable car conductor a few moments earlier. As her husband picked up the little girl and increased their stride, Lisa instinctively grabbed for her cell phone and dialed 9-1. She paused before dialing the final number, not knowing what she intended to tell the dispatcher who would answer her call.

"Hello. We are in grave danger! A man with dark skin is walking on the sidewalk behind us. Please send help!"

She instantly stopped herself. She was not prejudiced. She was merely reacting to probabilities. She did not want to be sucked in to the whole racial profiling thing, yet she recognized that this was not the time to be risking her family's life to make a point. For a brief instant, a moment of rational thought came over her. Maybe this man wasn't following them after all. Maybe this wasn't the same man who had been reported in the news. The night was so dark it was impossible to tell whether he fit the description of the suspect wanted by the police. All she could see was a dark face. She tried to remind herself that every dark-skinned man walking down the street isn't a criminal, but as she looked back and saw the man rushing faster toward them, rational judgment went right out the window. She could not get past the overwhelming fear that she felt when she saw this stranger's face.

Her thoughts were soon interrupted by the sound of traffic and the voices of other tourists walking along Fisherman's Wharf. No sooner than she began to feel relieved, Lisa felt a large hand press down on her shoulder. She turned around swiftly with her hands clenched, only to see the gentle, worn face of a man in his 50s.

"Excuse me ma'am, I think you may have left this package on the seat in the cable car. Is it yours?"

She looked down to the outstretched hand of the cable car worker offering the return of a small bag of stickers their daughter had picked out at a store earlier that evening.

As she tried to hide the trembling in her voice, she thanked the man for bringing them the bag. But underneath her emerging wave of relief, she felt an overwhelming sense of guilt and embarrassment. She was torn between walking away, pretending this never happened and offering this man an apology for misjudging him. She tried to look into his eyes to see whether they would reveal any hint of disdain. Maybe he didn't even notice. Or maybe it wasn't the first time. Her awkward hesitation was interrupted with a "Happy Holidays," as the man disappeared back up the deserted street.

To say that this experience overshadowed the merriment of her family's holiday shopping trip is probably an understatement. Since that December evening, she has walked down that foggy San Francisco street a hundred times in her mind wondering what she should have done differently. Although the entire episode lasted fewer than 10 minutes, it left her with many unanswered questions about race and her own prejudices that have occupied her thoughts ever since.

Her experience in the city instantly brought back a familiar fear that she had not felt so intensely since she was four years old. She vividly remembers waking up in the middle of the night and calling for her father, certain that there was a monster hiding in her room and watching her sleep through the wood slats in the closet door. When her father came in and turned on the lights, he opened the closet door and asked her what the monster looked like. She told him that she didn't know. The monster had no face. The fear was so real at the time her heart still begins to pound when she thinks of it today, even though she knows there is no such thing as monsters. After her experience in the city, she began to question whether the irrational fear of monsters conjured up in the mind of a four-year-old was so different from the "monsters in the closet" we perceive as adults, the only difference being that the "monsters" we see as adults have a face and the face is of those who are different or those whose skin color is darker than our own.

Regardless of our powerful instincts that segregate people by outward appearance, our rational thought process tells us that apart from our ethnicity, we all belong to one human race. Though modern science assures us that there are no internal differences or superiorities among us, we as a human species continue to use our most basic and primitive instincts and survival mechanisms to segregate people by skin color. As politically and socially incorrect as this practice has become, we all do it. We do it regardless of the color of our own skin. We may do it privately or to different degrees, but we all do it, and we do it every day. Some of us may do it quite subtly without even realizing it. We do it when we are driving down the road and look to see the skin color of the person who cut us off. We do it when we clutch our purse or wallet tighter in an elevator when there is someone standing next to us with skin color that is different from our own. Moreover, as Lisa learned firsthand, we do it when someone who is unfamiliar intrudes on an area around us that we consider our personal territory or "safety zone." Others may do it more flagrantly and may engage in obvious forms of racism such as the use of racial epithets or in actions analogous to hate crimes.

When racial profiling is examined in the context of law enforcement, it would be far too simplistic to suggest that this practice is limited to prejudiced cops or police corruption. Regardless of one's profession, education, class, or creed, prejudices will come out at times when we are the most vulnerable and will override rational thought and the ability to sort out myths and stereotypes from logic. It would be both simplistic and erroneous to suggest that racial profiling is the natural result of racism and prejudice. Rather, racial profiling is more about our human response to an instinctual and primitive fear buried deep in each one of us.

With this oversimplified definition of racial profiling aside, what exactly is it? It's what one young man reported feeling when he heard his parents talking about the black family that moved in down the street when he was five years old. It's about how another chose her friends in school. It's about watching TV sitcoms in the 1960s and '70s and making unconscious distinctions between different races and ethnicities. It's about the neighborhoods some may choose to live in and those they don't. It's about where one might drive after dark and where others won't even venture during the day. It's about whether a businessperson feels safe boarding an airplane with a young, Middle Eastern man. It's about whether we choose to lock our doors or roll down our windows when we drive down an unfamiliar street. It's about the lessons Lisa unwittingly taught her own child when she made her leave her candy cane on the ground to escape the threat of a dark-skinned man. It's about how we feel every day when we confront one of our most suppressed fears: someone who is different from ourselves.

Fear and Racism

In courses on racial profiling, we often ask the students a very simple question, "What is the underlying cause of racism?" "Prejudice," "ignorance," and "stereotypes" are usually common responses. Surprisingly, few students, and even experts for that matter, take racism back to the basic emotion of fear. Particularly in the law enforcement profession, fear is not allowed. By its very definition, fear is a sign of weakness and equates to a loss of courage. Officers arrive on the scene with a radio, a gun, a bulletproof vest, and an endless stream of backup. They are the police. Few civilians would arrive at a scene more prepared to do battle. Yet what one thing would cause this well-protected soldier of justice to shoot an unarmed man holding his wallet? Is it intuition or fear?

When fear is analyzed in its purest form, it generally falls into two categories. Fear in its most extreme form is classified as a phobia and tends to evoke responses that differ from person to person. Phobias can range from something as common as the fear of spiders (arachnophobia) to something as obscure as the fear of chickens (alektrophobia). Other phobias are more universal, such as the fear of heights (acrophobia) or the fear of being in enclosed spaces (claustrophobia). Although these extreme manifestations of fear may result in paralyzing phobias, this is more often the exception than the rule. Particularly in the context of law enforcement, fear can be energizing, motivating, and sometimes lifesaving.

On the other hand, fear may also cause one to do things he or she would not normally do, for example, fire several rounds from a gun when the first shot undoubtedly incapacitated the suspect or, as we have seen more recently, engage in questionable self-defense practices once a suspect is handcuffed and no longer a threat.

When we ponder the concept of fear in the comfort of a classroom, almost all would agree that to fear a person because of skin color, religious affiliation, or appearance is irrational. In the phobic sense, this fear is xenophobia, the fear and/or hatred of foreigners or anything that is foreign. In other countries, this sort of phobia is often associated with war and genocide. Despite rational thinking, this type of fear remains a strong emotion in our day-to-day decision-making process and becomes as valid as other fears that shape our lives, such as the fear of death, illness, or losing a job. To understand the complexities of prejudice, racism, and racial profiling, we must first explore the origin of fear and understand how it can dictate the way in which our body responds to outside stimuli long before we become consciously aware of the racial implications.

The word "fear" is derived from the Old English word for "danger." When we experience fear, our brain responds to the perceived danger by utilizing three distinct systems. The first, sometimes called the *primal* or *primitive fear system*, is found in most animals and mammals. This system is the first to react and is designed to alert the body to any potential threat. This automatic, unconscious "fight or flight" response alerts us to danger and becomes more intense when fueled by panic. This primal fear system is the most basic of the body's fear responses, evolving from man's lifestyle hundreds of thousands of years ago in his fight to survive his surroundings and his enemies. This primal fear system responded when Lisa's mind scanned the unfamiliar San Francisco neighborhood for potential threats. Likewise, this system engaged her body in a heightened state of alert and prompted an instinctive response to the man following her family. The outward manifestations of panic were almost instant: her rapid heartbeat, sweating, rapid stride, increased strength, and endurance. Her primal fear system alerted her to the danger even before she became consciously aware of it, and her body's response to the danger was set in motion long before she ever had time to contemplate whether this person was intending her any harm.

In the context of law enforcement, let's look to the example of officers who apprehend a suspect after a high-speed chase and then proceed to use force against the suspect even though he or she is handcuffed and no longer a danger. In this scenario, the primal fear system has detected a life-and-death threat. The primal fear system makes the unconscious decision to fight or flee. In the case of a police officer, the choice is usually to fight. When the fight response is initiated, the body's chemistry changes via the release of adrenaline and increased blood flow to other parts of the body, transforming the initial fear response into a combination of anger, panic, and aggression. With the increased blood flow comes increased strength and stamina. Often, the officer experiences a sensation known as "tunnel vision," the focusing of all of his or her attention on the matter at hand. The body's inability to control this sudden rush of strength effectively often culminates in the unlawful use of force against suspects once they are apprehended.

Once the body reacts to the early warnings from the primal fear system, the mind's *rational* or *logical fear system* takes over in an effort to assess the potential danger and weigh options for survival or escape. This system effectively plans the possibilities we need to consider in order to escape an immediate or future threat.

The third system, a person's *consciousness* or *awareness*, acts like a mediator between primal fear and rational thought. It will strike a balance between the mind's emotion and reason and become the ultimate decision maker in the entire process. Because this complex balancing mechanism comes relatively late in the fear process, it may ultimately prevent us from responding quickly to dangerous situations. For example, when we take time to think and analyze the potential threat instead of reacting immediately to the warnings of the primal fear system, we may put ourselves at risk for imminent danger or death.

Law enforcement is the perfect arena in which to observe the dangers inherent in this final decision-making process. Let's use the example of the officers who shoot the man holding his wallet. Had the officers taken the time to stop and allow consciousness to prevail over primal fear and their unconscious fight response (i.e., to shoot first), they would have undoubtedly risked imminent death had the wallet in fact been a loaded gun. Therefore, their decision to shoot, as mistaken and unjustified as it was, was probably the result of the officers' primitive survival instinct rather than a calculated and conscious decision to kill this man. Their survival depended on this instinctual reaction. Likewise, police officers will enter a mode of self-preservation when confronted with a dangerous situation, and they will look for a way to end the fear and regain control as soon as possible as opposed to waiting it out and risking imminent harm or death. Had the officers' rationale and conscious thought process balanced the panic response with logic and forethought, the result may have been different.

Once we attain a basic understanding of the fear process, it's important that we take the analysis one step further. Would the officers have had the same response had the suspect been white? Would the result have been different if the officers were the same ethnicity as the suspect? What if the suspect had been a woman or a child?

Similar to the behavior of primates, we try to read the minds of others. We try to evaluate whether the people we encounter are a potential threat to us. We look to the primitive stereotypes created in our minds that categorize people along racial, ethnic, or religious lines. This is true regardless of our own ethnicity. This phenomenon may even be true for those of the same race. For example, those of one minority group may segregate others within that group by using socioeconomic factors that distinguish these people as "different" from themselves.

The result is that these stereotypes, whether race-, class-, or appearance-based, cause us to judge people initially as members of a category as opposed to individuals. Some of these stereotypes may be as difficult to eradicate as a phobia, mainly because they are manifested preconsciously and draw from our mind's stored data, images, and experiences to determine who may pose a likely threat to our well-being.

It is the collection of this stored data that is the key to this complicated process. Because of our overwhelming exposure to the news, we often absorb a distorted perception of what is most likely to cause us harm. This media sensationalism keeps us in a constant state of anxiety and alarm and ultimately shell-shocks us into believing that the likelihood that these same events will occur in our everyday lives is high. This unrelenting flood of images becomes a dangerous distraction, causing us to focus our constant attention on unlikely risks rather than to tap our own intuitive abilities to process a dangerous situation. When our minds become filled with inaccurate information, our intuition will ultimately fail. Our intuition not only fails us concerning race, but it also fails us when we stop eating meat because of the mad cow disease outbreak. It fails us when we won't let our children play outside because of the risk of abduction. It will stop us from traveling in an airplane or attending events with large crowds because of the threat of terrorism. It will cause us to fear crime more than statistically called for when deluged with coverage of heinous crimes around the nation. Likewise, with respect to racism, when we go through our lives fearing everyone all of the time, there is no warning signal reserved for the times we may really be in danger.

Our minds work to gauge these potential threats in various ways. First, our minds take in outward clues, such as appearance, body language, and tone of voice, working like a large data center that scans memories and past encounters in search of similar events to draw upon. When the mind identifies a similar experience that is negative, it activates the *primal fear system* to alert the body to potential danger. This process is called *sensitization*, a complicated process in which the mind searches for past images that activate the early warning system when faced with the threat of danger. In our day-to-day endeavors, the experiences that sensitize us may be quite simple. For example, you're driving in the rain, and your car starts to hydroplane out of control, careening across three lanes of freeway traffic. This negative encounter will not only sensitize you and cause you to drive more carefully when it rains in the future, but it will likely sensitize those who witnessed you take the ride of your life.

When the system fails, however, it may trigger a fear response prematurely and may cause one to respond to a perceived danger that is simply not there. For example, on October 17, 1989, the San Francisco Bay Area experienced a magnitude 7.1 earthquake. When the earthquake struck, Michelle was shopping in a mall on the second level of a department store. As she stood in a doorway and tried to brace herself during the intense shaking, the lights went dark, and she heard loud crashes all around her. She was sure that the floor underneath her was about to cave in and that death was imminent. Although she experienced an eerie sense of calm during the actual earthquake, she suffered from terrible episodes of panic for months afterward any time there was a small aftershock or a loud noise causing the ground to shake. Even today, she feels that same instant panic if a truck driving by causes a building she is in to rumble, even before she can assess whether it is another earthquake.

The same is true concerning racism. When the mind carries a negative experience or image of one who is of a certain race or ethnicity, an irrational fear response may be triggered by anyone from that racial group rather than by just that one individual. This categorization process is the essence of the primal fear system, sorting our fears into broad categories that the system uses to scan our surroundings for potential danger. For Michelle, any shaking of the ground will always trigger fear of a catastrophic earthquake. For others, a fear of one spider will become a fear of all spiders. Likewise, a fear of one person from a certain race will equate to a fear of the whole race. These generalizations within the primal fear system will often prompt a person to react to a perceived threat long before his or her consciousness has the chance to recognize and assess the unique qualities of an individual within the suspect category.

This primitive alert system becomes especially powerful for those who work in professions that face imminent danger on a daily basis. The intake of negative information is astronomical and sensitizes the individual to many more dangers than the average human being might experience in a lifetime. For example, a police officer's past experiences with certain suspects or races may dictate how the officer will react to a dangerous situation in the future. The odds are quite high that someone who has worked in law enforcement for any length of time has probably had his or her share of negative experiences with suspects of all races. These negative experiences become "categories" programmed into an officers' primal fear system. In addition to experiences on the job, officers enter the profession with a lifetime collection of external stimuli such as media reports, crime statistics, and interactions with others. Whether it is a childhood experience, an unfamiliar neighborhood, or a negative encounter with a suspect of a certain ethnicity, the mind will tell the brain to remember the incident. This complex compilation of information will become the fear trigger when a similar situation arises in the future. This same system, drastically and sometimes tragically, fails if loaded with stereotypes and inaccurate information about certain races or ethnicities.

Without proper training in the ability to control and sort out the information in this powerful system, police officers may have difficulty distinguishing between irrational fear that is fueled by panic and rational fear that is borne out of good judgment and conscious reasoning. This internal tug of war may ultimately result in an inability to control or suppress the body's outward responses to the "fight or flight" impulse when facing a potential threat. Likewise, when the primal fear system is inundated with inaccurate information (racial stereotypes), inevitably the whole system fails, and its failure leads to decisions that are fear-driven (to fire a weapon) as opposed to those that are reasoned through conscious thought and rationale (assessing the actual risk).

One of the most common questions among students is whether we are born with certain genetic factors that make us more prone to racism or whether our attitudes about race are totally dependent on external forces. In order to answer this question, let us look back to this complex information-gathering system to examine some of the early stimuli the mind takes in.

Though none of us is born racist, it is important to note that from an evolutionary perspective, we are born with the instinct to survive. Just like prehistoric man, we naturally have a fear of outsiders. Our earliest instincts are similar to that of other animals—to protect our territory. Though not definitive, some experts suggest these early survival tools may have led to a genetic tendency to fear those who are different.

When we are infants, our primal fear system is not sufficiently developed to distinguish between these differences. This concept is probably best illustrated when watching young children playing in the schoolyard. To these children, the other kids are people just like them. As our cognitive thought process develops, however, we begin to take in outside stimuli that feed this large library of data. Some of these signals may be abstract, whereas others may be very specific.

Aside from any instinctual tendencies we are born with, we also begin to collect and process external data through our early introduction to language. Even by the age of one, we begin the amazing process of associating words with pictures and things. Through this discovery process, we begin to forge both positive and negative links in our minds to the objects around us. For example, a small child touching a hot stove will immediately associate this action with pain and will avoid it in the future, whereas a child who derives comfort from a certain blanket may gravitate toward this object when tired or upset.

In addition to trial and error, we learn by drawing inferences as we observe the world around us. Even at a very young age, we are able to draw conclusions about objects and people. For example, Steve's daughter Megan was three years old when the events of September 11, 2001, transpired. A few months after the terrorist attacks as Steve and Megan were walking through a store, Megan noticed two Middle Eastern men with long beards in traditional dress. Megan immediately grabbed Steve's hand and pointed to the men, yelling "Daddy, that's the Taliban! They're the men who knocked down the buildings." He was shocked to say the least, as he had not really talked to her much about the tragedy. Yet, through her independent observations of the television and newspaper, she was able to draw inferences from the images she had recorded in her mind.

This same process of inferences may work similarly as we start to develop language and vocabulary. As we learn a language, we begin to derive a word's meaning from the context in which it's used and the tone in which it is spoken. But when a word evokes different meanings, the result may be confusion and conflicting signals that inadvertently contribute to stereotypes and feelings of superiority among certain races later in life.

This confusion becomes readily apparent when looking at the words "white" and "black." By its very definition, the word "white" conjures up images of purity, such as new snow or a wholesome glass of milk. A direct quote from a dictionary describes an object "free from spot or blemish; free from moral impurity." We look to symbols and sayings in our culture that help us develop a visual image of this abstract concept: a white dress, a white lie, white magic, white Christmas. We often associate this color with a wedding, a baptism, or a new life. In contrast, the word "black" conjures up a much different set of images. The definition itself invokes an ominous sense of something "very dark in color; dirty; soiled; reflecting or transmitting little light; thoroughly sinister or evil; connected with or invoking the supernatural or especially the devil; sad; gloomy or calamitous." The expressions we use every day perpetuate these images further. For example, a black deed, black magic, black widow, or black Friday. We often associate the color with Halloween, fear, and death. When these images are embedded in the very essence of our communication system, it is inevitable that subconsciously, darkness becomes something that is associated with that which is bad, thus evoking an irrational fear of anything or anyone whose skin is dark.

Despite these early images, as we mature, we become better equipped to discern differences among people. In many respects, we become the products of our environment and readily absorb stereotypes and form biases that are largely based on the opinions and prejudices of those around us. We look to our surroundings to sort out and validate these opinions and observations independently. In school, we examine our classmates and categorize them in our mind. We mentally develop a picture of one another by measuring each other's strengths and weaknesses. We may notice that some races seem better in athletics, whereas others seem more proficient in academics. We notice that different parts of town have schools with more supplies, newer buildings, or better teachers, inadvertently sending a message to one group that they may be inferior to another. We begin to observe which races are treated as equals and which are not. We explore the socioeconomic differences between these groups and form generalizations and categorizations in our mind. We start filling in the details of our mental outline with images, stereotypes, and often misplaced rationale.

Though this collection of information serves largely as the baseline for our moral and social development, most children go through their entire childhood without discussing race and instead rely on this host of misinformation. Because race remains a taboo subject in our culture, children typically don't get to discuss these early observations about race and class. Parents are afraid to talk about it, largely because it's a topic that many of us really don't understand. Teachers are afraid to discuss it in the classroom because of the unsettling environment it may create. The result is that children tacitly learn about racism rather than race. When these childhood images and observations remain uncontested, they reinforce inaccurate generalizations and stereotypes that go unchallenged into adulthood.

Even as we enter adulthood, we look to messages in society that further frame our opinions about race. For example, why can Asians hail a cab while blacks cannot? Why are there more African Americans playing professional sports than whites, Hispanics, or Middle Easterners? We look to the hypocrisy of this whole skin color thing. On one hand, we have those with dark skin bleaching their skin to make it lighter, while on the other, those with light skin are spending a fortune in tanning salons to make their skin darker. These observations lead to the obvious question, Is it just about skin color, or is it about being different?

In a classroom exercise, we frame this phenomenon into a legal question. Let's say you go into the hospital for medical treatment, and you come out black. If you were to sue, what would the monetary damages be? Would they be more or less if you were transformed from black to white? What about from Hispanic to Middle Eastern (or vice versa)? If science tells us there are no biological differences among races, and skin color can be easily altered, would you be able to claim any damages at all? Would your friends and family members view you the same way, or would you be ostracized for being different?

Why do we feel differently toward certain individuals of one race as opposed to others? We love to listen to Bill Cosby's comedy, we try to model our lives around the advice of Oprah Winfrey, and we love to hear Jennifer Lopez sing or watch Kazuhisa Ishii pitch baseballs on Sunday afternoons. We read the novels of Tony Hillerman, whose mysteries centering on southwest Indian reservations keep us in suspense. We love these people who have become an essential part of our American culture. We would not be afraid of them if they were following us down a dark alleyway or sitting next to us on an airplane. We see them as "one of us" as opposed to people who are different or inferior. Yet if these same faces were unknown or unfamiliar to us, our minds may equate them with that of a drug dealer, a terrorist, or a white supremacist. In other words, our early warning system would be activated to alert us that there is someone nearby who might cause us harm. When we examine the very territorial nature of our primal fear system, we see that even through evolution, we as a species remain suspicious of people or things that are *different*. To varying degrees, we may even "attack" when we feel threatened, a response that is almost universal throughout the animal kingdom.

Although this ancient instinct may serve as a necessary survival tool in some cases, it may not always be accurate in practice. In fact, it may even expose us to greater harm. We recently interviewed a black law enforcement officer who related a story illustrating this theory. On his night off and out of uniform, he went to an instant teller machine to make a deposit. As he began to open his car door, he noticed a woman getting out of her vehicle at the same time. As soon as she saw him walking toward the instant teller machine, she immediately got back into her car and locked her door. Meanwhile, the off-duty officer made his deposit and walked back to his car. As he started to drive away, the officer noticed a well-dressed white man pulling up next to the woman in a newer vehicle. He recognized this man as a local doper, a methamphetamine user who was well known in local criminal circles. Unbeknownst to the woman, she began to exit her vehicle and walk toward the automatic teller machine. She and the doper stood side by side in the dimly lit parking lot while they conducted their banking transactions. Ironically, this woman would have been much safer with the off-duty police officer than with a known criminal; however, her instincts told her that the black man was a greater threat to her safety than the white drug dealer was.

Upon hearing this story, Steve, who worked with a San Francisco Bay Area organization, Bay Area Women Against Rape (BAWAR), reminded the officer that the woman did exactly what law enforcement teaches in rape-prevention trainings: take time to wait if you feel uncomfortable with your surroundings, and rely on your senses, whether justified or not. Even when we feel our instincts and fears are justified, we cannot avoid accusations of racism when we inexplicably feel threatened by those who are different from ourselves. The question is, Are we willing to risk harm by overriding this system, giving a potential perpetrator the benefit of the doubt? The logical answer would be "No."

The fact remains that regardless of race, skin color, or socioeconomic factors, the differences among us will remain broad classifications in our primal fear system that will trigger our fear response as we live and work in a civilized society. Whether we might someday be successful at circumventing this complicated system or whether we should even try remain unanswered questions that must be addressed before we can begin to eliminate racial bias in our modern world.

Taming the Primal Fear System

Unlike the rush of public support to develop miracle drugs or surgical procedures that cure our body's physical ailments, there has always been a marked caution when science begins to delve into the use of techniques and medications to alter the mind. The answer becomes simple when exploring cures for recognized diseases of the mind such as schizophrenia or depression. But what if the use of science and technology could tell us in advance which police officer candidates were prejudiced or whether a person committed a crime? What if a person's primal fear system could be reprogrammed to handle everyday stresses and stimuli differently? And what would happen if we became thoroughly successful at disrupting the primal fear system that our species has inherited from our early ancestors? These are important questions that must remain at the forefront when assessing techniques being developed that claim to alter the system in our brain to control fear effectively.

Undoubtedly, racism and prejudice remain the most dangerous byproducts of modern-day fear. Therefore, it is not surprising that some of the most effective behavioral techniques used to treat those with phobias may likewise be employed to lessen the effects of racism. One of these techniques, *desensitization*, is one of the most promising and readily accepted in this area. This process is based on the premise of learning by experience. In other words, the primal fear system may learn to rewire its preconceived generalizations about a certain race through the process of exposure, visualization, and modeling. This is not to say that fear should be eradicated. Some amount of fear is necessary for survival. Rational fear will alert us to danger, inspire us to be the best we can be, and help us deal with everyday stress. In contrast, irrational fears will hold us hostage and prevent us from maintaining our full potential as human beings. In extreme cases where fear has been eradicated, the results are typically unfavorable.

For example, we look to the mindset of the hijackers on September 11, 2001, when they flew planes into buildings. Most of us find it impossible even to contemplate how so many young men could willingly agree to embark on this suicide mission. We see striking similarities between these men and the mentalities of other suicide bombers who willingly strap on explosives and deliberately blow themselves up. In these troubling cases dealing in part with the fear of death, we have an example of desensitization taken to the extreme. Without achieving a delicate balance within our primal fear system, we are left with either the extreme form of desensitization on one side or an irrational phobia on the other.

One of the key steps toward managing our fears is to weigh the responses within our primal fear system with those in our rational thought process. To reeducate the primal fear system alone would not be successful, just as it would not work to explain to someone with a fear of flying why he or she should not be afraid to fly in an airplane. This person's primal fear system has been inundated with images of plane crashes, headlines that announce the number of dead in airline disasters, and media reports criticizing airline safety records. The fear response derived from this system is far more powerful than rational logic that suggests flying is one of the safest forms of transportation.

In order to overpower this process, the system that has been flooded with negative information must be reeducated by using repetition and behavior therapy under the supervision of a behavioral therapist. In the case of flying, the individual may be gradually exposed to airplanes on the ground. He or she may be taken inside an airplane and may eventually build up enough confidence to go on a short trip. The same repetition therapy can be applied to other fears as well. This gradual exposure to the source of the fear may be accomplished in many ways, depending on the specific fear. In the context of law enforcement, this goal may be achieved through a combination of therapy and computer-aided technology such as virtual reality or simulator exercises similar to those used by pilots. By experiencing fears in controlled settings, an officer may gradually become habituated and may become less fearful when encountering similar scenarios on the street. The result: deliberate actions based on rational information rather than fearful impulse.

We have learned that primal fears cannot be conquered by knowledge alone; however, this is not the case with the rational fear system. In conjunction with exercises to minimize irrational fears by desensitizing the primal fear system, we must supply the rational fear system with accurate information. In the example of the fear of flight, would-be passengers may have complex flight and safety systems explained to them so that they understand that the potential for disaster is minimal. In the case of racism, officers may be educated about different ethnicities and beliefs. Armed with this knowledge and training, the mind stands a better chance of being able to balance irrational and rational fear for an optimum outcome.

Predicting Fear and Racism

The use of a "mind-reading machine" is somewhat frightening, particularly if the machine could readily access one's innermost thoughts and feelings about a given topic. In other words, what if the machine could effectively tap into a person's primal fear system and detect the physical manifestations of fear even before the person was consciously aware of it? What if the system could alert an employer about whether a prospective employee is racist? The fact is such technology does exist, and it's used regularly in law enforcement to screen potential candidates for employment.

This system, known as the polygraph, or more commonly, the lie detector test, is routinely used to assess a person's fitness to become a law enforcement officer. When used in conjunction with the psychological profile, the system can detect falsehoods or, more specifically, measure a person's nervous system response long before he or she is consciously aware of it. When used correctly by an experienced polygraph examiner, this tool is designed to detect and measure subtle differences in the skin's ability to conduct electrical currents. Going back to our example of the San Francisco experience, before Lisa was consciously aware of the danger, she began to sweat. Her physical manifestation was almost instant and was activated long before she was able to process the danger consciously. Had she been hooked up to a polygraph machine at the time, the machine would have likely measured her fear response. Had the examiner then asked whether she felt afraid, a "no" answer would have been inconsistent with the signals given off by her body at the time she answered the question. It was the physical act of sweating, as slight as it was, that would give her away by reducing her resistance to the electrical current and would thereby alert the examiner to the falsehood. The examiner may also look to an elevation in pulse and blood pressure or an increase in breathing to detect whether a certain question elicited a verbal response that was inconsistent with her physical manifestations.

In the context of modern-day law enforcement, this tool is generally limited to screening candidates for honesty and probing areas of someone's background that the person might not otherwise disclose. Imagine the implications, however, if the scope of the questions were expanded to include inquiries into a person's attitudes about race. To take this concept one step further, what if this tool could be used to detect a person's opinions about race without even asking a question?

Perhaps this theory is best illustrated in the form of a classic experiment using the polygraph examination. Imagine an adult called into a room and given a polygraph in front of a blank screen. While the examinee was waiting for the test to begin, the examiner excused himself and proceeded to cause a number of pictures to flash in rapid succession on the screen in the room. In this case, the pictures were of snakes and spiders. The pictures flashed too quickly for conscious awareness; therefore, the examinee wasn't conscious of anything happening at all. (When asked later, all examinees would say they had seen nothing.) The polygraph examiner then returned to the room and proceeded with the verbal portion of the examination. Unbeknownst to the examinees, the polygraph examiner recorded an increase in skin conductance in individuals who had reported a fear of snakes or spiders. Those who had reported no fear of snakes and spiders had no increase in skin conductance.

Let's take the results of this experiment and apply them to race. What if the pictures of snakes and spiders were replaced with people of different ethnicities? What if the display of these photos and a person's subsequent reactions could predict his or her innermost feelings about those who are different? Although this mind-reading system might work in theory, the chances of it being accepted as standard protocol to screen law enforcement officers are virtually nil. Though some believe utilizing the polygraph examination in some limited form may be beneficial in determining whether an individual may have a propensity toward racism, others believe an intrusion so deep into a person's mind would not justify the overall benefit.

For instance, a candidate's response to one of these examinations may elicit a negative response that is not necessarily indicative of a bias against a certain racial group. The person may have had a past negative experience or altercation with an individual who looked similar to the person in the photograph. Likewise, five candidates may look at the same photograph and see something entirely different. The candidate may be reacting to the person's eyes, his or her clothes, the background in the photograph, or any number of stimuli that may elicit a response that could be interpreted as "negative" by the polygraph examiner.

Individual interpretation is not the only factor that could lead to inaccuracies in this kind of examination. Traditionally, polygraph examinations are given to uncover a person's background. For instance, whether a person has ever stolen another's property, whether the person has had sexual relations with a minor, or whether the person has ever used illegal drugs. The answers to these questions are easily quantifiable and determinable of a person's fitness for becoming a law enforcement officer. A "yes" response to any of these questions may justifiably disqualify a potential candidate or, at a minimum, call into question a person's respect of and adherence to the law.

Prejudice, however, is not a moral or a legal issue. In fact, prejudice in itself is not illegal. The rubber meets the road, so to speak, once prejudice is acted upon, a factor that is highly determinable by an individual's decisions. Whether a person chooses to act on these prejudicial tendencies is a variable that may never come into play, regardless of the emotions harbored in the individual's unconscious thought process. Since human beings have virtually no control over these unconscious thoughts, it would be difficult to justify holding someone accountable merely because a machine detects a slight aversion to someone of a different race. Rather, it is the combination of a discriminatory mindset coupled with and resulting in an overt act that equates to racial profiling. Independently, it is not illegal to have a discriminatory mindset, nor is it illegal to enforce legitimate violations of the law. When the two forces work in concert, however, the result is the illegal act of racial profiling.

Perhaps the only legitimate way a polygraph examination might be used to screen a person for racial bias would be through direct questions formulated to delve into one's past experiences or actions toward those of different races. For example, if someone had perpetrated a hate crime against a certain group in the past, there would be a high likelihood this person might do so again in the future. This line of questioning about the engagement in an illegal act would be highly relevant and probative of a person's fitness to become a law enforcement officer and would be well within the boundaries of a preemployment polygraph examination.

Though the use of polygraph examinations is standard protocol in most law enforcement agencies' hiring processes, questions about race rarely, if ever, come into play. Even though this line of specific questioning would be difficult to challenge, organizations tend to follow the lead of society and deem race a taboo subject that is traditionally left unexplored and unchallenged. By opting to treat the issue of racism as uncharted territory, law enforcement agencies continue to play the odds and hope that the problem will just go away, or at least not surface in the form of civil rights violations within their agency.

In law enforcement circles, there remains little or no safe haven for officers who may be on the verge of crossing the line. As it stands in most organizations, an officer would likely be terminated if he or she went to a supervisor and reported feelings of bias toward certain segments of the population, particularly if there was an indication that these feelings were manifested in inequitable enforcement actions directed toward the public. Rather than look at the problem as a weakness that can be corrected, organizations tend to see it as a liability that would make it unlikely for those in management to offer rehabilitation or counseling. This anticipated course of action may discourage an officer from coming forward when feelings of prejudice surface. When this hatred is allowed to build, the result is often subversive enforcement tactics that are clearly against the law. This historical "taboo" treatment of racism, and the ensuing pattern it perpetuates, is not unlike that which has occurred within society for hundreds and thousands of years.

As history has shown us repeatedly, fear is a powerful and destructive force. It has needlessly destroyed men, leaders, and entire civilizations. When looking back historically on the atrocities directed at a particular race, creed, religion or orientation, there is little sense or rationale that justifies our fear and treatment of those who are different. We cannot rationalize our fears of other races or religions any more than we can rationalize our childhood fears of monsters in the closet. Not even modern science can label one race as either superior or inferior to another. When the only difference among us is something as superficial as skin color, we are left to embrace the advice of President Franklin D. Roosevelt, who reassured us that we have nothing to fear but fear itself.

CHAPTER THREE

---•◦•---

Patterns of Racial Injustice:
Stepping into the Shoes

To better understand the impact of the ways in which our innermost fears of people who are different from us have evolved into our current attitudes about racism, we must start by examining the history of racial tensions in the United States. Historians might typically look to key turning points in our nation's history, with a particular focus on those that shaped the civil rights movement, in order to gain a better understanding of how these racial struggles have defined how we coexist within a diverse society. Our attitudes about others are challenged and shaped almost daily, as evidenced by continued terrorist threats to the United States since September 11, 2001, and the subsequent hunt for those with ties to terrorist networks. These incidents, coupled with the historical treatment of certain minority groups, continue to spark important questions about the legitimacy and effectiveness of racial profiling in a culturally diverse society.

Though it is not feasible to include a complete narrative of the civil rights movement in the confines of this book, its importance as it relates to the modern-day practice of racial profiling cannot be overlooked or underestimated. This correlation would be apparent to any scholar embarking on research, particularly when confronted with the inconsistent accounts of significant events in history that are perspicuously divided along racial lines.

In the search for a time in history when there was a common goal of equality for all, we took our research back to the drafting of the Declaration of Independence, in hopes that such a significant event would serve as a good benchmark and lead to an accurate, black-and-white account of our nation's history. To our surprise, it did—very black and white. It became quickly apparent that the historical overview could not be confined to the clear-cut approach we had originally envisioned.

With this in mind, we chose to recount key historical events with a combination of firsthand accounts, little-known facts, and sometimes sarcasm, in order to tell our nation's story from two different perspectives: black and white. Interestingly, these differing views have remained fairly constant throughout history and have perpetuated many of the biases and stereotypes that continue to challenge the premise of equality for all.

Though we will primarily be looking at relations between whites and African Americans in the United States, it should not be overlooked that other groups have suffered similar persecution both here and overseas. One need not look far to recognize that those of Jewish descent, Native Americans, Chinese, Japanese, Russians, and others have endured painful struggles to preserve their cultures in a nation that vows equality for all.

Although the arenas for prejudice have varied through time, the cycle of racism continues to replay itself in one form or another, from the days of slavery through to the aftermath of terrorist attacks on the United States. One of the groups that has been caught consistently in this cycle is law enforcement.

A Look Back

Those who do not learn from history are destined to repeat it.

It was the 1700s. British customs inspectors were routinely and randomly ransacking the homes of American colonists to search for contraband or evidence of a crime. These early search and seizure practices infuriated the colonists and served as one factor that led to their rebellion against the British government. This revolution prompted many early visionaries to leave Britain to come to America in order to forge a government in which such practices would be abolished. And the rest is history, or so they say.

Since its inception more than 200 years ago, the guarantee of freedom and liberty for all persons to live and travel within the boundaries of this great country unconstrained and unchallenged has been ingrained in all Americans. The idealism of the Declaration of Independence, that "We hold these truths to be self-evident, that all men are created equal, that they are endowed by their Creator with certain unalienable Rights, that among these are Life, Liberty and the pursuit of Happiness" have withstood the test of time. Our forefathers intended that these words would grant freedom to all Americans. Or did they?

July 4, 1776: The Declaration of Independence was adopted.
A section denouncing the slave trade was deleted.

As the United States formed its own government, it drafted the Constitution with one central theme in mind, equal justice. The colonists no longer wanted to bow to a royal figurehead or endure intrusions into their homes and their privacy. The Fourth Amendment was eventually drafted, thus limiting the power of the police to search citizens.

Unfortunately, equal justice for all, regardless of race or sex, would be long in coming.

> *January 8, 1811: 500 slaves led by Charles Dislondes revolted on a plantation near New Orleans. They marched from plantation to plantation and sent whites fleeing. They were finally stopped by militiamen and army regulars. Many were killed; many escaped. Those that were captured were beheaded and their heads displayed on the road from the plantations where they started to New Orleans as a message to other would-be rebel slaves.*

In 1865 and 1866, Congress passed the Thirteenth and Fourteenth Amendments, which, upon ratification, abolished slavery in America and granted all persons born or naturalized in the United States equal protection under the laws as U.S. citizens. Many blacks rejoiced, believing this would finally grant them the freedom white Americans had enjoyed for nearly a hundred years.

> *July 1, 1917: Race riot, East St. Louis, Illinois. Estimates of number killed ranged from 40 to 200. Martial law was declared. A congressional investigating committee said: "It is not possible to give accurately the number of dead. At least 39 Negroes and eight white people were killed outright, and hundreds of Negroes were wounded and maimed." "The bodies of the dead Negroes," testified an eyewitness, "were thrown into a morgue like so many dead hogs. There were 312 buildings and 44 railroad freight cars and their contents destroyed by fire."*

World War II brought a renewed sense of camaraderie in America. Brothers fighting side by side with brothers, black and white, on the battlefield. Fighting for those words written so long ago, "... all men are created equal." The fight against Hitler and his persecution of the Jews gave African Americans new hope that this type of oppression and genocide would no longer be tolerated. Blacks and whites were fighting together for one country, dying together, and ultimately, winning freedom. When the fight was over, these war heroes returned home to the land of the free, home of the brave, America the beautiful!

> *January 3, 1947: An NAACP report said that 1946 was "one of the grimmest years in the history of the National Association for the Advancement of Colored People." The report deplored "reports of blow torch killing and eye-gouging of Negro veterans freshly returned from a war to end torture and racial extermination" and said "Negroes in America have been disillusioned over the wave of lynchings, brutality, and official recession from all of the flamboyant promises of postwar democracy and decency."*

With the 1950s came a new excitement and renewed hope across America. The nation reveled in modern-day inventions such as the television, electric appliances, and the jet airplane. America's baby boom evidenced a renewed American spirit. Not only could women of suburbia efficiently do their housework and care for their families, but Americans could travel across the country in a matter of hours through the heavenly skies while looking down on purple mountain majesties and seeing nothing but brotherhood from sea to shining sea. *America, America, God shed his grace on thee!*

> *December 1, 1955: Rosa Parks arrested. Rosa Parks, a seamstress and activist, arrested after she refused to give her seat to a white man on a Montgomery, Alabama, bus.*

These were the best of times and the worst of times. With the advancement of travel came freedom for some and further oppression for others. Rosa Parks was perhaps the first victim of the modern-day pretext traffic stop. As does the modern motorist, Ms. Parks desired only to move from place to place by lawful means, unmolested and unchallenged, regardless of her race.

The civil rights movement of the 1960s was the dawning of a new day for all African Americans. With the passage of the Civil Rights Act, the promise of improving race relations was finally looking like it might become a reality. Unfortunately, the states did not waste any time in enacting legislation to circumvent the new federal law.

> *California responded by enacting Proposition 14, which moved to block the fair-housing components of the Civil Rights Act. This, along with other proposals, created feelings of despair and injustice, particularly among minorities living in inner cities.*

> *August 11, 1965: A routine traffic stop in Central Los Angeles turned deadly, sparking the Watts Riots. Lasting for six days, the riots left 34 dead, more than 1,000 injured, nearly 4,000 arrested, and hundreds of buildings destroyed.*

White Americans could not understand how a routine traffic stop could have started such deadly riots in Watts. Some believed that this was the result of giving blacks so much equality. Soon after the riots, the governor appointed a commission to study the cause of the deadly event. A report later issued by the commission concluded that the riots were not the result of thugs but rather an indication of much deeper problems within the community. High jobless rates in the inner city, bad schools, and poor housing were set forth as reasons for the unrest. Despite this conclusion, there was no substantial effort made to address the problems, nor was there much of an attempt to rebuild what had been destroyed.

> *January 3, 1966: Sammy Younge, Jr., 21, was shot to death by a 67-year-old white service station attendant. A Tuskegee Institute student*

and civil rights activist, Younge was shot after using the "Whites Only" restroom at the service station where the white attendant was working.

African Americans were desperately trying to make sense of the deaths of so many black men and women. These deaths finally began to mean something, as once again, hopes were raised for freedom and equality.

June 13, 1967: First black named Supreme Court justice. Thurgood Marshall, U.S. Solicitor General, named to the Supreme Court by President Johnson. He was confirmed by the Senate on August 30 and became the first black Supreme Court Justice.

Despite the unrest, many were encouraged by the emergence of remarkable black leaders such as Rev. Dr. Martin Luther King, Jr. Finally, the day was near when little black boys and girls would stand side by side with little white boys and girls, play together in the same schoolyard, and live together in the same neighborhoods as brothers and sisters. The vision was clear: equality for all colors—black, brown, red—all children of one God Almighty. With the shot of a gun, a haunting echo could be heard across the nation, "Free at last! Free at last! Thank God Almighty, We're free at last!"

With the death of Martin Luther King, no longer would the government turn a deaf ear to the cries of black Americans. The battle cry was no longer "We Shall Overcome" but rather "We Have Overcome!" We would not sit idly by and watch our brothers and sisters slaughtered like animals!

January 3, 1979: Los Angeles Police shot Eulia Love in a dispute over a $22.00 gas bill. The police shot her eight times after she refused to let the gas company turn off her gas. This, again, caused rioting and outrage across the nation.

In the 1980s, there seemed to be a decrease in the reports of racial incidents and disturbances, or perhaps the focus was elsewhere. The affirmative action programs instituted by the Nixon administration offered women and minorities brand new hope. Equality seemed inevitable as the number of minority leaders, politicians, and athletes flourished. It wasn't long before all hope was shattered, however, by a two-minute video tape of Los Angeles police officers viciously beating Rodney King, the grim result of a traffic altercation for suspected speeding and driving under the influence.

March 4, 1991: (Excerpts from police radio transcript in the Rodney King beating[1])

"I haven't beaten anyone this bad in a long time."
"Oh, not again...I thought you agreed to chill out for a while..."

(Excerpt from another call prior to the Rodney King incident)

"...Sounds almost as exciting as our last call...It was right out of Gorillas in the Mist.*"*

The Rodney King case resulted in an increasing minority distrust of police and the justice system and served as a vivid reminder of the injustices minorities had been complaining of for a long time.

Perhaps it was this outrageous example of discrimination that ultimately led to the acquittal of O.J. Simpson in 1995. It was a final vindication for all African Americans when a black man was found "not guilty" for killing a white woman and her white friend, in what the media dubbed "The Trial of the Century." Some said the proceedings were not a trial for murder but rather a trial of black versus white. The court of public opinion was likewise divided, with blacks promoting his innocence and whites asserting his guilt. On one side, it was the story of a black defendant, a black jury, and a black glove. On the other, it was the story of white victims, the alleged white police detective who some labeled a racist, and the white Ford Bronco. One might argue that this show of force between the two sides and O.J. Simpson's ultimate acquittal at the criminal trial finally brought long-awaited vindication for people of color. Others would argue that this was one giant step backward in a system riddled with racism, however subtle.

> *February 14, 1999: Amadou Diallo was shot at 41 times by four New York Police Department officers while standing in his doorway and holding a wallet, allegedly mistaken for a firearm.*

All four officers in the Amadou Diallo case were found not guilty of murder, manslaughter, homicide, and reckless endangerment. After the verdicts were read, protesters in the Bronx waived their wallets and jeered, "Looks like a gun!" One man raised his infant son into the air, and while pointing to the color of his son's skin, chanted, "Shoot him now!"

> *September 11, 2001: Nineteen men of Middle Eastern descent carry out the worst single terrorist attack in U.S. history when they crashed two commercial airlines into the World Trade Center in New York City, one into the Pentagon, and one into a Pennsylvania field, acts that killed thousands.*

Driving down the road after the terrorist attacks of September 11, 2001 was every bit like riding in a Fourth of July parade. From every car flew an American flag with a message of patriotism. Every building, home, and freeway overpass was draped with the stars and stripes. People of every race, color, and religion came together as never before to pray, cry, and remember those that lost their lives.

2001: Justice Department detains and questions hundreds of young Middle Eastern men about potential terrorist affiliations and intelligence information.

Christmas Day, 2001: An airline pilot refuses to take off with an Arab American Secret Service agent who was on his way to protect President George W. Bush at his ranch in Texas. The pilot refused to call the Secret Service or the White House to verify the agent's identity.

As current events unfold, we are reminded that the United States is still a young nation with a lot of growing up to do. We remain naive in many ways, trying to strike a careful balance between the fundamental goals of preserving freedom, diversity, and equality and maintaining a secure environment for our democracy to thrive, goals that are unprecedented in world history. Given the complexity of human nature, it may be impossible to eradicate racism. But history has taught us that if we cannot learn to understand its source and control its harmful effects, this great nation may never flourish to its full potential.

(Endnotes)

1. Gates, Daryl F., *My Life in the LAPD* 370-71 (Bantam Books, 1993).

CHAPTER FOUR

———•◆•———

Back to the Dinosaurs

Start with a good idea. Test it thoroughly, and use it with care. Put it in the hands of those who don't have the experience and training to apply it properly. Add a little discrimination and pressure, and turn up the heat for 20 years. What do you get? Racial profiling.

In a nutshell, this is the story of Howard Teten, a former FBI chief of research in the late 1950s who many criminologists credit with popularizing the concept of "criminal profiling." A man who lived the best of both worlds, Mr. Teten studied psychology at the University of California at Berkeley while working crime scenes in San Leandro, California. Back in the 1950s, cops typically looked for clues at a crime scene to try to tie the crime to a particular suspect. Teten took this concept one step further by looking at the *manner* in which the criminal committed the crime in order to develop a psychological profile. This profile ultimately helped officers identify a criminal's personality traits and mental state and led to a classification of potential suspects who could have committed the crime.

In this early form of profiling, these criminal composites were designed to identify specific characteristics, for example, a suspect's emphasis toward the use of a particular part of the body or a weapon that was uncommon among similar crimes. In its later forms, however, the concept was expanded to include geographic profiles, developed on the premise that criminals who commit serial crimes generally do so close to home, in areas with which they are most familiar.

In its purest sense, Teten's original concept of *criminal* profiling was a highly effective law enforcement tool used to identify and arrest criminals. But as law enforcement came under increasing pressure to battle drugs, crime, and terrorism, Teten's original concept quickly went awry.

Over the years, the science of criminal profiling was tampered with ever so slightly, eventually taking on a life of its own. Despite the parameters of its original use, those who did not have a clear understanding of the underlying science eventually applied race and stereotypes to the formula. When these variables were added to the mix, Teten's once highly respected science took on a discriminatory complexion, eventually becoming an illegal tool called *racial* profiling.

The War on Drugs

"It is difficult even to imagine a drug courier profile that singled out characteristics of well-off travelers, but one can be sure that if such a profile existed, either political pressure or judicial review would quickly bring its demise. Here, as elsewhere in the regulation of police practices, intrusive law enforcement tactics are tolerated precisely because the intrusion is not likely to affect the privileged among us."

—David Cole[1]

As a takeoff on Teten's early profiling efforts, one of the first drug profiles was developed in the 1970s for the Detroit Metropolitan Airport by DEA Special Agent Paul Markonni. By 1979, this profile was being used in more than 20 airports across the country, citing primarily behavioral traits as suspect. Characteristics that drew particular attention included whether the person appeared to be nervous; whether payment for an airline ticket was made in cash and in large bills; whether a departure or arrival was from a destination considered a place of origin for cocaine, heroin, or marijuana; and whether an alias was used to purchase airline tickets. In the 1980s, skin color was added to this profile and resulted in an emergence in the number of minority travelers in the nation's airports who were subjected to frequent interrogations and searches by DEA agents and the U.S. Customs Service.

Teten's brand of profiling, initially limited to the profiling of murder suspects, caught on like wildfire among his FBI trainees and by the 1980s was widely in use among local police departments in other types of cases. The downside of this rapid application was the misuse of the process by officers who did not have the psychological training to use it in the limited circumstances for which it was designed.

In the 1980s at the height of the crack cocaine epidemic, profiling was expanded in an effort to target low-level drug couriers in the Southwest and along the East Coast. A combination of pressure from politicians and inexperience within the law enforcement community resulted in the simplification and application of these complicated criminal profiles to cocaine couriers around Chicago. In no time at all, these dragnets began to target low-income minorities and resulted in the detention, questioning, and search of innocent victims about potential drug trafficking activities.

Although these drug intervention efforts represent one of the earliest and most public uses of racial profiling by law enforcement, it should be noted that as far back as 1967, the President's Commission on Law Enforcement and Administration of Justice recognized the potential harm such practices might have on law enforcement and community relations. A task force report published that same year acknowledged that field interrogations in some communities were becoming a major source of friction between the police and some minority groups.[2] Despite these early warning signs, law enforcement saw profiling as an exciting new crime-fighting tool to gain the upper hand on the government's war on drugs.

In 1982, the war on drugs once again escalated when President Ronald Reagan established the Task Force on Crime in South Florida under the direction of then–Vice President George Bush. The purpose of this task force was to escalate the government's air and sea operations to combat drug smugglers in the South Florida area. This action prompted the Florida Department of Highway Safety and Motor Vehicles to enter the fray in 1985.

Simultaneous with this intervention, guidelines were established for police on "The Common Characteristics of Drug Couriers." These guidelines identified possible targets for suspicion as those driving rental cars, people displaying "scrupulous obedience to traffic laws," drivers wearing "lots of gold" or those who do not "fit the vehicle," and people from "ethnic groups associated with the drug trade." Consequently, the traffic stops initiated by Florida state troopers were primarily based on this overtly race-based profile.

In 1986, crack cocaine use became a popular media topic as accounts of an inner city crack epidemic flourished. These reports often tied crack use to minority gangs, low-income housing projects, and geographical areas populated predominantly by minorities. In response to public concerns about this emerging trend, many urban cities heightened law enforcement efforts to tackle street-level drug dealing aggressively. New York began Operation Pressure Point in an attempt to rid the Hispanic Lower East Side of drug trafficking. Operation Invincible in Memphis, Operation Clean Sweep in Chicago, Operation Hammer in Los Angles, and the Red Dog Squad in Atlanta followed. All of these programs targeted poor, minority, urban neighborhoods where drug dealing seemed to be open and notorious, thus guaranteeing officers easy targets in their quest to rid the city of drugs and crime. These easy targets coincided nicely with the operations' primary goal, to make as many arrests as possible.

Success on this level was imminent and easily calculable. Nationwide, arrests for drug possession reported by state and local police agencies nearly doubled from 400,000 in 1981 to 762,718 in 1988. Comparable figures of arrests for drug sale and manufacture rose from 150,000 in 1981 to 287,858 in 1988. It was no surprise to anyone that minorities were disproportionately represented in these figures.[3]

In 1986, an enforcement campaign was also initiated on the nation's highways, prompted in part by a racially biased drug courier profile introduced to the highway patrol by the DEA. The product of this campaign was the launch of Operation Pipeline, a little-known highway drug interdiction approach that has to date trained approximately 27,000 police officers in 48 participating states to use pretext stops to find drugs in vehicles.[4]

In 1997, it was reported that of the more than 34,000 stops that were conducted, only 2% resulted in the seizure of narcotics. Though some may tout the 700 narcotics arrests Operation Pipeline netted, others are quick to point out that more than 33,000 motorists were detained and deprived of their constitutional freedoms in a dragnet largely based on a racially biased profile.

In recent years, the escalation of pretext stops across the nation can be directly attributed to the techniques taught and advocated in Operation Pipeline. In fact, the data used and circulated in connection with this and similar efforts have certainly suggested, and at times candidly encouraged, the targeting of minority motorists.

The long-term effect of these operations has been the proliferation in the law enforcement community of the "drug courier profile" that has resulted in the stereotyping of minorities in all segments of the population. Although the widespread use of this profile has been a critical tool used by law enforcement to respond successfully to the continued public pressure to escalate the war on drugs, it has likewise been met with harsh criticism because of its enormous racial overtones.

These racial overtones became even more pronounced as the public began to experience the wide reach of these drug courier profiles firsthand. The innocent victims caught up in this new law enforcement dragnet quickly recognized that these drug courier profiles, designed to guide officers in deciding who they should target for investigatory stops, were not limited to the highways. Similar profiles soon became widespread and were implemented nationwide in airports, bus terminals, and train stations. The downside of these profiles was the creation of a rather unorthodox collection of traits and mannerisms that was so all-inclusive it justified stopping every man, woman, and child that traveled through our nation's airports on any given day of the week.

At one time or another, federal agents have listed all of the following traits as part of a drug courier profile:[5]

1. Arrived late at night; arrived early in the morning; arrived in the afternoon;
2. One of the first to deplane; one of the last to deplane; deplaned in the middle;
3. Purchased ticket at airport; made reservation on short notice;
4. Bought coach ticket; bought first-class ticket;
5. Used one-way ticket; used round-trip ticket;
6. Paid for ticket with cash; paid for ticket with small-denomination currency; paid for ticket with large-denomination currency;
7. Made local telephone call after deplaning; made long-distance telephone call after deplaning; pretended to make telephone call;
8. Traveled from New York to Los Angeles; traveled to Houston;
9. Carried no luggage; carried brand new luggage;
10. Carried a small bag; carried a medium-sized bag; carried two bulky garment bags;
11. Carried two heavy suitcases; carried four pieces of luggage;
12. Overly protective of luggage; disassociate self from luggage;

13. Traveled alone; traveled with a companion;
14. Acted too nervous; acted too calm;
15. Made eye contact with officer; avoided making eye contact with officer;
16. Wore expensive clothing and gold jewelry; dressed casually;
17. Went to restroom after deplaning;
18. Walked quickly through airport; walked slowly through airport; walked aimlessly through airport;
19. Left airport by taxi; left airport by limousine; left airport by private car; left airport by hotel courtesy van;
20. Suspect was Hispanic; suspect was black female.

It is quickly apparent that these drug courier profiles do not represent good science, nor do they offer a sensible approach to productive law enforcement. In fact, most would agree that such a haphazard solution borders on the ridiculous. Using the above criteria, every airport traveler would be a drug courier suspect at one time or another, particularly if a member of a minority group.

Despite the apparent ineffectiveness, similar profiles are still in use in the law enforcement community. They are used at our borders, in our airports, on our roadways, and in our cities. Though the use of these profiles is generally not condoned in official department policy, they serve as an unofficial guide for many officers in the execution of their duties. In fact, many of the profiles currently in use may even contradict established policy. Regardless, the damaging effects to the community are just as apparent whether these investigatory tactics are practiced by an entire department or by an individual officer. Despite the obvious downsides, these practices once limited for use in the war on drugs soon expanded as an integral crime-fighting tactic.

The War on Crime

It wasn't long before police began employing tactics used in the war on drugs to fight the war on crime. Law enforcement organizations across the nation were coming under tremendous public and political pressure to reverse the skyrocketing crime wave plaguing major U.S. cities. In response to these calls for action, elite crime-fighting units were established within larger police agencies to target much of the violence. One such group, New York City's Street Crime Unit, was often seen patrolling the poorest neighborhoods after dark in search of criminal activity. Though the unit was independent and belonged to no one precinct, it quickly became a success by some measures and lived up to its motto, "We own the night." Based on one of the islets of the East River, the unit had free reign within the city to stop, frisk, and arrest would-be criminal perpetrators. Though it comprised only 2% of New York's police force, it accounted for more than 20% of the city's gun arrests. Estimates were that its practices reduced the number of weapons in the city by more than 2,000. As hoped, the murder rate plummeted as its size expanded from 150 undercover officers to nearly 400. Recruits for this specialized unit were given only three days of extensive training, and then sent out on the street to fight the war on crime.

Although many with political aspirations proclaimed the unit's efforts successful, others could not overlook the tremendous ramifications these aggressive crime-fighting tactics had on New York's citizens. In 1997 and 1998, the Street Crime Unit stopped and searched more than 45,000 men, primarily African Americans and Hispanics. Out of these 45,000 detentions, only 9,000 arrests resulted.

It is unclear whether the aggressive crime-fighting tactics would have been allowed to continue had it not been for the brutal killing of African immigrant Amadou Diallo as he stood in his doorway with his wallet in hand. His death sparked protests and legal action that ultimately resulted in the suspension and disbursement of the Street Crime Unit, with its members being reassigned throughout the police department. Perhaps the words of a Brooklyn sergeant said it best: "If there is anyone who should have been on trial, it is the department. Those guys went out for numbers—they didn't go out to kill anyone—but the department wants guns and numbers."

Similar high-profile incidents by elite crime-fighting and gang-intervention units have become the subject of increasing debate in the law enforcement community. Police chiefs are left to choose between launching these high-profile units that inevitably come with the potential for subversive crime-fighting tactics and attempting to reduce violent crime with their hands tied behind their backs. The challenge becomes even more of a balancing act under mounting public pressure that crime be reduced while officers shun tactics that involve stopping and detaining those who may fit a certain profile.

While many agencies have been successfully walking this political tightrope, others have chosen to continue unpopular enforcement practices despite varying public opinion. This is the case in Wilmington, Delaware, where Police Chief Michael Szczerba offers no apologies for the tactics used by the "Jump-out Squad," a highly controversial drug- and crime-fighting unit operating under Operation Bold Eagle. In the summer of 2002, as many as 18 agents began literally descending on individuals out of unmarked vehicles in search of guns and drugs. Most of those targeted have been African Americans living, working, or traveling through neighborhoods known for drug-infested street corners and high crime. Even if the frisk uncovers no evidence of wrongdoing, the detainee is photographed with a digital camera and the photo added to a database that can be accessed in the event of a subsequent violation. Though the police chief believes it is improbable that innocent people will be caught up in the sweep, police statistics reveal that of the 600 people detained and photographed thus far, nearly 20% were not charged with any offense.

Despite these statistics, public opinion remains split as to whether these efforts by police should continue, leaving many to question whether they are legal in the first place. According to the 1968 landmark case of *Terry v. Ohio*,[6] police are given almost unbridled discretion to stop and frisk a suspect if there is a reasonable, articulable suspicion that criminal activity is afoot. When the basic premise of *Terry* is misused, however, these investigatory stops are sometimes used as fishing expeditions for evidence of a crime. In the case of the Jump-out Squad, the reasonable, articulable suspicion required by *Terry* is satisfied in the form of surveillance, which police insist they engage in prior to initiating contact with a suspect.

Assuming the stop itself is constitutional, others remain troubled by the photographs taken for inclusion in a high-tech database. Though some experts argue that the photos violate a person's Fourth Amendment rights, others believe that the police are free to photograph these individuals despite the lack of evidence of any wrongdoing. The Supreme Court seems to support the latter belief, holding that people have no expectation of privacy in public places.

Regardless of the controversy surrounding this new crime-fighting tactic, the Wilmington Police Department intends to continue Operation Bold Eagle indefinitely.

Many law enforcement agencies are quickly learning that when the public sees or experiences similar crime-fighting tactics, allegations of civil rights violations quickly follow. In more extreme cases where there is evidence of a pattern of illegal enforcement tactics, agencies are quick to come under federal consent decrees that essentially set strict standards the agency must follow in order to remedy the harmful practices.

Though science and common sense both dictate that racial profiling does not lead to an increase in the successful apprehension of criminals, it remains a tactic that some officers use regularly, many for reasons having little to do with racism. While some might lack training and experience in the use of more scientific investigatory tactics, others may utilize racial profiling out of desperation, finding it difficult to keep up with the criminal element while satisfying the public's demand for crime reduction. Whatever the reason, we must look to factors such as fear and other underlying motives that may explain why race continues to surface as an alternative to good police work. Likewise, we must ask ourselves whether it is ever appropriate to use race as a crime-fighting tool, particularly in times of national crisis.

The War on Terrorism

Though the war on drugs and the war on crime in our nation's cities remain a top priority for both federal and local law enforcement, these efforts were largely overshadowed after the terrorist attacks of September 11, 2001. Fearing another terrorist attack by this new enemy, America was quick to outgrow the long-held premise that racial profiling was confined to the random stops of blacks or Hispanics on the highway. The far-reaching effects of this practice became painfully apparent and showed the world how we are all equally victimized by the fear and hatred of those who are different from us. In the span of a few hours, racial profiling went from what many viewed as an unacceptable practice, to a viable alternative for identifying those most likely to cause us harm.

Though this section as it relates to terrorism is by no means all encompassing with respect to America's war against this new enemy, it is included as further testimony to the extent and evolution of racial profiling as a means of identifying those suspected of criminal wrongdoing. It shows how attitudes toward the use of this practice change as current events unfold.

As America embarks on its quest for national security, the practice of racial profiling will undoubtedly continue to seize new victims, invoke new uses, and challenge long-held values of civil rights and freedoms.

Racial Profiling: A Help or Hindrance?

Prior to September 11, 2001, airports were prime targets for law enforcement and customs agents to use drug courier profiles to intercept would-be drug traffickers. The focus shifted post-September 11, however, from drug couriers to suspected terrorists. In response to this new threat, security personnel, law enforcement officers, and the National Guard embarked on an aggressive campaign to question and search individuals, particularly those of Middle Eastern descent, who fit the profile for suspected terrorists. In the campaign to identify and capture this new enemy, many freedoms enjoyed while traveling through the nation's airports, skies, and across its borders were stripped away, thus giving rise to restrictive and intrusive travel and immigration procedures.

Those of Middle Eastern descent who once traveled across the country unobstructed were subjected to the most scrutiny, sometimes even removed from planes when pilots refused to take off with them aboard. In one such instance, five minority passengers who looked Middle Eastern or Asian were kicked off flights after other passengers and crew members "felt uncomfortable" with them on board, even though all passed rigorous security checks. This new brand of fear led to resentment among many Middle Easterners detained in airports and at our nation's borders because of their race and prompted allegations of racial profiling.

Not surprisingly, the sentiments expressed by those most affected by these new security measures have not necessarily mirrored those of the public in general. In countless news reports and editorials, persons who do not fit into the terrorist profile seem to be more than willing to relinquish their rights when traveling through an airport for the sake of tighter security. In fact, soon after the September 11 attacks, a *Los Angeles Times* poll revealed that 68% of those questioned approved of law enforcement stopping people who fit the profile of suspected terrorists, which gave further credence to the power of fear. Perhaps the sentiments of many were summed up in a 2003 news editorial, ending with the well-respected commentator reminding the public that although not all Middle Easterners are terrorists, all terrorists have been Middle Easterners.

Though stereotyping and the resulting bias directed toward Arabs and Muslims in the United States have increased tenfold since September 11, many experts contend that this treatment began well before this tragedy.[7] Some point to a trend beginning as far back as the 1960s and 1970s, fueled in part by the well-publicized hijacking attempts by those of Middle Eastern descent. Others place the blame on political activists and individuals who boast anti-Arab sentiments and agendas. Some have even contributed these stereotypes to negative depictions in our popular culture, particularly those originating in the Hollywood film industry.[8] As one author notes: "[t]o my knowledge, no Hollywood WWI, WWII, or Korean War movie has ever shown America's fighting forces slaughtering children. Yet, near the conclusion of [the movie] *Rules of Engagement*, U.S. marines open fire on the Yemenis, shooting 83 men, women, and children. During the scene, viewers rose to their feet, clapped and cheered. Boasts director Friedkin, 'I've seen audiences stand up and applaud the film throughout the United States.'"[9]

Such open hatred toward these groups has led some to theorize that the "demonizing" of Arabs and Muslims frequently goes unnoticed, in part because it is entirely consistent with the widespread attitudes in U.S. society.[10] Many experts studying this phenomenon seem to concur with this theory and note that the recent trend to focus attention on those from certain Middle Eastern and religious groups has been met with little public resistance since September 11. Regardless of how widespread these attitudes are, few disagree that the most recent wave of anti-Arab and anti-Muslim sentiments represent but one chapter in a long history of misinformation associated with these groups.

Though many defend the government's terrorism intervention tactics as a necessary means for maintaining national security, the plight of those targeted has not gone unnoticed by other minority groups who have historically claimed similar treatment. As is true of any racially based stereotype, those directed at Arabs and Muslims are largely fueled by misinformation. One factor points to the frequent lack of differentiation between these groups, which prompts generalized hostilities toward entire communities instead of at the small group of Arabs or Muslims who perpetrated the terrorist attacks. As opposed to seeing the majority of these individuals as law-abiding, peaceful people, they are often categorized as terrorists and extremists who seek to wage a holy war against the United States. The ongoing tensions in the Middle East, the first Gulf War, and the more recent war in Iraq have further fueled hostilities in the United States, sometimes leading to hate crimes, vandalism, and violence against those perceived to be of Middle Eastern or Arab origin. These changing times have caused people of all colors and creeds to question how safe they really are living and traveling in America.

Flying the Unfriendly Skies

Contrary to public perception, the post–September 11, 2001 terrorist precautions now commonplace at U.S. airports are not new to veteran airport security personnel. Quite the opposite, this high terror alert is reminiscent of similar practices imposed on the airline industry in the 1960s and 1970s in efforts to thwart hijacking and hostage-taking attempts by Middle Eastern and Muslim perpetrators. Veteran security agents recall routine instances when Arabs and Muslims were taken out of line to be searched and questioned. Their suitcases were often marked with the word "SECURITY," clearly visible to other passengers.

Although current security measures seem to ring a familiar tone to those implemented nearly 40 years ago, the underlying mentality has changed dramatically. What was once the flagrant identification of those suspected of terrorist ties has evolved into a color-blind system that singles out no one. Allegations of racial profiling have caused airport security to take a politically correct route to keep our skies safe and have thus caused many to question at what cost.

While sitting at San Francisco International Airport waiting for a flight, a businessman's attention was drawn to a security checkpoint. He watched as a young mother was extensively searched. To the chagrin of those who had been waiting in line for nearly an hour, her infants were startled out of their sleep so that their stroller could be inspected and put through an X-ray machine. Likewise, there was no mercy for the 80-year-old grandparents boarding a plane to Las Vegas for the weekend, who had their golf bags torn apart in search of...perhaps a grenade launcher? While this scenario replayed itself throughout the terminal, it reminded him of an article he had read a few days earlier that took security checkpoint investigations to an entirely new level. The allegations accused airport personnel of forcing a young mother to drink from a bottle containing her own breast milk to prove that she was not boarding the plane with a harmful substance.

Watching this charade go on for nearly an hour brought about a wide range of emotions. Flight attendants, the handicapped, children, and pilots, all put through the same security searches. As much as he had sympathy for innocent Americans who were delayed simply because they had the misfortune of falling into a terrorist profile, he could not shake the fact that what he was witnessing was more of a "dog-and-pony" show wasting valuable resources than a real tool to intercept would-be terrorists. Reminiscent of the story of the emperor who had no clothes, one must question whether amidst the rituals and fanfare at the security checkpoints anyone really believes that race and ethnicity don't matter after the terrorist attacks of 2001. The fact remains that the suicide terrorists were all from al-Qaeda. They were young, male, Islamic, and Arab. Like it or not, anyone who boards an airplane since these horrific attacks will likely see those terrorists' faces transposed on every young Middle Eastern man traveling alongside him or her for the foreseeable future. The question is, Can we afford to assume that the next terrorist will fall into a certain profile?

Recent reports reveal that law enforcement's fear of racial profiling accusations coupled with pressure from civil rights groups are key factors that have led to the political correctness we are now experiencing in our nation's airports. Critics of this blanket approach argue that by employing such tactics, law enforcement's efforts to intercept actual terrorists have actually been hindered to a great extent. In the context of airport security, many complain that valuable resources are being wasted to search grandma rather than to investigate individuals who may really pose a valid security threat, and many believe that such efforts do nothing more than ward off racial profiling accusations.

With allegations of racial profiling becoming commonplace in the past few years, many government and law enforcement agencies have gone to great lengths to prove that their enforcement and investigatory tactics are indeed color blind. Despite praise of such policies and procedures by some civil rights groups, others are quick to suggest that these efforts may have inadvertently caused the government to miss investigating key terrorist suspects living in the United States prior to September 11, 2001. Others have theorized that the capture of these perpetrators would have prevented the attacks altogether. More specifically, one California senator suggested that fear of racial profiling accusations coupled with political correctness may have led to the FBI's reluctance to look into a tip by a Phoenix agent warning that Osama bin Laden might be sending people to U.S. flight schools to prepare for terrorist attacks. Other allegations point to key details, then construed as "racial profiling," that were removed from a search warrant whose rejection may have prevented the FBI from learning more about terrorism suspect Zacarias Moussaoui prior to the September 11 attacks. Have we allowed the pendulum to swing too far the other direction? In some cases, the answer may be yes.

The Changing Face of Terrorism

They say spending time in prison changes a person—perhaps in more ways than we ever dreamed. Terrorism experts point to a U.S. prison system filled with angry and alienated individuals as a fertile recruiting ground for terrorist organizations such as al-Qaeda. In a population filled with people looking for a common purpose or sense of belonging, experts continue to examine the close link between terrorists and gang life and draw analogies between the indiscriminate forms of attack prevalent in both organizations. This concept is not new; it has become a growing concern among those studying the overlap between terrorist organizations and street gangs here in the United States. Such links were observed as far back as 1980, when a Chicago gang known as El Rukin allegedly conspired with the Lybian government to blow up a U.S. airliner.

Though this attempt was thwarted, it directed experts to focus their attention on individuals such as José Padilla, the 31-year-old suspect who was arrested in 2002 as an enemy combatant in the war on terror for his alleged involvement in a dirty radiological bomb plot that was to have been carried out on behalf of the al-Qaeda terrorist organization. Padilla, a former Chicago gang member raised Catholic in the United States, converted to Islam while serving time in prison. Born in Brooklyn, this high school dropout spent much of his youth as a "gang banger" and eventually served time as a juvenile offender in connection with a murder case. Later, Mr. Padilla served time in Ft. Lauderdale, Florida, for a shooting in connection with a road rage incident. When finally released from jail in 1992, Mr. Padilla appeared as though he was finally interested in settling down. He married, had a child, began studying Islam, and even changed his name to Abdullah al Muhajir. He later left for Egypt and expressed to his friends and family his desire to teach there. His plans took a detour, however, when he was arrested May 8, 2002, at Chicago's O'Hare Airport after traveling from Pakistan via Switzerland.

Undoubtedly, law enforcement operating on a terrorist profile would have skipped right over Mr. Padilla. There was nothing about Padilla's race, origin, or history that made him suspect. Rather, he was caught when investigators uncovered information from an al-Qaeda operative and other sources that implicated him in the nuclear plot.

The story of José Padilla may not be as novel as one might think. United States intelligence agencies have become increasingly concerned that future terrorist attacks will be carried out by non–Middle Easterners in an effort to thwart racial profiles developed by law enforcement to apprehend terrorist suspects. For example, in December 2001, an attempted bombing of a jetliner by Richard Reid—a British national who is part black and part white—gave the government solid proof that the terrorist profiles it originally implemented to intercept suspects were already outdated.

The story of Richard Reid is not the only one prompting revised terrorist warnings. New alerts warn law enforcement to be wary of women who look pregnant because officials have suggested that some may be strapping bombs to themselves in a manner that would allow them to penetrate security checkpoints easily. Other terrorist alerts have been issued warning of children carrying explosives. With such trends on the rise, law enforcement is reminded that terrorists may gain the upper hand if they can successfully change their profile to circumvent long-held assumptions about the face of a terrorist.

Similar revelations have also led the government to focus new attention toward potential threats from Asia after terrorist suspects tied to al-Qaeda were arrested in Singapore and Malaysia. Government experts suspect that many of these terrorist networks may well be plotting to gain the upper hand by dodging these profiles all together, thus affording themselves a unique opportunity to strike where we are the most vulnerable. One senior U.S. official expressed the belief that "the next face of this is not going to be an Arab face but possibly Indonesian, Filipino, a Malaysian face, or even African...They understand the security profile we are operating on."[11]

Whether profiling terrorists, drug couriers, or common criminals, there is one thing universal to any race-based profile: fear will prevail over logic. America has learned in the past that these witch-hunts damage the innocent more than they reveal the guilty and that they are often counterproductive because they enable the real perpetrators to elude law enforcement altogether. The only true "profile" that will work to intercept terrorists is one that identifies fanatics of all persuasions. With the proven overlap of street gangs and al-Qaeda, future terrorists may well be Hispanic, Caucasian, Asian, male or female, and even U.S. citizens. As Timothy McVeigh proved when perpetrating the Oklahoma City bombing, there is no shortage of hate or discontent in America, even among its citizens, nor is there a shortage of people willing to do almost anything in the name of religion. At what point, however, does security begin and civil rights end? The answer may be at America's borders.

Racial Profiling in Immigration Enforcement

Few would disagree that the events of September 11 have had a profound impact on non-citizens living, working, and attending school within the United States.[12] Though not usually considered in the context of most racial profiling studies, experts remind us that racial profiling in immigration enforcement differs little in kind and substance from that employed in criminal law,[13] thus leading many to characterize the two as interchangeable.[14] Though racial profiling in immigration enforcement was a factor long before September 11, the tragedy raised many questions and concerns about U.S. immigration laws. In this vein, the use of race in the enforcement of U.S. immigration laws has emerged as one more battleground in the war on racial profiling that has historically been fought within our cities and on our nation's highways.

It is perhaps the fine line that separates the rights of citizens from those of non-citizens that some view as the reason immigration enforcement remains an area in which racial profiling practices remain somewhat unchallenged. As such, the rights of these individuals living in the United States will undoubtedly emerge as a topic of intense debate and legislation in the years that follow September 11.

Few will forget that the terrorist attacks left America with a tangible fear and a new enemy. The face of this perceived enemy became clear: young Middle Eastern men who legally came to America and lived among its citizens unrestricted while all the while plotting against its most visible symbols of freedom. With little effort or change in appearance, these young men entered our borders and became just another element of our diverse American landscape. In many cases, these men were our neighbors, our students, our business associates, and our friends. They were enemies that came from within. All of the benefits and education this country provided these terrorists, albeit for a short while, were used against us without warning in the most unthinkable way.

The blame and backlash for these attacks were swift and far reaching. Some responded instinctually, as would any threatened species in the animal kingdom when confronted with fear: they attacked. But with the hijackers dead, there were few places to direct the mounting fear and anger. With a surge in hate crimes against Middle Easterners, many demanded swift action by the government to prevent foreigners from entering the United States, particularly those who were from countries of suspected terrorists.

Local law enforcement was quickly called in to help fight this new battle waged on our homeland. Though immigration law has historically remained a field almost exclusively dominated by the federal government, this long-held tradition was quickly challenged when the post–September 11 administration considered expanding the role of local police to enforce immigration laws. One response was the new Department of Homeland Security, a government agency that, for the first time, actively began to include local law enforcement in the detection, questioning, and control of those it deemed suspicious.

One of the byproducts of this tightened security was the emergence of a new stereotype. Any person who appeared to be of Middle Eastern descent was a potential target, particularly those who were in America on student and work visas. Some Americans felt they could no longer trust their neighbors. Others were quick to support tighter immigration laws, border searches and, sometimes, even indefinite detentions and arrests. As part of this crackdown on terrorism, U.S. borders, particularly those in closest proximity to Canada and Mexico, became a swift target for law enforcement. Terrorism, and all the faces associated with it, was now public enemy number one. The desperate grab for national security and normalcy quickly overshadowed the more philosophical ideals of diversity, justice, and freedom for all.

The new restrictions placed on immigration were unfamiliar to most Americans. The public was largely unaware and unconcerned with immigration and border security prior to September 11, as it did not seem to pose an immediate threat. Even media reports were limited in scope and focused more on the deaths of Mexican citizens in U.S. border–enforcement operations as opposed to the threat of terrorism.

Ironically, however, in the years law enforcement was being criticized for using racial profiling in the criminal arena, the government's use of race as a factor in immigration enforcement was granted greater leeway in some cases and defended by its supporters as a necessary tool to aid law enforcement in identifying and apprehending illegal immigrants.

When reviewing cases decided prior to September 11, the court's role in immigration law was largely limited to the clarification of factors the Border Patrol could consider when stopping one suspected of immigration violations. This was one of the issues posed in *United States v. Brignoni-Ponce*[15] wherein the Supreme Court reasoned that "[t]he likelihood that any given person of Mexican ancestry is an alien is high enough to make Mexican appearance a relevant factor, but standing alone it does not justify stopping all Mexican-Americans to ask if they are aliens."[16] As such, many cases since *United States v. Brignoni-Ponce* have sought clarification as to the legal weight a Border Patrol officer may give to a person's "Hispanic appearance" when making the decision to stop and question him or her regarding a suspected immigration offense.[17] In more recent rulings, courts seem to suggest that race may be a relevant factor if other articulable facts are also present. This remains true despite the fact that roughly 90% of the Latinas and Latinos in the United States are lawful immigrants or citizens. The dynamic of race standing alone, however, would probably still be considered inadequate by most courts for an officer to use in determining whether to stop and question a person about his or her suspected undocumented status.[18]

Undoubtedly, many cases will emerge from this tragedy that will further clarify for law enforcement the boundaries of considering race in immigration enforcement. One guide for the courts has historically been to remain true to the founding fathers' original intent when they drafted the Constitution more than 200 years ago. It seems far too speculative, however, that even the courts will be able to predict what the founding fathers' intent would have been when faced with an event so inconceivable even by modern standards. In any case, as legal challenges emerge on behalf of non-citizens, it will be interesting to see how current immigration laws will evolve to meet the security demands of our post–September 11 world.

Regardless of recent legislation prohibiting racial profiling in law enforcement, its use as a national security safeguard has expanded tenfold since September 11. In the fight to keep America safe, there can be little doubt that race has played a significant role in targeting those to be detained and questioned as material witnesses in the terrorist attacks. Likewise, local police have, in many cases, been thrust into a precarious position when they were asked by the federal government to enforce immigration laws that are largely unfamiliar to them, thus leaving law enforcement with mixed messages about the use of race as a legitimate crime-fighting tactic. When mass government dragnets ensued under the guise of immigration-related violations, law enforcement was once again caught in the middle of a no-win situation and was left to choose between national security and abandoning laws and regulations prohibiting racial profiling.

Local law enforcement agencies were not the only ones left to walk this political tightrope. Similar to the sentiments historically expressed by other racial groups, those targeted in these terrorist dragnets became increasingly reluctant to cooperate with law enforcement investigations for fear of being detained, arrested, and deported. The probable and unintended result of these investigatory tactics was that those who may have been in a position to contribute important information to assist in terrorist investigations began to distrust law enforcement and opted instead to remain silent.

Moreover, this new brand of immigration enforcement sanctioned as a national security measure left many surprised at the seemingly unbridled power exercised by the government. Experts studying the impact of the United States' responses to September 11 as they relate to immigration law explain that "existing case law affords considerable leeway to the political branches of the federal government," and they note that the "Supreme Court has upheld immigration laws discriminating against non-citizens on the basis of race, national origin, and political affiliation that would patently violate the Constitution if the rights of citizens were at stake.[19] ... The doctrine thus allows the federal government, through the immigration laws, to lash out at any group considered undesirable.[20] Such authority increases exponentially when, as in the case of international terrorism, perceived foreign relations and national security matters are at issue.[21]"[22]

The use of race both within and at our borders is further testimony that racial profiling remains much more widespread than an automobile stop on the highway. As long as our nation is at risk, law enforcement will undoubtedly continue to be thrust into the forefront of this uncharted territory. The long-term role law enforcement will play in immigration enforcement and national security has yet to be determined. Presently, many local law enforcement agencies' involvement is limited to the receipt of weekly terrorist alert bulletins now sent to each agency by the Department of Homeland Security or their state's attorney general's office. For larger agencies, the involvement has been much more defined, particularly in times of heightened alert.

Regardless of size, there can be no doubt that the war on terrorism has been taxing on all law enforcement organizations. Despite budget cuts, understaffing, and escalating crime rates in some inner cities, law enforcement has been forced to stretch staffing levels and resources to the breaking point. For those agencies that have had to employ extensive security measures and personnel in response to the war/high-alert status, the costs have been staggering. A survey by the U.S. Conference of Mayors in March 2003 revealed that five major U.S. cities reported expenditures ranging from $1,500,000 to $5,000,000 per week on homeland security.[23] These numbers leave many wondering how long America can afford to operate in this heightened state of alert.

With the demand for local law enforcement to be on alert constantly for the potential and unexpected terrorist attack launched by an invisible enemy, many point to a shortfall of resources when it comes to protecting citizens from everyday crime, a factor that remains a daunting certainty in every city across America.

The American Way

The events of September 11 have undoubtedly challenged many of the ideals and freedoms that are unique to America. When American tourists travel abroad to "third-world countries," there are ominous warnings to stay away from corrupt police who have been known to fabricate criminal charges, haul innocent tourists off to jail, and throw away the key. No trial, no judge, no jury. The End. This kind of civil rights violation would be unthinkable in the United States, that is, until September 11, 2001. Civil rights groups have been joined by the American Bar Association in criticizing numerous "enemy combatant" arrests on U.S. soil. Many of these "dragnet" style detentions, designed to pick up and interview both foreigners and U.S. citizens alike, bear a frightening resemblance to those that would more likely occur in countries with no constitution or democracy or where police powers are routinely abused.

In addition to these aggressive detention tactics, many groups are likewise criticizing the U.S. Patriot Act of 2001 and other related legislation that gives the Attorney General unprecedented powers to detain and question noncitizens on the grounds of national security. Under this new anti-terrorism law, the Attorney General has the power to detain any noncitizens if there is a reasonable belief that the individuals "engaged in any broad range of terrorist acts or otherwise threatened national security." Certified aliens who are not deported could be held indefinitely until the Attorney General determines they are no longer a threat.

The thought of large numbers of innocent people being plucked out of society because of race, ethnicity, or religious beliefs and denied access to legal assistance for indefinite lengths of time flies squarely in the face of our democratic values. The practice has been openly criticized by several law enforcement agencies who've been asked by the Justice Department to conduct these dragnet operations. Many agencies have refused to cooperate with such operations and have cited policies that prevent them from engaging in racial profiling. Others voice their willingness to risk or give up whatever it takes to ensure that a tragedy the scope of September 11, 2001, will never occur on American soil again. In this vein, legislation is being proposed at an unprecedented rate that, if successful, will undoubtedly result in the further chipping away at our constitutional freedoms. Regardless, we must ensure that in finding the proper balance between security and civil rights, we are not trampling on the very freedoms we are fighting so hard to protect.

These unprecedented challenges will undoubtedly continue to perpetuate the internal struggle among law enforcement, government agencies, and citizens of all races. Undoubtedly, Congress must work to create and expand regulations that allow for investigations of those who may be a threat to national security. These regulations, however, must take into account constitutional safeguards that distinguish the United States from dictatorships and countries of rampant lawlessness.

Though the aggressive tactics employed since the 2001 terrorist attacks may be necessary in the interest of national security, we must be careful not to override both human and civil rights safeguards that distinguish us as a free democracy. The truth is that this internal turmoil we are creating in our country may come with a far more deadly price tag. When the vigorous campaign to fight terrorism ultimately turns Americans against each other, will we become a prime target for future attacks, particularly if we commit ourselves to the belief that terrorists are more likely to be those that fall into a limited profile?

More important, the use of fear, subversive tactics, and door-to-door investigations to interrogate and detain hundreds of people who had nothing to do with the terrorist attacks means that the terrorists have accomplished their mission of destroying our freedoms. This internal turmoil will hinder our strength as a nation and may make it impossible to defend ourselves adequately on a united battlefield. The hatred and fear some now have for certain ethnic groups will cause us to doubt our neighbors, our friends, and our coworkers. These misplaced fears will also condition the mind and body to react adversely when confronted with those we fear or view as different from ourselves. As we have seen throughout history, when the fear process is set in motion, responses to external stimuli often become more instinctual than logical.

We need not look far from the profession of law enforcement to see how our fears since the 2001 terrorist attacks have manifested into tendencies for all Americans to engage in racial profiling. Though no scientific poll has been released to date, one would guess that if five well-dressed, clean-shaven, young Middle Eastern men were seen by other passengers boarding a cross-country flight together, the plane would be virtually empty.

This new target of fear and hate has a familiar ring to that which has been directed at other Americans for hundreds of years. Whether these perceived threats are new or old, the fear and prejudice they perpetuate will undoubtedly continue to affect our nation in profound ways. It's yet to be determined whether these same fears contributed to the perceived failures in our intelligence gathering system, possibly preventing the unthinkable. There is no question that all Americans must remain united in order to circumvent a similar tragedy in the future. As a nation, we must refrain from employing race-based, dragnet-style tactics or those that pit neighbor against neighbor. Such a campaign will probably not be effective in uncovering our real enemies and may, in fact, put us at greater risk.

Looking Ahead to the Rising Cost of Travel

Though the potential for future terrorist attacks transcends far beyond our nation's airports, this limited venue becomes a good testing ground for new technology to fight the war on terrorism. The airport screening technology used to date to intercept potential terrorists relies mainly on human discretion. Its effectiveness is largely measured by an airport screener's ability to discern people or objects that may be harmful to other passengers. Whether they do so by a passenger's appearance, race, or other predetermined criteria, this method is highly subjective and has not proven successful in many cases. With the public becoming less and less tolerant of airport security breaches, there is little doubt that travel in the future will need to be made safer by new screening technologies. The cost of these intrusive new systems, however, may be more than many of us are willing to pay to travel from place to place.

Although still several years from implementation, the Federal Aviation Administration and screening technology companies may soon begin testing a passenger-screening system described by some as one of the largest monitoring systems ever created by the U.S. government. This complex computer network would combine vast data sources with predictive software to uncover passenger travel habits and link together obscure clues about passengers scheduled to embark on U.S. flights. Some of the obscure details this system hopes to uncover include links among passengers on the same flight, unusual travel habits among passengers on different flights, or how a passenger purchased tickets. Once these subtle patterns are ascertained, the system would assign a threat index or score for each passenger. Those who score highest on the threat index would be identified for additional screening by airport security.

Other security measures involve the use of a city's geographic data to interconnect disparate information and distribute it among several agencies within the city. Not only are these kinds of systems valuable in the context of homeland security, but they also play a key role in everyday law enforcement. Likewise, they have become an important tool for fighting natural disasters around the country.

While the government insists it is taking extreme precautions to protect privacy when developing these new systems, some believe such technology will severely erode the protections guaranteed to U.S. citizens by sanctioning a sort of government surveillance. Others predict that this same technology may be expanded to profile other targets such as drug couriers or deadbeat parents. Despite these criticisms, government officials hope to test at least two prototypes in the coming months.

Regardless of which systems are found to be the most effective, there can be little doubt that implementing such safeguards will come with a hefty price tag for all Americans. Whether this is a price we are willing to pay remains to be seen.

Coming Full Circle

The legal and legitimate practice of criminal profiling remains a valuable tool used by criminologists to identify and arrest criminals. Few could have predicted that a concept so pure could be transformed so quickly into an illegal and discriminatory means of targeting anybody who possessed characteristics that law enforcement considered suspicious. Experts have characterized this transformation as a fear-driven phenomenon, in direct response to the government's war on drugs, crime, and terrorism.

Though modernly, we tend to view racial profiling in these limited parameters, we can go back through history to see the often desperate measures undertaken to counter the powerful emotion of fear. There is no shortage of examples, most notably, the treatment of Native Americans, the Salem witch trials, slavery, the Japanese internment camps, the Holocaust, and the blacklisting of communist sympathizers. Though the targets of discrimination have varied, the results are viewed almost universally as some of the darkest times in world history.

Similarly, as we embark on the aggressive pursuit to keep our nation safe and free from new threats, we must ensure that the freedoms we are fighting so hard to protect are not trampled in the process. As history has taught us, any system that does not clearly distinguish between criminal profiling and racial profiling will fail in both policy and practice.

In our quest to keep America safe, some remain hopeful that science will once again emerge as a legitimate means to fight crime and develop predictions about suspects that are not dependent on human intervention and frailties. Whether the public will welcome such new technology remains to be seen. It is probably fairly accurate to predict, for example, that a system that extensively monitors a person's travel and spending habits will be highly unpopular. Other methods in the works, however, may be more appealing to the public and ultimately less reliant on human interpretation. Some look to promising new computers that will enable an airport screener to scan a person's eyes or unique physical characteristics and compare them with those of suspected terrorists. Similar high-tech screening systems are being either developed or tested nationwide in an effort for science to replace a system largely dependent on individual discretion.

The future of such technology and the impact it will have on law enforcement investigatory tactics is uncertain. The real question is whether these objective means of reading people will one day replace human intervention entirely, thus ridding law enforcement of the heavy burden of managing and defending racial profiling accusations.

Until science catches up to our vast and ever-changing law enforcement needs, we must continue to improve the policies and practices currently in place so that they will represent our diverse heritage and democratic values. With a better understanding of fear and racism and their evolution into modern-day racial profiling, we can now move forward to see how these underlying factors come together to frame much of our day-to-day encounters with both law enforcement and each other.

(Endnotes)

1. Cole, David, *No Equal Justice* 52 (The New Press, 1999).

2. President's Commission of Law Enforcement and Administration of Justice, Task Force Report, *The Police* 183 (1967).

3. Harris, David A., ACLU Special Report, "Driving While Black, Racial Profiling on Our Nation's Highways" (June 1999).

4. Harris, David A., ACLU Special Report, "Driving While Black, Racial Profiling on Our Nation's Highways" (June 1999).

5. List compiled by Cole, David in *No Equal Justice* 48-9 (The New Press, 1999) from the following sources: "Fluid Drug Courier Profiles See Everyone as Suspicious," 5 Crim. Prac. Man. (BNA) 333, 334-35 (July 10, 1991) (citing cases); *U.S. v. §129, 727.00 U.S. Currency*, 129 F.3d 486 490 (9th Cir. 1997); *U.S. v. Armstead*, 112 F.3d 320, 321 (8th Cir. 1997); *U.S. v. Small*, 74 F.3d 1276, 1282 (D.C. Cir. 1996); *U.S. v. $13,570.00 U.S. Currency*, 1997 U.S. Dist. LEXIS 18351, *8-*12 (E.D. La. 1997); Charles L. Becton, "The Drug Courier Profile: All Seems Infected That Th' Infected Spy, As All Looks Yellow To The Jaundic'd Eye," 65 N.C.L.Rev. 417, 438-54, 474-80 (1987) (listing and discussing drug-courier profile characteristics from reported decisions).

6. *Terry v. Ohio*, 392 U.S. 1, 88 S.Ct. 1868 (1968).

7. Akram, Susan M., "Scheherezade Meets Kafka: Two Dozen Sordid Tales of Ideological Exclusion," 14 *Geo.Immigr.L.J.* 51, 54 (1999).

8. Akram, Susan M. and Kevin R. Johnson, "Race, Civil Rights, and Immigration Law After September 11, 2001: The Targeting of Arabs and Muslims," *NYU Annual Survey of American Law*, Vol. 58:295 at 308 (2002); Shaheen, Jack G., "Reel Bad Arabs: How Hollywood Vilifies A People" (2001).

9. Shaheen, Jack G., "Reel Bad Arabs: How Hollywood Vilifies A People" (2001).

10. Akram, Susan M. and Kevin R. Johnson, "Race, Civil Rights, and Immigration Law After September 11, 2001: The Targeting of Arabs and Muslims," *NYU Annual Survey of American Law*, Vol. 58:295 at 310 (2002).

11. Pianin, Eric and Bob Woodward, *Washington Post*, "Officials fear terrorists will adapt to elude racial profiling," *The Valley Times*, January 18, 2002.

12. Akram, Susan M. and Kevin R. Johnson, "Race, Civil Rights, and Immigration Law After September 11, 2001: The Targeting of Arabs and Muslims," *NYU Annual Survey of American Law*, Vol. 58:295 (2002).

13. Johnson, Kevin R., "The Case for African American and Latina/o Cooperation in Challenging Racial Profiling in Law Enforcement," *Florida Law Review*, Vol. 55 at 341, 343 (January 2003).

14. Kennedy, Randall, *Race, Crime and the Law*, (1997).

15. 422 U.S. 873 (1975)

16. 422 U.S. 873 at 887 (1975). See also *United States v. Montero-Camargo*, 208 F.3d 1122 (9th Cir. 2000) (en banc) disregarding the language in *Brignoni-Ponce*, noting that the defendants' Hispanic appearance was not a proper factor to consider in determining whether Border Patrol agents had reasonable suspicion to stop them in light of the large number of Hispanics in the area. Agents in this case testified that the majority of persons passing through the checkpoint were Hispanic, the county in which the checkpoint was located was 73% Hispanic, and five southern California counties were home to more than one fifth of the nation's Hispanic population.

17. See *United States v. Cruz-Hernandez*, 62 F.3d 1353, 1356 (11th Cir. 1995); *United States v. Rodriguez*, 976 F.2d 592, 595 (9th Cir. 1992), *amended*, 997 F.2d 1306 (9th Cir. 1993).

18. See also Johnson, Kevin R., "The Case Against Race Profiling in Immigration Enforcement," 78 Wash. U.L.Q. 675 at 708-09, 712 (2000).

19. See *Harisiades v. Shaughnessy*, 342 U.S. 580 (1952) (allowing for deportation of immigrants based on their political views); *The Chinese Exclusion Case* (*Chae Chan Ping v. United States*), 130 U.S. 581, 599, 609 (1889) (upholding racial discrimination in immigration laws); see also *Nguyen v. INS*, 533, U.S. 53 (2001) (upholding gender discrimination in provision of immigration laws); *Reno v. Am.-Arab Anti-Discrimination Comm.*, 525 U.S. 471 (1999) (holding that courts lacked authority to review claim of selective enforcement of immigration laws against Arab and Muslim noncitizens); *Sale*

v. Haitian Ctrs. Council, Inc., 509 U.S. 155, 187-88 (1993) (holding that President's policy of interdicting Haitians fleeing political violence on the high seas and returning them to Haiti without hearing asylum and other claims, did not violate domestic or international law.)

20. See Johnson, Kevin R., "The Antiterrorism Act, the Immigration Reform Act, and Ideological Regulation in the Immigration Laws: Important Lessons For Citizens and Noncitizens," 28 St. Mary's L.J. 833, at 841-69 (1997) (same for political minorities); Johnson, Kevin R., "Public Benefits and Immigration: The Intersection of Immigration Status, Ethnicity, Gender, and Class," 42 UCLA L. Rev. 1509, 1519-28 (1995) (same for poor and working people); Johnson, Kevin R., "Race, the Immigration Laws, and Domestic Race Relations: A "Magic Mirror" into the Heart of Darkness," 73 Ind. L.J. 1111, 1119-47 (1998) (analyzing use of immigration laws to adversely affect racial minorities).

21. See *INS v. Aguirre-Aguirre*, 526 U.S. 415, 425 (1999) (recognizing "that judicial deference to the Executive Branch is especially appropriate in the immigration context where officials 'exercise especially sensitive political functions that implicate questions of foreign relations'" (quoting *INS v. Abudu*, 485 U.S. 94, 110 (1988)); *Mathews v. Diaz*, 426 U.S. 67, 81 n.17 (1976) ("'[A]ny policy toward aliens is vitally and intricately interwoven with contemporaneous policies in regard to the conduct of foreign relations, the war power, and the maintenance of a republican form of government. Such matters are so exclusively entrusted to the political branches of government as to be largely immune from judicial inquiry or interference.'") (quoting *Harisiades v. Shaughnessy*, 342 U.S. 580, 588-89 (1952) (footnote omitted)); see also Harold Hongju Koh, *Why the President (Almost) Always Wins in Foreign Affairs: Lessons of the Iran-Contra Affair*, 97 Yale L.J. 1255, 1258-63, 1291-1316 (1988) (analyzing the reasons why Presidents' foreign policy initiatives are rarely disturbed). Such deference combines with that ordinarily accorded agency action to create a most potent form of deference to the Executive Branch's immigration decisions. See *INS v. Elias-Zacarias*, 502 U.S. 478, 481 (1992) (stating that agency fact-finding could "be reversed only if the evidence presented...was such that a reasonable fact finder would have to conclude that the requisite fear of persecution existed"); *Aguirre-Aguirre*, 526 U.S. at 423-24 (relying on *Chevron U.S.A., Inc. v. Natural Resources Defense Council, Inc.*, 467 U.S. 837, 842 (1984) and deferring to INS interpretation of immigration law); see also Kevin R. Johnson, *Responding to the "Litigation Explosion": The Plain Meaning of Executive Branch Primacy Over Immigration*, 71 N.C. L.Rev. 413 (1993) (analyzing the impact of deference to agency action in Supreme Court's immigration decisions).

22. Akram, Susan M. and Kevin R. Johnson, "Race, Civil Rights, and Immigration Law After September 11, 2001: The Targeting of Arabs and Muslims," *NYU Annual Survey of American Law*, Vol. 58:295 (2002).

23. *Government West*, May/June, 2003 at 7. New York City, New York reports a weekly expenditure of $5,000,000 (population 8,008,278); San Francisco, California reports a weekly expenditure of $2,600,000 (population 776,733); Los Angeles, California reports a weekly expenditure of $2,500,000 (population 3,694,820); Atlanta, Georgia reports a weekly expenditure of 2,250,000 (population 416,474); and Fresno, California reports a weekly expenditure of $1,500,000 (population 427,652). Note that these expenses represent direct costs for homeland security. Many cities report significant, additional indirect homeland security costs.

PART II:

Is Jim Crow Alive and Well in America?

CHAPTER FIVE

In the Shadow of the Badge

You are driving down the road while minding your own business, as they say, when all of sudden, out of nowhere, red lights and sirens are breathing down your bumper. After the brief rush of adrenalin gives way to sheer panic, visions of spending an entire Saturday in traffic school dance in your head. For 10 minutes, you have been sitting on the side of the road fumbling miserably through the candy wrappers in your glove compartment to find your paperwork, only to discover that it's all expired. You feel like the opening act of a freak sideshow, humiliated by the police strobe light illuminating the inside of your vehicle. The only thing you are confident about is that at least 10 of your closest friends, relatives, coworkers, and neighbors have driven by. Without a doubt, you will be reminded about this moment at the next office party. Once you are handed the ticket, an almost pleasant voice can be heard drowning out all the expletives running through your mind, and to your surprise, it's your own, uttering a "Thank you" for the $200.00 speeding ticket. Sound familiar?

Let's look at this same scenario from another perspective. You are a young black man, and this is the third stop this month for a broken tail light. Stories you have read about "racial profiling" are playing out in your mind. You try to remain calm so your nervous demeanor and shaky voice won't be misconstrued as guilt. You don't dare open your glove compartment or search under your seat for your paperwork. You move slowly and keep your hands visible at all times. You can feel your heart racing, and you are overwhelmed with a combination of both dread and fear. You can feel the tension in the cold night air. Frustration and defensiveness are heard in your voice and are interpreted by the officer as "suspicious behavior." You know that nothing good can result from this encounter. The stage has been set, the stereotypes have been cast, and the curtain of doom has been lowered. What could have been a straightforward stop based on innocent motives will turn into a dangerous, out of control spiral, reinforcing both sides' suspicions about the other.

Regardless of color, these two scenarios have been experienced by most of the driving public, the latter serving as the focus of many publications on the issue of racial profiling. But it is likewise important to remember the side we don't hear—the one that often goes unreported and unconsidered when the stories of "traffic stops gone bad" surface. It is the story of "driver gone crazy."

> **WANTED: LAW ENFORCEMENT OFFICERS.** Must be a social worker, a mediator, a fighter, and a priest. Must be savvy to the criminal element yet have an unblemished criminal background. Candidates should be compassionate yet distant. Intimidating yet gentle. Aggressive yet always in control. Daily risk of death. Low pay. Must be willing to work all hours of the day and night in hazardous and extreme conditions. The faint of heart need not apply.

Unlike other professionals who have the luxury of choosing their assignments, police must be given extra leniency for their mistakes. As Jackson Toby, a professor of sociology at Rutgers University in New Jersey wrote in "Racial Profiling Doesn't Prove Cops Are Racist," which appeared in the March 11, 1999 issue of the *Wall Street Journal*: "They make house calls despite personal danger. They have to deal with not only criminals but also paranoid schizophrenics who have not taken their medication or suicidal people. The police come and do their best because the buck stops with them. Usually they succeed; occasionally, and sometimes tragically, they fail."

The public has a clear picture of what the police look like. Even those who have limited personal experience with the police need only turn on the television to watch the real-life cop dramas that accentuate and glamorize dangerous encounters with would-be criminals. Even in a routine traffic stop, it is easy to visualize the six-foot-tall, pistol-packing figure approach your car. It can be very intimidating and frightening, even when you know the only result will be a minor citation. But how do these images we see in the media compare with the real-life challenges faced by those in the law enforcement profession?

It is easy for the public to forget the people behind the uniforms and the tremendous sacrifices these husbands, wives, mothers, fathers, and siblings make daily. Most go through their workday never knowing who or what they will encounter when they stop a vehicle. This is especially true of patrol officers who respond to anything and everything ranging from a child fatality to a suicide. When was the last time you walked into your office at work and saw a badly mutilated dead body lying on the floor? A cop's office is the street, and he or she may respond to five dead body calls in a week or month and must do so without showing any emotion. It is unrealistic to think that any person would be able to work under such conditions for a period of years without it eventually taking its toll.

A few months ago, a veteran officer recounted a story about a young officer in his department who had stopped a motorist for a minor traffic violation (in case you're wondering, the man he stopped was white). As he approached the car, the driver, without warning, pointed a gun at the officer at point blank range and pulled the trigger. The officer had no time to react. The only reason the officer was not killed was that the driver's gun did not discharge. We'll call this encounter a case of "driver gone crazy."

How many of us go to work wondering whether we will have a gun pulled on us? This is a daily reality for officers. The stress is real and constant, and the sacrifice is great. Officers are conditioned by these negative events, which affect how they approach each call. We must remember that for every traffic stop that ends this way, there is a handful of others in which the gun did discharge and the officer never saw what was coming. Do you think this young officer will ever approach a traffic stop the same way again?

Most of us would not want to embark knowingly on a career path with such a high personal price; however, for others, it is this very promise of danger and excitement that is alluring about the law enforcement profession. The success often hinges on an individual's ability to manage these awesome powers and emotions and channel them toward the public good. Though many of these abilities are borne out of the individual characteristics and experiences the individual brings to the job, many of them are developed while working behind the scenes in a profession that is often shielded from the public.

All things considered, it is surprising that the police department, the branch of local government that has the most contact with the public, remains the most mysterious. Unlike hospitals and educational institutions that are under strict scrutiny and constant monitoring by other agencies, police departments are designed to work independently with little, if any, interference from outside auditors. Though this trait of law enforcement is often romanticized in TV dramas and the movies, it remains a source of intense criticism and public distrust in real life.

When used for the common good, this curtain of mystique can be a necessary and highly effective tool. It secures the anonymity of victims and perpetrators, allows police operations and investigations to be carried out safely and effectively, and protects officers and their families from retaliation by criminals. But as with anything good, it has its downsides when used to pursue political agendas and shield corruption, and it leaves many to wonder what role, if any, police politics plays in the practice of racial profiling. The answer may surprise you.

To understand this integral connection, there needs to be an appreciation of how a police agency operates. In this section, we will take a comprehensive look at what it takes to become a police officer, what goes on inside a police agency, the relationship between elected officials and the top brass, and the dynamics that govern the relationships between supervisors and officers. We will also examine common challenges faced by some organizations, including internal and external politics, training for new recruits, discipline, the infamous "code of silence," and the role of internal affairs divisions.

"Rogue" Cops

Most officers come to the force with very limited life experience. Those fresh out of high school or college see law enforcement as a glamorous profession that allows them to carry a gun and experience the real-life dramas that are reminiscent of the "cops and robbers" games played in their youth. Even though extensive testing, a rigidly controlled background-check process, and a psychological profile are performed prior to hiring new officers, many lack the maturity to handle the life-and-death decisions they face each day. These officers quickly realize that the job on the street is nothing like the Hollywood portrayals romanticized on television and in the movies.

This quest to become a police officer begins with about six months of rigorous academy training. Shortly thereafter, these young men and women are set loose with a badge, a gun, and nearly unbridled power. When the individual officer, often without a superior's scrutiny, begins to lose touch with the public's expectations and misuses this power, there is a chance that the officer's authority will be misdirected. It is within this gray area that fear and personal bias often overpower common sense and training and cause the officer to engage in practices that are beyond the lawful scope of his or her duties.

When the public witnesses officer misconduct, the whole system suffers. These incidents not only cost the officer the public's respect, but they also foster suspicion of the entire profession. We continue to be reminded how something as simple as a traffic stop can escalate and sometimes transform what should have been a minor incident into a national news event. If race is a factor, public outcry is sure to follow, sparking scenarios such as the Watts Riots and the uprising that followed the Rodney King beating verdict.

When these allegations of racial profiling and police violence surface, there is usually a clear distinction between the officer who has a clean record and the one who has a laundry list of citizen complaints and a reputation for being a "rogue" officer. In the case of the former, a sufficient remedy may be a comprehensive training program coupled with a review of department policies and procedures. Assuming the offense is minor, an officer with no track record of misconduct should remain on the force while undergoing a comprehensive training program unless the officer continues to exhibit a pattern of bad judgment. In other cases, however, the violation may be so serious that it warrants suspension of the officer while the allegations are being investigated. In the more extreme cases, the officer should be dismissed.

When officers become the source of repeated civil rights violations, it is questionable whether they should have ever been hired and doubtful whether any amount of training or counseling will change their pattern of behavior. These officers give the entire profession a bad reputation. In the wake of scandal, police organizations are quick to point the finger at these "rogue" officers and often dismiss the large percentage of citizen complaints and lawsuits a particular officer may have in his or her history. It is baffling to the public when these officers are exposed and it is revealed that the offender has a long history of complaints and legal action for similar violations yet remains on the force to continue the same pattern of behavior. Despite these early warning signs, many of these officers not only remain on the force but also are routinely promoted to serve as mentors, trainers, and supervisors for new officers. The trend to keep these rogue officers is particularly dangerous in the legal sense, often likened to a game of roulette. When administrators know of an officer's violent and dangerous propensities and fail to take any affirmative steps to intervene, they are, in effect, condoning the officer's actions. If a defendant can convince a jury that the police department either actually or implicitly condoned the behavior, the monetary ramifications can be significant. Given the irreparable damage one of these scandals can inflict on a police department, it is surprising that early warning systems are not more routinely implemented to identify these repeat offenders, followed by rehabilitation or, alternatively, dismissing the more serious transgressors from their duties altogether.

When an organization has an early warning system in place, it is usually triggered by numerous citizen complaints filed within a short period of time. Though most officers engaging in suspect practices will inevitably be exposed through this process, some organizations may still be slow to identify problem officers because of impediments for filing complaints and internal code of silence issues. Furthermore, these numbers are often skewed, in part because civil lawsuits are not always counted in the tallying of complaints, regardless of the outcome. Fortunately, this trend is beginning to change. In two consent decrees reached by the Justice Department with police departments exhibiting a "pattern or practice" of abuse, civil lawsuit data will be required in future oversight systems.

In Boston, the St. Clair Commission identified its concerns about the department's handling of "rogue" officers:

> "Our review of IAD files revealed a disturbing pattern of allegations of violence toward citizens by a small number of officers. The failure to monitor and evaluate the performance of police officers—particularly those with established patterns of alleged misconduct—is a major deficiency in the management of the department and results in an unnecessarily dangerous situation.... No police department and no community should tolerate a situation where officers with a long record of alleged misconduct, including some with histories of alleged physical abuse of citizens, remain on the street largely unidentified and unsupervised."[1]

The Christopher Commission investigating the Los Angeles Police Department echoed these findings:

"There is a significant number of officers in the LAPD who repetitively use excessive force against the public and persistently ignore the written guidelines of the Department regarding force."[2]

Investigations revealed that not only did the Los Angeles Police Department fail to deal with offending officers, but it also often promoted them and rewarded them with positive performance evaluations.[3] The testimony of former Los Angeles Police Department Assistant Chief Jesse Brewer acknowledged the overall findings of the commission: "We know who the bad guys are. Reputations become well known, especially to the sergeants and then of course to lieutenants and captains in the areas ...But I don't see anyone bring these people up..."[4]

Under new administration, the Los Angeles Police Department is working closely with the Department of Justice to remedy shortfalls identified within the organization.

In the current political and social climate, there should be no doubt that the systems in place in many agencies will not work in our ever-changing, diverse society. Just as in the private sector, employee performance must be closely tracked and assessed on a regular basis. These assessments should play a significant role in and correlate to promotions, pay increases, assignments, and the prospect of future employment. When inadequacies are revealed, the employee should be offered the opportunity to work toward improving performance. In cases where training and/or appropriate counseling does not yield results, the employee should be reassigned or terminated on the basis of the frequency and severity of the violations. When rogue officers are exposed early on, instances of police misconduct will certainly diminish, and the chances of these individuals moving up the ranks to serve in supervisory or leadership positions will be minimized.

The Code of Silence

When trying to understand the code of silence, one must first ask the obvious question, why does the code of silence exist? The answer is really quite simple: cops need cops to survive on the street. When a cop is outgunned or outnumbered, the only one that will be coming to his or her aid is a fellow officer. If a cop alienates himself or herself from other officers, the cop may be as good as dead.

It is this special brotherhood among police officers that distinguishes law enforcement from other institutions. In addition to this brotherhood, police officers are granted special powers unlike those conferred on other professions. Not only can the police put in motion a process to take away one's constitutional rights, but also they are permitted to use force, and sometimes even deadly force, to do so. Ideally, officers' primary loyalty is to the public they serve; however, this concept often goes astray as early as the police academy, where in some cases, officers are trained that their primary loyalty is to their fellow officers. It is this loyalty that sometimes takes a negative turn, particularly when officers conceal misconduct under a code of silence.

The code of silence, also known as the "blue wall of silence," is based on the premise that an officer does not reveal negative information about a fellow officer. In more extreme cases, officers may obstruct justice and lie under oath to save themselves or a fellow officer from discipline or prosecution. Many point to the code of silence as one reason officers can continue to engage in racially motivated practices without interference from their peers or supervisors.

A 2000 study examining officers' feelings about the code of silence revealed a significant gap between officers' attitudes about protecting wrongdoers versus actually turning them in. The study reported that more than 80% of officers surveyed rejected the code of silence as an essential part of the mutual trust necessary to good policing. Regardless, nearly one-quarter agreed that whistle blowing was not worth it, and more than two-thirds acknowledged that police officers who report instances of police misconduct are likely to be ostracized by fellow officers. Nearly 53% of all officers surveyed agreed that it is not uncommon for officers to "turn a blind eye" to other officers' improper conduct. The study also found that "a surprising 6 in 10 (61%) indicated that police officers do not always report even serious criminal violations that involve the abuse of authority by fellow officers."[5]

Experts studying this phenomenon have divided the types of incidents prompting officers to take part in code of silence practices into five parts. Of the five, anger was the most frequent incident in which the code of silence was used. In fact, out of 532 code of silence incidents, 41% were related to anger and the excessive use of force. Peer pressure represented 20% of the code of silence violations. The third most common motivation was greed; it represented 16% of the incidents. The fourth was lust at 8%, and the remaining 15% fell into other categories such as not arresting off-duty officers who were drinking and driving while intoxicated, illegal searches, hostile or defensive narrative, doing personal business while on duty, and perjury.[6] Similar studies have revealed that a majority of officers have participated in some form of code of silence misconduct in their careers.

Though code of silence practices are usually confined to line officers, they become even more dangerous when those in command turn a blind eye on misdeeds to protect their own. In cities where police corruption has been known to run rampant, code of silence practices have been uncovered far up the chain of command, all the way to the chief of police. In many instances, this conduct has even extended into the justice system. This may occur when a district attorney proceeds to prosecute a criminal case based largely on an officer's suspect testimony in order to gain a conviction rather than question the officer's candor. When this occurs, all sides suffer. The police become untrustworthy advocates of justice, and the public is left to wonder to what extent—if any—the police can be trusted.

Despite these risks, some officers are left with little choice when faced with a code of silence dilemma. The ramifications for officers who go against the code can be severe, usually leaving the officer with two choices: either keep quiet or quit. In many cases, offending officers have been the subject of ostracism and have had to endure threats of physical harm or even death. Perhaps even more troubling is the fear that fellow officers will not back them up in dangerous situations on the street.

A former NYPD officer testified in a hearing before the Mollen Commission that he never feared another officer would turn him in because there was a Blue Wall of Silence. "Cops don't tell on cops...," he said. "If a cop decided to tell on me, his career's ruined...He's going to be labeled as a rat." Another officer, testifying under hidden identity because of the code, stated that officers first learn of the code in the police academy, with instructors telling them never to be a "rat." He explained, "See, we're all blue...we have to protect each other no matter what."[7]

When the nature of police work is closely examined, it is not surprising that many officers choose to protect their own rather than risk being labeled a "snitch." The law enforcement profession is a lonely one; the tremendous physical and mental stress coupled with the unconventional days off and erratic work schedules often contribute to high divorce and alcoholism rates. In turn, it is quite common for officers to interact with each other socially outside of the workplace. These friendships, coupled with the great extent to which fellow officers must depend on each other in life-and-death situations, make it difficult to speak up against another officer when questionable practices arise. Officers who turn against their own not only risk destroying their careers but also often lose their entire social support system in the process.

Without critical testimony from fellow officers to substantiate citizen complaints about civil rights abuses, accusations of police abuse turn into a "he said, she said" match, and even the most rigid internal investigation process comes to a halt for lack of evidence of any violation.

Reports by veteran officers indicate that code of silence practices continue to dominate the profession. Though instances may be less blatant and less talked about than in years past, they still exist; the code of silence is a kind of unwritten rule for survival. In modern-day law enforcement, code of silence practices are a somewhat abstract concept for new officers and rarely surface in training or discussions within the organization. This curtain of mystique often leads to confusion among new recruits as to what constitutes a code of silence dilemma, thus leaving the inexperienced to learn the law of the land from those eager to cover up questionable practices. For example, does any moral or ethical transgression by another officer raise a potential code of silence dilemma, or must it be of a certain level of seriousness to warrant a fellow officer to come forward and advise superiors? Moreover, once an officer comes forward to report misconduct within an organization, how can he or she avoid being labeled a "snitch," particularly if the allegations implicate a supervisor or higher-ranking administrator?

Though specific solutions to the code of silence problem will be discussed in a later section, it should be noted here that training programs that teach officers to identify and address code of silence dilemmas must be integrated into the police academy and continuing education programs for veteran officers. Specifically, training must be tailored to teach officers when an instance of officer misconduct must be reported to superiors. Likewise, officers must be provided with assurances that when they report such instances, they will be protected from retaliation by fellow officers.

Even with the implementation of aggressive training programs, many in law enforcement doubt the code of silence will ever completely disappear. In some cases, officers have no incentive to tell the truth and every reason to lie. Experts and line officers alike point to weak administrations and supervision as one of the main reasons such practices are allowed to continue. Others blame the "us versus them" mentality prevalent in so many organizations. Some even point to highly suspect guidelines similar to that championed by a New York City police union, which gives officers a 48-hour "cooling off" period before they are required to give an official statement about an incident. Although not definitive, critics suggest that this 48-hour window is nothing more than a chance for officers to get their stories straight. Critics also suggest that when the police department itself conducts investigations, the likelihood that the public will view the proceedings as objective is slim.

Internal Affairs Divisions: Who's Policing the Police?

Unlike other professions that answer to governmental or independent oversight commissions, law enforcement institutions retain the right to police themselves. Though most law enforcement agencies are bound under the state's penal code to abide by certain regulations when handling complaints from the public, the systems in place are generally unique to each individual agency and may vary on the basis of the size of the organization.

In California, for example, agencies must establish a formal procedure to investigate citizen complaints against any personnel of the agency and must make a written description of the procedure available to the public. When a citizen complaint is filed, the organization must retain it for at least five years. [8] Many state penal codes may also direct organizations as to the proper method for maintaining the information in an officer's personnel file and establish guidelines about the purposes for which the information may be used in the future.

Though the general guidelines of the citizen complaint process are usually established by law, many agencies remain free to establish their own internal procedures for handling these contacts with the public. In small to midsize police agencies, citizens may be asked either to call or come in to the police department to voice their grievance. This process usually involves a meeting between the citizen and the supervisor, who acts as an intermediary to try to resolve the problem before a formal written complaint against the officer is initiated. If a consultation with the police supervisor does not resolve the problem, the citizen may proceed to file a formal written complaint.

On the complaint form, the citizen is asked to convey as much detailed information about the incident as possible. Once completed, the form is turned over to an investigator within the department, which sets the formal internal investigation in motion.

The internal affairs investigation process usually varies from state to state, in part because of state regulations that set forth an officer's rights when he or she is investigated for any sort of alleged misconduct. For example, in California, the Peace Officer's Bill of Rights[9] guarantees officers the right to legal representation, limits the use of compelled statements, bifurcates the criminal process from the employment process, and allows the officer an opportunity for a multiphase appeal before the imposition of termination proceedings or punitive actions.

Regardless of the specific statutes that govern this investigatory process, the job of the internal investigator is generally twofold. First, the investigator must provide the officer with notice of the complaint. Once the officer is aware of the complaint, the officer may choose to hire an attorney for representation prior to being questioned by the investigator. After the investigator obtains an official statement from the officer, he or she proceeds to contact witnesses, examine evidence, and gather any relevant information pertaining to the allegations in the complaint. The investigator will then make a formal finding and will assign one of four possible outcomes to the complaint: sustained, not sustained, exonerated, or unfounded. If a complaint is "sustained," the investigation disclosed sufficient information to prove the citizen's allegation. A finding of "not sustained" indicates that the investigation failed to reveal enough evidence either to prove or disprove the allegation. The officer will be "exonerated" if the investigation reveals that the actions of the peace officer that formed the basis for the complaint were not violations of law or department policy. Finally, the complaint will be "unfounded" if the investigation clearly establishes that the allegation(s) in the complaint did not occur as alleged.[10] In other states, complaints may be resolved as either frivolous, unfounded, or exonerated will be removed from an officer's general personnel file prior to any official determination relating to promotion, transfer, or disciplinary action by the agency.

Once the internal investigation portion of the complaint process is complete, the matter is turned over to the chief of police for review and disposition. The chief will review the findings, render a final determination of the resolution, and inform the officer and the citizen of the final outcome. In larger organizations, this internal investigation process may be fundamentally the same; however, the final outcome may be subject to review by an outside oversight committee such as a citizen review board or government oversight committee.

If the citizen's complaint is sustained, the officer may be subject to a wide range of disciplinary actions depending on the severity of the violation. Some alternatives include counseling, training, an oral or written reprimand, suspension, demotion, or dismissal.

Regardless of this thorough procedure, there are times when a citizen may not agree with the final disposition, thus further perpetuating the citizen's lack of trust in the internal investigation process. In most cases, the disposition is directly linked to a lack of evidence against the officer, which makes it impossible for the investigator to substantiate the complaint. When this occurs, the citizen is usually encouraged to initiate contact with the chief to try to resolve any concerns relating to the outcome. Alternatively, the citizen may choose to contact a civil rights organization, a private attorney, the state's attorney general's office, or the U.S. Attorney's Office for further investigation into the complaint.

Regardless of who is reviewing the matter, the job of investigating allegations of police misconduct remains particularly challenging in light of the evidentiary safeguards that are inherent in the investigatory process itself. Perhaps the most clear-cut case of officer misconduct occurs when there is some sort of physical act that the officer has been accused of committing. For example, if a citizen has been punched, hit, or dragged, there is usually physical evidence and witnesses to substantiate the officer's misconduct. Likewise, if a racial slur accompanies an enforcement action, there is evidence to substantiate an allegation of racial profiling. In many instances of racial profiling, however, the allegations are based entirely on a person's perception of the mental mindset of the officer. In other words, whatever may be the real motive for the stop cannot be measured or evaluated because the officer will likely choose to keep it secret. When the real motive for the stop is concealed, internal investigators simply do not have evidence of the officer's mental mindset to find him or her at fault. Merely weighing the probabilities or balancing the evidence is not the established standard for finding fault in this forum. Definitive proof that the officer was engaging in racial profiling is required, or the officer will be exonerated.

Despite public criticism, police agencies are not willing to give up this system of policing themselves. Similarly, nearly 95% of officers surveyed disagreed with the notion that investigations of police misconduct are usually biased in favor of the police.[11] When citizens and civil rights groups demand more accountability for police departments and officers, a common response is that there is an effective system already in place. If you feel you've been wronged, go to your local police department and file a citizen complaint. Sounds simple enough, right? Not necessarily.

A *Dateline NBC* investigation suggested that filing a complaint may not be as simple and painless as it sounds. To prove the point, *Dateline* sent a black undercover reporter into several New York police precincts to file a complaint. In each precinct, the reporter posed as a citizen, advising the desk officer that he wanted to file a complaint against an officer. In every precinct but one, the reporter was treated with hostility and sarcasm and was asked, "What did you do?" The reporter was also denied a complaint form until he was interviewed about the incident. There was only one precinct that treated the reporter right by giving him a complaint form and telling him how to fill it out.

It is no surprise that if citizens are put through this intimidating and degrading ordeal just to file a complaint, many will be deterred from doing so. Perhaps that is the point. This, coupled with the fact that some citizens never get a resolution to their complaints, may also be a key reason many acts of police misconduct go unreported. For many complainants, resolution amounts to the receipt of a form letter in the mail. Even the most effective internal investigation systems, hiding behind a cloak of secrecy, cause the public to question the legitimacy of the citizen complaint process and the validity of the resulting outcomes.

Citizens are not the only ones questioning the effectiveness of such a system. A 1998 Human Rights Watch report generated from a study of 14 major U.S. cities[12] revealed, "No outside review, including [their] own, has found the operations of internal affairs divisions in any of the major U.S. cities satisfactory."[13] Similar outcomes have been reported in other independent reviews of internal investigation divisions. Moreover, all three commissions reviewing police misconduct in three major cities[14] since 1991 identified serious shortcomings in the way in which internal affairs divisions handled complaints. Investigations by reporters and police abuse experts examining other major cities[15] produced similar results, indicating that internal investigations were not being properly conducted. Many of these examinations confirmed allegations of substandard investigations, sloppy procedures, an apparent bias toward fellow officers, a low rate of allegations sustained for excessive force, and a failure to identify and discipline problem officers with repeated complaints.

When flashed across the 6:00 news, reports of poor internal investigations in the police department often provide a tainted view of the scope of the problem and lead many to believe that all police departments are polluted with corruption. The result is analogous to racial profiling; it's what we'll call "police profiling."

To put this problem in perspective, it would be negligent to omit the fact that many departments *do* conduct satisfactory investigations and *do* take appropriate action when their own internal investigations uncover an abuse of power. More important, oversight commissions and journalistic investigations have revealed that many of the complaints reviewed by these divisions are related to a small number of problem officers. It takes only a few bad cops to perpetuate a negative image of police across the country, particularly in cities such Los Angeles and Philadelphia, where past corruption has been caught on videotape. Despite the aggressive efforts of these cities to regain citizens' trust, these troubling images remain ingrained in the minds of the public.

One of the biggest debates between law enforcement and the public is whether internal investigation divisions need to operate under a cloak of secrecy when investigating citizen complaints. Even when the secrecy seems legitimate and can be justified by an officer's right to privacy, this closed-door approach gives the public the *perception* that there may be something to hide. If and when information finally reaches the public, it generally takes the form of media reports of high-profile investigations into major scandals.

Studies have revealed that the public's perception of the complaint process often has a measurable and detrimental effect on the number of citizen complaints agencies receive. For example, after reviewing 250 internal affairs division cases, the St. Clair Commission in Boston concluded that the division was sustaining an abnormally low number of complaints:

> "Our investigation into the Department's handling of citizen complaints of police misconduct...was particularly troubling. Our study revealed an investigative and hearing process characterized by shoddy, halfhearted investigations, lengthy delays, and inadequate documentation and record keeping. The present internal affairs process is unfairly skewed against those bringing a complaint. Given the internal affairs division's ("IAD") failure to routinely provide thorough and timely investigations of complaints against officers, it is no surprise that the overwhelming majority of community residents we spoke to have little confidence in the Department's ability or willingness to police itself..."[16]

The Christopher Commission reported similar findings in Los Angeles. Its report revealed that the internal affairs division of the LAPD had sustained only 2% of its complaints of excessive force, thus indicating "that there are significant problems with the initiation, investigation, and classification of complaints." It characterized the internal affairs division investigations as "unfairly skewed against the complainant."[17] In Philadelphia, a review of more than 2,000 complaints filed from 1989 to 1998 revealed that most led nowhere.

It is important to interject here that a good number of the complaints filed against police officers have little or no merit. Citizens file complaints for numerous reasons, some of which include publicity; anticipated monetary gain; and retaliation against an officer who may have had a negative contact with them, a friend, or a family member. Additionally, many of the complaints stem from legitimate police actions taken in response to dangerous situations that are instigated by the suspect. Even if one factors in these variables, however, it is hard to rationalize the large percentage of citizen complaints that are ultimately found to be unwarranted.

Politics versus Progress

Elected Officials see the world through political lenses—with one eye on what their constituents value.

—*Working Together, A Guide for Elected and Appointed Officials,*
International City/County Management
Association (ICMA)

Despite accusations to the contrary, law enforcement is acutely aware that racial profiling exists. Pressure is being applied on all sides. One need not look far to see that it is often the political nature of the profession that puts both officers and administrators under tremendous pressure to acknowledge and address allegations of racial profiling and police misconduct within their organizations. Though most top law enforcement administrators work diligently to answer to the citizens they serve, others prefer to stay out of the limelight to keep the elected officials happy in order to retain their own high-ranking, well-paid positions. Similarly, these elected officials often rely on the political support and endorsement of local law enforcement agencies and politically powerful police unions, which makes them reluctant to construct demands that might alienate these groups.

Regardless, some politicians are under increasing pressure from civil rights groups to make changes within their cities' police agencies. Proponents argue that politicians who are closest to the communities' needs should step in and exert control on the upper management in an effort to eradicate any form of racial discrimination in law enforcement practices. In some governmental agencies, proposals are being implemented through the back door, by total dominance of the budget by elected officials, exertion of political pressure in the approval of hiring practices and equipment purchases, and the imposition of restrictions on the top at-will administrative positions. These steps alone have reduced the amount of control many police chiefs have over their own departments.

Although politicians have been hopeful that these practices would mold the organization's values to suit the political needs of the community, it has become increasingly apparent that these efforts have been unsuccessful at eliminating racial discrimination. This result reminds us that those at the top of the ladder do not necessarily have the most visible power in law enforcement. In the court of public opinion, the individual officer the public encounters on the street holds the power. The bottom line is that these encounters usually dictate the success or failure of those in ultimate control.

Particularly in larger organizations, police department administrators have only limited ability to monitor an officer's enforcement practices or contacts on the street. They are prohibited by law from setting quotas or disciplining for nonproductivity in custodial enforcement.[18] Moreover, the fundamental premise of police work is the officer's ability to work independently and use discretion and ethics when responding to calls and initiating stops. Unfortunately, many officers lack the skills to use these traits simultaneously and effectively. Not surprisingly, the absence of such traits on the street correlates directly to the lack of relevant training in many police academy and continuing education programs.

When unethical, improper law enforcement tactics practiced by a few officers surface in the media, the problem hits the whole department hard, with administrators looking for ways to circumvent the crime problem with approaches that will yield fast and quantifiable results. In several cities where aggressive policing tactics have been implemented, politicians often praise departments for their hard-line approach to law enforcement, yet they fail to recognize that these tactics usually correlate with a rise in police brutality complaints.

In 1994, for example, police in New York City began an experiment focused on "quality of life" policing. This tactic was based on the premise of reduced tolerance for nonviolent, petty crimes. Although many praised these efforts designed to make the streets of New York safer, not everyone shared the sentiment. Initially, minorities were happy with the increased police presence in their neighborhoods, but police-community relations soon turned sour when aggressive policing sometimes led to harassment of minorities. At the time this new quality of life policing took hold, citizen complaints rose 37% from 1993 to 1994. By the end of 1996, complaints increased 56% from the 1993 level.[19] One New York citizen complained "[the police] will bother you just for looking at them...[They] throw you against the car and start searching you like you're a criminal."[20]

In response to the protests, former Police Commissioner Howard Safir implemented a new program to reduce the number of citizen complaints. The aggressive program, aimed to teach officers courtesy, professionalism, and respect (CPR), was designed to hold police commanders accountable for such complaints. Though the number of citizen complaints dropped under this new program, they remained higher than they were prior to the initiation of quality of life policing.

Despite his efforts to improve relations with the community, Safir could not escape the unrest that overshadowed his aggressive stance on crime. Though instrumental in reducing homicide rates from 2,245 in 1990 to 671 by the time he resigned in 2000, many argue that these aggressive efforts by the police came at a price to those in minority communities, specifically, citizens' civil rights.

Though many critics are poised to discredit police, the public should not lose sight of the fact that a majority of police departments around the nation are run by upstanding police administrators who strive to serve the public and do so quite effectively. When problems surface, it is quite often the result of aggressive efforts by the police to combat crime and reduce crime rates in direct response to public demands. Though sometimes correlating to a rise in complaints of police misconduct, the most successful leaders are able to strike a balance between meeting crime reduction goals and preserving the civil rights of those they encounter in the process. When this delicate balance is not successfully achieved, however, the results are far reaching and often translate into media reports and public suspicion about the integrity of the entire profession. In more extreme cases of alleged civil rights violations, civil rights organizations stand poised to challenge police practices on behalf of the public.

(Endnotes)

1. St. Clair Commission report, p. iv.

2. Christopher Commission report, foreword.

3. Christopher Commission report, p. iv.

4. Christopher Commission report, p. ix.

5. Weisburd, David, Rosann Greenspan with Edwin E. Hamilton, Hubert Williams, and Kellie A. Bryant, *National Institute of Justice Research in Brief*, May, 2000 at 3. "The Police Foundation's nationally representative telephone survey of 925 randomly selected American police officers from 121 departments explores the officers' views on the abuse of police authority. Officers also provided information on different forms of abuse they have observed, the frequency of abuse in their departments, and effective strategies for controlling abuse. General findings, as well as differing attitudes of black, white, and other minority officers, are presented and discussed in this Brief."

6. Trautman, Neal, "Truth About Police Code of Silence Revealed." See other information from the National Institute of Ethics at http://www.ethicsinstitute.com.

7. Mollen Commission report, p. 53, 55, 58.

8. California Penal Code §832.5.

9. California Government Code §3200 and 3300.

10. California Penal Code §832.5.

11. Weisburd, David, Rosann Greenspan with Edwin E. Hamilton, Hubert Williams, and Kellie A. Bryant, *National Institute of Justice Research in Brief*, May, 2000 at 6. "The Police Foundation's nationally representative telephone survey of 925 randomly selected American police officers from 121 departments explores the officers' views on the abuse of police authority. Officers also provided information on different forms of abuse they have observed, the frequency of abuse in their departments, and effective strategies for controlling abuse. General findings, as well as differing attitudes of black, white, and other minority officers, are presented and discussed in this Brief."

12. *Shielded from Justice: Police Brutality and Accountability in the United States*

13. A footnote in this report indicates "[a]n exception to entirely negative reviews of internal affairs units may be a November 1997 report by the new "Integrity and Accountability" officer in Philadelphia. While noting continuing deficiencies, the officer found the investigations thorough and unbiased. His positive assessment was not shared by community activists who also viewed internal affairs files, as part of an agreement between the city and civil rights groups."

14. The cities examined included Boston, Los Angeles, and New York.

15. The other cities included Philadelphia, San Francisco, Chicago, Atlanta, and New Orleans.

16. St. Clair Commission report, pp. iii-iv.

17. Christopher Commission Report, p. 153.

18. See California Vehicle Code §41602: "No state or local agency employing peace officers engaged in the enforcement of this code or any local ordinance adopted pursuant to this code, may establish any policy requiring any peace officer to meet an arrest quota." Although this code addresses only the law in California, many states have similar legislation prohibiting arrest quotas.

19. Lii, Jane H., "When the saviors are seen as sinners," *New York Times*, May 18, 1997.

20. Pierre-Pierre, Garry, "Examining a jump in police brutality complaints," *New York Times*, February 22, 1995.

CHAPTER SIX

———◆·◆·◆———

One Perspective:
Civil Rights Groups Lead the Fight to End Racial
Profiling in America

Civil rights groups have long identified racial profiling as one of their highest priority issues. The problem is nothing new to civil rights proponents, with many organizations working for decades to stop illegal, race-based vehicle stops by law enforcement. More recently, however, the fight to end this practice has expanded to include the dragnet-style terrorist intervention and detention practices that are being conducted by some law enforcement and government agencies.

Despite the unyielding commitment by these organizations over the past few decades, their work became increasingly difficult in 1996 when the U.S. Supreme Court ruled that the constitutional reasonableness of a traffic stop does not depend on the actual motivations of the officers involved.[1] This blow to civil rights groups served as a vivid reminder that despite the illegality of racial profiling as a crime-fighting tactic, law enforcement could subversively engage in pretext stops to accomplish the same objective, as long as an officer could find a traffic violation that would justify the initial stop.

> *"There are some instances when a law is just on its face and unjust in its application. For instance, I was arrested Friday on a charge of parading without a permit. Now there is nothing wrong with an ordinance which requires a permit for a parade, but when the ordinance is used to preserve segregation and to deny citizens the First-Amendment privilege of peaceful assembly and peaceful protest, then it becomes unjust."*

—Rev. Dr. Martin Luther King, Jr.
Letter from the Birmingham Jail
April 16, 1963

The wavering law in this area has created an undercurrent within the legal community, with some experts criticizing courts for routinely finding that reasonable suspicion has been established by factors that are very close to those the Supreme Court originally found insufficient. This phenomenon becomes even more disturbing when in some cases "reasonable suspicion" equates to nothing more than being the wrong color or in the wrong place at the wrong time. When police equate "high-crime areas" with inner-city neighborhoods in which a high percentage of the community is black and Hispanic, those that reside in these neighborhoods begin any police encounter with one reasonable suspicion strike against them.

Though specific case law setting forth these guidelines will be discussed later in detail, it should be noted here that many court decisions over the past decade can be traced directly to the federal government's war on drugs and the deaths that are attributable to the illegal drug trade. Legal scholars project that similar cases stemming from terrorist intervention activities will be the next fertile ground for Supreme Court interpretation. If the trend to expand police discretion continues, many anticipate that tens of thousands of innocent people across the country will become victims of racial profiling. Despite objections from civil rights leaders, what constitutes "reasonable suspicion" continues to be expanded by judges across the country and leaves many to wonder whether there is any legitimate correlation between skin color, socioeconomic status, and criminal propensities.

Notwithstanding crime enforcement trends that seem to target those in these lower-income areas, case studies, in addition to a 1999 Gallup Poll study, seem to confirm that racial profiling victims are not exclusively the uneducated or poor. The problem is widespread and has been reported among prominent athletes, actors, members of Congress, attorneys, doctors, and business leaders. Some point to this phenomenon as more of an epidemic, which would suggest that racial profiling has become a national problem that singles out no one within certain racial groups. Whatever the scope, it has become clear that racial profiling is rejected by an overwhelming number of Americans and is seen as an unfair practice that continues to drive a wedge between law enforcement and the public.

This wedge has become increasingly deep in minority communities, particularly in the wake of countless media reports highlighting suspicious law enforcement tactics. In order to understand the real challenges posed by this problem, we will examine actual scenarios that range from arguably innocent mistakes by inexperienced officers to flagrant harassment of minorities by the very people sworn to protect them.

In the stories of those who believe they have been victims of racial profiling, we hear a mix of fear and anger. Many express the unsettling feeling they experience even during their most innocent encounters with police and the uncertainty over whether the person called to help them will end up being the one who causes them the most harm. Though most of the encounters between police and the public are uneventful, a small handful are not. In these instances, the fear process is set into motion, often fueled by the individual's own experiences with law enforcement and/or information they gleaned from media reports of police abuse. In some instances, victims express feelings of betrayal when they discover that officers who may even be part of their racial group are wrongfully singling them out as criminal suspects.

The reports of those who believe they have been victims of racial profiling serve as a powerful testament to the seriousness of the problem. Although the following accounts specifically deal with racial profiling as it pertains to law enforcement and pretext traffic stops, this practice is far more widespread than these limited examples suggest. We believe that these accounts that have gained national attention are probably the best way to illustrate the harmful outcomes that result when race or some other discriminatory factor is used as a means of segregating and classifying individuals. These stories also serve as a vivid reminder that regardless of your race, position in society, or activities, there is no safe haven from this practice. There are those that believe racial profiling is not harmful and, in fact, that it may be helpful in some facets of law enforcement. Civil rights groups vehemently disagree. We present you with actual case studies that will let you be the judge.

At one end of the spectrum is the case of Collie Brown, who was driving in New York from Albany to Bethlehem with his young daughter asleep in the car. Mr. Brown noticed that his headlights were dimming, so he stopped the car and got out to see what was causing the problem. A Bethlehem police officer pulled up behind him with lights flashing, walked up to the car, and asked if he needed any help. When Brown replied that he did not need any assistance, the officer told him to get behind the car and proceeded to handcuff him. The officer informed Brown that the car had been reported stolen, which was true. Brown had reported the car stolen many months earlier after it had been hot-wired in front of his home in Albany. The Albany police, however, had recovered the car a week after the theft. At no point prior to being handcuffed was Brown asked for his registration or driver's license in order to prove that he was the registered owner of the vehicle. The officer eventually retrieved Brown's wallet from the car and discovered that the car did belong to him, and Brown was released.[2]

Though some may defend the officer's actions during the stop as consistent with standard police procedure, others cite racial profiling. Law enforcement defends the tactic of handcuffing the suspect of an auto theft prior to determining whether the person is actually the owner of the car. In fact, many point to the procedure as necessary and cautionary, motivated by officer safety. Veteran officers contend that the officer was following standard procedure on the basis of his belief that the automobile was stolen and would have treated any driver similarly. The fact that Brown was African American, however, poses the question of whether a white driver would have been treated the same in a similar encounter. Although this situation could probably be analyzed either way, others are not so cut-and-dried.

The more commonly reported encounters are analogous to that of Arizona resident Laurel Riggs. Mr. Riggs, a 42-year-old marketing representative, was driving to a popular bar and restaurant in Scottsdale. He noticed a police car behind him as it flashed its emergency lights and indicated for him to pull over. He stopped his car and proceeded to get out but had no idea why he was being stopped. The officers approached his car with their hands on their weapons and instructed him to get back into the car. They demanded to see his driver's license and registration and kept their hands on their guns the entire time. Riggs was alarmed at the police officers' actions and could not understand why the officers were treating this as a "high-level" criminal encounter rather than a routine traffic stop. The officers eventually gave Riggs a citation for an illegible license plate and let him go after about half an hour.[3]

Without hearing the officers' side of the story, it's impossible to know what suspicions may have been aroused when the officers first stopped Mr. Riggs that warranted this kind of treatment, but this experience seems to be consistent with similar encounters that have been characterized by civil rights groups as racial profiling.

At the other end of the spectrum, we examine perhaps some of the most flagrant examples of racial profiling: pretext stops and police harassment.

Charles and Etta Carter, an elderly African American couple from Pennsylvania, were stopped by the Maryland state police on their fortieth wedding anniversary. The troopers searched their car and brought in drug-sniffing dogs. During the search, their daughter's wedding dress was tossed onto one of the police cars, and as trucks passed on I-95, it was blown to the ground. Mrs. Carter was not allowed to use the restroom during the search because police officers feared she would flee. Their belongings were strewn along the highway and trampled and urinated on by the police dogs. No drugs were found, and no ticket was issued by the state trooper. The Carters eventually reached a settlement with the Maryland State Police.[4]

A similar case involved Nelson Walker, a young Liberian man attending college in North Carolina, who was driving along I-95 in Maryland when he was pulled over by state police who said he wasn't wearing a seatbelt. The officers detained him and his two passengers for two hours as they searched for illegal drugs, weapons, and other contraband. Finding nothing in the car, they proceeded to dismantle it and removed part of a door panel, a seat panel, and part of the sunroof. They still found nothing. In the end, the officers handed Walker a screwdriver and said, "You're going to need this" as they left the scene.[5]

Though such flagrant examples of police misconduct are always egregious, racial profiling victims are not limited to the average citizen who may be in the wrong place at the wrong time. When this happens to those who we would consider the least likely among us to be suspected of criminal activity, the practice becomes especially shocking. As these examples illustrate, those who belong to a certain racial group have one strike against them, regardless of their status in society.

In Florida, Aaron Campbell was pulled over by sheriff's deputies on the Florida turnpike. The stop ended with Mr. Campbell being wrestled to the ground, sprayed with pepper spray, and arrested. It turned out that Campbell was a fellow police officer, a major with the Metro Dade Police Department, and had identified himself as such when he was pulled over for an illegal lane change and having an obscured license tag.[6]

Next, we examine the case of a 37-year-old man of Panamanian descent who was a highly decorated veteran of Desert Storm and Operation United Shield in Somalia.

While driving across the Oklahoma border in August 1998, U.S. Army Sergeant First Class Rossano Gerald and his son found that they could not travel more than 30 minutes without being stopped by the Highway Patrol on two separate occasions. The second stop, which lasted two and a half hours, resulted in Sergeant Gerald and his 12-year-old son being terrorized by state troopers.

On a hot summer afternoon, the troopers placed both father and son in a closed car with the air conditioning off and fans blowing hot air. The two were warned that if they tried to escape, the police dog would attack. Halfway through the episode, the troopers shut off the patrol car's video evidence camera in an apparent attempt to conceal their actions.[7] This case is similar to many that are under investigation by civil rights groups.

Needless to say, there is no shortage of horror stories to support the contention that racial profiling is alive and well in America. In fact, a majority of white as well as black Americans believe that racial profiling is widespread.[8] While civil rights groups are reporting some progress in their fight to end racial profiling, public opinion continues to be fueled by media reports of law enforcement at its worst. These countless reports leave many to wonder whether the problem is really confined to the actions of a few officers or whether it is a widely accepted practice rampant in the profession.

Reports suggest that in some agencies, administrators are not doing enough to intervene when officers are accused of errant law enforcement practices. One such case involved two New Jersey state troopers who were indicted in September 1999 on attempted murder and assault charges stemming from a shooting during a routine traffic stop on the New Jersey Turnpike. The traffic altercation with the troopers resulted in serious injuries for three young unarmed black and Hispanic men. Key to this controversy is that the two troopers involved were indicted only months earlier on 19 misdemeanor charges of falsifying activity logs to conceal the fact that they were stopping a disproportionate number of minority drivers on the highway.

The New Jersey scandal is one of many across the nation that led the public to wonder why officers with track records of dishonesty and discrimination are allowed to remain on the street only to continue patterns of racist behavior. These scandals that shatter the public trust and rock communities expose not only bad officers but a failed system as well.

When these accounts surface in the media, the entire profession suffers, regardless of the outcome. One such scandal, reported on July 5, 2000 by *Dateline NBC*, highlighted the accusations of racial profiling in the wealthy Chicago suburb of Highland Park, Illinois. The *Dateline* investigation uncovered serious allegations that pitted cops against cops and, once again, cast a dark shadow over the entire law enforcement community.

There are always skeptics that raise an eyebrow when allegations of racial profiling come from a minority citizen, but what about when the reports originate from fellow white police officers?

This is the question raised when three current and two former members of the Highland Park Police Department, with support from fellow officers, filed a federal civil rights suit against their own department.[9] The officers, who sued for an undetermined amount of money, alleged that their rights were violated when they refused to go along with an administration they claimed taught, encouraged, and rewarded racial profiling.

Though the lawsuit was later dismissed in June 2000 by a federal judge in Chicago, the scars left on this community were slow to heal, particularly in light of the national attention the story drew.

One unidentified officer claimed in the *Dateline* interview that "people in our department do it regularly as habit" and alleged that racial profiling, racial slurs, and mistreatment of minorities is routine in the Highland Park police force.

Allegations of racial profiling and the alleged cover-up by department officials left officers and police dispatchers in this 60-member force bitterly divided, with 10 of the plaintiff's colleagues swearing that the stories of racial profiling and racial slurs were true and more than 20 officers, commanders, and administrators claiming they never happened. One 20-year veteran probably described it best as a case of "your word against my word" and claimed that these officers "needed an issue…needed press…The racial issue was it. And it took off, and they're riding that horse all the way to the finish line."

Perhaps even more troubling than the allegations themselves were the shocking accounts of former patrol officer John Dabrowski, who recalled a common practice the cops called "shining."

"I witnessed officers who would sit perpendicular to the highway," he said. "He would have his brights shined on the vehicles. All of a sudden, he'd see one he likes because of the color of the person's skin. There was no other reason to pull out after him other than the fact that he was able to see who was driving the car." Mr. Dabrowski left the force and claimed he could no longer condone and participate in racial profiling.

Other allegations in the Highland Park lawsuit were equally troubling. Patrolman Rodney Watt described an unwritten rule called the "nut ordinance." Mr. Watt recalled one of his first experiences with racial profiling wherein his chief wanted to make sure that Watt was enforcing the "nut ordinance," a practice that allegedly stood for "niggers uptown." "You make sure this kid is enforcing that nut ordinance," he said. "We don't need those minorities up there."

Other officers on the force vehemently denied the allegations and claimed that the first they had heard of "shining" or the "nut ordinance" was when they read it in the newspaper after this story broke.

Though a lot of money was at stake in the litigation, the officers denied that their fight was about financial gain and claimed that the problem had been brought up for years, with nothing being done about it.

One piece of evidence that tended to support the officers' contentions was a computer communication referred to as "the hat transcript," which recounted a conversation occurring between officers on patrol in Highland Park:

"She has a driver with a cowboy hat."

The response: "Cool, we got a winner."

"You see the hat? It is a sombrero?"

"Twenty gallon, probably full of beer bottles."

Cindy Sanchez, a former Highland Park police dispatcher who signed an affidavit supporting the officers' allegations of racial profiling, clarifies the communication by explaining, "They're looking at someone through a car, and they're seeing that he has a cowboy hat on, and he's probably Mexican, and because he is Mexican, he's obviously drunk...They're not going by how he's driving. They're just assuming because he's Mexican that he's drunk, and he's going to be an easy arrest."

Although many claimed this "hat transcript" was conclusive evidence of racial profiling in Highland Park, the city manager limited his interpretation of this behavior as "inappropriate and unprofessional."

Tom Sullivan, a former federal prosecutor who was hired to investigate this matter for the city, concluded after 5,000 hours of conducting interviews and reviewing records that probably no more than five officers of the 35 assigned to patrol duties have stopped motorists on the basis of racial profiling. Although Mr. Sullivan found no evidence that racial profiling was the official policy of the police command staff, he concluded that police brass tolerated and participated in an atmosphere of racial jokes and slurs and failed to communicate the department's opposition to this practice. Mr. Sullivan also determined that the individual incidents of racial profiling resulted more from a lack of training than pervasive prejudice within the ranks.

In light of the national publicity and in response to the racial profiling allegations, Highland Park has taken aggressive steps toward pursuing diversity and tolerance initiatives. Along with the implementation of specific policies and procedures within the police department, Highland Park has also entered into a consent decree with the Illinois chapter of the American Civil Liberties Union (ACLU). Along with specific mandates contained in the consent decree, police officials have agreed to collect race, ethnicity, and gender data on all citizens they stop for any reason. The city will also have computer transcripts reviewed by the command staff and will initiate the installation of audio equipment and video cameras in all marked squad cars. These measures will coincide with additional training for officers and administrators.

Regardless of the outcome of these high-profile cases, the fact remains that allegations such as these have long-term implications on police departments across the country. When asked what the lawsuit has done to his department, one officer replied, "You go to a call, and people keep asking you if you're a racist cop."

Response to the Government's War on Drugs

Many experts attribute the police's abuse of power aimed at minorities to the government's war on drugs over the past decade. The use of "drug courier" or "gang member" profiles by police has been seen as nothing more than a misguided attempt to abate the escalating drug and crime problems that continue to spiral out of control in some communities. These tactics have resulted in the police targeting minority motorists, particularly blacks and Hispanics, for minor infractions. These individuals are generally not involved in any criminal activity and would probably never have encountered the criminal justice system absent the use of these racially biased police profiles. Some even link the use of these profiles to the disproportionate number of minorities that have been arrested and jailed, thus fostering the notion that people of color are more likely to violate drug laws. This notion, however, is one that the government's own statistics disprove.

Though drug interdiction efforts historically tend to target minorities, government statistics show that most drug offenses are *not* committed by minority perpetrators. In fact, experts indicate that five times as many whites use drugs, a statistic supported by the government's own report revealing that 80% of the nation's cocaine users are white middle-class suburbanites.[10]

These inaccurate perceptions held by both law enforcement and the public perpetuate a cycle that leads to a disproportionate number of minorities being detained and investigated for drug offenses. The cycle begins when law enforcement treats stereotypes as truth and uses them as a basis for targeting minorities or those who belong to a certain socioeconomic class. When a disproportionate number of minorities is arrested and jailed, both the police and the public are led to believe that certain groups are more likely than others to commit drug offenses. The cycle comes full circle when published crime data report a disproportionate number of stops, arrests, and prosecutions for minority offenders, thereby perpetuating the false impression among the whole population that drug crimes are more prevalent among these groups. The unintended outcome of these inaccurate, prejudicial profiles is that the real perpetrators often go unapprehended.

The astonishing demographics of the nation's prison population confirm the impact this cycle has had on minorities and serves as further proof that drug courier profiles are still in use by many police departments across the country. Statistics show that although only 13% of the country's drug users are black, they account for 37% of those arrested on drug charges, 55% of those convicted, and 74% of those sentenced to prison.[11]

Some reports attribute the upsurge of drug offenders in the nation's prisons and jails to increased drug arrests and harsher sentencing policies, which have escalated the total inmate population to a staggering 1.7 million—400,000 of which are either awaiting trial or serving time for a drug offense.

As these policies have been implemented, they have had a tremendous impact on African American and Hispanic communities. The African American proportion of drug arrests rose from 25% in 1980 to 37% in 1995. Hispanic and African American inmates are more likely than non-Hispanic whites to be incarcerated for a drug offense.[12]

The ultimate outcome has not been a successful war to combat drugs. For many, this war has done nothing short of trample the integrity of many law-abiding citizens and their constitutional rights. The corollary has been widespread humiliation and distrust of law enforcement in minority communities. For some, the practice has become all too common and has caused many to adjust their daily schedules, their routine practices, and the places they frequent in order to minimize their chances of being stopped by the police. This has left many to wonder when the priority shifted from enforcing the law to abusing it.

Even though the problem of racial profiling seems somewhat isolated on its surface, the reality is that this practice extends far beyond a citizen's contacts with the police. Many minorities believe that their treatment by law enforcement plays a significant role in how they are viewed by elected leaders and leads to the creation of policies that send confusing messages to youth about their worth in society. For example, in one Northern California city with a primarily African American population, one local politician summed up the problem of the escalating murder rate by calling it a case of "dopers killing dopers." Residents did not have to read very far between the lines to surmise the race of the dopers accused of perpetrating these rampant killings.

In the same vein, we look to the case of the 2002 East Coast sniper killings that left nearly 20 people dead. In response to these killings, the government joined forces with local law enforcement in a high-tech war to catch these perpetrators. Hundreds of officers were deployed along with agents trained to use the most advanced military technology in an effort to narrow the search for suspects. No one would suggest that these tactics were unnecessary; however, if we look to the total number of killings in this case compared with those occurring in this northern California city, the efforts used in pursuit of these sniper suspects should have been employed there long ago. Many minorities suspect that if it were whites being killed at the same rate, they surely would have. But the fact that the crimes are largely related to drugs and gangs suggests that the lives involved may not have the same value as those in other crime waves.

Although drug- and gang-related crimes remain top concerns for law enforcement, the focus has shifted somewhat with recent events. Though proven largely ineffective in the eradication of the nation's drug problem, racially biased practices continue to be used in an effort to investigate and detain hundreds of Middle Eastern men who have suspected ties to terrorist groups and activities. Whether these questionable practices will actually circumvent future terrorist threats remains unclear; however, if one looks at the track record of the efforts to win the war on drugs, one would hope that those in charge would implement a better model for success and stop the cycle of inequality these dragnets often perpetuate.

When looking to the whole system for answers, one must recognize that the cycle of racial disparity and inequality does not begin and end in the law enforcement community. Inevitably, the crime report statistics generated by law enforcement spill over into the entire judicial system and lead many to wonder whether justice is really blind at all. At times, these racially biased practices, justified under the cloak of the war on drugs, are so blatant that even judges have had to stand up and take notice.

In early 1990, a New York judge made the following statement after dismissing charges against an African American woman who had been stopped and searched at a bus terminal: "I arraign approximately one-third of the felony cases in New York County and have no recollection of any defendant in a Port Authority Police Department drug interdiction case who was not either black or Hispanic." In fact, a New York state judge, reviewing a drug interdiction program at the Port Authority bus terminal, reported that none of the three judges who arraigned felony cases in New York County could recall a single drug interdiction case where the defendant was not black or Hispanic.[13]

Even in those cases in which police motives are called into question, courts face a key obstacle: police are not likely to be forthcoming with testimony confirming illicit motivation. Judge J. Keith, in a dissent, noted that in his 26 years as a federal judge, "Although I have suspected discrimination by police officers, I have never heard an officer admit he stopped an individual based on the color of his skin."[14]

The reality is that officers are presumed to give truthful testimony under oath. An officer's honesty or integrity as a witness is rarely ever successfully challenged in court. This factor alone puts even the innocent victim at a severe disadvantage and is one more reality that cultivates a distrust of the entire justice system.

Concerns about Police Response to Racial Profiling Accusations

Perhaps the best analogy that comes to mind when claims surface alleging that racial profiling does not exist is the T.V. commercial footage of high-ranking tobacco company officials reassuring the public that "nicotine is not addictive." Such contentions insult the intelligence of the American public and raise serious questions about the integrity of those who defend such ludicrous claims.

Despite case studies, public outcry, and police departments' own traffic stop statistics, there are still those police agencies and legislators who will not acknowledge there is a problem. The denials range from assertions by some law enforcement administrators that its officers do not target or stop people on the basis of ethnicity to outright denials that racial profiling and pretext stops exist at all. Though some point to the independent acts of a few rogue officers, others see the problem as a national dilemma that extends far beyond the reaches of law enforcement.

> *"Law enforcement is a paramilitary organization. Law enforcement heads are aware of it [racial profiling] and are covering it up."*
>
> —Judge Mablean Ephriam of "Divorce Court"[15]

Although there have been some instances in which police agencies openly admit to practicing racial profiling in their traffic stops, few are willing to come forward and take the political risk that their definition of "good police work" might be construed by the public as practices rife with racial overtones.

As an example of the political suicide public figures risk when they candidly discuss racial profiling practices, in March 1999 then–Governor Christine Todd Whitman dismissed Carl Williams, New Jersey's chief of troopers, soon after a news article reported that Mr. Williams defended racial profiling because "mostly minorities" trafficked in marijuana and cocaine.[16] This admission came at a time when New Jersey officials were already under heightened scrutiny and facing public anger and distrust as a result of police mistreatment of black suspects.

Police agencies, particularly those serving racially diverse populations, have been put on the defensive about racial profiling practices in attempts to salvage reputations within their communities and rebuild public confidence in their integrity. For some agencies, this has been particularly discomfiting, putting many high-profile leaders in a position of having to respond to accusations from all sides.

However, leaders in some agencies should be commended for stepping forward to defend their officers and practices on the roadway. In a 2003 interview with California Highway Patrol (CHP) command staff, we learned about one such leader, CHP Commissioner Dwight "Spike" Helmick.

Commissioner Helmick's credo is for his officers to treat all people with dignity. If an officer does not treat a member of the public with dignity and respect, Commissioner Helmick and his command staff want to know why. They will not stop short of investigating and even prosecuting their own officers if they determine a civil rights violation has occurred. Commissioner Helmick considers this approach an operational necessity within his organization.

Despite the CHP's aggressive and proactive stand on racial profiling and civil rights violations, its practices were challenged by the ACLU in a class action complaint filed on June 3, 1999. The complaint alleged that the CHP engaged in a continuing pattern and practice of race-based stops, detentions, and searches of African American and Latino motorists due in large part to discriminatory drug interdiction policies and practices.[17]

More specifically, the ACLU lawsuit alleged that black and Latino motorists were three times more likely than Caucasians to be stopped and searched in some areas of the state. Though the lawsuit itself did not provide any insight about why this disparity might exist, the CHP points to several factors that may contribute to some limited enforcement discrepancies in certain parts of the state, including:

- ongoing investigations in which the race of the suspect(s) has already been determined,
- calls for service initiated by the public in locations that typically show an elevated rate of traffic accidents and crime, or
- officers responding to specific tips about drug trafficking along certain highways within the state.

Additionally, the CHP points to other dynamics in traffic stop data reporting that may lead to results that appear inequitable, for example, instances in which stops are initiated by the officer before the driver's race or sex can even be determined.

These factors are consistent with those presented in new research in the area of racial profiling that is often excluded or overlooked when discrepancies in automobile stops are identified.

Commissioner Helmick believed it was important for his organization and its officers to vigorously defend the allegations posed in the ACLU lawsuit. In addressing the specific allegations by Mr. Rodriguez and the other plaintiffs, the CHP pointed to a long-term drug investigation in progress on the stretch of highway at issue, where the race of the suspect(s) had already been determined. CHP officers also articulated the specific characteristics and actions of Mr. Rodriguez and/or his passengers that investigators were looking for and that made his vehicle suspicious to officers patrolling the roadway, including the following:

- the vehicle was traveling without headlights in a daylight test section where headlights were required,
- the vehicle reduced its speed to 35 mph in a 65 mph zone when it spotted CHP officers, and
- the exhibition of a shiny object out the door of the vehicle pointed at the CHP officers (later discovered to be a camera).

Though the CHP assured the ACLU its actions toward Mr. Rodriguez and his passengers were based on probable cause and correlated directly with the ongoing drug investigation, the ACLU perceived these practices as racial profiling.

In addition to defending the specific allegations in the lawsuit, the CHP took a proactive approach to educating the ACLU about its practices and provided the civil rights group with extensive information about its policies and traffic stop statistics long before the litigation ensued. Commissioner Helmick consistently defended CHP statistics and showed that out of 4.7 million annual contacts with the public, only about 2% resulted in the apprehension of illegal drugs. Commissioner Helmick specifically cited statistics from 1997 and 1998 that reported a total of 3,558 pounds of cocaine, 218 pounds of heroin, 58,975 pounds of marijuana, and 3,980 pounds of methamphetamine had been seized by CHP officers. "Every ounce taken off the highway is an ounce that didn't flow into our communities and didn't affect a driver on the highway."[18] This "just shows that we are doing our job—traffic safety and enforcement of the California Vehicle Code."[19]

Commissioner Helmick further confirmed that CHP has "a policy in place prohibiting the use of race as a basis to stop vehicles for any purpose."[20] The CHP command staff elaborated on this aggressive policy in our interview and noted that the CHP does not condone racial profiling and has prohibited the practice in its organization for many years. Likewise, CHP command staff assured us that CHP officers use only the vehicle code, not pretext traffic stops, to identify those who may be violating the law.

Though many agencies would consider such a high-profile legal challenge daunting, the CHP saw it as an opportunity to work in concert with the ACLU to extinguish any notions that the organization practices racial profiling. These cooperative efforts eventually led to the execution of a voluntary settlement agreement on June 6, 2003. With neither side admitting any wrongdoing, the terms of the settlement agreement reassured the ACLU that the CHP would continue to enforce its long-standing policies and practices prohibiting racial profiling in its dealings with the public. Some specific terms of the agreement require CHP officers to continue data collection on every motor vehicle contact, a practice that has been routine in the CHP for years. In fact, the CHP has, for some time, exceeded most nationwide data collection models and has required officers to document every public contact, whether the result of a vehicle code violation, a request for directions, or call for roadway assistance.

Additionally, the settlement agreement extends a temporary moratorium on some consent searches for three years. This moratorium is consistent with CHP's ongoing internal policies requiring all searches to be probable cause based. In other words, consent searches may not be initiated randomly as a fishing expedition. The officer must be able to articulate specific facts that led him or her to believe evidence of criminal activity would be uncovered in the search. Likewise, it is routine practice for CHP officers to advise a driver of his or her right to say "no" prior to initiating a consent search and to require the driver to sign a written form before the search begins.

Ultimately, the citizens of California are left with the most measurable benefit from the ACLU lawsuit: Commissioner Helmick's adamant and consistent assurance in both words and actions that he will do everything in his power "to make sure racial profiling does not happen here."[21]

There should be no mistake that many law enforcement agencies such as the CHP can be credited for their proactive efforts to eradicate racial profiling practices. Potential safeguards and solutions have taken many forms, with the most publicized being that of voluntary data collection. Although many of these programs are initiated with good intentions, public distrust of the profession runs deep, with some likening these voluntary data collection efforts to "the fox guarding the hen house." In some instances, public suspicion of these programs may be well deserved.

A closer look into these voluntary data collection efforts reveals that some lack internal checks and balances to ensure that the data collected is both factual and relevant. The identities of the officers and the violators sometimes go unrecorded, as do the license plate of the car and the time of the stop, which all make the accuracy of the data entirely dependent upon the candidness of the agency and its officers.

Hubert Williams, President of the Police Foundation in Washington, D.C., noted, in an interview, that "police departments that collect anonymous data may be tacitly admitting to the belief that a problem exists. By providing anonymity to officers who are abusers, they may be viewed as covering up an illegal practice and consequently, placing the department in greater jeopardy."[22]

Despite public pressure, the prospect of data collection has been a hard sell for many in law enforcement. In interviews with officers, the consensus is that cops do not want any independent oversight or, as more commonly expressed, no "big brother."

The concept of no oversight and no accountability is unique to the law enforcement profession. It is difficult to identify another vocation in which employees are given unbridled power and yet are not held accountable when mistakes are made or policies are not followed. Arguably, one would expect that public employees, or "public servants," should have greater accountability than the average employee working in the private sector.

The Underlying Problem

When we view the problem of racial profiling in the larger picture, it is shocking that nearly 40 years after the Birmingham police used vicious attack dogs and fire hoses against nonviolent civil rights protesters, racial profiling is still occurring. It may be argued that racists are just taking a different approach: promoting racial agendas using a small number of perpetrators in isolated incidences rather than initiating mass attacks that subject them to media exposure and public ridicule.

Although historically, battle lines were clearly drawn between black and white, it is becoming less and less acceptable in our modern society to attack some of this country's finest leaders and citizens. Racial profiling is a giant step backward, and recent numbers confirm that a majority of Americans—black, brown, and white—simply will not tolerate it.

> *"Discrimination is a hellhound that gnaws at Negroes in every waking moment of their lives to remind them that the lie of their inferiority is accepted as truth in the society dominating them."*

> —Rev. Dr. Martin Luther King, Jr.[23]

Unfortunately, the prophetic words of Martin Luther King still ring true more than 35 years after the day they were spoken. ABC News Anchor Peter Jennings, in a Martin Luther King Day interview, probably said it best when he expressed his belief that most Americans feel "we have come far but not far enough."

In recent high-profile cases involving suspect police practices aimed against minority defendants as well as in the reports following the September 11, 2001, terrorist attacks on America, the media have remained a powerful force in bringing racial tensions to the forefront and have reminded us all that racial tensions in America are still powerful enough to divide the public along the lines of color.

The Rodney King and O.J. Simpson cases forced the nation to see harsh reality and left it with new concerns: police treatment of minorities in general, stereotyping, playing "the race card," and loyalty to one's own minority group regardless of the moral and social cost.

In the years since these high-profile cases were decided, the media has taken hold of these issues and debated them in every possible forum. The larger issue of racism has been analyzed and critiqued on television and in most major newspapers and magazines from one end of the country to the other. The term "driving while black," used in the minority community for years, is now commonplace in the media circuit. Though not conclusive, the growing attention of the media, recent statistics, and the upsurge of legislation and lawsuits support the argument that the underlying problem of racism remains a nationwide epidemic.

Though the war on drugs can be credited with bringing the practice of racially biased policing to the forefront, it barely scratches the surface of the underlying societal problem. Whether the blame for the current civil rights crisis belongs with law enforcement, legislators, or the justice system itself, there can be no doubt that ending racial profiling is just the first step toward solving the much larger problem embedded within society: racism.

Racism

Racism and its destructive counterparts are nothing new to anyone who is black. It might be a little less unnerving if the practice of racism were confined to small numbers of skinheads or white supremacists. In some instances, however, the white sheets have been replaced by police uniforms worn by a chosen few with the power to put in motion the process of taking away one's freedom. When racist motivations are uncovered, the public is left to wonder just who it can trust.

The suggestion that racism exists within some facets of law enforcement and the criminal justice system poses a problem of such monumental implications that one can hardly begin to frame a workable solution. Most Americans would like to believe that racism is a thing of the past, something perpetuated by the naiveté of earlier generations. Modern-day practices, however, suggest a reality that most minorities have come to accept: racism is alive and well in America.

There is little disagreement that racial profiling undermines the legitimacy of our entire justice system. Minorities are afraid to report crimes to the police; they distrust law enforcement and are less cooperative as witnesses and jurors. In more extreme cases, these feelings of distrust and betrayal perpetuate violence.

Even some of the staunchest proponents of the campaign to end racial profiling don't seem to believe it will ultimately solve the larger problem of racism in America.

The Underlying Social Costs

"We are caught in an inescapable network of mutuality, tied in a single garment of destiny. Whatever affects one directly affects all indirectly. Never again can we afford to live with the narrow, provincial 'outside agitator' idea. Anyone who lives inside the United States can never be considered an outsider anywhere in this country."

—Rev. Dr. Martin Luther King, Jr.
Letter from the Birmingham Jail, April 16, 1963

The personal and emotional costs attributed to this epidemic are incalculable. Casualties of this attack on the minority segment of our population are mounting. Humiliation, stereotyping, and deprivation of personal freedoms leave deep scars that follow these individuals into other aspects of their daily lives. The fallout from these practices forces minorities to avoid certain parts of their cities after dark, drive low-profile cars to discourage police attention, and factor extra time into their daily commute for unwarranted traffic stops.

Stories continue to surface about people such as Mr. Paul Worthy, a 59-year-old retiree, who was stopped by white officers in Detroit and released without a ticket for a "tilted license plate" while driving his Cadillac. "I'm no criminal," Worthy told the *Detroit News*. "I worked at GM as a skilled tradesman for $25 an hour. I worked every day just like that police officer did."[24]

Many African American parents are well aware of the potential for deadly consequences when the police stop their young sons. Karen, a social worker, said that when her young son begins to drive, she knows what she'll tell him: "The police are supposed to be there to protect and to serve, but you being black and being male, you've got two strikes against you. Keep your hands on the steering wheel, and do not run, because they will shoot you in your back. Let them do whatever they want to do. I know it's humiliating, but let them do whatever they want to do to make sure you get out of that situation alive. Deal with your emotions later. Your emotions are going to come second —or last."[25]

Christopher Darden, the African American prosecutor in the O.J. Simpson case, reports that police stop him about five times a year.[26] He said that to survive traffic stops, he "learned the rules of the game years before...Don't move. Don't turn around. Don't give some rookie an excuse to shoot you."[27] Unfortunately, Mr. Darden's advice is not uncommon among minorities.

Perhaps Charles Ogletree, a black professor at Harvard Law School, expressed it best: "If I'm dressed in a knit cap and hooded jacket, I'm probable cause."[28]

The practice of randomly stopping people on the basis of skin color goes a lot deeper and is much more costly than the fine of a traffic ticket. Said an African American financial services executive in his early 30s: "When I see cops today, I don't feel like I'm protected. I'm thinking, 'Oh, shoot, are they gonna pull me over? Are they gonna stop me?' That's my reaction. I do not feel safe around cops."[29]

These feelings, once reported primarily by African Americans and Hispanics, have surfaced among a growing minority group composed of people of Middle Eastern descent. The questioning of men, women, and children suspected of having affiliations to terrorist nations has been likened by many to a witch-hunt. Only time will tell whether this knee-jerk reaction in the name of national security will evolve into a harmful, long-term practice similar to what other minority groups have endured for more than 200 years.

Regardless of skin color, the growing suspicion some feel toward their own police, coupled with escalating feelings of distrust toward the entire law enforcement profession, significantly undermines the validity of all law enforcement practices, whether they occur in the form of an automobile stop on the roadway or an encounter on the street. Suspicions of corruption and inequality trickle into other political structures and ultimately pollute the entire justice system, as suggested by the Rodney King and O.J. Simpson jury verdicts.

The underlying social costs are enormous and cause incalculable damage that affects people of all ages and walks of life. The fallout from these practices lead many to wonder what price Americans are willing to pay to eradicate crime or how many rights we are willing to give up to be free from the threat of crime and terrorism.

Civil Rights Groups' Proposals for Change

Though specific solutions will be discussed later in more detail, it is important to highlight some of the recommendations that have been suggested by civil rights groups to bring about change. It cannot be ignored that civil rights groups continue to actively promote awareness and facilitate change at every level of government. One group that has been the most vocal in this arena is the ACLU. Perhaps the most comprehensive compilation of proposals for change is outlined in the ACLU's special report on the problem of driving while black and those contained in a letter sent by the organization to former U.S. Attorney General Janet Reno. Both will be used as references to present one side of the issue.

1. Stop the Denials

Before any recommendations can be implemented, civil rights organizations want an end to the official denials that racial profiling is occurring. Given the heightened level of public awareness and the vast amount of information available, it is negligent for some elected leaders and police officials to continue asserting that racial profiling is not a problem. Gallup Poll statistics confirm the perception that this practice is widespread. These factors should make it clear to public officials that it is time to become accountable and admit that racial profiling is occurring.

2. End the Use of Pretext Stops by Law Enforcement

Through training and continuing education, law enforcement must eliminate the use of pretext stops as a crime-fighting tactic. In an attempt to accomplish this broad objective, civil rights groups are striving to pass legislation at both state and national levels that would make this practice illegal. More specifically, groups are looking for a total ban on racial profiling in all federally funded drug interdiction programs. This important first step, when coupled with subsequent strategies, will undoubtedly form the cornerstone of a realistic, effective solution to the problem of racial profiling.

In conjunction with ending pretext stops, there is increasing pressure for lawmakers to pass legislation pending in Congress that would outlaw the use of race in either traffic or pedestrian stops as part of routine, investigatory activities.

Though the federal government issued guidelines in 2003 barring federal agents from using race or ethnicity in their routine investigations, some point to loopholes in the policy that enable agents to use race and ethnicity in narrow circumstances to "identify terrorist threats and stop potential catastrophic attacks."

3. Expand Recruiting Efforts

Civil rights groups are looking to expand recruiting efforts so that the composition of police agencies is similar to that of the communities they serve. It is projected that a federal commitment of at least $5 million will be necessary to fund these improved recruiting strategies.

4. Initiate Whistle-Blower Protection Plans

In conjunction with aggressive training and recruiting efforts, it is critical that police agencies, with support from the U.S. Justice Department, initiate "whistle-blower" protection programs for police officers who report internal racial and sexual harassment incidents. The ACLU suggests the initiation of "federally supported integrity training" that would provide anonymity to officers reporting such incidents and give them an alternative to reporting these incidents to their superiors.

5. Eradicate the Code of Silence

Perhaps the most critical step is for law enforcement administrators to initiate programs that would do away with code of silence. This code of silence—the tendency for police to protect their own, even in the most deplorable circumstances—has remained a key obstacle in detecting and prosecuting acts of racially biased policing and abuse of police power. The ACLU has suggested that law enforcement training include anti-code of silence role playing similar to the scenario-based training that officers undergo to prepare for domestic violence situations, high-speed pursuits, and the like.

6. Expand Legislation and Data Collection Efforts

Comprehensive legislation must be passed at state and local levels that coincides with the legislation implemented by the federal government. The push for such legislation has sparked voluntary efforts by police agencies to collect statistical data in an effort to evaluate the scope of the problem. In California alone, a number of cities, including the major metropolitan cities of San José, San Diego, and San Francisco, have taken the lead to voluntarily implement these important programs.

Although state legislation may be effective to fight the problem on a more limited front, the public must recognize that the problem is a national one. As results are reported from voluntary data collection efforts around the nation, one certain outcome will be a growing public awareness that will ultimately force politicians and law enforcement agencies to take a stand on this issue. If civil rights agencies get their wish, mandatory data collection legislation will be enacted nationally, and routine traffic enforcement will be statistically monitored on an ongoing basis. Even though the current administration has spoken out against racial profiling in general terms, it is unclear whether it would support such all-encompassing anti–racial profiling legislation, particularly in light of continued terrorist threats in our nation and abroad. Though the administration barred federal agents from using race and ethnicity in routine investigations in 2003, many question whether the loopholes in this policy will prevent agents from engaging in pretext stops and using profiles to gain an upper hand in the war on terrorism.

At present, government response to legislation has been mixed, with some government agencies still hesitant to take a position and others showing support for initiatives requiring federal law enforcement officials to collect data on the race and gender of motorists they stop to question or arrest. In a survey of federal operations, the Justice Department concluded that profiling did not appear to be a systematic problem.

7. Initiate New, Proactive Measures

In conjunction with the systematic and independent review of federally funded drug interdiction training programs, law enforcement agencies are urged to implement mandatory safeguards to prevent, identify, and remedy abusive procedures and Constitutional violations. The ACLU has recommended six criteria that should be implemented in this regard:[30] "(1) the institution of 'early warning systems' that track officer behavior and that will help identify and deter officers who may engage in discriminatory practices; (2) an enforceable duty to notify dispatchers of the exact reason for the stop (unsafe lane change, speeding, etc.) before exiting the police vehicle; (3) systems to accurately monitor the exact duration of all stops; (4) the use of written 'consent to search' forms clearly informing drivers of their right to refuse consent, their right to be present during the search, and requiring a signature prior to any search; (5) an explicit ban on extending the length of non-consensual traffic stops so that drug-sniffing dogs can be brought to the scene; and (6) informing drivers that they are 'free to go' once the purpose for the traffic stop has been, or reasonably should have been, completed."

8. Develop Federal Oversight and Budget Controls

History has shown that when requests for voluntary compliance go unheeded, a hit in the wallet can produce amazing results. Some suggest that compliance measures target federal funding for Operation Pipeline and other highway drug interdiction programs by linking the receipt of funds to the collection and reporting of comprehensive race data on the individuals officers stop and search. Experts believe that such steps would help to ensure that Operation Pipeline and any other federally funded crime intervention programs are not encouraging or perpetuating race-based law enforcement practices.

In addition to collecting and reporting data, these programs would be required to submit to independent reviews by the Justice Department and civil rights experts in the community. These reviews would include investigations of federal, state, and local training programs to ensure that officers are not trained to use racial references or other racially biased tactics in conducting traffic enforcement. Such a stance by the Justice Department would send a clear message that the use of racial profiling will not be tolerated in federally funded programs. More important, it would reinforce to the law enforcement community that abandoning racially discriminatory practices is a higher priority than achieving drug interdiction goals.

9. Secure Federal Fund Allocations

It should not be overlooked that to implement these measures, government funding will be necessary. The recommendation is to provide the Justice Department's Civil Rights Division with at least $5 million to fund police accountability efforts. In conjunction with receipt of these funds, all law enforcement agencies from the Justice Department to the local police departments would have to commit to take a leadership role and implement a hard-line approach within their own organizations.

10. Involve the Justice Department

To coincide with the implementation of these recommendations, civil rights groups are looking for increased Justice Department involvement to support anti–racial profiling measures. As discussed above, some of these measures include the creation of an early warning system to detect problem officers and the utilization of *written* consent forms prior to an officer conducting a search. Without national support and assistance to implement such measures, the efforts of individual police agencies will remain fragmented and without clear direction.

Undoubtedly, racial profiling will remain a high priority for civil rights groups. Their message is clear: racial profiling is illegal and will not be tolerated as a crime-fighting tactic. Not only is it outdated, but also it is a completely ineffective means of predicting a person's criminal propensity in our modern world.

Many in law enforcement have heeded the call to eradicate racial profiling and have embarked on voluntary data collection programs to identify those who may be engaging in racially biased policing. But more work must be done. Many minorities continue to have their civil rights trampled, particularly in light of recent government antiterrorism policies designed to spy on those suspected of terrorist affiliations. While maintaining national security is essential, it is important that we do so without infringing on the rights of our citizens. If we continue to single out individuals on the basis of skin color, religious affiliations, or other discriminatory factors, we will continue to perpetuate the hatred and fear of those who some may view as different.

(Endnotes)

1. *Whren v. United States*, 135 L.Ed.2d 89, 116 S.Ct. 1769 (1996).

2. ACLU, "'Driving While Black' Horror Stories," <http://www.aclu.org/congress/dwbstories.html>; see also Lynch, Dan, "The Result of Following Procedure," *Albany Times Union*, January 19, 1997.

3. ACLU, "'Driving While Black' Horror Stories," <http://www.aclu.org/congress/dwbstories.html>; (originally published in *The Phoenix New Times*, July 3, 1998).

4. ACLU, "'Driving While Black' Horror Stories," <http://www.aclu.org/congress/dwbstories.html>; see also Brennan, Catherine, "Race-Profiling Again Attacked," *Daily Record*, Volume 212, No. 4.

5. ACLU, "'Driving While Black' Horror Stories," <http://www.aclu.org/congress/dwbstories.html>; see also Sullivan, John, "Raleigh Men Join Suit Against Maryland Police," *The News & Observer*, June 11, 1998 at B1.

6. ACLU, "'Driving While Black' Horror Stories," <http://www.aclu.org/congress/dwbstories.html>; see also "Police Profiling Goes on Trial," *Washington Times*, January 12, 1998.

7. Harris, David A., ACLU Special Report, "Driving While Black, Racial Profiling on Our Nation's Highways" (June 1999).

8. "The Gallup Poll. Gallup Poll Social Audit on Black/White Relations in the U.S.," Gallup Organization, Princeton, (December 9, 1999).

9. The lawsuit, originally filed in 1998 by the current and former officers, had alleged unfair labor practices. Later, however, allegations of racial profiling were added, including the controversial assertions of a department wide racial profiling policy.

10. "New ACLU Report on Racial Profiling Calls for Government Action and an End to Official Denials," ACLU Press Release (June 2, 1999).

11. Harris, David A., ACLU Special Report, "Driving While Black, Racial Profiling on Our Nation's Highways" (June 1999).

12. The Sentencing Project for the United States Commission on Civil Rights, Special Report (April 1999).

13. *People v. Evans*, 556 N.Y.S.2d 794, 796 (Sup. Ct. 1990).

14. *U.S. v. Harvey*, 16 F.3d 109, 114 (1994).

15. Interview with Judge Mablean Ephriam, *Larry King Live* (January 18, 2000).

16. "New ACLU Report on Racial Profiling Calls for Government Action and an End to Official Denials," ACLU Press Release (June 2, 1999).

17. Curtis V. Rodriguez, et al. v. California Highway Patrol, United States District Court, Northern District of California, San José Division, Case Number C 99-20895-JF/HRL.

18. "CHP Responds to Operation Pipeline Draft Report," (September 30, 1999) CHP Press Release #99-25.

19. "California Highway Patrol Responds to ACLU Lawsuit," (June 3, 1999) CHP Press Release #99-14.

20. "CHP Responds to Operation Pipeline Draft Report," (September 30, 1999) CHP Press Release #99-25.

21. "California Highway Patrol Responds to ACLU Lawsuit," (June 3, 1999) CHP Press Release #99-14.

22. Interview with Hubert Williams, President of the Police Foundation, Washington, D.C., December 11, 2000.

23. Rev. Dr. Martin Luther King, Jr., address at the Southern Christian Leadership Conference in Atlanta, Georgia (August 16, 1967).

24. Harris, David A., ACLU Special Report, "Driving While Black, Racial Profiling on Our Nation's Highways" (June, 1999) (excerpt from *The Detroit News*).

25. Harris, David A., ACLU Special Report, "Driving While Black, Racial Profiling on Our Nation's Highways" (June 1999).

26. Darden, Christopher with Jess Walter, *In Contempt* (1997).

27. Statement by Christopher Darden as quoted in David A. Harris, ACLU Special Report, "Driving While Black, Racial Profiling on Our Nation's Highways" (June, 1999).

28. Goodman, Ellen, "Simpson Case Divides Us By Race," *Boston Globe*, 10 July 1994 at 73 (quoting Charles Ogletree).

29. Harris, David A., ACLU Special Report, "Driving While Black, Racial Profiling on Our Nation's Highways" (June 1999). (Statement by individual identified as Emmanuel, early 30's, financial services executive.)

30. Letter to U.S. Attorney Janet Reno from Laura W. Murphy, ACLU dated June 4, 1999.

CHAPTER SEVEN

——•◦•——

Truth in Numbers

A Public Perception

In December 1999, a Gallup Poll reported that most Americans, particularly young black men, view racial profiling as extensive.[1] The race of those surveyed seemed to be a predominant factor in the study's results, with 77% of black respondents believing that racial profiling is widespread, compared with 56% of whites. Though racial profiling allegations tend to be more prevalent among those living in urban areas than those in suburban areas or rural America, the report reflects few regional differences in the *perception* of the incidences of racial profiling. Regardless of how closely these beliefs mirror reality, one cannot ignore the study's finding that an overwhelming 81% of Americans, both white and black, disapprove of the practice.

To understand the source of this discontent better, Americans were asked whether they felt the police had ever stopped them just because of their race or ethnic background. More than four out of ten blacks responded "yes." Moreover, about six out of ten who reported being stopped because of their race said it had occurred three or more times, including 15% who said it had happened eleven or more times.

The study revealed that almost three-quarters of *young* black men aged 18–34 were the individuals most likely to report being stopped by police because of their race. Comparatively, only 40% of young black women perceived themselves to have been the victims of racial profiling. An even smaller percentage of both black men and women aged 50 and older reported being stopped because of their race, a fact that left many to surmise that age and gender play a significant role in this practice.

Similar patterns were apparent when black men and women were asked how local police, state police, and police in other states treated them. The largest sense of unfair treatment was among young black men, particularly with respect to treatment by local police. For example, 53% of black men between the ages of 18 and 34 reported unfair treatment by their local law enforcement. That number dropped significantly to 23%

of black men between the ages of 35 and 49 who felt that they were not treated fairly and 22% for those over 50. Comparatively, among black women between the ages of 18 and 34, 26% felt that they were treated unfairly. This number dropped to 19% for those 35 to 49 and fell to 18% for those aged 50 and over. Perceptions of unfair treatment were less pronounced among these groups when asked how they felt about treatment by their state police.

Consistent with the suspicions of many minorities, the study suggests that education and income seem to be a negligible factor in this equation. Well-educated, higher-income blacks are as likely to report being pulled over as those with lower levels of education and income. Some theorize that factors of wealth or success may have a direct correlation to the lucrative nature of the drug trade, thus causing young men in high-profile cars to appear more suspicious to police.

Although this Gallup Poll study specifically dealt with racial profiling on the highways, similar studies tend to support the contention that this disparity is equally prevalent in our nation's airports. A 2000 General Accounting Office report on the U.S. Customs Service for 1999 revealed that black women who were U.S. citizens were nine times more likely than white women citizens to be X-rayed after being frisked or patted down. In reviewing the X-ray results, the black women were half as likely as white women to be found carrying contraband. The report revealed that the practices used by customs agents to identify passengers who are then subjected to more intrusive searches resulted in women and minorities being selected at rates that were consistently higher than the rates at which contraband was found.

After reviewing these statistics, one must ask whether skin color really does make minorities more prone for stops and searches by police or whether there are other factors not considered in the poll that may explain the disparity. Whatever the conclusion, these numbers bring to the forefront the importance of instituting a system of checks and balances to ensure that skin color is not being equated with probable cause in the enforcement of the law. At the same time, it also demonstrates the need for the public to work closely with law enforcement to determine whether racial profiling is truly a widespread problem or a simple misperception by the public that has been fueled by the media.

Officer Statistics

We know what the public thinks, but what do line officers think about allegations of racism in their profession? One study included in a report by the Christopher Commission in Los Angeles indicated that 25% of 650 officers responding agreed that "racial bias (prejudice) on the part of officers toward minority citizens currently exists and contributes to a negative interaction between police and the community... [and more than 25% agreed that] an officer's prejudice toward the suspect's race may lead to the use of excessive force."[2]

Both sides of the argument put a different spin on the statistics. The ACLU points to the numbers as a message to elected officials to "catch up with the voters and pass legislation to address this problem."[3] Yet some in law enforcement point to these statistics as nothing more than evidence of an escalating crime problem in minority communities, with the disproportionate stops representing police efforts to combat the growing problem. These statistics become even more challenging to analyze given other variables, such as the vast shift in population many communities are experiencing.

In the state of California for example, data released by the U.S. Census Bureau report that non-Hispanic whites make up less than 50% of California's overall population.[4] This population shift, attributed to the influx of immigrants from Asia, Mexico, the Middle East, and Central and South America in the past decade lead many to question whether the crime statistics reported are evidence of racial profiling or merely a reflection of a rapidly growing, diverse population.

When looking at the numbers for total arrests in diverse states such as California, law enforcement analysts point out that arrests for the race/ethnic groups of "White" and "Black" decreased while arrests for the race/ethnic groups of "Hispanic" and "Other" increased. Analysts defend these arrest statistics and note that the changes are consistent with the population growth among these race/ethnic groups.[5]

Similar conclusions were reached by former San Francisco Police Department Chief Fred Lau in response to a study revealing that blacks and Latinos are more likely than whites to be searched when stopped in San Francisco. The study results, reported in May 2002, revealed that blacks were 3.5 times more likely than whites to be searched, with Latinos being searched at a rate almost three times that of whites. Although the study raised a red flag for many civil rights advocates, former Chief Lau insisted that the numbers were not the result of racial profiling but rather reflective of other "sociological factors."

Regardless of these strong opinions, experts in the field have yet to definitively determine how much of a factor race is in everyday policing.[6] If the perceptions of police officers themselves are any indication, 17% of officers reported that they believed police treated whites better than blacks and other minorities. When black officers were asked the same question, however, 51% agreed that whites receive better treatment.[7]

The Facts about Force

When the public thinks about police officers' use of force against citizens, most immediately recount videos of officers "caught in the act" by an unsuspecting passerby with a video camera. These amateur films that inundate the evening news would lead one to question how widespread the problem has become. The reality is that most Americans believe that the use of force by the police is a common practice. Most would be surprised to learn that this widely held belief is not supported by any statistics we could find on police use of force. In fact, contrary to media reports and public perception, police use force in slightly less than one percent of their encounters with the public. And, Department of Justice reports indicate that when the police do use force or the threat of force, it is more often directed against white males.[8] In 1999 (the last year such statistics were available), a Department of Justice report revealed that law enforcement officers either used force or threatened to use force against about 422,000 citizens. Of this group, approximately 87% were males, and 13% were females. Contrary to widely held stereotypes, 59% of these citizens were white, and 23% were black. The report also indicated that the threat or use of force peaks at 37.5% among 20- to 29-year-olds and then declines steadily with increasing age. In summary, police officers refrained from using force or threats of force in 99.04% of all encounters with the public.

When force was used, about 40% of the cases resulted in injuries. More than half of those injuries were among whites. In use of force incidents by police, blacks reported injury in slightly more than 8% of the cases, compared with Hispanics who reported injury in 11% of the encounters and whites who reported injury in 20% of the incidents.

Consistent with these government statistics, one survey reflects that most police officers in the United States disapprove of the use of excessive force.[9] In fact, only 4.1% of officers believed that police regularly used more force than necessary when arresting a suspect, with 97.1% reporting that instances similar to that occurring in the Rodney King case in Los Angeles and the Abner Louima case in New York were "extremely rare" in their organizations.

Despite officers' disapproval of the use of force, more than 30% believed that they should be permitted to utilize more force than is currently permissible by law, with 25% agreeing that it may sometimes be necessary to use more force than legally allowable to control a person who is physically assaulting an officer. More than 40% of the officers polled agreed that following their agencies' rules in this regard might be incompatible with the goal of getting their job done.

Regardless of these statistics, the trend in public opinion implies that Americans are becoming less tolerant of police using any degree of force, even in self-defense. In 1973, Americans were asked, "Are there any situations you can imagine in which you would approve of a policeman striking an adult male citizen?" Nationwide, 73% of Americans responded "yes." By 2000, the Department of Justice reported that the number of citizens answering this question in the affirmative dropped to 64%. In 1973, Americans were asked, "Would you approve of a police officer striking a citizen who was attacking the officer with his fists?" Ninety-seven percent of those responding answered "yes" in 1973 compared with 90% who answered in the affirmative in 2000.

Although this study was not specifically designed to answer questions relating to the occurrence of racial profiling and violence against minorities by the police, one can infer that public perception relating to the use of force by law enforcement, particularly toward minorities, does not mirror reality. These flawed perceptions may be due, in part, to media reports sensationalizing accounts of white cops beating up black suspects without any apparent provocation. Perhaps these stories are deemed more newsworthy than the victimization of a white suspect by the police or, even rarer, a case in which a minority officer inflicted the harm. When armed with these images, any attempt by law enforcement to make even legitimate stops against minorities may be thwarted from the outset because of the underlying bias and animosity that inevitably taint the interactions between law enforcement and the community. Moreover, when an officer observes a person's anxiety and hesitation during a citizen encounter, it may be misconstrued as guilt and may set in motion a process that will reinforce the negative biases each side possesses about the other.

Battle of the Sexes

Studies that look at variables relating to police use of force point to a significant variance between male and female officers. A report by the National Center for Women and Policing indicates that female police officers are better at defusing potentially volatile situations than are their male counterparts. They rely more on verbal skills and less on the use of excessive force.[10] Other studies conducted by the center in collaboration with the Feminist Majority Foundation have revealed similar findings, reporting that male officers are more likely to be named as defendants in excessive force and police misconduct lawsuits than females.[11] In Los Angeles alone, claims alleging excessive force were paid out at a rate of 23 to 1 for male officers compared with female officers, despite their ratio of 4 to 1 within the patrol division.[12]

Even in smaller organizations, police use of force tends to be substantially less prevalent among female officers. In San José, for example, the independent police auditor reports that out of the 1,379 complaints lodged between 1997 and 2001, only 5% were against female officers, despite their 9% representation in the police force. The auditor also reported that of the 89 lawsuits resulting from police action from 1999 to 2001, two of the independent police officers named as defendants were female compared with 41 defendants who were male.[13]

Though many conclusions may be drawn from these data, one cannot minimize the importance of police organizations recruiting and employing a diverse workforce that is representative of the communities they serve. Recruits must work to develop not only optimum physical attributes but also superior communication and interpersonal skills that are critical for success. It cannot be overlooked that an officers' ability to engage in effective dialogue in volatile situations and refrain from the use of force may pay great dividends for the officer personally as well as for the organization and profession as a whole.

Dollars and "Sense"

The cost the public must bear for police misconduct is staggering. City and state governments spend millions of dollars annually to settle and defend lawsuits against officers. When does an officer begin to cost a police agency, and ultimately the public, too much money? Surprisingly, the answer in many organizations may be "never." In spite of the heavy price tags, many local governments continue to open their wallets, thereby justifying these exorbitant monetary awards as just another high cost of doing business. Contrast this approach to corporate America, where just one costly lawsuit would send heads rolling out the boardroom door. Better yet, consider the potential for reform if the same dollars were used proactively and rechanneled into research, new officer screening, and training.

How Much Is Too Much?

From 1994 to 1996, the New York City Police Department paid nearly $70 million to settle citizen complaints against police officers for assault, excessive force, false arrest, and police shootings. In approximately 90% of the cases, the lawsuit was not recorded in the officer's personnel file because the city's legal department and the internal affairs division determined that the officer was acting within the scope of his or her duties. In other words, this price tag came with no consequences to the officers involved.

During this same time span, the Los Angeles Police Department paid more than $34 million in settlements and lawsuit awards. Although all reports of misconduct initiate an internal investigation, the effectiveness of this process has remained the source of considerable controversy. Out of the 561 civilian complaints reviewed by the department in 1995, not even one was sustained.

From 1992 to 1997, the city of Chicago reportedly paid more than $29 million to settle 1,657 lawsuits stemming from allegations of excessive force, false arrest, and improper search procedures. Keep in mind that this figure is limited to criminal trials. Though the price tag would undoubtedly be that much higher if civil lawsuits were included, these figures have not been made available.

From July 1, 1995, to April 1, 1997, the city of Detroit paid nearly $20 million in cases stemming from wrongful death actions, excessive force allegations, and police misconduct. During the past 10 years, the annual monies expended by this department for similar litigation routinely average nearly $10 million.

Surprisingly, police supervisors in many organizations may never be informed of the complaints against officers under their command; thus, these charges rarely prompt any disciplinary action against those involved. With such a system in place, officers engaging in questionable practices may be getting a clear message from their superiors that such conduct is acceptable within the culture of the organization.

Although these numbers may seem excessive and the lack of disciplinary actions suspect, many attribute these figures to the system in place to handle such allegations. When viewed in its entirety, it is important to remember that officers are guaranteed certain procedural rights when confronted with misconduct allegations, all of which may result in a lack of disciplinary action. An officer misconduct allegation can be dismissed, for example, when a citizen's complaint cannot be substantiated to the required evidentiary standard. In other words, when there is simply not enough evidence to establish an officer's guilt, the complaint will be dismissed. For the officer to be charged, the evidence must clearly prove that the event did, in fact, occur. An officer's word against the citizen's word is not enough.

Another factor points to public misperceptions about what restraint and force tactics are considered proper and necessary when used in the apprehension of a suspect. Though some tactics may seem inappropriate when viewed by a bystander, officers are permitted to use some degree of force after weighing their own personal safety, the risk of harm the individual poses to the public, and the risk of harm to the suspect in light of the crime committed.

Federal Prosecution Data

Interestingly, the data reflecting internal investigation outcomes are fairly consistent with the data on prosecution rates for federal criminal civil rights violations under 18 U.S. Code, Sections 241 and 242 from 1992 to 1995.[14] A report compiled by the organization Human Rights Watch analyzed data from the following cities and reported on the trend:

- The federal district of Georgia North (including Atlanta) decided on how to proceed with 133 cases during this four-year period and prosecuted none.
- Rhode Island (including Providence) decided on 164 and prosecuted three.
- California North (including San Francisco) decided on 342 and prosecuted two.
- Louisiana East (including New Orleans) decided on 819 cases and prosecuted just nine.

In Central California and east Pennsylvania, prosecution efforts were more aggressive:

- In Central California (including Los Angeles), 39 cases were considered; 12 were prosecuted.
- In Pennsylvania East (including Philadelphia) 50 cases were considered, and 30 were prosecuted.

According to an analysis of the fiscal years 1994 and 1995, the Civil Rights Division declined to prosecute cases for a number of reasons. Many were declined for weak or insufficient admissible evidence (the most common reason for both years), lack of evidence of criminal intent, staleness, prosecution by other authorities anticipated, statute of limitations issues, and lack of investigative or prosecutorial resources. Some were declined per instructions from the Justice Department.

In the rare event that police officers are criminally convicted for federal civil rights violations, they spend little or no time behind bars. Out of 96 defendants convicted in 1994 and 1995, 25 were sentenced to three months or less in prison (including no time served at all), and 48 defendants, or 50%, were sentenced to 12 months or less.

Although these data may lend some credibility to similar trends in police agencies' internal investigation processes, it does not diminish concern over an alarming trend: the number of citizen complaints received by the Justice Department has risen dramatically. From 1995 to 1996 alone, the number of complaints soared from 8,864 to 11,721. An explanation for this 25% increase in complaints was difficult to determine, as the Civil Rights Division's data did not distinguish between types of civil rights complaints. By 2000, 12,000 civil rights complaints were submitted to the Department of Justice. In this same period, i.e., the year 2000, just 54 officers were either convicted of or pled guilty to crimes under the civil rights statute from complaints initiated in 2000 and previous years.[15]

When examining complaints of police abuse, several possible causes must be considered: an escalation in police violence, an increase in community awareness leading to an increase in complaints filed, or a large influx of new officers on the streets.

Last, data show that "law enforcement officers make up almost all of the acquittals in cases prosecuted by the Civil Rights Division, yet constitute only half of the indictments in civil rights cases. These data demonstrate juries' general unwillingness to hold police officers responsible for criminal acts."[16]

Civil Remedies

Although civil remedies are one way for victims to be compensated when their rights are violated, they often fall short of making the police agency and/or officer accountable for wrongful acts. Some organizations want these matters to go away quickly with as little publicity as possible and instead opt for early settlements that generally include provisions denying fault and requiring confidentiality of the final outcome. In many cases, it is easier for an organization to write a check to the victim to make the matter disappear, so to speak, than it is to address shortcomings in management, policies, or the organization as a whole. Additionally, economics frequently dictate that some cases are less expensive to settle than they would be to try in court.

When settlement efforts fail, many victims opt to litigate through to a jury verdict. The downside to litigation is that often juries are predisposed to believe an officer's account, particularly if the victim has a criminal record. In either scenario, even when the victim has been compensated, the question of abuse often goes unresolved in the minds of both the community and the law enforcement organization.

Historically, substantial amounts of money have been paid to settle police brutality cases:

- Los Angeles paid approximately $79.2 million in civil lawsuit awards and pretrial settlements against police officers from 1991 to 1996. These awards did not include those relating to traffic accidents.
- Philadelphia paid the most to settle such incidents. From July 1993 to November 1996, the city agreed to pay $32.6 million in settlements and civil jury awards. The *Philadelphia Inquirer* estimated in 1996 that the year's payouts would have paid the annual salaries of 250 police officers.

In contrast, other cities have paid considerably less to resolve similar incidents:

- Atlanta, a city known for its aggressive litigation of police abuse lawsuits, paid just over $1 million from 1994 to 1996. In 1997, however, the city paid a record $750,000 on a single case.
- From 1994 to 1996, Indianapolis paid approximately $750,000 in police misconduct lawsuits and pre-, and post-trial verdicts.

There is no doubt that city governments pay a high price for police misconduct, but what about the officers who commit such acts? In March 1992, Gannett News Service published a series of investigative reports examining the fate of police officers named in 100 civil lawsuits in 22 states in which juries awarded $100,000 or more to plaintiffs. The study encompassed awards rendered from 1986 to 1991. Of the 185 officers named in these lawsuits, only eight were disciplined. No action was taken against 160, and 17 were promoted. The reporter concluded that "Taxpayers are penalized more for brutality than the officers responsible for the beatings."

The Christopher Commission conducted a similar investigation of lawsuits in Los Angeles from 1986 to 1990 that resulted in settlements, judgments, or jury verdicts in excess of $15,000. In examining more than 300 lawsuits alleging excessive force with a combined price tag of more than $20 million, the commission found the department's internal investigation process deficient in many respects and uncovered that discipline against the officers was either nonexistent or relatively minor. Eighty-four percent of the officers investigated received positive ratings in their evaluations, and 42% were promoted following the incident.

Finding a Middle Ground

Without question, there must be a balance between the tremendous pressure put on law enforcement agencies to combat the drug and crime problem and the preservation of the rights and freedoms of all Americans to walk down the street without fear of being stopped, searched, and humiliated because of their skin color or appearance.

Above all, the public must demand accountability of its leaders, thus ensuring that tax dollars are spent to prevent these injustices rather than simply to make them disapear.

(Endnotes)

1. "The Gallup Poll. Gallup Poll Social Audit on Black/White Relations in the U.S.," Gallup Organization, Princeton, (December 9, 1999).

2. *Report of the Independent Commission on the Los Angeles Police Department*, 69 (1991).

3. ACLU Press Release, "New Poll Shows Public Overwhelmingly Disapproves of Racial Profiling" (December 9, 1999) (statement by Rachel King, ACLU Legislative Counsel).

4. *The Valley Times*, August 30, 2000.

5. Reports on Arrests for Burglary in California, 1998 State of California, Office of the Attorney General, Bureau of Criminal Information and Analysis, Criminal Justice Statistics Center Report Series, Volume 1, Number 2, August 1999. (Copy available at http://www.caag. state.ca.us/cjsc/cjscsrch.html.)

6. In "Race and Every-Day Policing: A Research Perspective," paper delivered at the Twelfth International Congress on Criminology, Seoul, Lorea, August 24-28, 1998:14, Stephen Mastrofski and his colleagues argue that, "Despite the obvious salience of race as an issue in policing over the last 30 years, there has been remarkably little rigorous research in this area." Mastrofski, Stephen D., Roger B. Parks, Christina DeJong, and Robert E. Worden.

Tonry, Michael, *Malign Neglect – Race, Crime, and Punishment in America*, New York, NY: Oxford University Press, 1995, 71. Mr. Tonry notes that "few or no reliable, systematic data are available that demonstrate systematic [racial] discrimination" in arrest practices.

7. Weisburd, David, Rosann Greenspan with Edwin E. Hamilton, Hubert Williams, and Kellie A. Bryant, *National Institute of Justice Research in Brief*, May, 2000 at 8. "The Police Foundation's nationally representative telephone survey of 925 randomly selected American police officers from 121 departments explores the officers' views on the abuse of police authority. Officers also provided information on different forms of abuse they have observed, the frequency of abuse in their departments, and effective strategies for controlling abuse. General findings, as well as differing attitudes of black, white, and other minority officers, are presented and discussed in this Brief."

8. U.S. Department of Justice Statistics, 1999, the last year such statistics were available. See http://www.ojp.usdoj.gov.

9. Weisburd, David, Rosann Greenspan with Edwin E. Hamilton, Hubert Williams, and Kellie A. Bryant, *National Institute of Justice Research in Brief*, May, 2000. "The Police Foundation's nationally representative telephone survey of 925 randomly selected American police officers from 121 departments explores the officers' views on the abuse of police authority. Officers also provided information on different forms of abuse they have observed, the frequency of abuse in their departments, and effective strategies for controlling abuse. General findings, as well as differing attitudes of black, white, and other minority officers, are presented and discussed in this Brief."

10. Lonsway, Dr. Kimberly A., "Men, Women and Excessive Force: A Tale of Two Genders," National Center for Women and Policing.

11. "More Women in the Ranks Would Stem LAPD Brutality," *Los Angeles Times*, October 2, 2000.

12. Lonsway, Dr. Kimberly A., "Men, Women and Excessive Force: A Tale of Two Genders," National Center for Women and Policing.

13. City of San José Independent Police Auditor's 2001 Year End Report.

14. Data provided by the Justice Department's Executive Office of United States Attorneys, analyzed by the Transactional Records Access Clearinghouse, a private data collection and analysis agency that has collected Justice Department records through the Freedom of Information Act. Data first appeared in a report by Human Rights Watch entitled "Shielded from Justice: Police Brutality and Accountability in the United States," July, 1998. Those prosecuted under these sections include all types of law enforcement officers: city, state, or federal law enforcement officers, sheriffs' deputies and correctional officers, as well as magistrates and judges.

15. Human Rights Watch World Report 2002: United States.

16. "New Data on Federal Prosecutions and Sentencing," from the report *Shielded from Justice: Police Brutality and Accountability in the United States*, (Human Rights Watch, 1998).

PART III:
Do You Want Crime to Prevail?

CHAPTER EIGHT

———•——

Law Enforcement Perspective: Cops Speak Out

"The American public needs to grow up. At some point, the public is going to have to adopt a more realistic view of the police. It needs to recognize what we are and what we aren't. The people pass laws to control traffic and pay the police to enforce laws. Then, when we stop them for a violation, they get mad at us...In Los Angeles, we have strict laws regarding jaywalking. Fifty percent of all traffic fatalities involve pedestrians. Yet whenever a police officer writes a ticket for jaywalking, the person whines and carries on as if the officer had just stolen his kid. It always amazes me that grown-ups can't follow simple laws. We didn't enact them; we're just supposed to enforce them. Right, says the public, but enforce them against someone else."

—Former Los Angeles Police Chief Daryl F. Gates
My Life in the LAPD

Just as accounts of racial profiling are shocking and troubling to the American public, accusations of civil rights abuses are equally disturbing to those in the law enforcement community. When these reports surface, everyone suffers. The erosion of public trust that these accounts promote hinders officers' efforts to form valuable alliances within their communities. Often, legitimate enforcement efforts are met with accusations of racism and threats of violence, which cause even the most seasoned officers to question how much they are willing to sacrifice to uphold the law.

Analysis of suspect traffic stops reveals that many veteran officers cite a variety of considerations including the actions of overzealous, rogue cops who are acting independent of department policies and police standards. Some also point to the lack of public understanding of police tactics used to ensure officer safety in stops. Others emphasize the fact that the stops in question represent merely a fraction of the millions of legitimate traffic stops that are made throughout the country daily.

Those in the law enforcement profession remain frustrated by the numerous media accounts that tend to paint only one side of the picture, which serve largely to incense the American public and lead people to conclude that no police officers can be trusted. Veteran officers criticize the media exploitation of shocking "racial profiling horror stories" and note that when viewed individually, these stories don't accurately portray the problem and are therefore not a real means of assessing its scope. Regardless of the one-sided tone of these stories, civil rights organizations defend the use of publicity by noting that they are too pervasive to be dismissed as random or rare and too persuasive to be disparaged as inconclusive.

Despite this fundamental disagreement, one point is indisputable in discussions with law enforcement officers: no one likes to be stopped by the police for any reason, regardless of his or her race. In fact, people who are stopped by police register the universal complaint that the officer made the stop for a trivial violation, often by asking the officer, "Don't you have anything better to do?" When the suspect stopped is a minority, accusations of racial profiling often surface, regardless of the legitimacy of the stop.

Experts argue that the sheer scope of traffic laws makes it easy for the police to stop almost any driver as a pretext to investigate those they suspect of criminal activity. It has even been suggested that some police officers routinely follow suspects around until they violate a traffic regulation, thus giving the officer the reasonable suspicion to pull them over.

The fact is, a large number of motorists are looking for someone or something to blame for the traffic stop. The stop is initiated either because the violator drives a red car, the officer is trying to "meet a quota," or the cop didn't like him or her. The list goes on. Occasionally, a suspect may even choose to play the race card in a desperate effort to "scare" the officer out of issuing a citation.

In the context of this discussion, it is important to look to the two groups complaining about this unfairness. On one hand are individuals who undoubtedly have a legitimate complaint. It would be irresponsible for the law enforcement community to deny that some officers misuse their power to further their own racial agendas. These officers must be exposed and dealt with on an individual basis. It cannot be ignored, however, that many complaining about this unfairness are those who are stopped for legitimate traffic violations. In the course of a given stop, evidence is uncovered either through observation or through a consensual search that provides the officer with probable cause that a crime is afoot, i.e., paraphernalia, contraband, or other evidence that suggests the driver may be under the influence. It is unfair to place the blame for a criminal's wrongdoing on the officer who is just doing his or her job.

Though many organizations have taken proactive steps to eradicate the use of racial profiling as a legitimate crime-fighting tactic, law enforcement's response in general to racial profiling allegations has been mixed. Some agencies have aggressively defended their right to conduct pretext stops, while others vehemently deny these practices exist. While there are many departments trying to dodge the political spotlight in hopes that media attention on a given complaint will dwindle, there is no shortage of others that have been hurtled into the media arena in the wake of litigation and scandals.

Although offensive to many, profiling and pretext stops are not uncommon law enforcement tactics. In fact, many describe these practices as good police work. Often, a well-trained officer proficient in his or her profession will become aware only through experience and training that an individual is in the process of committing a crime or performing an illegal act. In these instances, however, the officer will not have the requisite elements that a review court would demand to justify a stop. Should the officer then allow the individual to continue unchallenged or risk making a stop that may not be supported by sufficient articulable facts? The prudent and resourceful officer will find another legal way to continue the investigation or pursue the suspect until additional information or probable cause is developed. Would society expect any less of its law enforcement officers? Should the race of the person in the process of committing the crime be a factor in the officer's decision about whether to initiate the stop?

The public's perception of racial profiling and the resulting fear of police have been largely perpetuated by media reports of shocking encounters between the police and minorities. As troubling as these accounts may be, they fail to portray the positive uses of "profiling" by law enforcement. It is important for the public to distinguish between harmful *racial* profiling and *criminal* profiling, the first being illegal and the latter being an effective crime-fighting tool.

Criminal profiling is an important way for investigators to develop a unique blueprint on a suspect and is largely based on characteristics and behavior of a suspect perpetrating a crime. When these criminal profiles are used by law enforcement and released to the public, the potential for narrowing the search for and apprehending a dangerous suspect is greatly enhanced. Criminal profiles may also be used to determine whether the same suspect is responsible for carrying out similar crimes.

In addition to these *criminal* profiles, law enforcement routinely uses *geographic* profiles to predict where a suspect may strike next or to identify where the suspect lives in relation to the crime scene(s). For example, in the East Coast sniper shootings that took place in the fall of 2002, law enforcement looked at the location of the shootings and determined that the suspect probably committed the crimes in an area close to his or her home or in a very familiar area. Criminologists have developed similar profiles to pursue serial killers, rapists, and child abductors and have been instrumental in solving many of these difficult cases.

Once useful *criminal profiling* tactics are distinguished from the harmful practice of *racial profiling*, screening and training efforts can be sharply focused on developing the former and eradicating the latter. This approach is contrary to the views of many civil rights organizations that have proposed that "racial profiling" be defined in a broader sense to include any selective law enforcement practice directed at individuals because of their racial or ethnic composition. This all-encompassing definition will most certainly guarantee that many stops directed at minority drivers will fall under the guise of a racially motivated stop. The fact remains that race does play an integral role in many of the enforcement efforts undertaken by law enforcement, including race-specific gang intervention, the detention of illegal aliens, and the search for a suspect who has been described by witnesses as belonging to a certain race.

By adopting this overly broad definition of racial profiling, special interest groups are able to cite large numbers of minority traffic stops and categorize them as inappropriate, illegal acts by law enforcement that are inspired by a hidden motive to stop and harass minorities. Ultimately, this sweeping definition conceals the real problem and is highly prejudiced against the many law enforcement officers who work hard to enforce the law fairly and equitably. It also becomes the basis for recommendations that are flawed from their inception through to their implementation and generates radical ideas that hinder the enforcement of minor traffic violations and limit an officer's ability to use discretion to enforce the law on the street. Moreover, such proposals inadvertently initiate a type of quota system that predetermines who can legitimately be stopped on the basis of race and geography. Similar proposals also seek to promote the use of written "consent to search" forms, which would be required prior to any voluntary search. Rather than serve as a deterrent, these recommendations would severely handicap legitimate law enforcement objectives.

Probative police work is necessary for successful police operations and the safety of society. It is this aggressive stance against the criminal element that produces safer communities. A less aggressive approach would hinder these important objectives and would lead to an upsurge in crime, which in turn would result in public outcry. The criminal motive hinges on the successful commission of crime while eluding law enforcement in the process. It is only through the close observation of these activities, coupled with proactive tactics by law enforcement, that the means to keep pace with this elusive culprit will be achieved.

A Crime Is a Crime

It is true that most traffic laws are merely infractions that do not bear the serious consequences of misdemeanors or felonies; however, that does not make these laws any less significant in their application. The laws of the vehicle code share their origins with more serious criminal enactments. They are presented as bills before the legislature, and only those recognized by a majority are enacted into law. Why should these laws be any less enforceable than other legislation?

From the first day on the street, a police officer is sworn to enforce *all* laws of the land. There is no "level of enforcement" that distinguishes the enforcement of "minor" violations from the enforcement of more serious ones. Though enforcement objectives are sometimes prioritized on the basis of the risk to the public, it is important to note that many of the violations that appear minor on the surface may produce deadly consequences when perpetrators are permitted to skirt the system. In fact, in April 2001, the Supreme Court ruled in a narrow 5–4 decision that people stopped for minor offenses punishable by only a fine (i.e., not wearing a seatbelt or jaywalking) may be subject to a full-scale police arrest including handcuffs, booking, and jail.[1]

Contrary to the view of some civil rights groups, the initial stop for these vehicle code violations is not usually the culprit. In scrutinizing these stops, we need to focus our attention on the officers' actions *after* the stop has been initiated and the "clock is ticking." If the legislative intent is that traffic stops should not be made on regulatory violations, codes should be enacted to prohibit stops for these offenses. This would result in legislation similar to that of the early California seatbelt law under which a traffic stop could not be initiated on the basis of that violation alone but could be enforced in conjunction with a more serious violation.

Although a system such as this may be preferable to many, statistics suggest that to limit the discretion of police to stop drivers for minor violations may come with deadly consequences. Using the seatbelt law as an example, one must examine the disproportionate number of highway fatalities involving African Americans and Latinos. For young African American males 14 years and under, motor vehicle crashes are the leading cause of death. They are the second leading cause of death behind homicide for African American males age 15 to 24.[2] Undoubtedly, many of these deaths could be prevented if these drivers simply wore a seatbelt. Although the ACLU commends the Air Bag & Seat Belt Safety Campaign, the National Highway Traffic Safety Administration, and similar organizations in their concerted effort to get the message out in minority communities to "buckle up," this is simply not enough. Without the aggressive police enforcement of these laws, offenders would continue to suffer severe injuries and fatalities at an alarming rate. These offenses, regardless of how trivial they may seem, violate the law. The police are entitled to enforce this law, with benefits to society in the process.

It is important that civil rights organizations join with law enforcement to save lives rather than label every minor police stop part of a concerted effort to harass minorities. The two groups must work together to foster a mutual trust and cooperation if progress is to be made. Though law enforcement must take steps to ensure stops are conducted properly, officers should not be hindered by unrealistic restrictions that can produce deadly consequences on the street.

The court expressed its agreement with this premise by further empowering law enforcement in *Whren v. United States*[3] wherein the Supreme Court held that pretext traffic stops are reasonable and constitutional. Moreover, the court expressed that as long as an officer observes a traffic violation, a stop is constitutional even if the officer has no authority to make the stop and no intention of enforcing the law being violated. Though the Constitution prohibits the selective enforcement of laws on the basis of considerations such as race, police may legally stop any motorist if an officer believes a traffic violation has occurred. Unless the individual can prove that the officer's primary motivation for the stop was race, the stop will be deemed legitimate, and any evidence of criminal wrongdoing resulting from the stop will be admissible in court assuming that collection of the evidence was legal. Most law enforcement officers agree with the court's decision.

Though disagreeable to many, pretext stops can be a useful means of apprehending those who violate the law. For example, some states have enacted legislation that requires U.S. citizenship or legal alien status to obtain a driver's license. In a given time frame, officers may be directed to place an emphasis on the crime of driving without a license. In these states, however, a person generally cannot be detained or arrested "solely on the belief that the person is an unlicensed driver." But by using the pretext traffic stop, officers may legitimately investigate a driver's status while stopping the vehicle for a moving violation or an auto maintenance issue.

Though many may consider this type of enforcement activity trivial and discriminatory, the licensing requirement remains an important means of regulating highway safety and ensures the protection of those whose motor vehicles are insured and registered. On the basis of a profile of unlicensed drivers, officers may have a greater tendency to consider the race of the driver as a secondary factor in their probable cause analysis. All things considered, an officer may stop a greater ratio of Hispanics, for example, who are more likely to be illegal aliens than are Caucasians. This is not to say that an officer may stop all Hispanics on the basis of the generalization that race equates to a likelihood that the individual is unlicensed. Rather, the officer must examine the driving habits of the individual by using an observation of a traffic violation as the primary factor for the stop.

At first glance, it may appear that these stops are intended to target those of a particular ethnicity, since some Hispanics living in the United States have not yet satisfied citizenship requirements, a prerequisite for obtaining a driver's license in some states. However, a well-trained officer need not consider the race of the driver when targeting suspected violators. Rather, an officer can simply look to the individual's driving characteristics, which often provide the officer with enough reasonable suspicion to stop the individual for further investigation. An officer may look to a driver who has poor control of a vehicle or who seems unfamiliar with roadway markings and rules of the road. A person who is unlicensed will usually avoid making normal eye contact with an officer and will often "look at the dirt pile" instead. This obscure body language that seems insignificant to the average citizen can be invaluable in the pursuit of a potential suspect and signals to the officer that the person may be engaging in illegal activity.

In this context, it is important to emphasize that driving is a privilege, not a right. To obtain a license, a driver must meet residency requirements; demonstrate proficiency on a written and a behind-the-wheel test; and agree to submit to a blood, breath, or urine test upon arrest to determine potential drug use or measure blood alcohol levels. Additionally, automobiles operated on the roadway are subject to significant regulations that require mechanical inspections and proof of insurance, annual registration fees, fines, and penalties. These standards aim to promote public safety as well as to generate significant revenue used by the state, the Department of Motor Vehicles, and by law enforcement to support Peace Officer Standards and Training (POST). The privilege to drive should not be confused with an inalienable right, which comes with greater protections.

Quality of Life Policing

Pretext stops are often one component in a growing trend defined by many agencies as quality of life policing. Other elements of this trend include the use of routine, investigatory stops in high-crime areas; aggressive stop and frisk tactics; and arrests for quality of life infractions such as drinking in public, panhandling, or sleeping on park benches. The ultimate goal of these aggressive policing measures is for police to deter more serious crimes before they occur.

Many experts agree that the trend toward quality of life policing seems to be having a significant impact on crime rates nationwide. When introduced in New York City, the result was a 50% drop between 1990 and 1996 in the seven categories of serious crimes tracked by the FBI's Uniform Crime Reports. In 1990, New York City reported 2,246 homicides and 6,000 shooting victims. In 1996, there were fewer than 1,000 homicides and about 3,000 shooting victims. As one street vendor explained, "With all the police vigilance, nobody dares carry their guns."[4]

It is important to remember that when pretext stops are used as part of a special enforcement plan, emphasis is generally placed on specific crimes, with officers focusing their attention on areas with a high concentration of criminal activity. When the areas targeted are inner-city neighborhoods with a high minority population, officers immediately become the target of racial profiling accusations, when in reality, these special enforcement operations are usually a response to repeated complaints by the citizens themselves. Likewise, there may be other factors unrelated to race that account for the higher amount of police activity in certain geographic areas.

There should be no doubt that any individual, regardless of race, will have a higher criminal propensity if he or she is less educated, lives in a low-income neighborhood, or is involved in gang activity. This segment of the population generally drives automobiles that are in a state of ill repair, another prime target for enforcement. Unfortunately, some of these lower-income areas are populated by minorities. Regardless of race, often such unfavorable economic and living conditions breed a higher incidence of visible criminal activity than found in some of the more affluent suburban neighborhoods.

In addition to the challenges posed by socioeconomic issues, association with gangs is more predominant among minorities, whose members are lured into affiliations with groups composed of members of their own race. Therefore, if apprehending members of a particular gang during a special enforcement activity were emphasized, it would be ridiculous to think that race would be ignored when all of its members are known to belong to a specific minority group. Obviously, race and demographics would be significant factors in identifying potential gang members. This stark reality is often ignored in the context of these discussions.

With the rising crime rates in some inner cities, even the most unlikely proponents of pretext stops are beginning to defend these practices. In cities such as Oakland, California, where the homicide rate is dramatically rising, even the most liberal residents are beginning to embrace pretext stops in a desperate attempt to stop the violence. Under intense public pressure, politicians are also turning up the pressure and demanding that the police pull out all stops to end the violence.

The call of civil rights groups for nationwide legislation banning the use of pretext stops would probably not be very effective in eradicating its use. The fact remains that pretext traffic stops have been an integral law enforcement tactic for decades and have been a key tool used by officers to pursue those that they suspect of criminal activity. It is doubtful that law enforcement will give it up any time soon. Doing away with this practice may look good on paper, but the reality is that the loopholes created by the court would water down any proposal so significantly that the potential for success would be slight. As it stands now, the courts have permitted this practice to continue virtually unbridled and will probably continue to do so for the foreseeable future. The current system makes it easy for an officer to justify practically any stop under the guise of a minor traffic violation. This is all the courts require.

Political Emphasis on the Crime Rate

Local politicians and the public exert significant pressure on law enforcement to produce statistics that demonstrate officers are aggressively combating crime. These statistics, generally comprised of the number of citations issued and the number of arrests for various crimes, are important for three reasons. First, they provide the public with a means to measure the effectiveness of the local police. Second, these statistics serve as objective evidence to support a department's receipt of lucrative traffic and government grants that directly benefit the community. Third, these statistics are occasionally utilized to evaluate an officer's performance and to measure his or her commitment to eradicating crime in the community.

Often the inexperienced officer is the most vulnerable to the political pressure to produce favorable statistics. Rookie officers can be easily influenced by their newfound power and are often lured into a competitive arena by their peers to turn out the most arrests. Typically, this young officer will not have the requisite knowledge and skill to differentiate between the citizen motorist and the criminal element. The result is that minor traffic stops often become "fishing expeditions," with the officer hoping that arrestable violations will be found solely on the basis of the mere volume of stops.

In the course of these stops, it is not uncommon for officers to request permission to search a vehicle, mainly because they have nothing to lose. Veteran officers are quick to point out that it is rare for a citizen to refuse the search, usually because the average person is not aware that it is within his or her rights to do so. Race often becomes a factor in these random stops, sometimes a result of the mismatching of individuals to cars. For example, a 16-year-old driving a customized BMW may arouse more suspicion than a middle-aged businessman driving the same car. Likewise, some may equate the element of poverty to criminal demeanor, which results in prejudicial stereotyping that is brought to the workplace and occasionally fostered in locker room talk.

These law enforcement practices, when witnessed or experienced by the public, explain how accounts of unwarranted stops translate into allegations of racial profiling. Perhaps if the scope of detainable traffic regulations were minimized, the members of the general public would be assured that when they were pulled over, the seriousness of the offense would stand on its own and not be construed as a mere pretext for an officer to investigate whether a more serious crime is afoot. Preventing the police from judiciously making lawful stops could tragically result in a substantial number of criminals being allowed to continue their evil deeds. It is ultimately the public who must decide, through the legislative process, whether the reduction in crime rates justifies subjecting citizens to more frequent and intrusive searches, seizures, and pretext traffic stops.

Since September 11, 2001, the nation is wrestling with the same questions in the context of its war on terrorism. Government actions that limit freedoms, travel, and the ability to associate freely are tough enough to interpret when they are directed at those who are not U.S. citizens. When the rights and freedoms of our own citizens are infringed upon, however, the need to strike a balance between government security and constitutionally guaranteed freedoms must be added to this complex equation to ensure that any such infringements are within the confines of these essential protections.

Does Crime Determine Color?

It would be egregiously incorrect to theorize that terrorism, or any other crime, is more likely to be perpetrated by people of a certain racial or ethnic group. Though we typically hear about minorities who disapprove of profiling, it is important to note that this practice is used universally, regardless of race. Serial killings, white-collar crimes, savings and loan fraud, and tax evasion, for example, are crimes that usually enlist perpetrators from the male, Caucasian segment of the population. The reverse argument can be made that whites commit more of these types of crimes than minorities, thus the disparity in enforcement tactics against this group. The main distinction, however, is that many of these crimes are usually limited to wrongs against corporate shareholders or the government. Other than the rare case of murder committed by a serial killer, most of these crimes do not typically result in the loss of life that is characteristic of murders, rapes, and robberies and thus do not receive equal media attention.

One cannot avoid the reality that many crimes fall into a gray area, where officers are forced to balance the relevance of a suspect's race with the components of the crime itself. Although the crime may be the main target, race of the suspect becomes an unavoidable factor that must, at a minimum, be used as a secondary consideration when relevant. When the target is a gang whose membership is based in part on affiliation with a particular minority group, immigration violations, or drug trafficking in which suspects are known to originate from a particular country, factors such as race and the components of the crime itself become important considerations for the officers to use in narrowing the scope of potential perpetrators. In these specific instances, it is prudent for an officer to use race as a secondary factor to identify potential suspects and to maximize the effectiveness of special enforcement operations.

It is equally important to consider that many stops labeled "racial profiling" are initiated by an officer after a witness has provided a description of a suspect. For example, if the witness describes the perpetrator as a black male in his 20s, it would be prudent for the officer to restrict his or her detentions to black males in their 20s, focusing on race as one factor to identify the suspect. Would the public suggest that this is not "fair" and that white males in their 20s be stopped as well? This course of action would not only be silly, but it would also be a waste of valuable resources. The kind of "fairness" some civil rights organizations are searching for would severely undermine the underlying foundation of our justice system.

Perhaps Jesse Jackson said it best when speaking to a Chicago audience: "There is nothing more painful to me at this stage in my life than to walk down the street and hear footsteps and start thinking about robbery—then look around and see somebody white and feel relieved."[5] Apparently, Reverend Jackson's feelings are not the exception. A 1990 study at the University of Chicago revealed that more than 56% of Americans believe that blacks are "violence prone."[6] If one of the most powerful, highly respected black civil rights leaders feels this way along with a reported majority of Americans, how can society prevent police officers from feeling similar prejudices when making daily life-and-death decisions? This superhuman expectation of law enforcement is unfair and unrealistic.

Don't Shoot the Messenger

On the basis of the nation's prison demographics alone, one may be drawn to the assumption that blacks are more prone to commit crimes than whites are. The question is whether these demographics represent the cause or the effect of racial profiling by law enforcement. Does our tendency to suspect young black men as opposed to whites or women or the elderly have any legitimate basis? To equate prison demographics with a particular groups' criminal propensity is probably far too simplistic. However, one cannot ignore the findings of most criminologists, which suggest that blacks, men, and young people do in fact commit crime at a higher per capita rate than do whites, women, and older people. Statistics tend to support this hotly debated theory. In 2000 alone, almost 10% of black non-Hispanic men aged 25 to 29 were in prison compared with 1.17% of white men in the same age group. Although blacks comprise only 12% of the population, they accounted for 56% of the arrests for murder, 42% of the arrests for rape, 61% of the arrests for robbery, 39% of the arrests for aggravated assault, 31% of the arrests for burglary, 33% of the arrests for larceny, and 40% of the arrests for motor vehicle theft. Forty-six percent of state prison inmates were black, and another 17% were Hispanic, even though they represent only 24% of total U.S. residents.[7] By virtue of these statistics alone, some might conclude that one should be more wary of a young black man than an elderly white woman. But what do these statistics really tell us when we look at the problem in the bigger picture?

Random surveys conducted among thousands of drivers across the United States have revealed that African Americans are more likely to fail breath tests for alcohol than whites are. Although Hispanics were less likely to fail the test than whites in 1973, the study revealed that in 1986 and 1996, a greater number of Hispanics failed similar tests.[8] Other limited studies reveal dissimilar trends when looking exclusively at drug possession, thus indicating that blacks and Latinos are *not* more likely than whites to possess narcotics or other contraband.[9] Despite these studies, blacks constitute 57.6% of all drug offenders in state prison, Hispanics 20.7%, and whites 20.2%. These figures continue to fuel the debate among experts over whether this trend directly correlates to racial profiling efforts by law enforcement or emerging trends in black and Hispanic communities. Some experts studying the phenomenon have even suggested that the numbers reflect nothing more than minority population shifts in certain geographic areas, usually those with a predominately minority population.

Probably the soundest theory in this regard is that which suggests that some minority groups may be more prone to stops than whites because of their own safety habits. Some experts propose a cause and effect theory—the cause being safety habits and the effect being discrimination. For example, federal studies have shown that only 51% of blacks wear seat belts versus 62% of whites. Assuming these statistics are consistent with seatbelt trends in states that have enacted mandatory seatbelt laws, blacks would be 11% more likely than whites to be stopped by police for this reason alone. Once the officer makes the legitimate stop for the seatbelt violation, he or she can lawfully look for other variables that may become apparent in the course of the stop to suggest that another crime may be afoot. Though the initial stop may be lawful under the umbrella of safety, sometimes discriminatory motivations prompt the ensuing investigation. These investigations are often based on inaccurate stereotypes and generally do not occur when the perpetrator is white. When these stereotypes are acted upon as if they were facts, they inadvertently permit the real perpetrators to continue unchallenged. As a result, law enforcement and the public are left with prison demographics that do not mirror the reality on the street, consequently perpetuating the misinformation about certain racial groups' propensity to commit crimes.

Despite these revelations, officers insist that the perceived propensity of a certain race to commit a crime does not alone guide them in determining enforcement priorities. These statistics are often secondary to pressure by citizens and community leaders for officers to focus attention on particular high-crime areas or roadway violations within a community. Often, these "high-crime areas" are inner-city neighborhoods whose citizens represent a diverse segment of the population. Thus, when these areas become a priority for special enforcement action, minorities may be targeted disproportionately.

To illustrate this point, let's use the example of illegal drugs. Studies reveal that more whites than blacks are cocaine users.[10] Until cocaine use among the affluent has a significant impact on the quality of life in a community, the public simply will not demand that police officers barge into conference rooms of major corporations to arrest CEOs and executive board members for cocaine use. The average cocaine user is typically a white businessman who can afford to support a drug habit and who tends to fade into society at the end of the day.

On the other hand, young drug users tend to be more "high profile" because of their frequent affiliations with gangs and in the extent of their deleterious effect on the community. They often engage in theft to support drug habits and deal drugs in schools and on the streets. The very essence of these gangs is the members' affiliation to a specific racial group, which likens these associations to pseudo-families for wayward youth. Because of the high visibility of these groups in the community and the resulting public outcry, the attention of self-initiated police is often directed toward these individuals.

Regardless of how one interprets crime statistics, it is important that they be put into context as they relate to the bigger picture of race. For example, even though statistics may suggest that a disproportionate number of blacks are arrested and convicted for committing violent crimes, only about 2% of blacks are arrested for committing *any* crime in a given year. In other words, nearly 98% of blacks are not arrested for committing any crime at all.[11] Regardless, many civil rights groups argue that although a small percentage of blacks may actually be convicted of a crime, they are nevertheless stopped at a disproportionate rate. It is these stops, many say, that are the real injustice by law enforcement against the minority community.

Even the officers themselves realize that their suspicions will not be confirmed every time they become wary of criminal activity. Regardless of an officers' training or experience, the fact remains that many traffic stops that begin under a cloak of suspicion reveal that a suspect's activities are entirely legitimate. Even the *Terry v. Ohio*[12] court recognized that officers may stop innocent people. As is the case with any system dependent entirely on human discretion, there will inevitably be some casualties.

The discretionary system used by law enforcement and sanctioned by the courts is not 100% error proof. In fact, almost every aspect of our legal system is highly dependent on one's interpretation of a set of laws or facts. This process of human discretion and interpretation begins on the street and ends in the courtroom, with the wild card of race always looming. Our entire legal system—from legislators to officers to prosecutors to judges—relies on human beings who naturally have biases and prejudices. Often, we forget that "[w]e are men and women as imperfect as the society we are drawn from."[13] Though many criticize the system in place for affording officers too much discretionary power, there is no better system.

The Two Extremes

Though specific solutions will be addressed later in depth, it should be noted here that even the noblest efforts to minimize some of the inequalities that come with officer discretion have come with unavoidable downsides. In New York City, for example, former Mayor Rudolph Giuliani instituted an aggressive police tactic called "zero tolerance," through which arrests were made for minor offenses. Although this tactic was implemented to change public attitudes and support crime control, one must ask whether this is really what the public wants—a system that gives police officers no discretion to issue tickets. It is doubtful. This is no more tolerable than the inexperienced officer stopping everyone in the hopes of making an arrest. The officers' ability to warn and to obtain voluntary compliance is often far more beneficial in the long run than the negativism of issuing a citation.

Should the public outcry banning pretext stops be heeded? Is that what society truly wants? What would result in communities such as Oakland, California, where the citizens are trying to take back their neighborhoods from drug dealers and stop the rising homicide rate? How can the police work to eradicate the drug problem without appearing racist when the demographics of the community demanding more enforcement are largely minority?

Police are at a severe disadvantage in the war against drugs and the war against crime and must use every avenue that the law provides to gain the upper hand. To take away officers' ability to do their jobs would severely hinder law enforcement efforts. Ultimately, doing away with pretext stops would come with a heavy price tag that many in society may not be willing to pay.

Playing It Safe

When unwarranted pressure is exerted on the police by outside sources, all Americans suffer. Often, when the police believe they have been maligned and unjustly accused, they display the human tendency to play it safe and do less. This is best illustrated by looking back to past riots in Los Angeles and New York City's Central

Park, where police officers have allegedly been afraid to get involved for fear of being labeled a racist every time they stop or arrest a minority.

This concept has also played itself out in Cincinnati, Ohio, where the lethal police shooting of a 19-year-old black man with outstanding misdemeanor warrants prompted destructive race riots around the city. Neighborhoods and businesses were torn apart, and white pedestrians and motorists were beaten by black mobs. One radical attorney applauded the rioters and likened their actions to giving "whites a better understanding of what it feels like to be a random target of violence just because of the color of your skin."

A look back on the destruction revealed that the majority of the rioting took place in predominantly black neighborhoods. Experts reviewing the aftermath of these unnerving events point to the withdrawal of police from these black neighborhoods as the reason the riots gained in intensity in these areas.

Following the rioting and the harsh public criticism of the police, the crime rate in Cincinnati skyrocketed. An August 2001 commentary in the *Washington Times* reported that Cincinnati had recently experienced 74 shootings that left 86 people wounded or killed, compared with 9 shootings and 11 victims for the same period the previous year. Experts point to these numbers as one example of the new trend in police work that is taking hold across the country: selective disengagement by law enforcement.

Selective disengagement is the unintended outcome in the cycle of racial profiling. When police officers risk facing federal probes and investigations on the basis of their discretionary conduct in high-crime neighborhoods, many will choose to pull out of those neighborhoods altogether. In the current climate, police are finding it impossible to enforce the law in minority neighborhoods without being branded "racists" regardless of how legitimate or lawful their enforcement actions may be. Once charges of racism surface, the ball is set in motion, and the officer risks public ridicule, lawsuits, investigations, and even the loss of his or her career. In some respects, the damage to the officer, his or her family, and the department is done whether the accusations are ever substantiated. In some cases, it is simply easier to step back and let the criminals win.

Unfortunately, these sentiments toward disengagement are growing among officers across the country and have become an increasing source of frustration among those committed to the profession. The trend to sit back and do nothing is not confined to bad officers. Dedicated veteran officers who have been on the force for years are deciding to play it safe and pretend they don't see anything rather than running the risk of losing everything. They are paid the same amount of money whether they enforce the law or not.

It has become predictable and almost inevitable that stopping a minority for even the most minor violation will result in accusations of racial profiling. It has come to be viewed by many officers as a minority's way of "playing the game" when stopped by the police. The new buzzwords "racial profiling" are like a live grenade brandished in the officer's face, the accuser hoping their mere utterance will intimidate the officer into just walking away.

The dangers of this new trend will undoubtedly affect many unintended victims. The neighborhoods of law-abiding minorities will suffer. Police will not patrol their streets. Crime will run rampant because the criminals will know that they have a safe haven to conduct their lawlessness. Officers will hesitate to respond to calls in these communities and will subconsciously hope that the perpetrator will escape before law enforcement arrives to intervene. Other law-abiding citizens will also suffer anytime the perpetrator is a minority. It may even become commonplace for the victim of a violent crime to endure the horror of wondering whether anyone will come to help.

Unfortunately, the police have been placed in a no-win situation. Officers all across the nation are ready to give the people what they want: nothing.

These new challenges, together with the demoralization of the law enforcement profession, have severely hampered police departments' ability to recruit new officers. Agencies nationwide are experiencing an alarming decrease in the number of new recruits. This comes at a time when many have taken on aggressive campaigns to add officers to their force, particularly women and minorities. The impact of this trend weighs most heavily in the larger U.S. cities. For example, in Chicago, 5,263 applicants applied to take the police examination in the year 2000. By comparison, there were 10,290 applicants in 1997 and 36,211 in 1991. In New York, more than 1,700 officers left the force. The number of captains leaving the force increased three times from the previous year. In a similar pattern, the number of new applicants dropped sharply from 32,000 in 1996 to 13,136 in 2001. It has become the rule for cities to operate with well below the authorized number of officers. Veteran officers are opting for retirement rather than promotion, and they justify the decision by citing a profession that is much different from the one they entered more than 20 years earlier.

Even the once coveted spot of police chief has become far less desirable to many. Major cities around the nation are finding it increasingly difficult to recruit qualified individuals for this political hot spot. Many would-be chiefs cringe at the thought that the power of the chief—once so strong that the position offered unbridled control over a city's police agency—could be extinguished when it is signed over to the Justice Department in the form of a consent decree.

If the current trends are allowed to continue, the public will see firsthand the unintended casualties of the "do less" philosophy. The question we must ask ourselves is as plain as black and white: do we want a safer society in which law enforcement detains anyone and everyone they find suspicious, or do we want total chaos and lawlessness, where law enforcement looks from afar with its hands in its pockets until officers get the "okay" to intervene? More important, is there a middle ground we can all agree on?

Weapons for Change

Idealistically, law enforcement's solution to the problem of racial profiling is easy. It is found in almost every lobby of modern-day police departments: the mission statement and creed of conduct. Following these established ethics and standards would guarantee equal and fair treatment for all. In his book, *My Life in the LAPD* 424, Daryl F. Gates writes, "Every police officer fresh out of the Academy knows what our mission is. The mission…is to achieve a safe environment free of crime and to promote the well-being of all people while demonstrating integrity, diligence, sensitivity, and compassion."[14]

But finding a solution to racial profiling may not be as simple as many civil rights organizations suggest. What many forget is that racial profiling is a product of the mind. As such, identifying racial profiling may not be as simple as looking at the circumstances surrounding an officer's contacts with the public and drawing a conclusion as to whether the officer's actions were motivated by racial bias. Though the facts and circumstances of two separate incidents may be identical, an officer's mindset may be completely different. Unless the officer makes some outward admission or statement that reveals his or her true motives, the public is left to wonder whether race was the primary motivation for the stop.

The unfortunate reality is that racial profiling will never be totally eliminated from law enforcement, just as it will never be eliminated from society as a whole. The important role law enforcement plays in the community, however, positions police and citizens to work together toward solutions that will minimize this harmful practice in both arenas. In order for these efforts to succeed, law enforcement must target some key areas for change.

1. Stop Police Profiling

Although racial profiling is prevalent in all facets of society, many civil rights organizations see law enforcement as an easy target that offers blanket recommendations broadly focused on the whole institution rather than on narrowing the scope of proposals to the small group of individual offenders who are tarnishing the reputation of the entire profession. Just as racial stereotypes are unfair, so too are those that label all police as racists. The public must become informed about its local police and learn to view reports of police misconduct in the context of the many examples of good police work.

2. Redefine Harmful Profiling

Racial profiling is no doubt a complicated issue. Even the definition of racial profiling used by the federal government, the states, the numerous law enforcement agencies, and civil rights organizations is inconsistent and sometimes even contradictory. This inevitably leads to great confusion among law enforcement officers about what actions constitute racial profiling. In addition to the confusing and sometimes conflicting definitions, most are quite broad and leave specific details relating to an officer's actions on the street up to the officer's individual interpretation. To avoid this confusion, many in law enforcement suggest that these broad and conflicting interpretations of racial profiling be replaced by a unified, narrower definition that does not permit such a myriad of interpretations. The definition proposed should set forth explicit standards about which actions are permissible and which are not. Absent such detail, officers are forced to use their own discretion to interpret "gray areas," which results in many situations where officers are unsure whether their actions are legally or procedurally acceptable.

Those with the task of developing such a definition must keep in mind that racial profiling is the specific thought process of an officer that results in a discriminatory act directed at an individual based *solely* on prejudice. This definition requires that race be a dominating factor, not just an auxiliary observation. As with any prejudicial conduct, the thought process will be specific to the officer, with the resulting act fueled by preconceived stereotypes, misplaced hate, and animosity. Without this discriminatory mindset, racial profiling has not occurred.

3. Address the Larger Problem

Civil rights groups must expand their focus from law enforcement to other areas of society where racial disparities and socioeconomic conditions put minorities at a disadvantage from an early age. For example, it is often overlooked that a higher percentage of African American and Hispanic children in this nation grow up in poverty. Often raised by single parents, many return home from school with little to no supervision because of a parent's extended work schedule. Others live in dilapidated housing projects with gunfire ringing through the streets both day and night. Some studies have pointed to the quality of employment, education, and health care as other factors that are sometimes inconsistent among certain racial groups. For the percentage of those who endure these societal challenges, crime is learned at a young age and becomes a survival strategy rather than a conscious choice. These social and economic disparities often correlate to adults who are more prone to encounter the criminal justice system.

These numbers in and of themselves obviously do not translate into open season on a particular racial group; however, neither can they be ignored. While some incidents of profiling undoubtedly equate to racism, others may be evidence of a system that is mistakenly equating class with race. In neighborhoods with poverty, broken windows, high crime, and gang problems, it is often the residents who seek an increased police presence and ask the police to take more aggressive steps to rid their communities of crime. In many cases, these neighborhoods are populated largely by minorities.

4. Redirect Resources

Funding for police agencies must be redirected to creating and implementing officer training programs that cover cultural diversity, changing demographics, and ethics. As with many large organizations, within law enforcement, resources are commonly directed to projects that are more "visible" than "necessary." Training, for example, is frequently offered to all officers in a blanket fashion. Rather than receiving training tailored to his or her needs and experience level, a veteran officer may be forced to sit through a course in an elementary subject like report writing designed for rookie officers. Obviously, a 20-year veteran who has been writing reports for his or her entire career would not find this elementary information useful. Regardless, the department will be able to claim that every officer has participated in a certain amount of training hours, even though many of the hours may have been completely irrelevant to the officer's professional needs and, likewise, to the achievement of the organization's goals. Alternatively, organizations must explore offering courses that are highly relevant to the officers' position and responsibilities within the organization. For example, the veteran officer may benefit from courses on people skills, supervisory ethics, and leadership.

In smaller organizations, it may not be feasible to have an independent section of the police department solely responsible for training, nor would it be practical to run a separate training class for three or four veteran officers on the force. But by setting standards for training and identifying which officers are lacking information or skills in certain subject areas, several smaller departments can work together to offer appropriate training courses for officers that fill a critical void as opposed to just an empty seat.

Though redirecting resources may be valuable in some areas, in others there are greater challenges. For example, some groups suggest that officers who make a traffic stop notify dispatchers of the reasons for their stop prior to initiating contact with the citizen. In many of the larger organizations, it may not be feasible for officers to initiate contact with dispatch every time a traffic stop takes place. Though this proposal may seem logical to the average citizen, those on the street recognize that such a practice may be hindered by other considerations, for example, the limited amount of radio time available. Even if such a program were feasible, the accuracy of the information being conveyed is once again dependent on the honesty and integrity of the messenger.

5. Preserve Officer Discretion

"Begin with one of the most important ideas in modern criminology, and one that has revolutionized police practice—the belief that a good way to prevent robberies, murders, and other serious felonies is to go after minor offenses."

—Jackson Toby[15]
Wall Street Journal, March 11, 1999

Officers must be allowed to use their discretion to investigate and enforce the law while adhering to proper police practices that coincide with community expectations. The institution must look toward developing the appropriate use of this powerful tool through training and example. Though laws and statutes cannot be drafted to cover every situation, officers should not be left to operate in a vacuum. Guidelines for police operations should be set and procedures implemented that hold officers accountable for inappropriate, independent decisions and misuse of discretion.

The most compelling argument for preserving officer discretion in the enforcement of minor offenses is the case of the former chief of the transit police in New York City and the current Los Angeles Police Chief, William J. Bratton. Bratton directed his officers in New York City to target offenders for small infractions—fare beating, panhandling, graffiti, smoking, and boisterous behavior—as part of a strategy to control violence in the subway system. "Within two years of the policy's adoption," he said, "the number of felonies in the subway declined by more than 30%. Why? Well, one out of every six fare evaders stopped by the transit police in 1991 was either carrying a weapon or wanted for another crime on an outstanding warrant. By paying attention to behavior that most people regard as not worth bothering about, the transit police prevented many violent crimes on the subways."[16]

6. Use Race as a *Secondary* Factor

Regardless of how unpopular it may be to use race as a factor in profiling suspected criminals, the practice should not be portrayed as synonymous with racism. Though it is true that most minority citizens are law abiding, it is inevitable that police may need to direct enforcement efforts toward a specific racial group as a *secondary* factor to the underlying offense. Crime is not always generic, and race will remain an unavoidable factor in many situations. When police target racially segregated gangs, drug trafficking to and from a particular country, or Immigration and Naturalization Service (INS) violations, race becomes an important part of the equation.

7. Eliminate Voluntary and Mandatory Data Collection Efforts

When racial profiling is defined in a narrower sense, one quickly realizes that it cannot be solved simply by keeping track of the number of minority drivers stopped by officers and calculating by volume whether an officer is targeting one race over another. Even when the data reveal a disproportionate number of minority stops, many fail to consider other variables that would drastically change the outcome. When such variables are ignored, the data reported are of no real use in determining the scope of the problem. For example, few of these studies look to the demographics of a given enforcement area or the arbitrariness of where an officer may be at a given time. Moreover, the anonymity of the collection efforts makes it highly unlikely that the true violators will turn in any "cards" at all. Those who do may choose to fabricate data in an effort to hide their activities. When data collection is viewed in the broader sense, this all-encompassing solution oversimplifies the problem and often bypasses the true violators. Police officers even jest about this approach as if they were talking about a parlor board game, i.e., "I have used up all my minority cards, so I guess this one can go free." More often, the result is reverse racial discrimination, which occurs when officers stop a nonminority in an effort to "break even."

Under a revised collection and reporting system, it may be possible for data collection to establish whether racial profiling is occurring and even to prevent it. Under many of the current systems, however, these objectives will not be met.

8. Redirect Efforts of Citizen Review Boards

Many experts suggest that when racial disparities become evident, the police should answer to a citizen review board. One might question, however, how the utilization of people with their own racial biases will add to the mix and influence the systems already in place: a law enforcement organization's own review process, the court system, grand juries, civil remedies, and the federal government's commission on discriminatory practices. Above all, there is the Constitution itself. More important, how can one evaluate this type of "data" and determine what "disparities" are reasonable if it is determined that there is a disparity in the number of crimes committed by minorities versus whites or vice versa? Isn't it logically impossible to start with a disparity and end with equality?

It should be emphasized that law enforcement is not particularly opposed to constructive involvement of the community. In fact, a 2000 survey reported that nearly 70% of black officers and one-third of white officers found citizen review boards an effective means of preventing police misconduct.[17] Perhaps the efforts of these oversight groups would be better placed within the community and would thus bring law enforcement and the public together rather than construct another wall that law enforcement likens to "big brother." If the efforts of these oversight groups were redirected to address the problem on the front end rather than after the wrong has been committed, each side would be more willing to accept the involvement of the other.

9. Maintain the Current "Consent to Search" System

One of the most controversial arguments surrounding data collection is whether officers should be required to advise a citizen of his or her right to say "no" to a search of their person or vehicle. The theory is that minority citizens are at a greater disadvantage when asked to agree to a consensual search, in that many are less likely to be aware of their right to say "no."

Perhaps the most debated of these proposals is whether to require the use of a written "consent to search" form to advise drivers of their right to refuse to grant consent to a search. If such a system were implemented, police officers would be required to advise citizens of their right to say "no" before conducting a search of their vehicle or person. If the citizen had no objection to a search by the officer, he or she would be asked to sign a written consent form voluntarily.

As with the *Miranda v. Arizona*[18] admonishment, no substantial effect was experienced by law enforcement obtaining voluntary statements; thus, one would anticipate merely advising a person of his or her right to say "no" would not diminish the number of voluntary searches performed. At it stands, the Supreme Court has ruled that law enforcement is not bound to advise a person of his or her right to say "no."[19] Most in law enforcement would agree with this ruling.

10. Reshape the Image of Law Enforcement

"Fairness requires that mistakes be looked at in the context of the more numerous examples of good judgment."

—Jackson Toby[20]
Wall Street Journal, March 11, 1999

Law enforcement practices are historically rooted in rigid "take it or leave it" practices steeped in tradition. It is sometimes this hard-line, unwavering approach that results in negative contacts between the public and the police, particularly among minority groups who may view law enforcement differently on the basis of their own experiences in their native countries. In response to this diversity, organizations must engage in aggressive marketing tactics usually reserved to large corporations in an effort to promote the positive aspects of the profession.

While many agencies are developing these marketing tactics on their own, others have reserved this controversial approach as a defensive measure. For example, in New Jersey, state troopers have responded to an ACLU billboard aimed at recruiting plaintiffs for racial profiling lawsuits by erecting highway signs with a toll-free number for motorists to compliment helpful state troopers. Adorned with an American flag on one side and a state trooper on the other, these billboards want to know: "Have you ever been helped by a New Jersey State Trooper?"

The highway is not the only forum law enforcement can utilize to reshape its image. Agencies must look to schools, cultural centers, and religious groups as partners in this marketing approach. More important, law enforcement must listen to those within their own organization. Gaining the respect and trust of its own employees is probably the most important step in fostering a positive attitude that officers can carry over into their contacts with the community.

11. Promote Interdepartmental Unification

Despite law enforcement efforts to portray a unified alliance to the public, race remains a predominant factor that inadvertently divides those within many organizations. Though the segregation inherent in some organizations can take on many forms, one that is the most visible is that occurring among police unions. In smaller police agencies, officers of all races may belong to one police union that represents their interests in various forums. In larger organizations, however, police officers generally divide into race-specific unions and seek a forum that will represent their views along racial lines. Whether a member of the White Officers' Association, the Black Officers' Association, or the Hispanic Officers' Association, just to name a few, this division by race may inadvertently send a clear message to the public that race does matter and that officers within the organization may not be as unified as one might hope with respect to the organization's goals and objectives. Perhaps one citizen said it best: "I've always been suspicious of white cops. I would feel much better if a black cop comes to my house when I have a problem. When you look at what's going on in these police unions, even the black officers themselves don't believe that a white officer can represent them properly."

Though many officers believe these police unions offer minorities a stronger voice within an organization, one must not overlook the perception these affiliations may inadvertently leave with the public. On the contrary, when unions are designed to benefit all officers and look out for the interests of the entire profession, officers can reinforce to themselves and the public that people of all colors can work together toward one common goal.

12. Rebuild Public Trust

Before law enforcement embarks on any path to change, one thing remains certain: any efforts must first be directed toward rebuilding the trust that is the basis of the relationship between the police and the public.

When we talk about trust, we refer to several elements that are essential to the success of any partnership. Qualities such as full disclosure, honesty, timeliness, an unblemished track record for truthfulness, and high ethical standards are just a few that must exist in any successful cooperative exchange.

Though these qualities are essential building blocks, the public must recognize that law enforcement is at an extreme disadvantage with respect to fulfilling these expectations, mainly because of the privacy restrictions within the profession. Particularly in the context of full disclosure to the public, officers are often compelled by law to protect a suspect's rights, other officers' rights, the rights of juveniles, or the rights of innocent citizens, and they are prohibited from disclosing pertinent information that may compromise any of these privacy mandates. Liability and political sensitivity may also prohibit law enforcement from full disclosure and honesty, thus leaving the decision about whether to inform the public in the hands of police administrators, city attorneys, politicians, or risk managers employed to assess potential liability. When these factors interplay, the reasons law enforcement has difficulty building trust with the public become apparent.

Despite these challenges, there are several steps law enforcement can take that may actually work to achieve the same objective. By choosing effective and ethical leaders, officers will be held to a higher standard of public service. When officers who are respected by the public assimilate into the community and establish a rapport with its citizens, each side will be in a better position to understand and trust the other.

In interviews with police officers of every race, age, and sex, one sentiment was universal: officers enter the profession for the purpose of protecting society. Most officers do so for their entire careers, despite the high personal costs. Regardless of an officer's training or experience, the job of confronting the worst of society on a daily basis never becomes routine. This aspect of the profession inevitably chips away at a person and routinely forces officers to shift their mindset from that of preventative police work to a fight for survival. Whether pursuing a murderer, a drug dealer, or a child molester, officers must stay ahead of those who are void of conscience and, frankly, less human than the rest of us. When confronting those with nothing to lose, officers must continue to play by the rules. Most officers do so very successfully. In some cases, however, fear, stress, or desperation lead a small percentage to engage in practices that are inconsistent with the fundamental tenets of police work. When these cases of impropriety surface, the entire profession suffers. We must remember that for every officer who engages in improper conduct, there are thousands more whose tenacity and good judgment legitimately take criminals off the street.

These success stories deserve to be told.

(Endnotes)

1. *Atwater v. Lago Vista*, 195 F.3d 242 (2001).

2. *Saving Lives and Liberties*, statement of Laura Murphy, Director of ACLU Washington National Office dated Friday, October 15, 1999.

3. *Whren v. United States*, 166 S.Ct. 1769 (1996).

4. Krauss, Clifford, "Shootings Fall as More Guns Stay at Home," *New York Times*, July 30, 1995 at 29.

5. *Perspectives*, *Newsweek*, December 13, 1993 at 17 (quoting Jesse Jackson).

6. Smith, Tom W., *Ethnic Images*, 9, 16 (Dec. 1990) (General Social Survey Topical Report No. 19), quoted in Armour, Jody D., "Race Ispa Loquitor: Of Reasonable Racists, Intelligent Bayesians, and Involuntary Negrophobes," 46 Stan. L. Rev. 787.

7. Toby, Jackson, "Racial Profiling Doesn't Prove Cops Are Racist," *Wall Street Journal*, March 11, 1999.

8. *Time Magazine* report, July 30, 2001, citing 1998 study in *Accident Analysis and Prevention*.

9. "National Household Survey on Drug Abuse," at 16, (1998), National Clearinghouse for Alcohol and Drug Information, Research and Statistics, Washington, DC: U.S. Department of Health and Human Services.

10. "New ACLU Report on Racial Profiling Calls for Government Action and an End to Official Denials," (June 2, 1999) ACLU Press Release (indicating that the government's own reports indicate that 80% of the nation's cocaine users are white, middle-class suburbanites).

11. Statistics from "Developments in the Law: Race and the Criminal Process," 101 Harv. L. Rev. 1472, 1508 (1988) (noting that 97.9% of blacks and 99.5% of whites in any given year are not arrested for committing a crime.).

12. *Terry v. Ohio*, 392 U.S. 1 (1968).

13. Gates, Daryl F., *My Life in the LAPD* 363 (Bantam Books, 1993).

14. Gates, Daryl F., *My Life in the LAPD* 424 (Bantam Books, 1993).

15. Mr. Toby is a professor of sociology at Rutgers University. He was director of the Institute for Criminological Research at Rutgers from 1969 to 1994.

16. Toby, Jackson, "Racial Profiling Doesn't Prove Cops Are Racist," *Wall Street Journal*, March 11, 1999.

17. Weisburd, David, Rosann Greenspan with Edwin E. Hamilton, Hubert Williams, and Kellie A. Bryant, *National Institute of Justice Research in Brief*, May, 2000 at 8. "The Police Foundation's nationally representative telephone survey of 925 randomly selected American police officers from 121 departments explores the officers' views on the abuse of police authority. Officers also provided information on different forms of abuse they have observed, the frequency of abuse in their departments, and effective strategies for controlling abuse. General findings, as well as differing attitudes of black, white, and other minority officers, are presented and discussed in this Brief."

18. *Miranda v. Arizona*, 384 U.S. 436, 86 S.Ct. 1602 (1966).

19. *Schneckloth v. Bustamonte*, 412 U.S. 218 (1973).

20. Mr. Toby is a professor of sociology at Rutgers University. He was director of the Institute for Criminological Research at Rutgers from 1969 to 1994.

CHAPTER NINE

An Equation for Success

An Inside Look
at Phoenix Police Chief Harold Hurtt
and the Phoenix Police Department

One recurring theme that has framed many of the discussions throughout this book is quite simple: to comprehend the scope of racial profiling in law enforcement fully, the public must first develop a complete understanding of the larger picture as it relates to society. The issues posed are complex and cannot be understood merely by looking to the cause and the effect in the limited context of crime enforcement and traffic stops. Rather, all sides of the controversy must be explored in order to gain an insight into some of the underlying social issues involved. It is important for those who have never been victims of racial profiling to become educated on the challenges faced by many minority citizens and to realize what it means to have one's civil rights taken away by an officer who has been sworn to uphold the law. On the opposite end of the spectrum, individuals of every race must appreciate the tremendous demands and pressures that are inherent in the law enforcement profession and must work in partnership with these agencies to develop programs that will be successful in minimizing the potential for racial profiling in all facets of life.

It is common for the media to oversimplify the issue by often implying in colorful and sometimes shocking reports that the problem begins and ends with corruption in law enforcement. The concept of racial profiling is commonly linked to law enforcement, mainly because its high visibility makes it a likely target for intense public scrutiny. This erroneous oversimplification of the problem suggests to the public that if this corruption can be eradicated, racial profiling will disappear. Although racial profiling is inherent in every aspect of society, it is at law enforcement that some repeatedly point the finger of blame. Others look to law enforcement for an unequivocal solution. Those in law enforcement, however, will tell you it's just not that simple.

In our extensive review of countless media reports and publications on this controversial issue, we were struck by the overwhelming tendency to "bash" law enforcement and to expose officers and police administrators that were experiencing problems within their organization. Although this avenue certainly must be explored in order to understand fully one part of this complicated issue, it is equally important that the public meet and hear the words of the unsung heroes in law enforcement that are just as committed to stop racial profiling as many civil rights organizations.

Our research led us to one major U.S. city police chief who is working toward such a goal: Police Chief Harold Hurtt of Phoenix, Arizona. We were so impressed after our interview with him that we have devoted this chapter to his philosophies and strategies. We'll examine his innovative approaches to the challenges in his city and explore his opinions about race, racial profiling, and potential solutions.

We believe the following information and discussion derived directly from our interview with Chief Hurtt lends valuable insight into the problems surrounding the issues of race and racial profiling, and we would like to thank him and the Phoenix Police Department for their important contribution to this project.

Background

The city of Phoenix, Arizona, with a population of about 1.25 million people, is the sixth largest city in the United States. Phoenix, Arizona's capitol city, covers an area of approximately 476 square miles. It is located in the south-central portion of Arizona, its population is one of the fastest growing in the nation, and its minority demographics are rapidly rising.

In 2000, the Hispanic community comprised about 26.37% of the Phoenix population and was the largest minority representation in the city, probably due, in part, to the city's close proximity to the border. African Americans comprised about 5.17% of the population, Asians about 1.94%, and Native Americans 1.78%. Although the Hispanic populous will probably remain prevalent in the community, the city of Phoenix is becoming more and more like a reflection of the world's population.

During the past 30 years, the demographics of Phoenix have changed significantly. Phoenix is rapidly becoming a melting pot similar to other major U.S. cities experiencing growth in the size of its Russian, Bosnian, Vietnamese, and Ethiopian communities. Law enforcement in Phoenix has been especially challenged by these new demographics, as this desert community is beginning to reflect the diversity and experience the growth of an East Coast metropolis.

The one person who has seen these changes firsthand and who is probably the most personally challenged by the city's changing demographics is its own police chief, Harold Hurtt. One of a small handful of African American police chiefs in major U.S. cities who have climbed through the ranks to success, Chief Hurtt is no stranger to the challenges presented by race. Overseeing more than 3,500 officers, there is no question that he is dedicated to doing what's right to benefit his employees, his department, and most of all, the Phoenix community.

Originally recruited into the Phoenix Police Department from the Air Force, Chief Hurtt initially intended to go through the police academy just long enough to save money for college and never intended to become an officer on the street. Nearly 35 years later, however, he compares the love of his profession and his long tenure to that of playing golf by explaining, "If you play it for three months, you're hooked for life."

Surprisingly, law enforcement was not the first career choice of this popular chief. After going through the police academy, he decided to stay in the profession a little longer, mostly because he enjoyed working in an organization in which he could be part of a team. "You start getting the instant reinforcement from the community and find out how many people are out there really supporting you," he said. "When you get the support from your political leaders, and financing, and they give you the training and facilities that you need, it's not a bad place to be."

Although Chief Hurtt has been with the Phoenix Police Department in the capacity of chief only since 1998, his long career with this department has led him through the ranks as a valuable asset to the organization. In 1992, he retired from Phoenix and moved to California to become police chief in Oxnard, a suburb of Los Angeles, a position he held for about five and a half years. In April 1998, he returned to Phoenix as chief and has been one of the instrumental forces in this department's success ever since. Chief Hurtt also remains active in other law enforcement organizations, some of which include the International Association of Chiefs of Police and the National Organization of Black Law Enforcement Executives.

Though no organization is without its problems, the Phoenix Police Department seems to have a long history of doing things right. If the accomplishments of its leaders are any indication, the department has been a springboard for many successes and credits its values and culture with the promotion of many of its officers to positions of prominence nationwide, including positions in major cities in California, Utah, Texas, Oklahoma, and Virginia.

Although Chief Hurtt can take a lot of the credit for his department's success, he makes it clear that others before him have worked equally hard to make the organization what it is today. His modern philosophies promote a team effort from the police dispatchers and line officers up through the command staff while instilling the values of honesty and integrity in all who serve under him. Chief Hurtt's philosophies and innovations have changed the way this police department operates, which likens it to a profitable corporation that is successfully marketed to the public it serves.

One of this organization's most unique qualities is the fact that it represents a small handful of law enforcement agencies that have become voluntarily accredited by the Commission on Accreditation for Law Enforcement Agencies, Inc., and it is nationally recognized as a model organization. Although the voluntary accreditation process has existed for only a few years, it is often recognized as something that should be mandatory for all law enforcement agencies. In studying the benefits of mandatory accreditation, one need not look far to see that professionalism in law enforcement is not always defined the same. With an oversight system such as accreditation in place, many theorize that the profession would be forced to become more accountable and would join other sectors within society that are monitored in a similar fashion.

The present system of voluntary accreditation imposes different requirements for an organization on the basis of its size. Because the Phoenix Police Department is one of the largest organizations to become accredited, it must maintain certain policies and procedures for training employees, conducting citizen investigations, and impounding property, just to name a few. The requirements run the gamut of what is required to operate a large department successfully and are closely monitored to ensure that the organization maintains measurable standards. Chief Hurtt compares the process to accounting procedures for an accountant and notes, "We all need a benchmark to determine where we stand as far as the profession."

The process of becoming and remaining an accredited organization raises the bar by requiring organizations to submit to auditor reviews of their records and paperwork, as well as to facilitate local meetings open to the public so that citizens in the community can come forward and testify about whether the department is meeting certain standards. These data are then analyzed by the accrediting organization to measure the level of trust and confidence the citizens have in the police organization and to gain an overall assessment of how well the department is relating to its citizens.

Recruiting New Officers

Perhaps an organization's most important link in the chain of success begins with the challenging and often difficult process of hand-selecting the line officers that serve the city. The Phoenix Police Department does not leave much to chance when recruiting new officers, and Chief Hurtt makes it clear that it cannot afford to.

Traditionally, the recruiting process for law enforcement has not evolved to keep up with the changing technology, with many organizations relying on systems that have been in place for more than 30 years. The changing climate in the nation, however, has prompted the overhaul of many recruiting programs, most notably in the hiring of women and minorities. Although the ultimate goal of many organizations is to have a police force that is a true representation of the diversity in the community, Chief Hurtt's own experience has shown that achieving this kind of representation may not be as easy as it sounds.

In many communities such as Phoenix, even the most aggressive recruiting efforts have not changed the fact that the city's makeup has made it difficult to hire as many minorities to fill openings as one might like. Chief Hurtt is the first to acknowledge that although the department has done a great job recruiting African Americans and Hispanics, it is still not where it needs to be, mainly because of the lack of minority candidates applying for such positions. He recalls a meeting with community members to address hiring more Hispanic employees in the department. The chief agreed to do his part and challenged the group to help him recruit more minorities by saying: "Between now and a year from now, bring me 50 people. Help me. And we never had that end-of-the-year meeting."

Despite aggressive efforts, it is no secret that the law enforcement profession is finding it increasingly difficult to attract qualified individuals. Though much of this may be due to the inherent dangers of the job itself, one cannot ignore the negative publicity this profession has endured over the years. Even though the tragedy and aftermath of September 11, 2001, reminded the nation of the unselfish dedication of these unsung heroes, media attention has more frequently focused on the corruption and scandal surrounding a few bad apples, which have inevitably tarnished the image of the entire profession.

Law enforcement agencies that want to remain competitive have had to rethink their approach to recruiting and come up with a new game plan to lure potential candidates into this ever-changing field. Though every agency has its own process for recruiting new officers, we have looked to Phoenix to find out what challenges this department has faced, what changes have been made, and how these changes have helped this city increase its pool of candidates by nearly 50%.

Though many smaller agencies tend to entice potential candidates from within the state to test for open positions, many of the larger agencies will often look outside the state for new recruits. Similarly, Phoenix, one of the larger U.S. cities, frequently sends its recruiters out of state to look for individuals who may be interested in joining the ranks of the Phoenix Police Department. Traditionally, Phoenix's approach had been somewhat straightforward, not unlike that of many other large organizations. If a potential candidate came to the Phoenix Police Department recruiting booth, the candidate was given a study guide to take home and fill out. If the individual was truly committed to pursuing the position, he or she would have to pay to travel to Phoenix, take the test, pay for a hotel, and travel back home to await the test results. If the candidate passed the written portion of the test, he or she would again have to pay their own way back to Phoenix to continue the application and screening processes. In a review of its recruiting program, the police administration quickly realized that this often expensive and burdensome quest resulted in many candidates being left out, particularly those in the very sector that the department was trying so hard to attract. In an effort to address this dilemma, Phoenix did what most law enforcement agencies are better known to avoid: it changed.

The significance of change in the law enforcement profession should not be underestimated. In the day-to-day administrative operations, law enforcement has traditionally operated more like a governmental body as opposed to a private entity. In many of the larger corporations in this country, success is often measured by the number of innovative products released and the successful risks the company takes. Profit is generally the driving force that determines who stays and who goes.

But this proactive approach has not necessarily been the norm in the law enforcement community. Leadership is often reluctant to initiate change, mainly because of the political risk involved. In this arena, success is not measured in dollars and cents. It's measured by one's ability to keep the department out of trouble with the media and the public. Often, management finds it safer to stay in the shadows to avoid making waves in their organization while clinging to the old adage of "If it ain't broke, don't fix it."

This archaic approach is far from reality in Phoenix, where new, proactive ideas and innovations appear to be the rule rather than the exception. In response to the dwindling recruitment numbers for example, the department identified the need to revamp its approach to mirror that of many large corporations in the private sector, and it focused on marketing the benefits of a profession in law enforcement, as well as "selling" potential candidates on coming to work for the city.

In order to recruit new officers successfully, it became clear that one of the immediate challenges was to overcome a problem reported in many other large agencies across the country. Law enforcement would need to remain competitive with careers in the private sector.

> *"If you could go to work at Hewlett Packard or Motorola and start off at 50K–60K and nobody is going to shoot at you and you don't have to wrestle anybody down and face some of the challenges that law enforcement has to, why wouldn't you?"*

The philosophy in the city of Phoenix is essentially to go out and ask candidates what they are looking for in a job. Armed with this information, the organization makes a concerted effort to match the culture of the department and expectations of police work to what the candidates want in a career. Chief Hurtt notes the "one mistake many organizations make. They try to sell their organization and profession without finding out what the candidates are looking for, and I think we've been very successful in doing that." This shift in philosophy, coupled with the recruiting changes from an administrative perspective, has increased the number of candidates coming to take the entrance examination from about 200 to 300 every other month.

Chief Hurtt insists that this policy shift has not lowered the standards for new officers; rather, it has changed the process so that the funnel is widened at the beginning and encourages more candidates to apply. Recruiters now carry the test with them when they travel out of state, and they sit down with potential candidates to take the test at the recruiting site rather than require the candidate to pay for costly travel up front. This new approach in the out-of-state recruiting process has permitted people to apply who may have been excluded under the old system.

In addition to enlisting some of the more obvious tactics to attract recruits such as raising the pay for new officers, they realized that to better serve the needs of the city, they had to do more to increase the number and broaden the diversity of the candidates applying for law enforcement positions Chief Hurtt wasted no time embarking on an aggressive marketing program for Phoenix by employing his philosophy of "selling" the organization, as well as the law enforcement profession. To the chagrin of some of the neighboring police chiefs, it would not be uncommon to drive through city or the outlying areas and be confronted with advertising billboards, taxi cab signs, and various print ads, all designed to entice the public to join the ranks in the city of Phoenix. Although this hiring approach is nothing new to the private sector, it is virtually unheard of in the law enforcement community, and thus it represents one of the innovations organizations are exploring to better their position as employers and ultimately become more competitive with corporate America.

The efforts in Phoenix have not gone unnoticed. The Phoenix Police Department has been recognized by organizations such as PERF (Police Executive Research Forum) and served as a model for other large cities around the country. Chief Hurtt is proud of these accomplishments. He notes: "We're not just controlling traditionalists. I think we're the innovative risk takers, and I think our recruitment and selection process are really what gets us over."

While marketing the positives, many departments are undoubtedly feeling the effects of the negative publicity that have overshadowed the profession over the past few years. The media reports have exposed corruption at every level that ranges from the fabrication of evidence against the innocent to the blatant abuse of citizens and their civil rights. This negative publicity poses some of the greatest challenges recruiters are faced with when trying to entice Generation Xers into this demanding profession. Chief Hurtt does not underestimate the fact that, in his words, "A lot of these people are no different than anybody else in that they have wants and needs, and fortunately for them, there's a lot of places out there other than police work that can provide that for them."

> *"Why would anyone want to be a police officer? That is one of the many questions we ask ourselves when we go out recruiting today. And that's what the candidates ask, 'Why would anybody want to recruit me? Why would I want to be a police officer?' ...and you've got to be able to respond to that."*

Although recruiting, screening, and hiring objectives are fundamental to the ultimate makeup of any police department, the methods used to implement these processes vary substantially from city to city. Some of the variations seem to be segregated by state, while others differ depending on the size of the department. The lack of qualified or diverse candidates may not be as noticeable in a major city such as Phoenix, which may be in a better position to pick and choose those at the top of the list, so to speak, than other communities are. In smaller organizations that have few qualified individuals applying for positions, management may sometimes be forced to compromise and deviate from the "ideal" candidate in order to keep staffing at safe levels.

One example of such sacrifices focuses on the "make or break" psychological test and evaluation that candidates must undergo prior to hiring. These psychological tests often probe areas of a candidate's personality to anticipate his or her mental stability when handling potentially volatile situations and to predict how the officer may interact with the public. These tests may also help weed out candidates who seem more prone to dishonesty or criminal behavior. In Phoenix, a candidate that fails this test is automatically taken out of the running. In some smaller departments, however, applicants may remain viable candidates after failing the psychological profile. When candidates are not mentally able to endure the rigors of the job, misconduct such as racial profiling and discrimination often surface.

Training

"We do a lot of training and we give them a lot of skills. We teach them how to drive. But we don't give them a lot of education. We need to look at the cultural stuff; we need to talk about it. We need to have this discussion about race."

It should be no surprise that in order to become a police officer, one must be well trained in the use of weapons, force, and the legal system. New officers are trained in a boot camp setting to ensure that they possess the physical agility and skills needed to fight crime on the street. Although these physical attributes are essential in the profession, the skills taught in training offer only minimal preparation for officers to serve the public well. Without comprehensive and ongoing training in the psychological aspects of the job, officers may be unprepared to deal with stress, ethics, and cultural dynamics such as race or class that are often more prevalent in the job than physical combat. This becomes most apparent when officers respond to calls well trained in the use and application of force, sometimes using these alternatives prematurely for lack of a better approach, particularly when the suspect is a minority.

Chief Hurtt recognizes the lack of understanding of the different cultures as one of the major challenges within his agency and emphasizes that training in these areas is critical for any organization's long-term success. Tools and training must be implemented so the officers understand the dynamics of the various cultures and learn effective communication skills that will yield the most positive results when dealing with the public. When these skills are applied at the front end of a conflict, the confrontation may come to a peaceful resolution rather than escalate out of control. He cites conflicts involving Hispanics or African Americans as one example: "They will, in a conflict situation, usually have a great deal of words before there is any action, as far as veiled threats and how bad they are and what they're going to do. There's always some type of exchange, and a lot of times, it doesn't get past that exchange. If officers are not aware of this, they will overreact to the circumstances and create a confrontation versus letting them talk, letting them get it off their chest. Then intervene some, and de-escalate the situation versus plowing in and saying OK, this is out of control, when really, this is part of the process within those cultures to have these types of exchanges and discussions before the fight starts."

His philosophy about race extends far beyond the challenges he faces in his position as chief. As a nation, he points to our unwillingness to discuss the underlying problems stemming from our diversity by saying: "We need to have the discussion about race. We need to have the discussion about bias, crimes, and discussions about culture and ethics and community. We need to do this without putting people on the defense, and without saying, 'Oh, those poor people.' In America, we don't want to have the real discussions. We'll do anything to keep from having those discussions."

He looks to the example of apartheid in South Africa and the rebellions that took place when Mandela was elected. He points to the blacks and whites sitting down and discussing apartheid and being able to get past the bitterness and anger to move the country forward. "In America," he said, "we have never had that discussion about slavery and the inequities. We will do anything to try and mask that discussion."

He points to both his own experience and government statistics that reveal a larger representation of minority youth in the criminal justice system. He finds this interesting given the fact that these kids are not even driving yet. He contributes this disparity to the lack of understanding many officers have of the minority cultures they serve. "An officer may be responding to a home as a result of a radio call, and because the home is not like the officer's with two parents living in a nice neighborhood, there could be a tendency to automatically assume that this is an unfit place for this child and that the best thing for the child would be to introduce them into the criminal justice system or some other social services system in order to take them out of that environment. In most cases, this may not be the best thing to do." Officers who lack the training and insight into these cultures may think that they're helping the child, but what they're really doing is more damaging to the youth and to the entire family.

> *"When most people key in on racial profiling, they key in on traffic stops. There is a great deal more to police work than traffic stops. If you're going to look to the relationship between law enforcement and the minority community, I think you need to take a broader approach and look at the concept of biased policing."*

Chief Hurtt is quick to caution people about focusing too narrowly on the issue of racial profiling without seeing it in the broader picture as it relates to biased policing. The premise of fair and equitable treatment relates not only to minorities but also to officers' interactions with the elderly, people with special needs, and the handicapped. It is important to look at the focus America is putting on people with special needs. For example, do you exert the same level of force on an 85-year-old man that has committed a felony as you would on a 25-year-old man? The policy says to handcuff all felons. But do you take this 85-year-old person to the ground and put his or her hands behind his or her back and handcuff them as you would a 25-year-old? Under the current system, the answer would probably be "Yes."

"And these are some of the greatest challenges we have as leaders in law enforcement. How do you train into an individual that this minute, you need to be Superman, and the next minute, you need to be Mr. Rogers?"

Chief Hurtt insists that you do it by providing training in professionalism. "No matter what the circumstances that exist as a result of the call or the response or the contact, we cannot forget that our responsibility is to maintain professionalism." The concept of professionalism encompasses many things. It includes taking charge and acknowledging that "I need to de-escalate here; I need to start communicating; I need to start building rapport."

Although there is always more work to be done, the Phoenix Police Department is one of a small handful of organizations that does quite a bit of training in this area, particularly in educating the officers how to interact with the public. This training is also offered to management, supervisors, and command staff, supported by the chief's philosophy that the way the officers are treated is the way they will treat others. Rather than focusing on external forces and the bottom line, the training efforts are directed toward, in Chief Hurtt's words: "How we get along with our people. How do we build trust? How do we raise expectations? How do we successfully continue to raise the bar and have them respond? Because there is more than a supervisor, manager, leader relationship—there is a personal relationship."

For these programs to be successful externally, the chief is not afraid to look within his own organization to address potential racial and gender tensions on his staff. He is quick to admit that there is probably no organization that has totally eliminated this kind of internal discrimination; however, he believes that Phoenix has largely outgrown these kinds of problems. "If you listen to the stories that were told 25, 35, 50 years ago about the Phoenix Police Department, and you talk to individuals today, there has been change," he said. "Because we train people to respond as a team and act as a team, you don't have the privilege to have your biases interfere with your decision making because your team is there and you're depending on an individual to be there for your back and they're depending on you."

With so many successful internal training programs in place, Phoenix is developing a more innovative approach to educating many of its officers in the area of cultural diversity. One training option currently available for select officers includes immersion programs that enable officers to take Spanish classes and live in a Hispanic community for two weeks while speaking the language and studying the culture. Although Chief Hurtt would love to have the budget to send all officers through this program, he believes the officers that do have an opportunity to go will benefit from the experience of living with and learning about the largest minority group the department serves.

Community Policing

Community policing, often touted as the new political "buzz words" in the law enforcement profession, has been incorporated into the philosophies of many police organizations across the country. Promoted to the public as a new way of doing business, the concept often looks good on paper but in practice has met with skepticism. Probably one of the greatest reasons for its mixed reviews has been the limited number of officers who usually work in these "community policing" assignments. It may look great politically; however, when some other sector of the department meets with bad publicity, its short-reaching success is quickly undermined.

"You can't have effective community policing if you look at it as a program. It has to be a philosophy."

Chief Hurtt is no stranger to the challenges of developing a successful community policing program that truly improves and fosters the department's relations with the public. Before becoming chief, he was in charge of the community relations program in Phoenix for five years and was well aware of the importance of community interaction long before community policing became mainstream. His efforts and philosophies in this regard exceed the norm, and his innovative approach has turned an often watered down concept into a way of life at the Phoenix Police Department.

He credits the success of his department's program in part to the foundation that was laid back in the early 1960s during the height of the civil unrest in the United States. During this volatile time, Phoenix established a community relations bureau to enhance the department's relationships with special interest groups. The current program has evolved from this early concept into a department-wide philosophy that the leaders and employees are committed to practicing on a daily basis.

This philosophy focuses largely on the community, local businesses, the media, social services, and other city departments and resources working together with the police in a full partnership. It goes far beyond having specific people in the organization assigned to do community policing. In Phoenix, community policing is both policy and practice. Chief Hurtt explained: "The detectives are doing community policing, the people that answer the phone in the chief's office or the 911 call understand the philosophy of community policing. I think the mistake that a lot of agencies make is that they assign a handful of people to do community policing, and the majority of the department is doing police work. Big mistake."

The chief's philosophy is not merely an abstract concept that gets lost in a large department. It is a value at the foundation of the organization that is integrated into training programs for new recruits, in basic training, and in the policies and procedures of management, all the way up to the chief.

"Anything we do that is significant in the Phoenix Police Department, our community is involved. And they're not involved by receiving information from us. They're involved at the front end of the system."

The city of Phoenix looks to its citizens to work in concert with the police department to establish policy. For example, one of the chief's advisory groups, the

Hispanic Community Advisory Group, helped the police administration draft the department policy concerning immigration and how officers are to interact with the city's undocumented individuals.

This new and proactive philosophy has led to changes in the hiring process as well. At one time, candidates were interviewed by sworn personnel, generally sergeants, lieutenants, or line officers. Now there are people from the community who take an active role in the selection process of new officers. "I think it's very appropriate for the citizens to sit there and look at candidates and interview them to help make the decision as to whether this person is okay," Hurtt said. "'This is my community and my neighborhood; come to my house and take a report,' or 'I have concerns about that person, and I don't think you should hire them.'"

He credits this program with bringing a new perspective to the department. When new ideas and perspectives are borne from the people affected the most, the concept of community involvement has a much further reach. Much of the time, citizens who are not directly affected by a problem do not get involved in their communities. In his role as chief in California, Chief Hurtt feels he was successful at enhancing the leadership that was already out there at the neighborhood level. "I've seen people really shy and uninvolved get involved and block watch and neighborhood watch," he explained, "and after six months or a year, they're ready to run for president, because they've had an opportunity to grab a hold of something and see change made and take ownership and realize that there's a lot of other partners out there willing to be supported. They're getting recognition." This kind of empowerment within a community leads to a renewed sense of confidence toward the police department. For an officer, said Hurtt: "It makes you a problem solver, a conflict resolver, a facilitator of leadership. It makes the officer king of that beat. He gets immediate gratification and gets it from people he sees every day."

Uncovering the Real Issue

"I don't think there would be a police chief in this country who would say 'I've never had an issue of racial profiling in my city.' It happens in the schools, it happens in the businesses, it happens in the churches, it happens everywhere. So what's going on? How do we get past this concept that race doesn't matter anymore in our society? When we are able to address those issues in our general society, we can address them in policing."

In our interview with Police Chief Hurtt, one common theme emerged: race does matter, and the focus needs to be broadened substantially beyond police agencies. Without a discussion of the real problems, Chief Hurtt sees the issues of racial profiling and data collection as nothing but knee-jerk reactions to what is going on in society as a whole. Although he acknowledges that the police may have more powers than those in the private sector in that they can take away one's rights, he sees this type of behavior as "no different than an African American walking into a car lot and looking at a Lexus SUV. Because of who they are and because people see who they are, no salesman will approach them to say, 'Hey, what kind of car do you want?' They automatically assume that the person is just coming in to kick the tires, when in reality, the person could be a multimillionaire. So when we're able to get rid of that kind of thing, we can get rid of it in policing. But I think we do it in policing because we have a system that follows up."

Using juveniles as an example, they may be introduced into the criminal justice system by the police department, but when one looks to racial profiling and the inequities in the whole system, it usually gets worse the further down they go. Without the nation sitting down and saying "Okay, what are the real issues?" we are left with the reality that race does matter.

> *The discussion of race would be most appropriate in "a forum that is led by the president, the administration, the governors, and the appointed and elected leaders of our country. It should be everybody's responsibility."*

Troubling for many leaders is the attempt to sidestep the discussion about race and shift the blame for race-related problems to someone else. Chief Hurtt recalls watching Secretary of State Col. Colin Powell in a TV interview at a time when he was a potential candidate for president. He said if he were elected, he would be judged on how well he handled the minority crime issue. Chief Hurtt found this comment appalling, wondering: "Isn't that something that Nixon and Ford and Carter and all the previous presidents should have been judged on too? Why was that an issue for him because he was African American?"

Anyone who talks with Chief Hurtt immediately recognizes that he is a leader who is not afraid to do the right thing and make tough decisions for his organization. He recognizes the subject of race is sensitive for government as a whole, but this does not seem to extinguish his hope that our leaders will take the initiative to sit down and talk. Having these discussions about race without offending the public in the process is a dicey challenge and not one readily tackled by many in public office. Chief Hurtt suggests that one way to overcome this kind of hesitation is to "elect leaders with courage. Elect leaders that say, 'While I'm in office, I want to do the right thing' versus 'while I'm in office, I want to run to get elected.'" Not only is this ambition one that Police Chief Hurtt wishes leaders would incorporate into their political platforms, but it is also a personal philosophy that he lives and works by every day.

> *"One thing that we suffer from greatly in this country is the courage to deal with the real issues. We will build the courage for war. Just give us an enemy. But the war is right here. We talk about the war on crime, the war on drugs. The war is not with Columbia or Mexico. The war is with the social toxicity that exists in our cities and in our communities. The things that we have let fall by the wayside. That's where our war is. We just don't have the leaders in place with the courage to say, 'Hey,*

*we've got to have this discussion; we've got to have this talk. If we don't
do anything about it, let's just talk about it.'"*

The consensus as to whether the nation is better or worse off now than it was in the midst of the civil rights movement of the 1960s varies depending on whom you ask. Not surprisingly, these opinions are usually segregated along racial lines. Chief Hurtt offers an interesting insight to this debate and suggests that the process goes in cycles. At times in history when the economy looked up and people felt better, there appeared to be measurable progress. In times of economic downturn such as during the early 1970s oil embargo and the upsurge in gasoline prices, however, things went right back to where they were. The progress of these movements in the 1960s and 1970s can be compared with a pendulum swing. Historically, said Hurtt, "When there's not much food on the table, table manners change."

Affirmative Action

Despite efforts to abolish affirmative action programs in hiring and education, these programs continue to flourish in both the public and private sectors. Usually, the debate is divided. Many suggest affirmative action is a necessary form of retribution for the persecution and oppression of a particular race or gender in past generations. Others argue that all races and genders should be treated equally and that an individual should be allowed to compete for a job or an education without special considerations or quotas that may permit a less qualified candidate to prevail.

In the context of affirmative action, it is often considered ironic that minorities usually represent the side seeking special treatment, while the largely Caucasian populous seeks equality across the board. Interestingly, these views are quite opposite of the overall position of these two sides on other issues related to race.

One view suggests that minorities want race to be a factor when it is beneficial to them, yet they want to be treated equally in the context of racial profiling. This argument is further complicated by the opposing position, which suggest that the outcome of affirmative action persecutes those that may not fall into a special category of race or gender and in turn results in the very evils that the program is designed to redress.

Police Chief Hurtt is quick to defend the affirmative action programs in place around the nation.

*"Affirmative action is needed because there is one thing in America that
we do. We obey the law. We are a lawful society in most cases. If the law
is there, we will obey it."*

When there is the opportunity to avoid doing what's socially responsible, some will take advantage of it. Often, the decision to hire, promote, or educate a minority takes a back seat to other considerations. "In most cases, we won't do it," said Hurtt, "because we don't possess what I call that unselfish giving and sharing. There are a lot of good things that happen in this country, but there's an awful lot that needs to be done."

Hurtt sees some areas as particularly susceptible to abuse: equality in education, equality in opportunity for business development, and the ability for one to attain the skills and advantages needed to become an entrepreneur. Without affirmative action to enhance a minority's chance to succeed, the person, said Hurtt is "trying to catch an airplane going down the runway when you're on foot. Unless you've got an airplane too, your chances are not as good."

Racial Profiling versus Criminal Profiling

When asked whether his department engages in any type of profiling for major crimes, Chief Hurtt was quick to distinguish between racial profiling, which is prohibited by department policy, and criminal profiling, which can be a helpful tool used to identify and apprehend specific suspects. Guided by department definitions of racial profiling and criminal profiling, the chief looks to his supervisors and management to ensure that officers' activities fall within policy guidelines.

In some circumstances, the line between the two forms of profiling is clear, but that's not always the case. Most crimes are not race specific; perpetrators of any race can commit rape, murder, or robbery. To direct officers to look out for Hispanics because they are more prone to commit rape or to target African American youths driving expensive cars because they are more prone to theft equates to racial profiling. In these cases, race is being used as a predominant consideration rather than an element—one of many—in the investigation of a crime.

In other scenarios, profiling practices may be somewhat less distinguishable, particularly when the crime is very specific and involves the activities of a particular group, for example, Jamaicans who are trafficking narcotics from Jamaica to the United States or criminal gang activity within a specific Hispanic gang. Although racial profiling may be suspected, those in law enforcement point to the need to criminally profile in some instances where race may be *one* factor used to identify a specific perpetrator as opposed to the *only* factor used in a general sense to fight crime.

Like many large cities around the United States, Phoenix has experienced its share of gang problems. The increasing public pressure to eradicate this highly visible problem, coupled with the fact that gangs are typically segregated along racial lines, makes this challenge one of particular interest to many civil rights advocates. Often, agencies are more receptive to a solution that will result in a "quick fix." Tactics such as racial profiling may be tempting. It is important, however, that these agencies reconsider this approach and develop creative, innovative solutions that address the problem at the front end as opposed to taking the "easy route" that may only perpetuate the erroneous perception that racial profiling is rampant within law enforcement.

As a substitute for racial profiling, the Phoenix Police Department has worked closely with the statewide Gang Task Force to identify gang membership through other criteria and to stiffen the penalties so that gang activities in Arizona will be very unattractive to would-be gang members. Their program is designed to act as a deterrent regardless of race and looks to prevent gang affiliation rather than take a "wait and see" approach to address the problem after it becomes rampant.

Under this program, the state has set up five criteria for gang membership. The suspect is prosecuted as a gang member when two of the five criteria are met. For example, if the person is an admitted gang member or has been apprehended in a gang operation, he or she would be deemed a gang member and prosecuted accordingly. Once gang members and gang leadership are identified, they are investigated as members of criminal syndicates, which carries the potential of a seven to fifteen year sentence as opposed to the normal three to five years. If the members can be prosecuted federally for gun violations, they are sent out of the state. With this effective system of in place, Phoenix has seen a tremendous decrease in its gang problems, without having had to resort to racial profiling.

Chief Hurtt is not afraid to admit that racial profiling is a real problem in law enforcement. In his own department, he works closely with the community to develop proactive approaches to the problem to avoid having to rely on more reactive measures such as data collection that many groups are pressuring organizations to incorporate as a mandatory safeguard.

> *"I think where we missed the boat is the willingness of people to admit there's racial profiling. Not the collection of data. We're doing some things wrong, and we should be ashamed of ourselves. We need to correct it, and we need to hold people accountable so that they're serving all citizens and not just some."*

There should be no mystery about why minorities distrust the police. The suspicion and anger directed toward the police during the civil rights movement has not, in many cases, diminished with time and has carried over into new generations. Looking back at history, it would be hard to convince many that the police can now be trusted. During the civil rights movement in the 1960s, for example, who stopped the marches? The police. Who represented the majority? The police. These vivid memories are difficult to overcome when coupled with media reports and videos of police officers beating African American citizens or detaining and questioning young men of Middle Eastern descent.

Although we as a society must live with these events, Chief Hurtt sees great promise in giving the police the credit they more often deserve. He points to examples in his own organization of police going into the schools and neighborhoods and partnering with social agencies to educate the public and improve the image of law enforcement within the community. By emphasizing the hiring of more women and minorities, he hopes his officers and his organization will continue to reflect the department's commitment to excellence and diversity.

While acknowledging that there are some agencies under consent decrees for not hiring and promoting minorities, he points to many that are promoting them and cites an increase in the number of minority leaders in law enforcement. "I just came back from a Major Cities Police Chief's meeting," he explained, "and as you look around, there's about 54 major city chiefs represented in the U.S. Out of that, you're looking at 12–15 African Americans and Hispanics that are sitting at the top of very large organizations in some of the largest cities in this country, and if we're allowed to sit there long enough, I think there will be some changes made."

Though many of the perceptions about race and law enforcement come from external sources, Chief Hurtt points to the internal challenges and focuses on the importance of balancing the two. Many officers will complain about the chiefs and the management claiming a lack of support; however, he said, "One of the things that we as CEOs must have is the courage to tell the officers: 'We care about you. We know you do a dangerous job, but our first responsibility is to the citizens we serve.'" Once that gets through to the officers and management, the organization can evolve to prove to the public that there is a concern for not only the downtown areas and the gated communities but also for all of the citizens.

Leadership, upper management, and supervisors must have mutual goals and a shared focus to achieve this goal; all have a role to play. For his part, Chief Hurtt is fully committed to leading the charge actively. In keeping with his philosophy of attacking problems before they occur, the chief gets regular briefings from the assistant chief that are related to ongoing investigations. He looks to specifics such as who is involved, what precinct, and what detail as a sort of early warning system to identify potential problems with supervision, leadership, and the work unit. The department is also initiating another type of early warning process, called a performance assessment system, in order to identify and track officers with numerous complaints, attendance issues, questionable work habits, and irregular use of sick leave and commendations. With such a system in place, a better assessment of individuals can be made and appropriate intervention can be initiated early on to avoid more serious discipline problems in the future.

Data Collection

"We don't have to look at any data. We have to look at our past. There is nothing that data can tell us that we all can't figure out by reaching inside of our souls, looking at our experiences, and listening to the stories that are told about organizations."

Data collection, touted by many as the first step in combating racial profiling, is criticized by others who see this process as a knee-jerk reaction that won't tell us anything we don't already know. Chief Hurtt acknowledges that he has been under some pressure to start data collection in his department and reports that the most of the pressure comes from his peers and other major city police chiefs. These advocates suggest that such efforts look good to the community and show the public that there is nothing to hide.

The problem with data collection is not the data collection itself but rather in the efforts to determine what the data actually reveal. In questioning the supporters of data collection programs about what the numbers mean, the chief often meets with the response, "Well, we haven't really figured that out yet." Without departments engaging in a standardized method of data collection, the public lacks any sort of uniform system to figure out what any of these data really say about a department's treatment of a certain minority group.

Chief Hurtt cautions us to be very careful with data collection and cites as one of the main problems the anonymity of the officers reporting the statistics: "I applaud those organizations that want to do something to enhance their relationship with the minority community, but it's important to do the right thing. If you want to do something, it's important to do it correctly. If you look at the officer who's going to do racial profiling, is he going to be the one who fills out the form and says, 'Hey, I pulled over this African American here this weekend, and I treated him wrong, and I violated his rights, and I searched him, and here is his name and phone number. Would you call him so you can fire me?' That's how much sense that makes."

Another problem is the limited scope of time covered by the data collection statistics. Most departments embark on three-month collection programs rather than looking at the history of the organization over a prolonged period. The data obtained from these limited three-month collection programs may or may not be representative of the overall problem within an organization. Once reported by the media, however, these statistics become the numbers the agency has to live by in its efforts to determine whether racial profiling is a problem.

He prefers to develop a method that would look to the paths, patterns, and practices in a particular organization by going back to evaluate, for example, five years of data, and focusing on criteria such as who has been arrested, who has received citations, and who had search warrants served on them. "Look at that past data," he suggested. "Look at the officers and the supervisors that were involved and who was arrested, and that will be a better indicator than saying 'Okay, now we are trying to catch guys who are doing racial profiling, and the only way we are going to be able to catch them is by having them fill out this form and telling us that's what they're doing.'"

The data collection procedures imposed by many departments result in nothing more than "garbage in, garbage out." There is no way to know whether the officers are filling out the data collection forms, turning them in, or even collecting the data for that matter. In most cases, the information won't come to light unless a citizen files a complaint or tells someone about it.

Although not entirely opposed to the idea of data collection, Chief Hurtt cautions that in order to do it properly, a department needs to take an all-or-nothing approach. The one group that will stand in the way of such an approach will be the police unions that, to date, have been only supportive of anonymous data collection, which has proved ineffective in most cases. Even if an open reporting system could be implemented, other statistical considerations would need to be evaluated. These could substantially affect the accuracy of the outcome. For example, if an officer were assigned to a beat that was 80% to 90% Hispanic and African American and a look back on the officer's statistics for a specified time frame identified that 80% to 90% of the officer's stops were minorities, would the officer be engaging in racial profiling or just stopping the people that he or she sees on a regular basis? Often, the present reporting systems do not sufficiently narrow the parameters to reveal the activities of certain officers or specific beats. Instead, these systems analyze them in the context of the entire department.

There is no doubt that we have these issues in our society. The question is, How do we address them in a more proactive manner rather than go out, try to collect data, and not know how or why we're going to collect it? What is the benchmark?

Likening data collection to the "welfare to work" program, Chief Hurtt anticipates that it will ultimately not be successful in solving the much bigger problem, the social toxicity that is prevalent in our society. For example, when looking at the "welfare to work" program, you're dealing with a group of people who have never been socialized into a work atmosphere. You tell them that they have two years to be on welfare, and then they need to go out and get a job. In most cases, these people have never been in a real integrated environment for an 8 to 10 hour period of time, so how do they socialize? They may have the job skills, but they lack the social skills. One just needs to look at the tremendous number of people that are fired for poor job performance. Often, they aren't fired for not knowing how to drive the truck or to lift the package or fly the plane. They are fired for their inability to become part of the team in an environment that is foreign to them. "We can give people all the technical skills and all the work know-how," Hurtt explained, "but if we don't give them the social skills to integrate into those new arenas, they're going to fail." The result is a group of people who are off welfare, had a new job, and failed. Now where do they go? Usually the answer is into the criminal justice system. "And we're so proud of ourselves because of the welfare to work program," Hurtt said. We look to programs such as this to fix the ills in society. And now, one more time, we find ourselves looking to a program such as data collection to fix the ills in society. "'Let's do data collection, and we won't have crime or violence or people on welfare, and we won't mistrust and hate each other.' And we give it to the most visible part of the government to do that. And that's the police."

Chief Hurtt proposes the better approach of looking at the organization as a whole. If the Justice Department wants to do something, have them help to establish early warning systems within the departments. Help departments train officers, supervisors, and administrators in various intervention programs. Provide more funds to assist in the recruiting, testing, screening, and selection processes and to expand ongoing psychological training. Chief Hurt believes that these measures will help law enforcement become more professional and efficient at the front end of the system and avoid having to pick up the pieces on the back end.

Officer Accountability and Discipline

Even with aggressive early warning systems in place, it is almost inevitable that some officers in larger organizations will fall through the cracks unnoticed by those in upper management. Chief Hurtt acknowledges that some of these rogue officers may be able to float for a while in his organization but does not believe it would be too easy for them to do so for the long term because of the tremendous degree of accountability demanded of the officers and supervisors in his department.

> *"I tell the officers, 'Don't be accountable to me; be accountable to each other. Be accountable to the community. Because those are the people you have to look in the face every day.'"*

Chief Hurtt points to the many avenues available for information to come to his office. He and his assistant chiefs are always available to the community, and there remains a concerted effort by the organization to develop and maintain those critical relationships. He insists that if he does not find out about a problem internally, he finds out about it externally. Chief Hurtt credits his open-door policy as one of the reasons data collection would not be advantageous within his department. Although it may appease the public, the same things are happening in the organization with or without data collection. "You've either got the data or you can go down through the organization and ask people."

Generally, most information is discovered through internal sources, frequently from the officers themselves. He cites two recent examples of officers who were commended for coming forward. In one instance, he recalls an officer who was involved in a shooting who came forward to say, "We were involved in a shooting, and we were wrong." In another instance involving a canine unit that acted outside of policy, officers came to him on their own initiative to say, "Hey, it wasn't right." All of the officers involved were given commendations to reinforce the importance of accountability and taking responsibility for their own actions. The community does not see these things. These officers came forward on their own. The complaint did not come from a citizen or a supervisor; it came from another officer who was there.

Instances such as this are probably not the norm in many agencies, as the majority is still run similar to the military, particularly in the larger cities. Though some have relaxed the heavy discipline policies over the years in order to run their department similar to a corporate entity with a "feel good" approach, many cite this new lax environment as one reason for the problems within many law enforcement organizations. Regardless of how these organizations choose to handle personnel and discipline issues, one thing remains constant: sworn officers continue to have special rights in discipline proceedings that are not available to an employee working in private industry.

"When we have to severely discipline someone, it never fails that someone in the organization will come up and say, 'It's about time. That guy's been screwing up for years. He was a bad recruit in the academy, he was bad in training, he was bad as a detective, he was a bad motor officer. It's about time.'"

In any organization, it usually comes as no surprise to others when an officer is disciplined or terminated. In Phoenix, management goes one step further by promoting a policy and atmosphere that encourages and rewards officers for coming forward to report potential problems before they turn into actual ones. Under this policy, it is often the information brought to upper management by others in the organization that leads to the identification and discipline of officers who may be engaging in questionable practices on the street.

If there is one thing that is certain, officers in Phoenix know the expectations of their chief. When an officer deviates from these expectations, he or she is subjected to a thorough investigation by one or more agencies acting independently to safeguard the rights of both the offending officer and the community. "They know if they lie, they are more likely to get fired than if they have a bad shooting," Hurtt said.

At the start of the internal investigation process, management is guided by a set of procedures designed to investigate allegations of officer misconduct fairly, as well as to demand truthfulness and accountability. Under this system, officers are not just hit cold with questions when they are brought into internal investigations for questioning about an incident. "We tell them, 'Here are the allegations against you, and we're going to ask you questions about these allegations,'" said Hurtt. "'One of the things that we're going to insist on is that you are truthful in your responses. If you are not truthful, you can get some severe discipline up to the point of termination. Now, go get yourself a drink of water, go use the restroom, call your union rep, your wife, your family, your mother, your father, your priest, whoever you need to talk to, and you have 10 to 15 minutes, and then its all business.'"

Chief Hurtt said this system gives the officer a chance to think about the allegations and the ramifications of lying before the questioning begins. It also diminishes the chance of an officer later coming forward and admitting to lying during the investigation because he or she was "hit cold." "When officers lie," Hurtt explained, "they may come back one hour later, two hours later, or they may never come back, and they get in very serious trouble."

The success of Phoenix's internal investigation process is not merely theoretical. Unlike many police departments that substantiate less than 10% of the complaints against officers, Phoenix's statistics send officers a clear message: if they engage in questionable conduct, there is a high likelihood of being caught. In 1998, for example, the city initiated 512 internal investigations against officers. Of the 512 investigations, 40% were initiated by supervisors. Sixty-six percent of those resulted in discipline. Among the citizen complaints, 23% were sustained, and 51% were unfounded. The top areas for discipline were failure to prepare reports properly, brut conduct toward citizens, and the improper use of computer systems.

When a citizen has a complaint against an officer, often a civil rights group will file the complaint on the citizen's behalf to alleviate concerns of intimidation or retaliation by other officers. An undercover investigation by a major news program found that "Citizens who were sent to file complaints against some major city police departments found this task difficult, if not impossible, because of the deterring and intimidating nature of the process." Similar studies have brought many civil rights organizations forward, demanding citizen review boards to oversee the complaint and internal investigation process within a city's police agency.

> *"I don't think [civilian review boards] are very effective, and I think it's a waste of time to build in a procedure on the back side of the system such as review. I tell people all the time, 'If you want me to spend some additional money, help me spend that money in my selection, recruitment, and training of individuals.'"*

Chief Hurtt does not believe that the existence of these internal review boards will be an effective tool to fight internal corruption. He points to the majority of high-profile corruption cases coming from cities with more civilian oversight than Phoenix. He prefers to focus on the front end of the process itself. In Phoenix, citizens can pick up a complaint form at any city office or walk in and make a verbal complaint at any police facility. Once the department becomes aware of the complaint, the citizen is kept in the loop about the time frame for investigating the allegation through to the final outcome. If the citizen receives a decision that he or she believes is unsatisfactory, the citizen may go the city council or the mayor or choose to pursue the matter through proper legal channels.

Regardless of the procedures in place, Chief Hurtt is a believer that intervention by management early on is the key to avoiding major problems down the road. With this goal in mind, the Phoenix Police Department aggressively incorporates its philosophies about discipline, forthrightness, and truthfulness into the overall culture and values of the organization. There is no question about what is acceptable and what is not, as department policy clearly establishes directives relating to racial profiling and the use of force, just to name two. Officers are given every opportunity to come forward when there is an alleged violation of the policy, and they know that if they don't tell the truth, they are in the same spot as the officer who is violating the policy and may even be subject to termination.

Getting to the truth of the matter is a high priority for the chief, even if it means subjecting the offender to a polygraph examination. In some states, using a polygraph could be questionable in hiring or internal investigations. In Phoenix, however, Hurtt explained: "For hiring, you have to take a polygraph, and for internal affairs, it's not an option. If we feel you should take a polygraph, you're given a polygraph."

It has become apparent in many organizations that when leadership does not clearly lay out expectations or fails to follow through with discipline, the result is often an internal sort of corruption better known in the media as the "wall" or "code of silence" discussed at length in Chapter 5. The code of silence can be a deadly game that prevents fellow officers from coming forth to report civil rights violations or criminal activities perpetrated by other officers. Those who do come forward and break this "code" may find that others will not come to their aid if they are in need of backup on the street.

When asked how peers react to the type of forthrightness exhibited by officers in the department, the chief reported that there has been no backlash from officers coming forward because it's all part of the culture in his organization. "When people step up, we recognize them," he explained. "We recognize them by saying this is acceptable behavior that we look for in our employees, and we try to reward them as far as training opportunities and assignments. We do this because these are the people we want leading the organization in the future. If you don't build that into an organization, it just won't happen."

"We know what our problems are and what our issues are. It's having the courage to do not what will make you successful but to do what is correct and what is right."

Chief Hurtt insists that although some may view his internal investigative tactics as coercive or intimidating, the approach is essential given the important job the police do to protect civil rights and ensure the safety of the community. The motto in his department is: "We have to do things right the first time. We just don't have the ability or the privilege of trampling on civil rights and the rights of search and seizure and the use of force because our actions can really have a significant impact on the lives of others and the quality of life in the community." He points to communities in which police departments are suffering because of all the corruption. These kinds of activities attract media attention and have a significant impact on all facets of life in that community, including the success of local business and its citizens' lack of confidence in their police force.

Though this type of negative publicity often casts a shadow of suspicion over the entire profession, Chief Hurtt works hard to get his message out and to instill in his officers a philosophy that goes to the essence of the job. He said: "We don't look at police work as if, 'It's our job to catch criminals, that's it.' We look at what we do as adding value to the quality of life for the citizens and those that come to work and play in the city of Phoenix."

The chief has been instrumental in seeing that his philosophy is a reality within his organization. It is important to note, however, that Phoenix is not the only Arizona city that takes the integrity of the state's law enforcement officers very seriously. Statewide, all officers are under the watchful eye of Arizona Peace Officer Standards and Training (Az POST), an organization that provides services to 170 law enforcement agencies and 16 academies and has certified more than 13,200 sworn peace officers and 9,000 correctional service officers statewide. The Az POST Board is comprised of individuals from all professions and represents both rural and large metropolitan areas in Arizona. Although its members are appointed by the governor, the organization is somewhat free from the local political pressures that sometimes inhibit similar oversight entities. Unlike many national POST organizations that have the power to certify officers working within a given state, Az POST is unique in that it also has the power to decertify officers who serve within Arizona.

As an Az POST board member, Chief Hurtt has been instrumental in ensuring that his high standards are carried through to other organizations around the state. One of the main concentrations of Az POST's efforts is to instill in the officers the importance of truthfulness in internal investigations, as well as in their day-to-day conduct while serving Arizona citizens. In addition to its work as an oversight organization, Az POST is responsible for investigating and disciplining officers who have been accused of improper conduct. The process of disciplining an officer through Az POST usually begins within an individual agency, when an officer is involved in misconduct that warrants an internal investigation. In Phoenix, the internal investigation process is extensive, designed to give the officer involved every chance to get a fair hearing.

Upon completion of the formal internal investigation process, the officer is sent to a disciplinary review board. The Disciplinary Review Board is made up of the assistant chief, some commanders, three citizens from the community, a peer rep, and representatives from training and legal that sit in to identify any changes that need to be made from either a legal or educational perspective. Once the board reviews the results of the internal investigation, it makes a recommendation to the chief. For example, the Board may recommend up to 240 hours of suspension, a demotion, dismissal, or a written reprimand. The matter may also be sent back through the chain for lesser discipline. Once the chief reviews and agrees with the Board's recommendation, the officer can either accept the discipline or appeal to the city of Phoenix Civil Service Board. The Civil Service Board will either agree with the decision made by the chief or suggest a lesser punishment, for example, a 240-hour suspension rather than a dismissal. At any time during this process, Az POST may elect to step in if the conduct in question is in violation of one or more of the Az POST rules.

Interestingly, Az POST may not always find out about questionable conduct through official channels and may even choose to initiate an investigation on the basis of information it obtains from a media report. The Az POST hearing process is not directly linked to the outcome of the department's own internal investigation or the appeal process of the Civil Service Board; thus, its involvement is an independent safeguard to ensure that investigations are conducted fairly and that the outcome is proper. The hearing officer, usually from the Attorney General's office, will ultimately make a recommendation to POST as to the type of discipline warranted. The Az POST Board, comprised largely of civilians, will consider the recommendation from the Attorney General's office and determine whether an officer's certification should be revoked or suspended or whether no action should be taken at all. Once an officer's certification is revoked, it can never be reinstated.

This three-prong check-and-balance system has been a successful deterrent in

Arizona and has left no doubt within the state's law enforcement community that if you lie, or if you do something that disrupts an organization or brings distrust to the profession, your certification will more than likely be taken away.

Marketing the Police

Despite many challenges the profession faces, law enforcement is putting a high priority on reshaping its image. At the forefront of these efforts is the concept of marketing the police—a newer idea that many larger agencies are experimenting with as a means to restore public trust in the profession. In Phoenix and other major cities, agencies are embarking on risky and sometimes aggressive public relations campaigns to unveil the mystery that has historically shrouded the law enforcement profession.

One of the primary objectives of these programs is to reach out to the community and inform its members about the availability of police-sponsored opportunities and programs. In the aftermath of a police-related shooting, the community turned to the Phoenix Police Department to find out what programs were available for young people. It was a surprise to many that the police were involved in a significant number of youth-oriented programs throughout the community. It became immediately apparent that without an aggressive marketing program in place, the community would remain in the dark about the wide range of community involvement and education programs offered by the department.

The marketing efforts in Phoenix are largely focused on implementing and publicizing programs designed to educate a vast segment of the population, often beginning in grade school and continuing through high school and adulthood. These programs are particularly important in Hispanic communities where the fear of the police often hinders resolution of the large number of homicide investigations in the city. The department finds it very difficult to solve many of these cases because many of the suspects and witnesses are non-English speaking and do not trust the police. These barriers can be attributed to the relationships and experiences these people have had with the police in their native lands. When they come to the United States, they often come with preconceived ideas about the police that are difficult to penetrate.

As part of its aggressive approach to cross over these barriers, Phoenix has hired a firm to do image building for the police department among the non-English speaking communities. Chief Hurtt is eager to get the message out to these groups and tell them, he said, "who we are and what we do, the fact that we will listen and will let you participate, and you just need to come forward."

> *"We could very easily sit back and say, 'You come to me; come down, and we'll talk.' We go to the community."*

And that he does. As much as time permits, he makes it a point to go out to different communities and just walk the blocks to talk to people. "No one has been offended by that; they have been very grateful," he said. "I learn a lot about the relationships that exist between the officers and the citizens in the community, and it serves as a wealth of information for me."

Though marketing to the community may seem like a major challenge, the department is often called to answer to an even tougher audience, that of many civil rights organizations. Chief Hurtt has found that the best way to do that is to keep an open line with everybody. The Phoenix Community Relations Bureau has offices that regularly communicate with the NAACP; the ACLU; and activists in the Hispanic community, Asian community, gay and lesbian community, and the elderly community, just to name a few. The bureau has people working closely with these groups on a daily basis and making contacts and building relationships and goodwill. "They know they can come in and say, 'We want to look at your files, we want to look at your budget, we want to have a meeting, we want to talk.'" Chief Hurtt's well-publicized open-door policy also ensures that when a citizen calls, whether there's a complaint or a commendation, someone from the department will get back to that person the same day.

Chief Hurtt laughingly recalls a recent meeting he had with all the advisory groups' leadership to talk about issues in the organization and to identify ways for these groups to expand their roles. "You know the thing that they want to do?" he said, laughing. "They wanted to be invited to our banquet!" He goes on to explain that these groups are not just interested in the community and in knowing that they are working with the police department, but they also want the officers to know as well.

In addition to establishing positive relationships between police organizations and the community, departments such as Phoenix must continually work to maintain a good partnership with the U.S. Justice Department in order to combat crime effectively.

> "We, as police, are in the ideal position to be the vanguards of civil rights, so we shouldn't be afraid of the justice department because what they are trying to do is respond to the civil rights issues. That puts us in a perfect position."

Though the Justice Department generally maintains good relationships with law enforcement, there is universally some concern that it may be hitting everyone with the same size hammer. Rather than taking an aggressive posture toward law enforcement, the general consensus is that the Justice Department should come in and offer assistance in the form of financing for early warning systems, training for both police personnel and community members, and coalition building, and it should also bring in facilitators rather than lawyers to have these discussions about race. Chief Hurtt is a firm believer that the government needs to initiate different levels of responses for organizations that may be having internal problems. At present, the government's approach is the consent decree, which often costs the targeted agency millions of dollars over a number of years and often does nothing to enhance the relationship between the police and the community.

Perhaps the first step toward enhancing these relationships is for the police to take accountability for the shortfalls within their own organizations. From a broader perspective, Chief Hurtt looks to the federal government to address the racial tensions that are present within both public and private sectors. As long as these underlying racial tensions go unchallenged, progress for minorities will be difficult to achieve.

Despite the underlying problems, progress for minorities has become more measurable. In the past five or ten years, for example, minorities and women have become a rising and powerful force in every facet of government. The small ratio of minorities in these positions, however, makes measurable change more of a long-term goal than a quick fix for the racial tensions and bias that exist nationwide. "I think the majority goes in with good intentions," Hurtt said, "but I think you're swimming upstream—and there's a lot of other big fish in that stream." Regardless of these good intentions, inevitably, initiatives that benefit minority communities do not receive the political backing or publicity that is typically enjoyed by initiatives benefiting the majority. Absent support from the major political financial backers, change will continue to move at a snail's pace.

Chief Hurtt reiterates that any measurable change will be impossible without looking at the past and discussing race. Until this occurs, the country will not be able to move forward to resolve these issues. He recalls the words of a speaker at a conference who pointed to "one thing that keeps us from getting where we want to be in this country. In some of our communities, especially in our minority communities, we are afraid of the police. We have a great fear of them. And the police are afraid of us; they have a great fear of us." Until we as a nation have the courage to engage in these important discussions about race and identify the real problems that are corroding our society, we will continue to grasp at issues on the surface such as racial profiling. When efforts such as data collection do not solve the problem, ultimately a deeper wedge will be driven between minorities and the police.

CHAPTER TEN

———•◦•———

Scales of Justice

"No right is held more sacred, or is more carefully guarded by the common law, than the right of every individual to the possession and control of his own person, free from all restraint or interference of others, unless by clear and unquestionable authority of law."

—*Union Pac. R. Co. v. Botsford*[1]

Much of today's modern law is based largely on the English legal system. Although we will not go into considerable detail in this regard, it is important to acquire a general understanding of how our laws are established in order to appreciate the evolution and significance of the cases relating to pretext stops and racial profiling.

Our current legal system originally evolved from colonial courts and served as the basis for what we modernly refer to as *common law*. Common law is best defined as a body of rules setting the social standards society must follow. These rules have emerged over time through judges' decisions in actual legal controversies and have formed the basis for many of our current local, state, and federal statutes.

Under this system, judges are routinely asked to interpret established law as it relates to a new set of facts or circumstances in a criminal or civil case. Though judges are usually compelled to follow previous case decisions from the same or higher jurisdictions that involve the same question of law, they may choose not to follow these precedents in cases where the facts are distinguishable, and thereby they establish new law. As you will see in the cases presented in this chapter, judges may depart from precedents if they believe these precedents should no longer be followed. For example, a judge may overturn all or part of a finding in a previous case if it is outdated or if the judge believes it no longer represents good law. Judges may also look to precedents and either expound on prior case law or present a different point of view when the facts vary from those in the original case. Often a case may be brought before a judge for which there is no legal precedent, whereupon the judge will decide what new rules should be applied given a particular set of facts and circumstances.

Although case law plays a significant role in framing our legal system, a police officer's ability to stop, detain, and investigate is primarily regulated by the Fourth Amendment of the U.S. Constitution.[2] The Fourth Amendment ensures the right of people to "be secure in their persons, houses, papers, and effects, against unreasonable searches and seizures," and it establishes a system based on probable cause for the issuance of warrants. Moreover, in *Schmerber v. California*, for example, the court has interpreted the Fourth Amendment's function as "to constrain, not against all intrusions as such, but against intrusions which are not justified in the circumstances, or which are made in an improper manner."[3] It is these exceptions that the court has carved out of the Fourth Amendment that some argue grant unchecked power to law enforcement officials.

In the context of racial profiling, the court may also look to violations of the Equal Protection Clause of the Fourteenth Amendment[4] and the Fifth Amendment's Due Process Clause which prohibit the government from making classifications based on race, sex, alienage, illegitimacy, wealth, or any other characteristic and guarantee that all people similarly situated are treated the same. In order for any race-based classification to be upheld, the court must determine whether the classification was necessary to promote a compelling governmental interest. It must also involve a fundamental right of the individual, for example, the right to travel.

Although the guarantees for all citizens under the Constitution remain constant, racial profiling is one subject on which case law and legal interpretations are constantly changing. More specifically, judges are frequently asked to hear a set of facts in order to decide what constitutes probable cause for a stop and what, if any, factor race plays in this equation.

One of the most recent controversies requiring judicial review and interpretation sought to answer the question of whether running from the police constitutes enough reasonable suspicion or probable cause to detain a suspect. Judges have also been asked to hear cases dealing with consent to search and the scope of consent in order to determine whether evidence has been legally obtained and can be used against the defendant in a criminal proceeding.

The following cases represent some of the major legal precedents in the areas of pretext stops and searches. Though many do not specifically deal with racial profiling, they have paved the way for current law in the areas of police discretion and probable cause for traffic stops. It should be noted that the law presented is current as of press date; however, it is subject to change depending on the composition of the courts and the mood of the nation when new cases are heard. There is no doubt that cases will begin to surface as a direct result of both the 2001 terrorist attacks and in light of future terrorist threats that will establish new laws in the areas of terrorism and the governments' ability to stop and detain potential suspects.

Legal Background

Terry v. Ohio[5] is one of the earliest cases addressing serious questions about the role of the Fourth Amendment as it relates to confrontations on the street between law enforcement officers and citizens. Perhaps this case is best known for recognizing officers' need to protect themselves and other potential victims of violence in situations in which the officers may lack sufficient probable cause for an arrest. More specifically, *Terry* addressed whether it was reasonable for the police to seize a person and subject him or her to a limited search for weapons in the absence of probable cause for an arrest. Limited searches conducted in the interest of officer safety are commonly known by police as "Terry searches."

Terry involved suspects who were stopped and frisked by a 39-year veteran police officer who had observed them pacing up and down the street and peering into the window of a store. Although the suspects' acts in and of themselves were not illegal, the officer, on the basis of his observations and experience, believed that the individuals were casing the store and possibly armed and dangerous. When the officer approached the suspects to investigate their behavior further, he grabbed defendant Terry and conducted a pat down of his clothing, wherein he found a pistol. The court ultimately held that the officer's act was justified and that a "stop-and-frisk" was constitutionally permissible despite the absence of probable cause for either a full-scale search or arrest.

Although ruled constitutionally permissible in the confines of *Terry*, the court did place certain limitations on "stop-and-frisk" police activity and required that to justify "the particular intrusion, the police officer must be able to point to specific and articulable facts which, taken together with rational inferences from those facts, reasonably warrant that intrusion."[6] The court went on to clarify the *Terry* limitations and cited *Beck v. State of Ohio*,[7] establishing that "good faith on the part of the arresting officer is not enough.... If subjective good faith alone were the test, the protections of the Fourth Amendment would evaporate, and the people would be 'secure in their persons, houses, papers and effects,' only in the discretion of the police."

Since *Terry*, there have been many cases that critics argue continue to chip away at the protections of the Fourth Amendment. The first of those cases, *Adams v. Williams*,[8] significantly broadened the Terry "stop-and-frisk" exception to the probable cause requirement by extending it to include suspicions that are *not* based on the officer's own observations and, further, by allowing the stop of a vehicle.

Nevertheless, the decisions in *Terry* and *Adams* seemed to leave unclear what degree of probability had to exist that criminal activity was occurring before a stop would be justified. Several Supreme Court cases followed that shed some light on the problem.

In *Brown v. Texas*,[9] the court determined that a person may only be stopped if the officers have a "reasonable suspicion, based on objective facts, that the individual is involved in criminal activity."

In *U.S. v. Sokolow*,[10] the court further broadened the decision in *Terry* by holding that a modest degree of suspicion would be enough for a Terry-like stop.

The guidelines set forth in these "stop and frisk" cases eventually carried over to cases involving *detentions* by officers and extended the requirement that the officers must have a "reasonable and articulable suspicion of criminal activity" for the *detention* to be valid under the Fourth Amendment.

Courts further broadened these standards to encompass automobile cases and held that a law enforcement officer who initially detained a motorist for a traffic violation could investigate matters not related to the traffic violation.[11] For example, the court found that in carrying out a routine traffic stop, a law enforcement officer may request a driver's license and vehicle registration, run a computer check, and issue a citation. Any further detention for questioning is considered beyond the scope of *Terry* and therefore illegal unless the officer has reasonable suspicion of a serious crime.[12] The court further expounded on the guidelines for an automobile detention and found a continued detention lawful even though an officer had a subjective intention not to issue the defendant a ticket. In *Ohio v. Robinette*,[13] the court cited several "specific and articulable facts," which, taken together with rational inferences drawn therefrom, were sufficient under the standard set forth in *Terry* to justify reasonable suspicion on the part of the officer that criminal activity was afoot: (1) the inability for the driver to produce a valid driver's license; (2) the driver's lack of any identification whatsoever; (3) the large quantity of cash the driver and the passenger were carrying; (4) the fact that the truck had been rented to an unknown third party; (5) the fact that the driver and passenger maintained their complete ignorance regarding the contents of the truck's cargo hold; and (6) the driver's and passenger's claims that they did not have a key to unlock the cargo hold's door when in the officer's clear view was a key that appeared to fit the door's lock.

Similarly, the court found that an officer did not unreasonably detain a motorist in violation of the Fourth Amendment when he spotted what appeared to be a handgun on the floor of the vehicle as he was issuing a warning for a traffic violation. This "reasonable suspicion," coupled with the fact that the driver was a convicted felon who was prohibited from possessing a firearm, led the court to find the continued detention reasonable.[14]

In contrast to the above cases, some courts have been more willing to limit the scope of *Terry* stops. For example, in *Knowles v. Iowa*,[15] the court held that an officer was not authorized to conduct a full search of a vehicle stopped for speeding even though the officer had probable cause to make a custodial arrest under the Fourth Amendment but chose instead to issue the driver a citation. The scope of *Terry* was further clarified when the court held that reasonable suspicion is determined by the totality of the circumstances and must be more than an inchoate "hunch."[16]

A more recent landmark case, which some argue has been the most damaging to the rights of minorities in their fight against pretext traffic stops and racial profiling, is *Whren v. United States*.[17] While patrolling a high-drug area, plainclothes police officers in an unmarked vehicle observed a truck stopped at a stop sign for an unusually long period of time. The truck, driven by Mr. Brown, suddenly turned without signaling and sped off at an "unreasonable" rate of speed. The officers stopped the vehicle, presumably to warn the driver about traffic violations. Upon approaching the truck, however, the officers observed plastic bags of crack cocaine in Mr. Whren's hands. Both Brown and Whren were arrested. Petitioners moved to have the evidence against them suppressed, arguing that the plainclothes officers had neither reasonable suspicion nor probable cause to believe petitioners were engaged in illegal drug dealing activity. Moreover, the petitioners argued that the officers' traffic violation grounds for approaching the vehicle were pretextual.

Though *Whren* did not specifically rule on the constitutionality of pretext traffic stops, the U.S. Supreme Court affirmed the Court of Appeals' ruling that "regardless of whether a police officer subjectively believes that the occupants of an automobile may be engaging in some other illegal behavior, a traffic stop is permissible as long as a reasonable officer in the same circumstances could have stopped the car for the suspected traffic violation."[18]

The U.S. Supreme Court further held in *Whren* that the temporary detention of a motorist upon probable cause that he or she has violated a traffic law does not violate the Fourth Amendment's prohibition against unreasonable seizures, even if a reasonable officer would not have stopped the motorist absent some additional law enforcement objective.[19]

Although the *Whren* case essentially held that the constitutional reasonableness of a traffic stop does not depend on the actual motivations of the officers involved, it likewise represents a culmination of earlier key decisions that laid the framework for the treatment of pretext traffic stops. As discussed by the *Whren* court, these cases served as important precedents for the standards that currently guide the actions of law enforcement.

The first of these key decisions set forth in *United States v. Robinson* foreclosed the argument in *Whren* that "ulterior motives can invalidate police conduct justified on the basis of probable cause."[20] *Robinson* further led the *Whren* court to caution that "[s]ubjective intentions play no role in ordinary, probable-cause Fourth Amendment analysis."[21]

The *Whren* court was not willing to consider petitioners' argument that questioned whether the officers' conduct deviated materially from standard police practices and believed that "petitioners' proposed test [was] plainly designed to combat the perceived danger of pretextual stops."[22] The court further criticized petitioners' argument as being inconsistent with prior cases, such as *Robinson*, "which make it clear that the Fourth Amendment's concern with 'reasonableness' allows certain actions to be taken in certain circumstances, whatever the subjective intent."[23] Moreover, "police enforcement practices, even if they could be practicably assessed by a judge, vary from place to place and from time to time. We cannot accept that the search and seizure protections of the Fourth Amendment are so variable...."[24]

The *Robinson* court also set an important standard concerning pretext stops by police officers and provided substantial guidance for the *Whren* court as well as courts in later cases.[25] More specifically, the key holding in *Robinson*, that "a traffic-violation arrest...would not be rendered invalid by the fact that it was a mere pretext for a narcotics search[26]...and that a lawful post-arrest search of the person would not be rendered invalid by the fact that it was not motivated by the officer-safety concern that justifies such searches,"[27] was seen as a major victory for police agencies and further broadened the scope of their investigative tactics.[28]

The *Whren* court ultimately credited *Robinson* for establishing the theory that just because "the officer does not have the state of mind which is hypothecated by the reasons which provide the legal justification for the officer's action does not invalidate the action taken as long as the circumstances, viewed objectively, justify that action."[29]

Delaware v. Prouse, another important case relied on by the *Whren* court, represented another key victory for law enforcement officers. The *Whren* court acknowledged that although the "temporary detention of individuals during the stop of an automobile by the police, even if only for a brief period and for a limited purpose, constitutes a 'seizure' of 'persons' within the meaning of [the Fourth Amendment],"[30] the court, relying on *Prouse*, reasoned that "as a general matter, the decision to stop an automobile is reasonable where the police have probable cause to believe that a traffic violation has occurred."[31]

The *Whren* court emphasized that the foregoing cases "foreclose any argument that the constitutional reasonableness of traffic stops depends on the actual motivations of the individual officers involved." Although they agreed that "the Constitution prohibits selective enforcement of the law based on considerations such as race," they concluded that "the constitutional basis for objecting to intentionally discriminatory application of laws is the Equal Protection Clause, not the Fourth Amendment. Subjective intentions play no role in ordinary, probable-cause Fourth Amendment analysis."[32] Ultimately, the *Whren* court was not willing to entertain Fourth Amendment challenges based on the motivations of individual officers and expressed instead that "there is no realistic alternative to the traditional common-law rule that probable cause justifies a search and seizure."[33]

Last, in *Illinois v. Wardlow*,[34] the U.S. Supreme Court sided with judges in seven other states in a ruling that fleeing at the sight of an officer creates enough reasonable suspicion to warrant a stop.[35] Respondent Wardlow fled upon seeing a caravan of police vehicles converge on an area of Chicago known for heavy narcotics trafficking. When Officers Nolan and Harvey caught up with Wardlow on the street, Nolan stopped him and conducted a protective pat-down search for weapons because in his experience, there were usually weapons in the vicinity of narcotics transactions. Discovering a handgun, the officers arrested Wardlow. The Illinois trial court denied Wardlow's motion to suppress the evidence and found that the gun was recovered during a lawful "stop and frisk." Although the Illinois Appellate Court and the Illinois

Supreme Court reversed the trial court's decision, the U.S. Supreme Court upheld the lower court's decision and ultimately ruled that the officers' actions did not violate the Fourth Amendment.

The *Wardlow* case reaffirms the premise established under *Terry* that a brief encounter between a citizen and a police officer on a public street is reasonable when the officer can establish an articulable suspicion that criminal activity is afoot. In the facts set forth, it was Wardlow's unprovoked flight that aroused the officers' suspicion. Nervous, evasive behavior is another pertinent factor in determining reasonable suspicion,[36] and headlong flight is the consummate act of evasion. Officer Nolan was justified in suspecting that Wardlow was involved in criminal activity and was likewise justified in investigating further.

Surprisingly, such a holding was found to be consistent with the decision in *Florida v. Royer*,[37] which established that an individual, when approached, has the right to ignore police and go about his or her business. The *Wardlow* court distinguished unprovoked flight as the exact opposite of "going about one's business." While flight does not necessarily indicate ongoing criminal activity, *Terry* recognized that officers can detain individuals to resolve ambiguities in their conduct,[38] thus accepting the risk of officers stopping innocent people. Although courts have not specifically ruled on fleeing in an automobile, it appears the ruling in *Wardlow* would apply to this scenario as well.

In California, a divided Supreme Court further extended a police officer's ability to search a suspect's vehicle. In a split decision, justices ruled that police may search a vehicle without a warrant if the driver is not able to produce proper identification or proof of ownership. The justices permitted police officers to search "within a vehicle where such documentation reasonably may be expected to be found" but made it clear that the ruling does not "condone the equivalent of the full-scale search for contraband." *In Re Arturo D.*[39]

These legal precedents have established government regulations and directed law enforcement tactics for the past several decades. Moreover, the cases discussed above, particularly *Whren*, have granted an incredible amount of discretionary power to law enforcement, which some concede laid the foundation for the government's current tactics in its war on drugs and war on terrorism. Undoubtedly, in the years that follow the September 11, 2001, terrorist attacks on America, we will see new cases that will either expand or limit the discretion law enforcement officials have to fight crime. This ever-changing area further emphasizes the need for law enforcement to conduct regular legal updates so that officers on the street are better equipped to perform their jobs within the confines of the law.

Selective Enforcement

Though the Supreme Court undoubtedly recognizes the seriousness of forceful and intrusive contacts by the police, it has historically balanced this concern with the notion that too many restrictions on law enforcement impede justice. For the most part, the trend of the judiciary has been to expand the amount of discretion given to police officers to stop, interrogate, and detain a suspect. Although this expansion of a police officer's rights has broadened the scope of traffic stops that fall within the confines of the law, it has also left the court to decide whether the police selectively enforce certain laws.

In the context of racial profiling, selective enforcement comes into play when an officer stops a minority for a rarely enforced violation as a pretext to investigate whether a more serious crime is afoot. When the stop uncovers criminal activity, a defendant may choose to bring a selective enforcement claim against an officer and may allege that a law has been enforced against one person whereas the same law has not been enforced against others "who appear equally culpable and apprehensible."[40]

Perhaps the most common selective enforcement claim arises when a minority driver is stopped for a minor traffic violation that is either obscure or rarely enforced. The charge of the minor traffic violation will usually occur while the driver is under investigation for a major crime. On its face, it would appear that the only reason the officer chose to enforce the minor offense was to satisfy a renewed interest in the major offense. The result is that officers target the driver in a pretext stop, sometimes by special agents who don't even enforce traffic violations, in order to obtain information pertaining to the major offense.

When evaluating this type of claim, the court might look to what the department standard is for enforcing the type of violation, the circumstances and/or frequency with which the violation is charged, and how the police were attracted to the minor offense, particularly if the officers in question are members of a special task force designed to undertake specialized investigations unrelated to the offense. As many cases reveal, it is not uncommon for the police to become aware of a minor violation during a large-scale investigation in which the defendant is coincidentally a prime suspect.[41]

The first case to establish the law on selective enforcement was *Yick Wo v. Hopkins*,[42] in which petitioners challenged a local ordinance that granted licensing discretion to a board of supervisors. Basing their argument on equal protection grounds, petitioners alleged that 200 applications submitted by Chinese individuals for laundry licenses were denied, while all but one of 80 applications submitted by Caucasians were approved. Though the Supreme Court ruled that a certain amount of discretion in the administration of the law was acceptable, it reasoned that the exercise of discretion "directed so exclusively against a particular class of persons...administered...with an evil eye and unequal hand" is not constitutionally permissible.

Later selective enforcement cases held that a defendant must establish that the treatment inflicted upon him or her was purposeful and systematic. This showing may be made by "specifying instances in which the plaintiff was singled out for unlawful oppression in contrast to others similarly situated."[43] The defendant must further show that the discriminatory effect of the selective enforcement practice was motivated by the decision maker and that the decision maker intended the discriminatory result.

In other words, the defendant must show that the officer's decision to enforce the violation was a direct result of his or her prejudice toward a particular group.

Achieving a successful outcome in these types of claims can be difficult, particularly in the context of a traffic stop. Most defendants will find it difficult to establish requisite proof that a particular law is not usually enforced. Likewise, absent a confession by the officer as to his or her discriminatory motivation, even the most suspicious enforcement activity will be difficult to establish on the basis of circumstantial evidence alone.

Though the Supreme Court has never clarified whether a pretextual stop or arrest renders the search incident to a Fourth Amendment violation, the *Whren*[44] court indicated that the act of stopping a motorist for a traffic violation on the basis of pretextual reasons does not mean that any evidence garnered as a result of that stop was unlawfully obtained or inadmissible.[45]

Experts predict that the court will expand on and further clarify the issue of pretext traffic stops when deciding allegations of selective enforcement claims stemming from the September 11, 2001, terrorist attacks. Although there has not yet been much precedent set by case law, there is a growing debate about whether individuals of Middle Eastern descent were detained for INS violations in an effort to locate and interrogate potential terrorists in the weeks and months that followed the initial attacks. Many in the Middle Eastern community were offended by these detentions and claimed in effect that the government was holding these individuals for motives other than the immigration violations charged. As case law in this area continues to develop, it will be interesting to see whether the discretionary standards set forth in *Whren* will be limited or expanded under the new threat of terrorists living among us and what safeguards will be established to preserve the rights of citizens and noncitizens alike.

Selective Prosecution

"Just as police officers no longer simply make arrests, prosecutors should not simply try cases. Rather, they should become problem solvers who are looking to improve the quality of life for the communities they serve."

—Eric J. Holder, Jr.
Deputy Attorney General
U.S. Department of Justice[46]

Just as law enforcement may choose to enforce laws against citizens selectively, prosecutors may likewise opt to prosecute certain cases selectively. When this occurs, the inequitable treatment alleged takes place at the prosecution stage rather than at the enforcement stage.

When initiating a selective prosecution claim, the defendant may directly challenge a prosecutor's motive for bringing charges for a particular crime. In order to be successful, a defendant must prove that the offense charged is one that is rarely prosecuted and, therefore, the claim is being influenced by a discriminatory motive.

In *United States v. Berrios*,[47] the Second Circuit developed a formulation to establish a claim of selective prosecution and set forth certain requirements a defendant must meet to prove a prima facie case: (1) that, while others similarly situated have not generally been proceeded against because of the conduct of the type forming the basis of the charge against him or her, he or she has been singled out for prosecution, and (2) that the government's discriminatory selection of him or her for prosecution has been invidious or in bad faith. A defendant cannot merely allege that others have not been prosecuted for the same crime. In order to establish a federal constitutional violation, a defendant must meet both prongs of the *Berrios* test.

In a later case, *Wayte v. United States*,[48] the Supreme Court established additional guidelines for the defendant to prove a claim of selective prosecution and specifically showed that the government's decision to prosecute was "deliberately based upon an unjustifiable standard such as race, religion, or other arbitrary classification... including the exercise of protected statutory and constitutional rights."[49] Likewise, the *Wayte* court established that a defendant must show both a discriminatory effect and purpose behind the prosecutorial scheme.

When considering such factors, it is important to understand that prosecutors have broad discretion in determining whom to prosecute. Courts will generally presume that a prosecutor's discretion is exercised in good faith and in accordance with the laws and the Constitution. In order to overcome this presumption, a defendant must show that his or her prosecution is the result of "intentional and purposeful discrimination"[50] on behalf of the prosecutor.

Such a showing may be made by the defendant at an evidentiary hearing, during which the defendant must (a) set forth only "some facts tending to show that he has been selectively prosecuted and (b) raising a reasonable doubt about the propriety of the prosecution's purpose."[51] In cases where the prosecutor is able to present "countervailing reasons" to justify the prosecution, the district court may refuse to grant the defendant an evidentiary hearing, and the case will proceed accordingly. Typically, such cases of selective prosecution are difficult to prove, in that almost all crimes have been charged at one time or another, a fact that makes it difficult to prove that a prosecutor acted differently with respect to other defendants who were similarly situated. The limited success of such claims leaves the defendant to rely on other safeguards that have been established by the courts to ensure fairness for the accused at both the arrest and prosecution stages.

Consent Doctrine

Despite the court's best efforts to ensure that safeguards exist to protect citizens' rights, many argue that the protections currently in place typically fail. One of the most widely used safeguards, the consent doctrine, prohibits an officer from searching a vehicle absent a warrant, probable cause, or consent from the suspect. The reality is that this doctrine, designed to give potential suspects the freedom to reject a police search, generally fails in everyday application and often reflects race and class divisions.

These divisions result in the segregation of potential suspects into two distinct groups. First, there are those who are well aware of their rights and know that they may refuse to allow a police officer to consensually search their person, vehicle, or home absent a warrant or probable cause. Next, there are those who are unaware of their right to refuse a consensual search by police or who may feel pressured or intimidated into allowing police to conduct a search in order to prove their innocence. Most veteran officers agree that when a citizen is asked for consent to search, officers are rarely told "No," for fear this may imply guilt. The fact is that both minorities and those who belong to lower socioeconomic classes may be less apt to know their rights when confronted by the police, whereas those who are white or upper class may feel more confident to assert their rights without fear of retaliation by the police.

Since September 11, 2001, this law enforcement tactic has become especially controversial in contacts between the police and noncitizens, who may be unaware of the law or their rights and fear detention or deportation by the INS if they refuse consent.

Despite the legitimacy and legality of these consensual searches, they often have the unintended effect of perpetuating the distrust minorities typically feel toward the police. The long-term residual effects manifest in the form of noncooperation by minorities when police are called into the community to investigate crimes.

Vocal efforts by civil rights organizations have demanded changes in the way consent searches are initiated; they suggest safeguards that would essentially place all citizens on an even playing field, regardless of race or class. The first of these proposals is that the citizen be asked to sign a written consent form prior to the officer conducting a search. This measure is designed to ensure that the officer did, in fact, obtain consent for the search, and this becomes particularly important when English is a second language for the citizen. Other proposals being explored would require the officer to tell the suspect about his or her right to say "No" to the search. Despite vigorous efforts to initiate these measures, courts have repeatedly rejected any changes to the current system and cite the exclusion of tainted evidence as one safeguard that deters officers from conducting unconstitutional searches and seizures.

Exclusionary Rule

When a citizen's rights are violated, the exclusionary rule takes effect, thus prohibiting the use of evidence that has been obtained in violation of a defendant's constitutional rights. Though not mandated under the Constitution,[52] "ever since its inception, the rule excluding evidence seized in violation of the Fourth Amendment has been recognized as a principal mode of discouraging lawless police conduct."[53]

Some commentators suggest that evidence exclusion is the leading solution to the pretext problem.[54] The court has characterized the exclusionary rule as a "judicially created remedy designed to safeguard Fourth Amendment rights generally through its deterrent effect, rather than a personal constitutional right of the power of the party aggrieved."[55] "Experience has taught us that it is the only effective deterrent to police misconduct in the criminal context, and that without it the constitutional guarantee against unreasonable searches and seizures would be a mere 'form of words.'"[56] The origin of the Fourth Amendment, however, seems to support some commentators' argument that it offers a broader right to be free from unlawful searches and seizures[57] and "the imperative of judicial integrity."[58]

Although the exclusionary rule is used daily in our courts to deter and punish police misconduct, it has nevertheless been the target of criticism for its serious weaknesses. Perhaps these weaknesses are one reason the rule has been steadily cut back in the Burger and Rehnquist years. One of its most significant shortcomings is its "after the fact" effect on the defendant; i.e., it will not stop the search. Although the illegally obtained evidence may ultimately be thrown out at the defendant's trial, the defendant has already been subjected to an illegal search, embarrassment, and harassment. Even though vindication may be the ultimate outcome after the defendant has his or her day in court, the damage has already been done. Upon close review, it would appear that the intent of the Fourth Amendment drafters was that it prevent the search itself rather than have its provisions come into effect after an officer's abuse of power has occurred and the constitutional wrong is committed. The exclusionary rule circumvents this theory, however, and provides retribution for the victim at the prosecution stage instead.

The exclusionary rule has also been criticized for encouraging officers to commit perjury by fabricating causes for a stop and thus avoiding the inclusion of incriminating evidence. Although this possibility has been recognized by the courts, one judge concluded that the "exclusionary rule was designed to deter unconstitutional conduct, not perjury."[59]

The *Terry v. Ohio* court likewise acknowledged the limitations of the exclusionary rule as a tool for judicial control and recognized that "it cannot properly be invoked to exclude the products of legitimate police investigative techniques on the ground that such conduct which is closely similar involves unwarranted intrusions upon constitutional protections."[60] Moreover, the *Terry* court questioned the effectiveness of the exclusionary rule as a deterrent and cited that "encounters are initiated by the police for a wide variety of purposes, some of which are wholly unrelated to a desire to prosecute for crime."[61] The court further noted that "regardless of how effective the rule may be where obtaining convictions is an important objective of the police, it is powerless to deter invasions of constitutionally guaranteed rights where the police either have no interest in prosecuting or are willing to forgo successful prosecution in the interest of serving some other goal."[62] Ultimately, the *Terry* court did not believe that merely excluding evidence from a criminal trial would stop the "wholesale harassment by certain elements of the police community, of which minority groups, particularly Negroes, frequently complain."[63]

The concepts of selective enforcement and selective prosecution are both byproducts of our justice system that frame how we live and work within a diverse society. Implanted in this system are also safeguards such as the consent doctrine and the exclusionary rule that are designed to ensure fairness in interactions between the police and the public. Despite the challenges inherent in maintaining this check-and-balance system, there remains the idealism that regardless of our color, religion, or place in society, we as a civilization are accountable to one another. Whether we draft the laws, vote for them, enforce them, prosecute them, or serve on a jury to apply them, we must do so on the basis of merit as opposed to our own personal bias concerning race and class. When our laws are enforced or prosecuted inequitably, it is detrimental not only to the accused but also to the entire system on which our society is based. As citizens of a thriving democracy, each of us is equally responsible for ensuring that our justice system remains truly color blind to serve our diverse society effectively.

(Endnotes)

1. *Union Pac. R. Co. v. Botsford*, 141 U.S. 250, 251, 11 S.Ct. 1000, 1001, 35 L.Ed. 734 (1891).

2. Fourth Amendment of the United States Constitution: "The right of the people to be secure in their persons, houses, papers, and effects, against unreasonable searches and seizures, shall not be violated and no Warrants shall issue, but upon probable cause supported by Oath or affirmation, and particularly describing the place to be searched, and the persons or things to be seized."

3. *Schmerber v. California*, 384 U.S. 757, 768 (1966).

4. Fourteenth Amendment: (Section One) All persons born or naturalized in the United States, and subject to the jurisdiction thereof, are citizens of the United States and of the State wherein they reside. No State shall make or enforce any law which shall abridge the privileges or immunities of citizens of the United States; nor shall any State deprive any person of life, liberty, or property, without due process of law; nor deny to any person within its jurisdiction the equal protection of the laws.

5. *Terry v. Ohio*, 392 U.S. 1, 88 S.Ct. 1868 (1968).

6. *Terry v. Ohio*, 392 U.S. 1, 21, 88 S.Ct. 1868, 1880 (1968); this demand for specificity in the information upon which police action is predicated is the central teaching of this Court's Fourth Amendment jurisprudence. See also *Beck v. State of Ohio*, 379 U.S. 89, 96-97, 85 S.Ct. 223, 229, 13 L.Ed.2d 142 (1964); *Ker v. State of California*, 374 U.S. 23, 34-37, 83 S.Ct. 1623, 1632, 10 L.Ed.2d 726 (1963); *Wong Sun v. United States*, 371 U.S. 471, 479-484, 83 S.Ct.407, 416, 9 L.Ed.2d 441 (1963).

7. *Beck v. State of Ohio*, 379 U.S. 89, 97, 85 S.Ct. 223, 229 (1964).

8. *Adams v. Williams*, 407 U.S. 143 (1972).

9. *Brown v. Texas*, 443 U.S. 47 (1979).

10. *U.S. v. Sokolow*, 490 U.S. 1 (1989).

11. *United States v. Cummins*, 920 F.2d. 498 (1990).

12. *U.S. v. Sullivan*, 138 F.3d 126 (1998).

13. *Ohio v. Robinette*, 117 S.Ct. 417, 136 L.Ed.2d 347 (1996).

14. *Valance v. Wisel*, 110 F.3d 1269 (1997).

15. *Knowles v. Iowa*, 119 S.Ct. 484, 142 L.Ed. 2d 492 (1998).

16. *United States v. Tapia*, 912 F.2d 1367 (1990); *Com. v. Cardoso*, 46 Mass.App.Ct. 901, 702 N.E.2d 398 (1998).

17. *Whren v. United States*, 517 U.S. 806, 116 S.Ct. 1769 (1996).

18. *United States v. Whren*, 53 F.3d 371, 374-375 (1995).

19. *Whren v. United States*, 517 U.S. 806, 116 S.Ct. 1769, 1772-77 (1996).

20. *United States v. Robinson*, 414 U.S. 218, 221, n.1, 236, 94 S.Ct. 467, 470, n.1, 477, 38 L.Ed.2d 427 (1973).

21. *Whren v. United States*, 517 U.S. 806, 116 S.Ct. 1769, 1772-74 (1996).

22. *Whren v. United States*, 517 U.S. 806, 116 S.Ct. 1769 (1996).

23. *United States v. Robinson*, 414 U.S. 218, 236, 94 S.Ct. 467, 477 (1973).

24. *Whren v. United States*, 517 U.S. 806, 815, 116 S.Ct. 1769, 1775 (1996); see also *Gustafson v. Florida*, 414 U.S. 260, 265, 94 S.Ct. 488, 491, 38 L.Ed.2d 456 (1973); *United States v. Caceres*, 440 U.S. 741, 755-756, 99 S.Ct. 1465, 1473-1474, 59 L.Ed.2d 733 (1979).

25. See *United States v. Villamonte-Marquez*, 462 U.S. 579, 574, n. 3, 103 S.Ct. 2573, 2577, n.3, 77 L.Ed.2d 22 (1983) (held that an otherwise valid warrantless boarding of a vessel by customs officials was not rendered invalid "because the customs officers were accompanied by a Louisiana state policeman, and were following an informant's tip that a vessel in the ship channel was thought to be carrying marihuana.").

26. *United States v. Robinson*, 414 U.S. 218, 221, n. 1, 94 S.Ct. 467, 470, n. 1 (1973).

27. *United States v. Robinson*, 414 U.S. 218, 236, 94 S.Ct. 467, 477, (1973).

28. See also *Gustafson v. Florida*, 414 U.S. 260, 266, 94 S.Ct. 488, 492, 38 L.Ed.2d 456 (1973).

29. *Scott v. United States*, 436 U.S. 128, 136, 138, 98 S.Ct. 1717, 1723 (1978) (also held that "[s]ubjective intent alone...does not make otherwise lawful conduct illegal or unconstitutional.").

30. *Whren v. United States*, 517 U.S. 806, 809-10, 116 S.Ct. 1769, 1772 (1996).

31. *Delaware v. Prouse*, 440 U.S. 648, 659, 99 S.Ct. 1391, 1399 (1979); see also *Pennsylvania v. Mimms*, 434 U.S. 106, 109, 98 S.Ct. 330, 332, 54 L.Ed.2d 331 (1977) (per curiam).

32. *Whren v. United States*, 517 U.S. 806, 813, 116 S.Ct. 1769, 1774 (1996).

33. *Whren v. United States*, 517 U.S. 806, 819, 116 S.Ct. 1769, 1774, 1776 (1996).

34. *Illinois v. Wardlow*, 120 S.Ct. 673 (2000).

35. Robinson, Mike, Associated Press, "High Court to Hear Case on Police Power to Frisk Someone Who Flees," *The Valley Times*, November 1, 1999.

36. *United States v. Brignoni-Ponce*, 422 U.S. 873, 885, 95 S.Ct. 2574, 45 L.Ed.2d 607.

37. *Florida v. Royer,* 460 U.S. 491, 498, 103 S.Ct. 1319 (1983).

38. *Terry v. Ohio*, 392 U.S., at 30, 88 S.Ct. 1868.

39. *In Re Arturo D.*, 115 Cal.Rptr.2d 581, January 24, 2002.

40. Reiss, Steven Alan, "Prosecutorial Intent in Constitutional Criminal Procedure," 135 U. Pa. L. Rev. 1365, 1369 (1987).

41. *United States v. Scopo*, 814 F. Supp. 292, 294-95 (E.D.N.Y. 1993), rev'd, 19 F.3d 777 (2d Cir.), cert. denied, 115 S. Ct. 207 (1994).

42. *Yick Wo v. Hopkins*, 118 U.S. 356 (1886).

43. Contractors Against Unfair Taxation, 1994 WL 455553 at *6.

44. *Whren v. United States*, 517 U.S. 806, 116 S.Ct. 1769 (1996).

45. Emmanuel Law Outlines, *Criminal Procedure* 81.

46. "Community Prosecution," *The Prosecutor,* May/June 2000.

47. *United States v. Berrios,* 501 F.2d 1207 (1974).

48. *Wayte v. United States,* 470 U.S. 598 (1985).

49. *Wayte v. United States,* 470 U.S. 598, 608 (quoting *Bordenkircher v. Hayes,* 434 U.S. 357, 364 (1978) (quoting *Oyler v. Boles,* 368 U.S. 448, 456 (1962)) and citing *United States v. Goodwin,* 457 U.S. 368, 372 (1982)).

50. *United States v. Berrios,* 501 F.2d 1207, 1211 (2d Cir. 1974).

51. *United States v. Saade,* 652 F.2d 1126, 1135 (1ˢᵗ Cir. 1981).

52. *U.S. v. Leon,* 468 U.S. 897, 104 S.Ct. 3405 (1984).

53. *Terry v. Ohio,* 88 S.Ct. 1868, 1875 (1968); see also *Weeks v. United States,* 232 U.S. 383, 391-393, 34 S.Ct. 341, 344, 58 L.Ed. 652 (1914).

54. See Smith, M.H., the *Writs of Assistance Case* 1-2 (1978); Amsterdam, "Perspectives on the Fourth Amendment," 58 Minn. L. Rev. 349, 433-36 (1974). The use exclusion rule differs from the exclusionary rule. In an effort to deter unconstitutional police conduct, the exclusionary rule denies admission of evidence that has been obtained illegally. By contrast, the exclusion rule treats the search as constitutionally permissible, but denies admission of any evidence obtained that is considered beyond the scope of the search's justification. This is aimed to discourage police abuse.

55. *United States v. Calandra,* 414 U.S. 338, 348 (1974).

56. *Mapp v. Ohio,* 367 U.S. 643, 655, 81 S.Ct. 1684, 1692, 6 L.Ed.2d 601 (1965).

57. See, e.g., Amsterdam, supra at 432 (criticizing the Court for solely focusing upon an 'atomistic' view of the Fourth Amendment, thereby not recognizing its role in keeping citizens 'collectively secure' against unreasonable searches and seizures); Schock & Welsh, "Up From Calandra: The Exclusionary Rule as a Constitutional Requirement," 59 Minn. L. Rev. 251, 302-07 (1974) (arguing that Justice Day's Fourth Amendment interpretation in *Weeks v. United States,* 232 U.S. 383, 391-92 (1914), compels the conclusion of a personal constitutional right to exclusion).

58. *Elkins v. United States,* 364 U.S. 206, 222, 80 S.Ct. 1437, 1447, 4 L.Ed.2d 1669 (1960).

59. *United States v. Hawkins,* 811 F.2d 210, 215 (3d Cir.).

60. *Terry v. Ohio*, 88 S.Ct. 1868, 1875 (1968).

61. *Terry v. Ohio*, 88 S.Ct. 1868, 1876 (1968).

62. *Terry v. Ohio*, 88 S.Ct. 1868, 1876 (1968).

63. *Terry v. Ohio*, 88 S.Ct. 1868, 1876 (1968).

PART IV: What's the Score?

CHAPTER ELEVEN

———•◦•———

Data Collection and Analysis

Data collection efforts by law enforcement agencies have become one of the most controversial issues surrounding racial profiling. To collect or not to collect? What will it prove? How accurate is it? Is it a deterrent, a burden, or neither? Despite these unanswered questions, data collection efforts have skyrocketed in the past few years. Although most of these collection programs are voluntarily implemented because of pressure by outside sources, some agencies are collecting data under new legislation or by mandate of consent decrees with the U.S. Department of Justice or other entities.

In many cases, law enforcement agencies are implementing these voluntary data collection programs to prove to the public that their officers are not engaging in race-based traffic stops. Unfortunately, both sides are often so anxious to get to the result that the accuracy, integrity, and usefulness of the data are often lost somewhere in the process.

Of those organizations already collecting data, few know what to do with it once it's been compiled. Though the results of most data collection efforts cannot be considered statistically valid, many view them as such when raw numbers are reported. When the media report this statistically unsound data, law enforcement organizations are forced to live with the negative consequences, namely an inaccurate picture of whether law enforcement is engaging in racial profiling. Whether errors occur in the data collection itself, in the analysis, or by factors related to demographics and socioeconomics, many organizations engaging in voluntary data collection are no better off than those not collecting data at all.

It should be noted here that data collection must not be confused with a scientifically based statistical analysis. Unlike a bona fide study with checks and balances, data collection has, in many cases, surfaced as a "wolf in sheep's clothing" in an effort to draw conclusions about whether the use of racial profiling is prevalent in law enforcement. The fact is racial disparities in traffic stops do not in themselves prove a given agency practices racial profiling.

To break this premise down systematically, we can start with one basic assumption: in order to establish evidence of racial profiling, *two* factors need to be proven, assuming all other things are equal. First, it must be demonstrated that blacks and Hispanics (or some other racial group) are no more likely than whites to violate traffic laws and, second, that police routinely pull over one of these minority groups at a higher rate than whites. To the public, this simple and straightforward explanation may seem quite logical; however, those analyzing data must not assume all other things are equal when using raw traffic stop data to draw conclusions about racial profiling practices.

Despite emerging research in this area, some experts still view the nexus of data collection and racial profiling far too simplistically. In many of the published data collection studies, this linear approach to collection and analysis focuses on establishing the rate at which minorities are pulled over in comparison with whites. If one were to look no further, most studies would probably appear quite factual in their reporting of raw numbers that show, for example, that 100 whites were stopped in a given time frame compared with 120 African Americans or 65 Hispanics. But to draw inferences from these raw numbers is, in most cases, irresponsible. More importantly, it produces poor and inaccurate analysis.

Though most data collection efforts can be credited with arriving at some benchmark against which to measure the raw data, these benchmarks often vary substantially from one jurisdiction to another. Complete and accurate analysis of the data would have to consider more complex factors that often contribute to a disparity in traffic stop demographics. The actual rate at which each racial group breaks traffic laws and the disproportionate assignment of officers to high-crime areas within a jurisdiction are examples of two such factors. Either of these or a multitude of others unique to a given jurisdiction can account for discrepancies in traffic stop demographics.

When traffic stop demographic studies use these data to make generalizations about an entire organization, they harm the organization as a whole and do little to address the problem of racial profiling. Few of these studies are designed to look for *individual* patterns of racial profiling and biased policing within an organization and force the entire rank and file to live by results that are conclusory, at best.

A 2002 study released by the CNA Corporation (CNAC) through funding from the U.S. Department of Justice Office of Community Oriented Policing Services (COPS) reported findings from its review and analysis of more than two dozen published reports encompassing more than three million records of police stops from 700+ federal, state, and local law enforcement agencies. This study, one of the most comprehensive to date, reported that "Most of the analyses reported show that police traffic stops are not proportional to the racial distribution of that jurisdiction's resident population, but most studies do not conclude that the police are engaged in racial profiling." The study also reported that "Every study that examined police searches found some racial disproportionality, at least in certain types of police searches, but the majority of the report authors concluded that police search behavior does not indicate racial profiling."[1]

While some of the reports studied by CNAC cited findings as definitive proof of the existence or nonexistence of racial profiling,[2] others were inconclusive, in that they failed to adequately establish proper comparison models and statistical analyses by which to measure the effect of race on traffic stops and searches.[3] Another group of studies analyzed by CNAC failed to address many of these challenges altogether and reached conclusions despite substandard data or analysis methods.[4]

As this examination suggests, when critical variables inherent in traffic enforcement remain unknown and unexplored by those collecting data and publishing traffic stop studies, the results that purport to establish the existence or nonexistence of racial profiling within an organization are incomplete and, more likely, inaccurate.

Interviews with officers revealed an almost universal belief that current data collection studies do not prove whether racial profiling is occurring. Most experts seem to concur with this opinion. Some point to flawed reporting and evaluation methods used by many agencies that result in data that are statistically unsound from the outset. Others point to human intervention that may circumvent the integrity of the data either in the reporting or the analysis. In fact, experts publishing data collection studies themselves acknowledge the challenges posed by using data collection as a means to measure whether racial profiling or biased policing is occurring within an organization.[5] Even the most detailed studies express "the reluctance of using the traffic stop data to draw conclusions about the existence of racial profiling...."[6]

While not completely opposed to data collection, we believe its value in identifying racial profiling practices is quite limited. It is important that users of traffic stop data be vigilant and cautious in drawing conclusions from the data and weigh the benefits of its use against the danger of reporting or relying on inaccurate results.

Although many studies set forth appropriate disclaimers about the accuracy and implications of the reported data and analyses,[7] others blindly report data and draw conclusions on the basis of a process that's flawed from start to finish. Some studies are so riddled with disclaimers that cite factors that may contribute to the unreliability of the data that people attempting to extract some value from them may wonder why the studies ever proceeded at all. Some readers often skip over disclaimer language and go straight to the raw numbers to make their own assessment about whether a jurisdiction is engaging in racial profiling. Even more disquieting is the media's tendency to frame conclusions and craft sensational headlines based on raw data without responsible explanation of the intricacies and high probability of error inherent in the collection and analysis processes.

Though some studies that acknowledge the difficulty of assessing individual officer motives with respect to race-based enforcement may be in the offing,[8] when there are disparities in the data reported and the headlines reveal these disparities, the public's perception that officers may be engaging in racial profiling is inevitably fueled, driving a deeper wedge between law enforcement and the public.

Though data collection may be a valuable internal early warning system for police organizations themselves or a process that can yield information to support the development and evaluation of training curricula within an organization, as a means of establishing with some certainty whether racial profiling is being practiced, it remains largely unreliable. This is true simply because human discretion cannot be measured. It is unlikely that a third person will ever be able to assess definitively *why* an officer made one decision over another, an assessment the officer himself or herself may not always be able to make or articulate.

To illustrate, assume two officers in City X make two separate traffic stops. Everything about each stop is identical: the time of day; the make and model of the vehicle; and the gender, race, and age of the driver. Let's also assume that the outcome of each stop is identical: each driver is issued a citation for a broken tail light.

If traffic stop data are collected in City X, the data from both of these stops would be identical in every way. Let's assume now, however, that Officer A stopped the vehicle after noticing a broken tail light. Officer B, on the other hand, first noticed that the driver of the car was black. Officer B is very suspicious of blacks and believes the driver of this car is probably a drug dealer. Officer B then looks for some reason to stop the driver to investigate his or her suspicions further. Officer B finally notices the broken tail light and uses this mechanical violation as the reason for stopping the driver.

In the first stop, Officer A's motives were above reproach; Officer A may not have realized the driver's race prior to the stop, nor was it relevant to him or her. Officer B, however, was clearly racially profiling the driver. Though the data collected from these two stops would yield the same information, they would fail to capture whether racial profiling occurred in either instance. In other words, no study would be able to reveal the *mindset* of the officers at the time the stop was initiated. Absent information on this critical variable, any study attempting to determine whether racial profiling exists in City X would overlook Officer B entirely and draw a specious conclusion.

Perhaps in part because of these known hurdles, it's been next to impossible for either experts, civil rights groups, and the government—either independently or collaboratively—to agree on a nationally standardized data collection study model. Instead, these endeavors are more often left to the discretion of individual law enforcement organizations that can sometimes act as the facilitator of the process from implementation and collection through reporting and analysis.

Clearly, data collection is far more complicated than one can appreciate from this overview of the topic. To expand upon some of the challenges posed by data collection, the following sections delve into the two components of data collection in detail: the data collection process itself and the data analysis.

The Collection Process

One of the essential challenges in this process is ensuring the accuracy of the data collected by the line officers. Though almost all agencies collecting data mandate that the information be complete and accurate by policy, two factors cause concern for those analyzing traffic stop data: 1) the anonymity granted to the officers on the collection forms and 2) the lack of independent checks and balances in many models. In fact, even in some of the most respected traffic stop studies, the authors acknowledge, "The percentage of auto stops for which officers did not accurately fill out a data form is unknown."[9] In fact, "Some departments nationwide report that up to 50% of their traffic stops were not captured by a data collection system."[10]

It should be noted here that inaccurate data collection may be attributed to several factors. The most obvious, of course, is a conscious decision by the officer to avoid collecting data altogether or to collect it haphazardly. When interviewing officers around the country, two scenarios seemed to play out most frequently in this regard. One officer talked about the efforts his own department was undertaking as a result of pressure by civil rights organizations and community leaders. The command staff's directive was for one officer within the department to implement a data collection system. With no training, input, or guidance, the officer printed hundreds of 3″ by 5″ cards that enabled fellow officers to record the approximate age, race, and sex of the person stopped. The card also included a line for the officer to record the violation that initiated the contact.

The cards were made available to all officers within the department. Officers were directed to fill out these cards anonymously when they conducted a stop and to turn them in accordingly. After four months, many officers within the department admitted they had never turned in a card. Others that did so said their efforts were intermittent at best. Some officers admitted filling out a stack of cards before their shift started, always making sure the "white" stops exceeded the "black" stops they reported. The command staff never questioned the minimal response to the data collection program, nor did it seem to notice that the cards that had been turned in did not even represent a single-digit fraction of the total number of traffic tickets issued by the agency over the four-month period. A few months later, upon the natural demise of the data collection program, the command staff proudly reported their statistics to the ACLU and the media as "proof" that racial profiling was not occurring within the organization.

Particularly in smaller agencies, these substandard data collection efforts are more often the rule than the exception. The haphazard approaches don't necessarily indicate that the organization has something to hide; they underscore the low priority of such efforts for many law enforcement agencies and their officers. Unfortunately, the real motivating factor for some agencies to collect the data may be to alleviate political pressure rather than to identify the one or two officers who may be engaging in suspect practices. In some cases, these pressures may even tempt officers to circumvent the system altogether in order to avoid racial profiling accusations.

Another factor that may compromise data accuracy is the conscious decision by the officer to "regulate" the process in an effort to turn in favorable statistics, a phenomenon that is acknowledged in some traffic stop studies: "...traffic stop studies traditionally do not include information about the individuals who could have been stopped but weren't..."[11] The very nature of these discretionary encounters makes it possible for the officer to regulate consciously the number of minority stops compared with the number of white stops he or she may make in a given day.

In one such instance that took place in the Midwest, a state trooper pulled over one of our family friends. The Caucasian middle-aged man could not figure out why he was being stopped while traveling along a deserted highway at night. When the officer approached his car window, he was surprised to learn that he was receiving a ticket for traveling five miles per hour over the posted speed limit. The man indicated that his brother was a police officer in another state and could not believe that exceeding the speed limit by five miles per hour on a deserted road warranted a ticket. The officer was quite matter-of-fact when he returned to the man's car with the citation, indicating to him that he had already stopped two black guys that night and he needed to stop a white guy so he would "break even." When similar variables are thrown into the mix, even the most well-intentioned officers may be forced to circumvent the data collection process to create a system artificially that was not fair to begin with. One of these critical factors is whether certain minority groups have a greater likelihood of being stopped for reasons other than race.

To understand this concept, it's useful to look at the two most common types of violations targeted by the police: moving violations and equipment or registration violations. Some experts suggest the drivers who are stopped for equipment and registration violations are more often minorities who, for economic reasons, may be more likely to drive cars in a state of disrepair. Others may be less likely to wear seatbelts, particularly young males. Likewise, certain ethnic groups tend to equip their vehicles so that they are unique and easily distinguishable from nonaltered vehicles. This might be done by lowering the frame, adding hydraulics, changing lighting systems, or tinting windows. Some suggest these vehicle alterations attract greater attention from law enforcement, which results in a greater number of stops per capita. In some instances, the probability of being stopped by the police for these discretionary violations may be higher in certain parts of a city. Some also point to specific dynamics within many ethnic populations, for example, a higher percentage of new immigrants who may have less experience behind the wheel than the average driver.

On the contrary, whites are thought to account for more speeding violations than nonwhites. On some roadways, these types of violations may be given limited attention absent an increase in accidents or citizen complaints.

Consider these differences, and then consider the fact that when enforcement priorities—which do change from time to time—emphasize one type of violation over another, data are skewed at the outset for factors that have little to do with skin color. Absent definitive data that establish whether whites and nonwhites commit moving and mechanical violations at equal rates to use for comparison purposes, analysts will be unable to draw any sound conclusions as to whether the police may be unfairly targeting one racial group over another or whether these disparities are consistent with the rate at which these groups commit traffic violations. Though some of these variables are quite complex, others are more simple. For example, some people may live in or travel through neighborhoods with a greater police presence, which would logically increase the likelihood of an encounter with the police. Let's assume, for example, 100 officers are on patrol in Town X. Eighty officers are deployed to the downtown area, which, unfortunately, is known for its high crime, drug, and gang activity. The other 20 officers are deployed to patrol the outlying neighborhoods. In Town X, blacks represent 8% of the overall population but 90% of the downtown area. Traffic stop statistics for Town X would undoubtedly reveal a disproportionate number of blacks stopped if for no other reason than the unequal deployment of officers throughout the city. Though a traffic stop study conducted in Town X might show a disproportionate number of blacks stopped compared with whites, these results would not be effective in determining whether officers were using race as a primary motive for enforcement stops. If the study were more narrowly focused on the outcome of each *individual* officer contact, however, the local police would be better equipped to detect patterns of inequality.

Likewise, it is important to remember that unintentional mistakes may occur in the data collection process that would be difficult to account for in the final tabulation of the data. Most studies, for example, require that officers record the race of the driver on the basis of their own perception. Though some predict that accuracy rates in this respect may be quite high, other unscientific studies have reported accuracy rates as low as 2% when officers were asked to identify the race of the driver. In terms of data collection, some indicate that this variable need not be accurate to measure an officer's activities toward a particular race; the analysis should be based on whether the officer treated the suspect fairly on the basis of his or her subjective *perception* of the person's race. This argument may be valid if the traffic stops are evaluated on an individual basis. However, when the percentage of stops within a city is compared one dimensionally to the racial demographics and reported in terms of the entire department, these errors in perception can quickly add up to inaccurate results.

Finally, many traffic stop studies face a far more straightforward question, what to do with incomplete data collection cards. Though some studies exclude any incomplete cards from the analysis, others include these data even though their incompleteness casts doubt on their reliability. Either way—whether incomplete cards are included or excluded—results are once again skewed, likely painting an inaccurate picture that law enforcement is left to defend later in the process.

Though these variables pose some of the most daunting challenges to the data collection process, experts are exploring new ways to ensure that the data collected are as accurate as possible. Some of these efforts include substantial oversight and auditing by the organization, often overseen by study facilitators or special interest groups.

For example, data collection logs might be compared with in-car police video camera recordings or to police dispatch records to compare the details of each stop to what was recorded by the officer. Others have developed internal supervisor audits of activity logs to identify areas of discrepancy. Though many of these oversight measures most certainly have improved the integrity of the data, we must continue to explore new and innovative approaches that will yield a level of accuracy and completeness such an important endeavor must demand.

Accurate data collection and stringent check-and-balance systems are crucial to the success of any traffic stop study. It is important to remember that even the most rigid scientific data analysis will be inaccurate if the data it is based upon are flawed at the outset.

Data Analysis

Data analysis is the second critical component of any successful traffic stop study. Though data collection can be accomplished with limited interference and oversight by study coordinators, data analysis is far more complicated and should be undertaken as a cooperative endeavor. While some organizations still choose to analyze data internally, others have turned to academic partners, police research organizations, and statisticians to assist in this complex process. Although the importance of involving academics and other outside partners in this process cannot be underestimated, of equal importance is the contribution of law enforcement, particularly line officers. Though law enforcement administrators frequently provide feedback and participate in the data analysis, there can be no substitute for the insight and street experience that a line officer can contribute to the process. Often, the line officer can educate academics about practical factors that would not otherwise be apparent to those with little or no law enforcement experience. For example, officers may inform study coordinators about variables that would make the race of the driver almost impossible to discern prior to the initiation of a stop, for example, when a stop is made at nighttime or at times of poor visibility or when the stop is initiated solely on an objective factor, i.e., the violation is detected by radar before the race of the driver can be determined. Though these factors may be irrelevant when evaluating traffic stop data as factual matters, they become critical when analyzing and drawing conclusions about the existence or nonexistence of racial profiling within an organization. The inclusion of line officers throughout the analysis process may be one of the single most important variables in arriving at an accurate study model but one that is often overlooked.

Establishing a Benchmark

A *benchmark* may best be defined as a point of reference from which measurements, evaluations, and comparisons can be made. Therefore, before conclusions can be drawn from the data and directed to any useful purpose, appropriate benchmarks must be incorporated into the system to derive real meaning from these raw numbers.

Many organizations currently utilize census data as benchmarks for comparing the racial demographics within a community to traffic stop data. When challenged statistically, however, census data cannot be considered accurate benchmarks against which to compare roadway demographics. This is because in most cases, population demographics vary substantially from roadway demographics.

This logic suggests, for example, that if census figures report 5% of the population in a given location is African American, stops of African Americans in this jurisdiction should not exceed 5%. This logic is flawed for many reasons. First, the driving population may vary substantially from the residential population. Variables such as age are usually not factored in to the equation to determine the percentage of those of a particular ethnicity who are of driving age or who are licensed to drive. Census data also don't account for variables inherent in census reporting such as margins of error, nor do they capture the numbers of people who may be commuting through a given location who do not reside in the area. When these and other factors aren't considered, no analysis based on census data alone will lead to an accurate assessment of traffic stop data, even if the data collection methods themselves are flawless.

Some experts have suggested that a location's driving population as reported by Department of Motor Vehicles (DMV) records would be a better benchmark. (It should be noted here that many states' motor vehicle departments do not currently collect racial data or have outlawed the collection of these data.) In some states, DMV data would provide a breakdown of the driving public within a certain city or precinct. Some experts have proposed that where applicable, these data be made available to law enforcement for purposes of traffic stop analysis. There are a few downsides, however, to using DMV data for this purpose. First is the inability to measure the varying rate at which individuals with drivers licenses actually drive. This important variable would increase a frequent driver's risk of being stopped by the police simply by virtue of the amount of time he or she spends driving on the roadway. Second, DMV records are not always known for their accuracy, nor do they account for the transient nature of the driving public. Though a driver's address may reflect a residence in Town A, the driver may spend 95% of his or her time driving in Town B.

Some more recent studies utilize a combination of demographic and transportation data to calculate a community's roadway demographics. Others have incorporated rolling or stationary roadway and video observations to determine the racial breakdown of roadway demographics and violations. These roadway observations usually consist of an observation car traveling on the roadway while its passengers record the race, sex, and age of the driver.

Though some rolling or stationary observations provide the best alternative to arriving at an accurate benchmark, others criticize them as costly and time consuming. Likewise, these rolling observations are largely dependent on the observers' ability to assess and record a person's race and age correctly. Though some studies purport to have a 95% accuracy rate with respect to race observations,[12] others have opined that a person's ability to assess another's race accurately in this limited time frame may be as low as 2%.

Regardless of a person's training or abilities in this regard, human intervention and perception remain variables that are never certain. In the case of arriving at an accurate benchmark, even the slightest margin of error may result in analysts comparing data to an inappropriate benchmark, which would produce inaccurate and unreliable analysis.

We appreciate the frustration most experts express as they seek to establish an appropriate and accurate benchmark to measure traffic stop data. Though not perfect by any means, we believe that the optimum benchmark at this point in time is a combination of multiple models: census reports, DMV records (where available), transportation data, and/or a close analysis of business and retail traffic patterns through a given location. Though studies are slowly evolving to reflect a more multifaceted benchmark, this task still remains challenging at best.

Assigning a Risk Factor

Once experts agree on a benchmark believed to represent the roadway demographics in their survey area most closely, they must shift their focus to other factors that may alter these demographics from time to time. One of these factors is whether certain racial groups own vehicles or drive at different rates, in different parts of the city, or at different times of day. For example, there are differences between those who work and those who do not. The members of the working class are normally on the roadway during commuting hours while the unemployed have a far more variable driving schedule. A closer examination of these important factors would enhance experts' ability to analyze and predict patterns in the data that may be attributed to factors other than race.

In addition to considering variables that may cause roadway demographics to vary, experts must take their analysis one step further to determine a driver's risk of being stopped by police. Though 100% of drivers may make up the roadway demographics, there is a quite different subset of drivers who are at a greater risk of being stopped by the police for one reason or another. Though all may be numerically represented as drivers on the roadway, some individuals in this group may have been driving for 20, 30, or 40 years without a single contact with the police. On the other hand, there are some drivers in this group who may complain of monthly stops by the police. Therefore, it becomes apparent that in order to derive at an accurate picture of roadway demographics, all drivers must not be treated equally. It is important for experts to break out roadway demographics and assign appropriate risk factors to narrow this broad category further and better approximate a benchmark by which to compare data for reliable results.

Let's assume, for example, that in City A minorities account for 15% of the drivers on the roadway. Raw data compiled for City A reveal officers stop minorities at a disproportionate rate compared with whites between the hours of 9:00 p.m. and

3:00 a.m. Though this raw data may distinguish stops by time of day, the benchmark of 15% used to measure all traffic stop data remains constant, with the final analysis broadly encompassing data from all shifts. When no other factors are considered, this skewed data may lead to the assumption that any disparity is race based. Many reports may never look beyond this conclusion.

Upon further examination, however, it is revealed that there are activities that take place within City A between the hours of 9:00 p.m. and 3:00 a.m. that may elevate the risk factor for minorities to be stopped by the police. One of these unreported factors in City A's study is the large industrial district with several assembly plants. When one looks to the workforce during these late night and early morning hours, it is discovered that 500 employees—75% of those minorities—are employed by these assembly plants and work the graveyard shift. These employees travel to and from work during these hours and use the roadways during multiple break and meal periods throughout the evening and early morning hours. Is there a disproportionate number of minorities stopped during these hours? Yes. But there is also a disproportionate number of minorities using the roadways during these hours. When broad conclusions are drawn from data collected in expanded survey areas, these seemingly insignificant factors may never be uncovered. The result is that City A police will likely be forced to defend results that (inaccurately) suggest that its officers stop minorities at a rate that is disproportionate to their representation in the community.

Let's take this analysis one step further and relate it back to establishing roadway demographics for City A. How would this study approximate the roadway demographics if most of the employees from these assembly plants traveled to City A from cities outside of the survey area? Some studies have attempted to predict just that by identifying factors that may "push" drivers out of surrounding cities and "draw" them into target cities. There is some skepticism, however, as to the ability to quantify such factors with any degree of certainty, in part because these factors may also vary along racial and socioeconomic lines. Though the accuracy rate of these endeavors remains somewhat uncertain, the endeavors do illustrate the complexity of and the challenges posed by these studies.

"Blind" Stops

Time of day may also play a critical role in data analysis for reasons that are rarely considered in traffic stop studies. For example, in the evening hours, an officer may observe a violation and stop a vehicle *before* the officer can ever discern the race (or the gender) of the driver. Yet data from these "blind" stops are combined with data from stops in which the driver's race is predetermined by the officer. Though the driver's race may arguably play a role in whether the officer decides to initiate a stop during the day, stops at night are frequently based solely on the violation. Yet a study may lump data on day and night stops together and draw conclusions about whether officers are engaging in racial profiling. Clearly, data on the stops in which the officer could not predetermine the race of the driver should either be excluded from the analysis or segregated from the balance of the data and analyzed separately.

These "blind" stops are not limited to those officers make during the day versus the night. Officers may be unable to determine the race of the driver before initiating a stop for several reasons, including roadway and weather conditions, window tinting on the vehicle, or the observation of a violation from a distance.

"Blind" stops also occur when officers rely on radar to detect vehicle code violations. For example, officers may position themselves on a busy stretch of roadway and monitor the display of a radar gun or other speed measurement device. When the device detects a vehicle traveling at an excessive rate of speed, the officer will often decide to stop the vehicle before it is close enough for the officer to determine the driver's race.

Again, these stops are treated equally in the data collection process, with the race of the driver recorded on the data collection form and used to determine whether the officer or the department is engaging in racial profiling. As with some nighttime stops, the data in which the race of the driver plays no role in the stop itself should not be included in the analysis or, alternatively, should be reported and analyzed as a subset.

When these "blind" stops are removed from the data, the impact on studies trying to link a disparity in traffic stop data to racial profiling can be significant. This is particularly true in states that attribute nearly 50% of their traffic stops to speeding.[13] Though all speeders may not be detected by radar, the drivers that are detected by this objective means are unlikely to be targets of racial profiling. Even in many nonradar initiated speeding violations, it is likely that the vehicle's speed may make it impossible for the officer to ascertain the race of the driver in advance of stopping the vehicle, particularly when the observation is made from a stationary location. It should be noted here that one of the only times these blind stops should be seen as insignificant is when a traffic stop study is measuring, as a factual matter, how many individuals from any racial group are being stopped for any reason. Unfortunately, the data from these "blind" stops are often combined with data from stops in which the race of the driver is known to the officer and are used to draw the sometimes specious conclusion that officers are engaging in racial profiling.

Who Initiated the Stop?

In addition to these "blind" stops, there are other types of police encounters that most data collection analyses fail to capture. Though officers may report data on every public contact, there is usually no opportunity for the officer to distinguish between stops that he or she initiated and stops initiated by a citizen. Examples of these citizen-initiated stops are calls for roadway assistance, requests for directions, and requests for the officer to sign off on mechanical violations. Though the process of recording citizen-initiated stops is identical to the process of recording discretionary contacts, these stops provide no information about whether the officer might be engaging in racial profiling. Yet, the fact that a stop was citizen initiated is rarely reported or considered in many data collection studies. All data from these stops should be excluded from reporting and analysis of the data collected when the study is being used to determine whether police are engaging in racial profiling.

Statistical Significance

Finally, once the data are collected and analyzed, experts must determine what variance is statistically significant/acceptable in order for the data to be considered reliable and predictive. For example, let's assume Hispanics represent 10% of the roadway demographics in City X. When experts in City X compare traffic stop data to this benchmark, they find that Hispanics are stopped at a rate of 14%, or 4% more than their representation on the roadway. Is a 4% variance significant for purposes of determining whether officers in City X are engaging in racial profiling, or would another variable be more predictive? Many published data collection studies report acceptable variances that usually range between 3% and 5%. Other studies fail to provide any reference point by which to assess the significance of the data reported. Likewise, a variance that may be viewed as acceptable in one jurisdiction may be considered unacceptable in another. Regardless, one must look at this narrow margin in the context of each study to determine whether such a limited window is appropriate for determining whether officers disproportionately stop one race over another. Some experts have proposed that such an assessment be left up to legislators and policy makers.

Despite data collection's vocal critics, many civil rights organizations still hope that data collection will be nationally mandated and required to be used by all law enforcement officers when conducting traffic stops. Regardless of this ambitious goal, there continues to be persistent resistance among many law enforcement agencies to implement mandatory collection programs. It would appear that before such an aggressive approach could be successful, current models must be studied to determine what works and what doesn't. It would also seem prudent for the system to be uniform nationwide and take into account, of course, limitations smaller organizations may have to invest in costly equipment and additional staffing. Most important, a plan must be developed to determine what will be done with the data once they are collected. Assuming such efforts would reveal that racial profiling is a nationwide problem, how do we go about fixing it?

To answer some of these questions, we looked to studies on data collection that highlighted larger agencies' efforts to implement successful programs. Northwestern University's comprehensive research guide on the subject, developed with partial funding from the U.S. Department of Justice, is one study that analyzes specific data collection programs that have been implemented around the country.[14] The Department of Justice hopes that this information will encourage law enforcement agencies to begin data collection programs and alleviate some of the concerns that currently surround the concept. This guide explores four data collection systems being used in the United States in San José, California; San Diego, California; and throughout North Carolina and New Jersey. In an effort to determine which systems are the most effective, we will look to the specifics of these programs and review some of the findings and recommendations from the Northwestern University guide.

Prior to reviewing these selected programs, it should be noted that there are several reasons law enforcement is reluctant to initiate data collection programs. For some organizations, the reluctance is related to specific enforcement challenges and demographics within the community. For others, the concerns are more universal and fall into eight major areas:

1. Data collection forms require the officer to list the race or ethnicity of the driver stopped. How can officers obtain accurate information about the driver's ethnicity without being perceived as either intrusive or confrontational?

2. Any comprehensive data collection effort usually involves substantial changes in the way officers conduct traffic or pedestrian stops. Such changes may result in new departmental procedures; officer training; and a collection, analysis, and reporting means. How can these data collection programs be implemented with the fewest budgetary, time, and paperwork burdens for an organization?

3. Some fear that police officers who are required to adhere to stringent documentation procedures will refrain from conducting as many stops, which would result in a decrease in enforcement efforts for legitimate stops and searches. How should this potential for disengagement be addressed?

4. Many of the current data collection efforts are anonymous and do not have checks and balances to ensure data accuracy. These efforts may inadvertently enable officers engaging in racial profiling to submit erroneous information or, alternatively, to fail to report any data at all. How can officers be held accountable without violating their privacy rights?

5. The scope of data collected must be sufficient to assess the problem accurately. How can those drafting data collection procedures develop systems that collect a sufficient amount of useful information without unduly burdening line officers?

6. Organizations must develop methods to ensure that officers comply while addressing the resistance of individual officers and police unions. Can these two objectives be balanced effectively?

7. Once data are collected, how will they be used? In other words, will organizations be limited to using the data for general analysis and training, or can the information be used to establish blame or for discipline and lawsuits?

8. What would be the most accurate statistical benchmark for analyzing the data?

A Look Inside Four Data Collection Programs

San José, California

The city of San José, located in the heart of Silicon Valley, is the third largest city in California and the eleventh largest in the nation. Geographically, its incorporated area consists of about 177 square miles. It's population is about 920,000 and represents diverse demographics comprised of 36% white, 30.2% Hispanic, 26.9% Asian or Pacific Islander, 3.3% African American, and 3.6% other.[15] In 1999, data revealed that San José conducted approximately 100,000 traffic stops.[16] In the year 2001, the number decreased to 89,889.[17] The independent police auditor Teresa Guerrero-Daley reports that the city of San José recorded about 461 complaints in 2001, a 34% decrease from 694 in 2000. Of those complaints, 143 were related to serious misconduct allegations. The Independent Auditor's 2001 Year End Report found a direct correlation between the number of complaints officers received and the percentage of the San José Police Department their own ethnic group represented. For example, European Americans made up 55% of the force and received 58% of the complaints. Hispanic/Latinos made up 26% of the force and received 31% of the complaints, and Asian Americans comprised 8% of the force and received 9% of the complaints.

In response to racial profiling allegations, San José began a voluntary data collection program in June 1999. The system is based primarily on the use of letter codes, whereby the officer conducting the traffic stop either verbally relays information via radio to a dispatcher or manually types it into a mobile data terminal. There are no written reports or forms used in the data collection process. When relaying the data to a dispatcher, an officer might, for example, use a letter code ("H" for "Hispanic" or "B" for "African American") to identify the race or ethnicity of the driver. In order to avoid asking the driver to identify his or her ethnicity, an officer can essentially guess which predetermined ethnic category the person falls into. Whether the officer guesses incorrectly is not seen as especially significant, as the main objective is to determine whether the person is treated fairly in light of the officer's perception about the driver's race.

In addition to ethic information, officers must convey the age and gender of the driver and the reason for the stop. These variables are reduced to a letter code system in which "V-Victor" indicates a vehicle code violation, "P-Paul" represents a California Penal Code violation, "M-Mary" indicates a municipal code violation, and "B-Boy" represents an all-points bulletin broadcast or description of a suspect or car by another police agency.

When a call is complete, the officer must report the final outcome by assigning it another letter code. For example, "A" indicates an arrest was made, "D" is used if a traffic citation is issued for a hazard, and "H" indicates a courtesy service or assist by the officer, just to name a few. It is estimated that the information takes only about three seconds for an officer to complete in order to clear a call. An officer will not be allowed to clear a call either by dispatch or via the computer until all of the information has been completed.[18]

San José has estimated the cost of implementing this data collection system as relatively low, less than $10,000 including training, training materials, and plastic pocket-sized reference cards to enable officers to identify the appropriate letter codes. This amount does not include other expenses such as the cost of data analysis.

When the system in San José was implemented, some were skeptical, voicing concern that officers would conduct fewer stops to avoid engaging in burdensome data collection. But this has not been the case. In fact, San José reports that stops have increased rather than decreased since the data collection system was put into effect.[19]

Experts credit this positive trend to the development of an extensive training program and, more important, to the assurance given to the officers and the local police union that the data would not be used for discipline or individual performance assessment. Rather, the data are generated for the sole purpose of evaluating the department on a system-wide basis.[20] Presently, the data collection program is used only for traffic stops; however, there is some hope that it will eventually be extended to pedestrian stops as well.

Though San José's data collection system has been praised by some local officials, it has its share of skeptics. Some point to the absence of any systematic mechanism for spot-checking or cross-checking the data. In other words, if no citation resulted, what would prevent an officer from reporting inaccurate data? Others point to the scope of the data collected and suggest that the department identify whether the officer initiated a search during the stop. Partly in response to these concerns, San José indicated in June 2002 that it would soon begin recording whether motorists and/or their vehicles were searched during the traffic stop.

Despite accolades for the data collection process itself, questions remain as to how the data collected are interpreted and reported. On December 17, 1999, the San José Police Department reported on preliminary data collected from July 1, 1999, to September 30, 1999. The data were analyzed by comparing the racial demographics of the San José area with the racial and ethnic origins of those stopped. The following trends were reported:

Race/Ethnicity	San José's Population (%)	Total Vehicle Stops (%)	Variation
African American	5	7	+2.0
Asian	21	16	-5.0
Hispanic	31	43	+12.0
White	43	29	-14.0

The results of later studies supported a similar trend, with statistics remaining largely unchanged:

Race/Ethnicity	San José's Population (%)	Total Vehicle Stops (%)	Variation
African American	3.3	7	+3.7
Asian	26.6	16	-10.6
Hispanic	30.2	41	+10.8
White	36	31	-5.0

In 2001, the San José Police Department reported that of the 89,889 drivers stopped, African Americans and Latinos were stopped at rates higher than their percentage of the city's population.

The San José Police Department defends its statistics by citing various socioeconomic factors for the disparity in the data. Some of the dynamics cited by the department include higher unemployment and poverty rates among certain minority groups, which result in more stops for vehicle maintenance issues.[21] Similar factors have also been linked to an increase in calls to African American and Hispanic communities. These disparities have undoubtedly resulted in more officers per capita patrolling these lower income areas.

Even ACLU attorney Mark Schlosberg is quick to point out that "The data in the report, while interesting and helpful, doesn't...prove one way or the other whether San José Police Department officers engage in racial profiling." Many civil rights advocates who are closely watching the data collection efforts in San José believe the new data pertaining to searches during vehicle stops will be much more definitive, supporting efforts to determine whether racial profiling is occurring in this community.

Some experts remain cautiously optimistic when looking to these data as proof of a trend in traffic enforcement efforts, and they voice concerns that are almost universal about similar programs around the country. For example, some point to statistical flaws inherent in the use of residential population demographics as a benchmark by reasoning that these numbers do not necessarily correlate to the demographics of those traveling on the city's roadways. This is particularly true in San José, whose highways and city streets are traveled by many San Francisco Bay Area commuters who may or may not live in the San José area. Likewise, the residential data do not distinguish residents who are of legal driving age from those who are not. Some have also suggested that although San José's data indicated that blacks and Hispanics were stopped at a rate higher than their representation in the city's population, that was not the case when the data were analyzed by patrol district. As discussed earlier, there are several other factors that were not considered in this study that may account for a disparity in San José's traffic stop data.

Regardless of this trial and error, many experts agree that San José appears to be on the right track in developing a system that is cost effective and relatively simple for the officers to incorporate into the traffic enforcement program. Other agencies will benefit from the lessons learned in San José, particularly that of simplicity and cost effectiveness in a data collection program. Moreover, this system was effectively integrated into the current traffic program with very little burden to officers conducting traffic enforcement activities and has been fairly well received throughout the organization.

San Diego, California

San Diego, California, is the state's second largest city and the nation's seventh. Located at the southwest tip of California about 125 miles from Los Angeles, its population is about one and a quarter million people, who represent a diverse population comprised of 55% white; 26.7% Hispanic; 5.5% African American; 9.1% Non-Hispanic, Asian, Native Hawaiian, or other Pacific Islander; and 0.5% American Indian/Alaskan Native.[22] The police force has approximately 2,683 officers patrolling the San Diego area.[23] Regardless of its reputation for being one of the most lightly policed cities in the nation, San Diego boasts a decrease in crime for 11 successive years from 1989 to 2000 and a 75% decrease in its homicide rate.[24] Some of this success may be a direct result of the city's 1,100 civilian volunteers who donate more than 200,000 hours of service annually to the department.[25]

In 1998, San Diego Police Department initiated more than 200,000 vehicle stops and issued about 125,000 citations.[26] In February 1999, San Diego became the first police department in the nation to record voluntarily the race and ethnicity of the drivers its officers stopped.[27] In order to implement this data collection program, the agency issued each of its 1,300 patrol, traffic, and canine officers a laptop computer to enter the relevant data. These laptop computers provide the officers with flexibility so that the data can be entered either inside or outside of the officer's patrol vehicle. In addition to the laptop computers, San Diego issued its motor patrol units wireless, hand-held computers to collect the data. The importance of including the motor officers in the data collection process could not be underestimated; its motor officers routinely write 50% of all traffic tickets.

Officers are directed to record data from all traffic stops, regardless of whether the stop resulted in a warning or a citation. San Diego's system is more comprehensive than most and requires the collection of 14 data elements:

1. The district in which the stop was conducted;
2. The date and time of the stop;
3. The cause for the stop (moving violation, equipment violation, radio call or citizen complaint, personal observation or knowledge, suspect information from bulletin or log, or municipal/county code violation);
4. The race of the driver (on the basis of officer's perception);
5. The gender of the driver;
6. The age of the driver;
7. The disposition of the stop (citation issued, oral or written warning, field interrogation, or other);
8. Whether there was an arrest;
9. Whether the officer conducted a search;
10. The type of search conducted (vehicle, driver, passengers);
11. The basis for the search (contraband visible, odor of contraband, canine alert, inventory search prior to impound, consent search, Fourth Amendment waiver search, search incident to arrest, observance of evidence related to criminal activity, or other);
12. Whether the officer obtained a consent to search form;
13. Whether contraband was found; and
14. Whether any property was seized.

Upon initiating a traffic stop, the officer is directed to advise the dispatcher by calling in the location of the stop. The officer will generally run the automobile's license plate and obtain the driver's license and vehicle registration from the driver. After reviewing all the information, the officer will return to his or her patrol car to determine the final disposition. For example, the officer may decide to give the driver a verbal warning rather than a citation for the violation. After the officer initiates the final contact with the citizen, he or she will complete the data entry. The data entry must be completed before the officer will be permitted to clear the call and return to service.

San Diego has been successful in overcoming many of the difficulties inherent in establishing a comprehensive data collection program. The cost to implement San Diego's program has been minimal, as the department was able to use a previously installed, in-house data system for data collection purposes. The only expenses reported by the department have been to bring on line two additional computer servers at a cost of about $30,000.[28]

Likewise, the burden on officers to collect the traffic stop data has been nominal, with the task of recording the data via pull-down menus taking only about 20–30 seconds. Interestingly, San Diego does not significantly emphasize traffic enforcement, so disengagement by the officers under the new system was not a major concern. Although traffic stops have decreased by 50% in recent years, San Diego reports that this has nothing to do with the new data collection system. Rather, management has diverted resources to more important enforcement activities within the city.

Despite San Diego's proactive approach to data collection, it has not yet initiated an independent method to check the data's accuracy. San Diego has attempted to implement safeguards to minimize any potential compromise of the traffic stop data. For example, in addition to the data entered on the officer's computer device, officers are required to record the data in a daily journal. Officers are reminded that entering false information is a violation of department policy and may result in disciplinary action.

The data collection efforts in San Diego have been relatively well received by its officers, with only about 10% voicing concerns about the program. Some of the key concerns included whether there would be disciplinary actions associated with the data collection, whether the data collection would discourage officers from conducting stops, and whether officers would be labeled "racists" if the traffic stop data revealed they were stopping too many minority drivers.

Although San Diego's system is more comprehensive than most, experts still point to the lack of information available on the nature and quantity of contraband seized during searches. Additionally, the data collected remain difficult to verify because of the anonymity of the officer and the motorist involved in the stop. Regardless of the these flaws, San Diego appears to be taking concrete steps to ensure that the data collected accurately reflect the enforcement activities. In cooperation with academic partners such as the University of San Diego and San Diego State University, the city analyzes the data by the eight divisions that comprise the department. San Diego is working closely with these academic partners to develop appropriate benchmarks that can be used to analyze the data collected accurately and form useful conclusions about the patterns and practices of its officers. Similar to the San José Police Department, San Diego looks at the data in the context of the whole department rather than using the information to assess the performance of individual officers.

North Carolina

North Carolina, the eleventh most populous state in the country, is comprised of both rural areas and medium-sized metropolises. In the 2000 census, the state reported a population of more than 8 million people, with ratios of 75.6% white, 22.2% black, and 2.2% "other."[29] The North Carolina Highway Patrol serves as the primary law enforcement entity in the state and employs more than 1,400 troopers and a 12-member interdiction team. In 1999, the North Carolina Highway Patrol issued about 737,724 traffic citations. In 2000, that number increased to 780,973. In 2001, about 897,891 "enforcement charges" were reported.

One of the factors prompting the agency to begin data collection was the negative publicity it received in 1996 and 1999 about its traffic stop practices. On July 28, 1996, the Raleigh News and Observer reported that the North Carolina Highway Patrol's drug interdiction team stopped and charged black male drivers at almost twice the rate of other troopers patrolling the same roadways.[30] A similar report appearing in the Raleigh News and Observer in February 1999 revealed that blacks were twice as likely as whites to have their cars searched by the drug interdiction unit.[31]

Partly in response to this negative publicity, State Senator Frank Balance and State Representative Ronnie Sutton joined forces with the ACLU in 1999 to introduce a bill that required state law enforcement officers to begin collecting traffic stop data. North Carolina subsequently became the first state to enact a mandatory data collection program.

North Carolina's collection system is similar to San Diego's in that officers are required to enter traffic stop data into a mobile data terminal. With the use of pull-down menus, officers are required to record the following information:

1. The race/ethnicity of the driver (on the basis of the officer's perception);
2. The age of the driver;
3. The gender of the driver;
4. The reason for the stop;
5. The type of enforcement action taken as a result of the stop;
6. Whether any physical resistance by the driver is encountered; and
7. Whether a search is conducted.

If a search is conducted, the trooper must record the type of search; the basis for the search; whether the vehicle, driver, or passengers were searched; the race, ethnicity, and gender of those searched; and a description of any contraband found or property seized. Undoubtedly, this system can be credited with being one of the most comprehensive employed to date.

Data collection efforts in North Carolina have been met with little criticism, as their comprehensive scope alleviates many of the concerns encountered in similar data collection programs. Even though the scope of the data collected far exceeds that of other agencies, North Carolina reports that the electronic form takes less than five minutes to complete. Estimates suggest that the system cost North Carolina about $50,000 to implement, including the cost of new computers, hardware, and software. Not included in this estimate is the cost of equipping each vehicle with a mobile data terminal, which is about $8,000 per unit. Although these systems play an integral role in the data collection process, they are also used for other purposes. Because the previous data collection system recorded only the number of written citations and warnings, it is unclear whether officers have reduced enforcement efforts under the new system.

Similar to other data collection programs, North Carolina has no immediate plans to audit or verify any of the data collected, nor is the officer's identification number recorded. Although most officers have responded favorably to the program, some have been insulted by the "big brother" approach to law enforcement. Most of the internal resistance has been effectively countered with comprehensive training workshops that emphasize the use of data to measure the organization's overall performance as opposed to initiating officer discipline.

The future prospects for reporting and analyzing the data collected in North Carolina look hopeful. The Highway Patrol is working closely with the Center of Crime and Justice Research at North Carolina State University to identify a statistical benchmark with which to analyze the data. Preliminary figures released by the Highway Patrol in January 2000 indicated that black motorists were stopped in proportion to their representation in the state's population.[32] It was also revealed, however, that black motorists were more likely to be searched and arrested compared with other ethnicities within the state.

It is important to remember that even the most comprehensive data collection systems make it difficult or impossible to ascertain an officer's ultimate motivation for a traffic stop. The programs currently in use revolve largely around a rigid number-gathering system that often fails to provide an adequate context for the stop. In an effort to correct this problem, some experts suggest that agencies install cameras in patrol units that would serve as a valuable supplement to even the most sophisticated data collection systems.

Despite its ongoing challenges, North Carolina should be praised for its proactive approach to mandating data collection across the state. Although no system is perfect, its widespread approach is a positive starting point that exhibits to the public and to other agencies that data collection and racial profiling are important issues to the law enforcement community.

New Jersey

New Jersey is a diverse eastern state consisting of medium-sized cities and rural areas. According to the 2000 census, New Jersey's population comprises about 8.5 million people.[33] Despite its rank as the eighth most populous state, it is one of the most densely populated states, the fifth smallest in the nation. The U.S. Census Bureau reported that in 2000, the state's demographics consisted of about 72.6% white, 13.6% African American, 5.7% Asian, 0.2% American Indian/Alaskan Native, and 5.4% other. The state's primary law enforcement agency is the New Jersey State Police, which employs nearly 2,800 state troopers. Fourteen percent of the New Jersey State Police are minorities, and 3% are women.

The problems faced by the New Jersey State Police relative to racial profiling have been significant. One report revealed that in a review of two selected months in 1997, three out of four motorists arrested on the New Jersey turnpike were minorities.[34] Later that year, additional studies revealed that four out of five motorists arrested were minorities.[35] To complicate the matter further, the then–New Jersey superintendent made a public statement and explained: "The drug problem is cocaine or marijuana. It is most likely a minority group that is involved with that."[36] Shortly thereafter, he was fired.

These high-profile practices on New Jersey's highways resulted in a federal investigation of the allegations and ultimately forced the state into a consent decree with the U.S. Department of Justice to collect and monitor traffic stop data. Many point to these problems in New Jersey as a major contributing factor in the increased public awareness of the racial profiling problem in law enforcement.

The resulting data collection system the state implemented in May 2000 is under close scrutiny by the federal government. It's used primarily by state troopers engaged in patrol activities within the state and does not include pedestrian stops.[37] By using the existing computer aided dispatch system (CAD), officers must report the following information to the CAD officer:

1. The name and ID number of all the troopers who actively participated in the traffic stop;
2. The location, date, and time the stop commenced and ended;
3. The license plate number and state of vehicle registration;
4. A description of the vehicle;
5. The gender, race (on the basis of trooper's perception), ethnicity, and date of birth of the driver, if known;
6. The gender, race, and ethnicity of any passengers;
7. Whether the driver was issued a summons or warning;
8. The category of the violation (moving violation or non-moving violation); and
9. The reason for the stop (moving violation or probable cause).

The consent decree also specifies that if practical, an officer engaging in a traffic stop should first place a call to the communication center before approaching the vehicle. This will allow CAD officers to input the appropriate data into the system at the time of each stop. New Jersey is working toward installing laptops in all patrol cars so that officers can enter this information directly. If the trooper chooses to initiate a search of the vehicle, the consent decree specifies that the officer should first advise the communication center of his or her intention to do so.

If any post stop enforcement action is necessary, a trooper must complete a Motor Vehicle Stop Report. This form specifies the occupant's race, gender, and date of birth and is used any time an officer orders an occupant out of his or her vehicle, requests a consent search, conducts a search, requests a drug detection canine, frisks an occupant, makes an arrest, recovers contraband or other property, or uses force.

In addition to the detailed data officers must collect after each stop, the encounters are tracked via an incident number. These numbers can be useful for future tracking and auditing by the organization or the government.

Unlike the voluntary data collection systems discussed previously, New Jersey's mandatory program directed by the consent decree has placed a significant financial burden on the agency. For example, modifications to the existing CAD system cost the state about $130,000. Nearly $1.43 million was spent on officer training, and $12.581 million was budgeted to install mobile video recorders and mobile data computers in each patrol vehicle.

New Jersey is also unique in that the implementation of the data collection system correlated with a dramatic drop in patrol-related arrests, according to the New Jersey Attorney General's Office. The reasons for this drop are under review.

Also unique to New Jersey are the stringent processes in place for data analysis and review. Internally, supervisors are required to review post stop enforcement actions and videotapes to ensure officers are conducting traffic stops properly within department guidelines. In addition to this internal check-and-balance system, the Department of Justice directives contained in the consent decree establish that the Attorney General remain responsible for conducting an audit of the data. In conjunction with the internal review of videotapes and reports, the Attorney General's office must conduct a random sampling of persons who were stopped by state troopers to assess the accuracy of the data reported and to determine whether the trooper acted appropriately.[38]

Unfortunately, New Jersey's data collection program has come with a high emotional price tag for the officers in the state. One of the primary concerns state troopers expressed involves the publication of traffic stop data. Bad press often leads to allegations of racism and increases the potential danger for those officers involved in traffic enforcement. Unlike other agencies in which voluntary data collection statistics are monitored on the basis of the entire organization, the Attorney General in New Jersey can monitor agency-wide problems and identify suspicious patterns of individual officers. Regardless of this reporting system, the Attorney General indicated in an interview that these numbers alone will not lead to disciplinary action. "What we tried to move away from with the Justice Department was the idea that numbers alone dictate results," he said. "If it were the case that an officer had some proportion of a certain kind of stops, that would not trigger a conclusion of any kind, rather, it would trigger further investigation. So the numbers don't dictate results; they raise a red flag that we then pursue to see if there is a problem."[39]

The problems faced in New Jersey may exemplify a police agency experiencing system-wide problems as opposed to problems with a few officers. Experts believe that certain patterns and practices from the past may have inadvertently helped to create an environment conducive to profiling within the department. For example, officers were awarded the Officer of the Year on the basis of the highest number of arrests as opposed to looking at the quality of arrests made. Additionally, ineffective stop and search practices have been documented throughout the state, and they represent a "find" rate of only 10% that did not vary among races. In 1999, nearly 500 seizures by New Jersey law enforcement netted only $60,000 in contraband.[40]

Lessons Learned

These data collection programs represent a small sampling of the data collection efforts taking place nationwide. A review of these particular programs was included so that other organizations can use the lessons learned as a guide to implement similar programs. Though specific recommendations relating to data collection as a solution to racial profiling will be addressed in a later chapter, these examples are important in that they demonstrate that data collection can be integrated into current traffic stop programs for little added cost and effort. More important, these programs have shown that the real work may actually begin after the data are collected.

(Endnotes)

1. McMahon, Joyce, Joel Garner, Ronald Davis, and Amanda Kraus, "How to Correctly Collect and Analyze Racial Profiling Data: Your Reputation Depends On It, Final Report for: Racial Profiling – Data Collection and Analysis," at 23. (Washington, DC: Government Printing Office, 2002).

2. McMahon, Joyce, Joel Garner, Ronald Davis, and Amanda Kraus, "How to Correctly Collect and Analyze Racial Profiling Data: Your Reputation Depends On It, Final Report for: Racial Profiling – Data Collection and Analysis," at 23. (Washington, DC: Government Printing Office, 2002).

3. McMahon, Joyce, Joel Garner, Ronald Davis, and Amanda Kraus, "How to Correctly Collect and Analyze Racial Profiling Data: Your Reputation Depends On It, Final Report for: Racial Profiling – Data Collection and Analysis," at 31. (Washington, DC: Government Printing Office, 2002).

4. McMahon, Joyce, Joel Garner, Ronald Davis, and Amanda Kraus, "How to Correctly Collect and Analyze Racial Profiling Data: Your Reputation Depends On It, Final Report for: Racial Profiling – Data Collection and Analysis," at 31. (Washington, DC: Government Printing Office, 2002).

5. Farrell, Dr. Amy, Dean Jack McDevitt, Shea Cronin, Erica Pierce, "Rhode Island Traffic Stop Statistics Act Final Report," at 6-7, June 30, 2003 (Northeastern University).

6. Farrell, Dr. Amy, Dean Jack McDevitt, Shea Cronin, Erica Pierce, "Rhode Island Traffic Stop Statistics Act Final Report," at 6, June 30, 2003 (Northeastern University).

7. Farrell, Dr. Amy, Dean Jack McDevitt, Shea Cronin, Erica Pierce, "Rhode Island Traffic Stop Statistics Act Final Report," at 6, June 30, 2003 (Northeastern University).

8. Farrell, Dr. Amy, Dean Jack McDevitt, Shea Cronin, Erica Pierce, "Rhode Island Traffic Stop Statistics Act Final Report," at 6, June 30, 2003 (Northeastern University).

9. Farrell, Dr. Amy, Dean Jack McDevitt, Shea Cronin, Erica Pierce, "Rhode Island Traffic Stop Statistics Act Final Report" at 10, June 30, 2003 (Northeastern University, Institute on Race and Justice).

10. Farrell, Dr. Amy, Dean Jack McDevitt, Shea Cronin, Erica Pierce, "Rhode Island Traffic Stop Statistics Act Final Report" at 10, June 30, 2003 (Northeastern University, Institute on Race and Justice), citing Sacramento Second Annual Report, 2002, Los Angeles Police Report to Monitor, 2002.

11. Farrell, Dr. Amy, Dean Jack McDevitt, Shea Cronin, Erica Pierce, "Rhode Island Traffic Stop Statistics Act Final Report" at 36, June 30, 2003 (Northeastern University, Institute on Race and Justice).

12. Farrell, Dr. Amy, Dean Jack McDevitt, Shea Cronin, Erica Pierce, "Rhode Island Traffic Stop Statistics Act Final Report" at Appendix 4, June 30, 2003 (Northeastern University, Institute on Race and Justice).

13. Farrell, Dr. Amy, Dean Jack McDevitt, Shea Cronin, Erica Pierce, "Rhode Island Traffic Stop Statistics Act Final Report" at 16, June 30, 2003 (Northeastern University, Institute on Race and Justice). In Rhode Island, the most common cited legal basis for traffic stops was speeding (48.6%).

14. Ramirez, Deborah, Jack McDevitt, Dr. Amy Farrell, "A Resource Guide on Racial Profiling Data Collection Systems. Promising Practices and Lessons Learned," (November, 2000).

15. 2000 U.S. Census Report.

16. Lynem, Julie "San José Police Study: Race in Arrest Patterns," San Francisco Chronicle, March 25, 1999.

17. City of San José Office of Independent Police Auditor Annual Report.

18. San José's analysis of its data collection revealed that many calls were cleared with incomplete information. Sometimes, this information was lacking when special enforcement activities were being conducted, for example, radar patrols.

19. Lynem, Julie, "San José Police Study: Race in Arrest Patterns," San Francisco Chronicle, March 25, 1999.

20. It should be noted that the officer's name, the date and the time are recorded along with the other required information. Although this information is potentially available to the department, it is not presently collected and analyzed.

21. It should be noted that the overwhelming majority of the stops conducted were for speeding violations, as opposed to equipment failures or vehicle code violations.

22. 2000 U.S. Census Report.

23. San Diego Police Department, Budget and Personnel, 1999.

24. San Diego Police Department, Historical Crime Rates, 1950-1999.

25. Will, George, "Takes More Than Good Policing to Cut Crime," Houston Chronicle, August 23, 1999 at A18.

26. Bejarano, David, "Racial Profiling: The San Diego Police Department's Response," Internal Memo, Chief of Police, San Diego Police Department, November 9, 1999.

27. Stetz, Michael and Kelly Thornton, "Cops to Collect Traffic Stop Racial Data," San Diego Union Tribune, February 5, 1999 at A1.

28. Stetz, Michael and Kelly Thornton, "Cops to Collect Traffic Stop Racial Data," San Diego Union Tribune, February 5, 1999 at A1.

29. North Carolina Office of State Planning, State Demographics, 1997.

30. Neff, Joseph and Pat Smith, "Highway Drug Unit Focuses on Blacks," Raleigh News and Observer, July 28, 1996 at A1.

31. Neff, Joseph, "Who's Being Stopped?" Raleigh News and Observer, February 19, 1999 at A2.

32. Jarvis, Craig, "Spotlight on Stops," Raleigh News and Observer, March 9, 2000 at A16. Jarvis, Craig, "Traffic Stops Aren't Linked to Race, First Report Shows," Raleigh News and Observer, March 3, 2000 at A3.

33. Actual number is 8,414,350 as reported by U.S. Bureau of the Census for New Jersey, 2000.

34. Raphel, Michael and Kathy Barrett Calter, "State Police Reveal 75% of Arrests Along Turnpike were of Minorities," Star-Ledger, February 10, 1999.

35. Raphel, Michael and Joe Donahue, "Turnpike Arrests 73% Minority," Star-Ledger, April 8, 1999, at News 01.

36. Donahue, Joe, "Trooper Boss: Race Plays Role in Drug Crimes," Star-Ledger, February 28, 1999 at News 01.

37. Consent Decree, see note 25 at 29-33.

38. Joint Application for Entry of Consent Decree, see note 85, at section 110.

39. Ramirez, Deborah, Jack McDevitt, Amy Farrell, "A Resource Guide on Racial Profiling Data Collection Systems. Promising Practices and Lessons Learned," (November, 2000). (Interview with John Farmer, as recounted by authors of report.)

40. Ramirez, Deborah, Jack McDevitt, Amy Farrell, "A Resource Guide on Racial Profiling Data Collection Systems. Promising Practices and Lessons Learned," (November, 2000).

CHAPTER TWELVE

Call to Action

"The struggle is grander but more microscopic."

—ABC News Anchor Peter Jennings[1]

Mounting public pressure and media attention have forced many law enforcement agencies to take a stand on racial profiling. Whether in the form of data collection systems or the implementation of new policies and practices, the issue of racial profiling has affected virtually every law enforcement agency to some extent. While it is impossible to calculate the exact progress toward eradication of the practice, there have been some notable improvements in the relationship between law enforcement and the public due in part to the joint efforts toward change.

One area of measurable progress is the decline in the use of violence by law enforcement toward those in minority communities. Justice Department statistics report that the number of African Americans killed by police since 1976 has decreased by more than half, from a rate of about 11 per million to 5 per million. Although even one death is too many, the trend suggests that law enforcement agencies are becoming more educated and aware about the use of force against suspects and consequently more cautious and accountable than they have ever been.

Though some of these improvements can be attributed to positive changes within the very culture of law enforcement, others may be a direct result of recruiting and hiring practices. From 1990 to 2000, large cities serving 250,000 or more residents reported an increase in the representation of Hispanic officers from 9% to 14%, blacks from 18% to 20%, and women from 12% to 16%. Likewise, the percentage of agencies requiring new officers to have at least some college rose from 19% to 37%, and the percentage requiring a two- or four-year degree increased from 6% to 14%.

Despite these promising statistics, some organizations still have not done enough. For those agencies unwilling to police themselves, accountability has been but a stone's throw away, with the federal government becoming more vigilant about overseeing police agencies than it has been historically. As of November 15, 2000, the Department of Justice initiated 14 ongoing "pattern and practice" investigations involving racial profiling allegations. In addition, it filed five "pattern and practice" lawsuits, with four of the cases being resolved by consent decrees. In conjunction with these efforts, lawmakers are drafting and enacting state and national legislation to address the problem, including new enforcement standards and training mandates for officers around the nation.

Within the shadow of these larger triumphs are others that deserve equal praise. In addition to supporting racial profiling legislation and working with law enforcement to improve the quality of community relations, civil rights organizations and special interest groups around the nation are vigorously campaigning to end racially biased policing. One such group is the ACLU, whose nationwide campaign has been instrumental in bringing this issue to the forefront. In addition to the release of a major public policy report outlining the problem,[2] the ACLU has been a driving force in support of anti profiling legislation in more than 20 states. The ACLU has also reached out to minority communities by launching local and national hotlines for alleged victims to report acts of racial profiling.[3] As a mouthpiece for those who may not ordinarily feel secure in asserting their own rights, groups such as the ACLU have stepped forward to ensure that those who feel they have been victimized have their day in court. More important, these groups continue to form valuable alliances with community groups and law enforcement agencies to develop new policies and procedures and to initiate programs for collecting and reporting traffic stop data.

In an effort to reach out to those most likely to have negative encounters with law enforcement, the ACLU remains an important resource for minority communities, particularly with regard to its nationwide public awareness and education campaign. To bring attention to the problem, for example, the ACLU distributed 50,000 "Driving While Black or Brown" kits to attendees of the McDonald's Heritage Bowl (also known as the "Black College Super Bowl") in Atlanta. These resource kits included information on what to do if you're stopped by the police, stickers with the ACLU's toll-free national hotline number to report pretext stops,[4] sample letters to Congress urging support for bills that would end racial profiling, and a summary of national and state efforts to combat the problem.[5]

Another component of this broad-based educational campaign is the placement of informative ads targeted at minority groups. Public service radio announcements are broadcast nationwide in both English and Spanish, and they urge victims of racial profiling to call in to report their experiences with police. The ACLU of Southern California has generated materials for the Asian American community in six different languages. ACLU wallet cards entitled "What to Do in a Police Encounter" are being distributed nationwide in at least seven different languages.

The ACLU reports that its concentrated efforts in the past few years are paying off:

- Officials in Eagle County, Colorado, paid a settlement of $800,000 to 402 black and Latino defendants who were stopped along Interstate 70 because they fit a "drug courier profile." This settlement was the result of a class-action lawsuit filed on behalf of defendants by the ACLU and included a provision that prohibits the police from stopping, seizing, or searching a person "unless there is some objective, reasonable suspicion that the person has done something wrong."[6]

- The state of Rhode Island passed the Traffic Stops Statistics Act on July 13, 2000, in part to explore whether minorities are unfairly targeted by the police on the local interstate. Data collection of all routine traffic stops made by the Rhode Island State Police and all municipal police departments began on January 15, 2001. To evaluate the data, the Act designated the formation of a Traffic Stop Study Advisory Committee to assist with the analysis and interpretation of the data. On June 30, 2003, a final report was issued, entitled "Rhode Island Traffic Stop Study" that incorporated new and existing theories about data collection and methods for establishing benchmarks to measure raw data derived from these collection efforts.

- In Oregon, leaders of the State Police, in conjunction with 23 Portland-area police departments and police alliances, took a forceful stand against race-based profiling by signing a resolution designed to ensure the community that this type of policing would not be tolerated. LeRon Howland, the former Oregon State Police Superintendent, assured the public, "If you have a police officer out there who uses his badge for racially motivated conduct, it will not be tolerated by police agencies or the leadership of the unions."[7]

- The governor of North Carolina signed into law a bill requiring data collection on all traffic stops. It was the first law anywhere in the nation to require officers to compile data portraying a detailed, statistical picture of the use of traffic stops.

- In June 1999, *Emerge*, a popular magazine for black audiences, ran a cover story on the problem of DWB. In response to an ACLU full-page ad in this issue, a lawsuit was filed in Oklahoma on behalf of a black Army officer.

Although this battle has become very personal for the ACLU, it is not fighting it alone. Joining its efforts are other prominent civil rights groups and police organizations, including the NCLR,[8] the NAACP,[9] the National Black Police Association, the National Organization of Black Law Enforcement Executives (NOBLE), the Hispanic American Police Command Officer's Association, CopWatch, and the National Latino Peace

Officer's Association.[10] More recently, the ACLU teamed up with the three largest organizations representing Hispanic law enforcement officials to fight improper police practices. The National Council of La Raza, the Hispanic American Police Command Officer's Association, and the National Latino Peace Officer's Association characterized the partnership as "another powerful blow against racial profiling."[11]

In addition to these notable efforts by civil rights groups, other organizations are likewise joining the fight to end racial profiling. One of the groups leading this effort is the Police Foundation of Washington, D.C., one of the five leading law enforcement organizations implementing community policing for the Justice Department. For more than 30 years, this group's research and training have helped to upgrade the level of police services in the nation through studies and reports, conferences, seminars, technical support, and training.

The Police Foundation's president, Hubert Williams, regards data collection as a first step, with the acknowledgment that "Data analysis, progressive policies, and monitoring systems to prevent and deter abuse are necessary." Toward this end, Mr. Williams is guiding his organization in the development of software to be used in conjunction with training and monitoring systems. He hopes that these efforts will contribute to the implementation of a clear and concise strategy that provides for early intervention.[12]

Other notable entities involved in similar endeavors are the Police Executive Research Forum (PERF) and the U.S. Department of Justice Office of Community Oriented Policing Services (COPS), which both provide research and guidance to several data collection endeavors nationwide. In addition, the International Association of Chiefs of Police (IACP), the National Sheriff's Association, along with some state-based entities such as the California Organization of Police and Sheriffs (COPS) and the Peace Officer Research Association of California (PORAC), which together represent 650 law enforcement associations and 45,000 officers around the state, are working hard to address many of the ongoing challenges posed by racial profiling.

These groups can be praised for their collaborative efforts with law enforcement to implement proactive measures for investigating and addressing racial profiling allegations. These joint endeavors have encouraged cities and states nationwide to implement policies designed to improve relations between the police and the community.

- Minnesota, a state that has ranked among the worst in disparities between blacks and whites in arrests and incarcerations, is gathering data for potential use in future legislation addressing the issue. In an attempt to study whether racial profiling is happening in the state, police departments in St. Paul and Minneapolis became the first to track the race of motorists stopped and set a precedent for a handful of other cities nationwide.

- In Massachusetts, the State Police will join Boston Police in collecting traffic stop data to determine whether racial profiling is an issue in the state. The decision to collect data came just one week after a meeting of the Massachusetts Chiefs of Police Association vote to add anti-racial profiling training to the police academy curriculum. The chiefs also issued a statement acknowledging that "[T]he first and most important step in addressing the issue of racial profiling in traffic stops is to acknowledge that a problem exists...[T]he use of racial or ethnic stereotypes has no place in law enforcement."[13]

- San Francisco is the 34th city in California to collect racial data on police traffic stops voluntarily. In response to the growing controversy over racial profiling and the urgings of local ACLU officials, San Francisco officers will be required to fill out a four-question form after each traffic stop. Officers will identify the driver's race, the basis for the stop, whether the vehicle was searched, and whether the driver was cited or arrested. Officer Sherman Ackerson, a San Francisco police spokesman, told the *San Francisco Chronicle* that any sort of racial profiling is not tolerated by the department and cited the agency's general orders that specifically prohibit officers from making race-based traffic stops. "We feel comfortable that our officers are acting properly," he said.[14]

In a 2003 interview with CHP command staff, the CHP emphasized the importance of data collection as a means of evaluating each officer's stops—a practice that has long been the standard in the organization. Similar to other data collection efforts underway, the CHP has implemented a voluntary tracking program aimed at identifying the race of the driver (or person in control of a vehicle) in any public encounter.

To ensure the accuracy of the data derived from its collection program, the CHP has devised an internal check-and-balance system so that each public contact can be examined on an individual basis. By its own initiative, the CHP holds supervisors accountable for their officers' actions on the roadway. This internal mandate has been carried out successfully by requiring supervisors to review each officer's activity and data collection logs each day to identify any areas that might be cause for concern. The officer and the supervisor attest to these daily logs under penalty of perjury before submitting them to the command staff for further review.

In addition to compiling traffic stop statistics, CHP Commissioner Helmick has taken a vocal stand on the issue and has assured the public that the CHP has never condoned racial profiling by citing the CHP's long-standing policies and practices specifically prohibiting this activity. "It is the policy of the CHP to treat every citizen equally, and we will continue to maintain this approach," he explained. "If the data shows any variance from this standard, we will take immediate action to rectify it."[15]

In addition to undertaking proactive steps to combat racial profiling within its own organization, the CHP has been instrumental in encouraging other agencies around the state of California to collect traffic stop data voluntarily.[16]

Despite the combined efforts of law enforcement, civil rights groups, and community leaders to end racial profiling, the public remains cautious in its optimism.

A letter signed by the ACLU, the Hispanic American Police Command Officers Association, the National Association for the Advancement of Colored People, and a number of other civil rights organizations was unequivocal: "As many law enforcement organizations and public officials have come to recognize, it is not enough just to be 'against' racism and racial profiling. Concrete steps must be taken to identify where discriminatory practices exist and to root them out. No branch of government can be blind or passive with respect to discriminatory police practices."[17]

While civil rights advocates are generally pleased with law enforcement's cooperation, some have characterized the efforts as modest steps toward dealing with the problem. Though few view data collection as the panacea for ending racial profiling, many believe that such efforts will help agencies better identify the number of people being pulled over by police and monitor how they are treated afterward.[18]

Despite the aggressive measures implemented at local and state levels, no campaign would be complete without the involvement of the U.S. Justice Department, whose efforts to eradicate racial profiling remain in the national spotlight. Though some local police agencies have not openly welcomed involvement by the federal government, one cannot ignore the fact that its involvement has motivated many to take a stand against racially biased law enforcement practices.

- In December 1999, the state of New Jersey and its Division of State Police entered into a comprehensive settlement with the U.S. Justice Department.[19] This settlement included the appointment of an independent monitor to ensure that racial profiling by state troopers will cease. The decree provided that "State troopers may not rely to any degree on the race or national or ethnic origin of motorists in selecting vehicles for traffic stops and in deciding upon the scope and substance of post-stop actions, except where state troopers are on the lookout for a specific suspect who has been identified in part by his or her race or national or ethnic origin." Additionally, the decree requires that any request by State Troopers to search a motorist's vehicle be limited to situations in which they have reasonable suspicion that the search will reveal evidence of a crime.

- In an effort to comply with a U.S. Department of Justice consent decree, the Los Angeles Police Department has begun to collect data to determine whether officers are engaging in racial profiling. In addition, the department is installing a computer system to track performance evaluations, complaints, disciplinary actions, and other data on police personnel.

- In April 2002, a year after the Cincinnati Police Department became the target of racial protests and street violence following the fatal shooting of a young black man, an agreement was reached to implement new tactics for the police to deal with the public. The settlement proposal included the appointment of a court-sanctioned monitor to oversee the proposed changes in police training and patrolling. This unusual collaborative effort between police union negotiators and civil rights groups was also overseen by the federal court and served as a preferable alternative to full-scale litigation.

In addition to efforts by the federal government, members of the legal community and judiciary are emerging as strong advocates in the fight to increase minority presence in the courtroom. Some of these efforts include rallying support for affirmative action in law school admissions so that more minority judges will be available in an increasingly diverse population.

One high-profile advocate of increasing the minority presence in the courtroom is Superior Court Judge Lance Ito,[20] who has been working for the past several years to integrate more interpreters into the courts for the benefit of minority defendants.

Likewise, the court system is sending a strong message to officers that engage in racially motivated encounters with citizens.

A federal appeals court upheld a $245,000 damage award to three young men who were stopped by Torrance, California, police.[21] The three 17-year-old boys, two black and one white, had graduated from an elite private high school earlier in the day and were driving home from a movie when they were stopped and harassed by Torrance police officers. The youths were ordered out at gunpoint, subjected to pat down searches that included squeezing one of the boys' genitals, and ultimately had their car searched. When the search turned up nothing, the boys were ticketed for nonworking turn signals and seat belt violations. The white passenger was asked whether he knew the two black men. Unfortunately for the officers, the youths' parents included a Los Angeles assistant city attorney, a partner in a major law firm, and a probation officer.

Contrary to the images portrayed in the media, the public must be reassured that the fight to end racial profiling and biased policing in law enforcement is a battle fought by many. It is not limited to the efforts of civil rights advocates or victims. Rather, it has become one of the highest priorities for many law enforcement entities across the country. People of all walks of life and all colors and creeds are joining the fight by working with law enforcement, the Justice Department, and the legal community in true partnerships to foster better relationships between the police and the public. Despite the progress made to eliminate racial profiling in law enforcement, the fight to end this practice remains just one small battle in the war to end racism in America.

A National Campaign

"[Racial profiling is] a form of race discrimination and should be treated as such. Congress needs to enact legislation with strict penalties."

—Judge Greg Mathias[22]

The national campaign to end racial profiling is a slippery slope, at best. On one side of the spectrum are civil rights groups and victims demanding changes to law enforcement practices and procedures that are often contrary to the desires of police unions and sometimes contrary to the law itself as it relates to police discretion. On the other side are law enforcement organizations that are seemingly fighting an uphill battle to eradicate any sign of biased policing within their ranks. Even with aggressive recruiting campaigns in place to increase minority representation in law enforcement, administrators are compelled to balance these objectives with the need to maintain safe staffing levels and keep crime rates down.

This tenuous balancing act is not limited to those in law enforcement. Caught in the middle of this tug of war are politicians who cannot afford to abandon police organizations that have supported them politically yet who are under growing pressure to acknowledge widespread racial profiling publicly and to implement and support legislation to correct it. These lawmakers also recognize the need to avoid taking a stance that could alienate minority supporters and other politically powerful groups such as the Rainbow Coalition and the NAACP. In more extreme cases, some lawmakers have preferred to remain in the dark, with some even questioning the need to gather "Driving While Black" statistics, which might suggest that preliminary statistics were overblown.[23]

Regardless of its critics, the public has demanded that politicians take a stand on racial profiling and introduce legislation to address the problem. In an ambitious effort to answer the public's calls for action, a flurry of legislation has been introduced in the House of Representatives and the Senate to address the problem on a national level. One of the first pieces of legislation was introduced on April 15, 1999, entitled the "Traffic Stops Statistics Study Act of 1999."[24]

The bill provided, in part, that the Attorney General conduct a nationwide study of stops for traffic violations by law enforcement officers. This study was designed to comprise an initial analysis of existing data, including, but not limited to, complaints alleging traffic stops motivated by race and other bias. At the completion of the initial analysis, the bill directed the Attorney General to gather more specific data relating to traffic stops from a nationwide sample of jurisdictions, particularly jurisdictions that were identified in the initial analysis. The specific data sought included:

1. The traffic infraction alleged to have been committed that led to the stop;
2. Characteristics of the driver stopped, including the race, gender, ethnicity, and approximate age of the driver;
3. Whether immigration status was questioned and immigration documents requested or an inquiry was made to the Immigration and Naturalization Service with regard to any person in the vehicle;
4. The number of individuals in the stopped vehicle;
5. Whether a search was instituted as a result of the stop and whether consent was requested for the search;

6. Any alleged criminal behavior by the driver that justified the search;
7. Any items seized, including contraband or money;
8. Whether any warning or citation was issued as a result of the stop;
9. Whether an arrest was made as a result of either the stop or the search and the justification for the arrest; and
10. The duration of the stop.

Once compiled, the data were to be reported to Congress and the resulting report made available to the public.

This proposed legislation provided for a grant program that allowed law enforcement agencies participating in the study to receive federal grant money to support their data collection efforts.

Finally, the bill ensured anonymity for any officers or motorists involved in a traffic stop.

Though the U.S. House of Representatives and the Senate were under increasing pressure to adopt this legislation, the bill was criticized for placing an unnecessary burden on law enforcement that would result in the collection of random, inaccurate data that would not adequately address the problem.

One of the main criticisms of the proposed legislation related to the anonymity requirement for the officer conducting the stop as well as the driver of the vehicle. Although this was certainly a "safe" approach designed to gain the support of police unions, the obvious downside was that the data were subject to the honesty and integrity of the officer reporting the incident. The measure provided no way to track whether the data provided to the Attorney General was accurate and complete or totally fabricated in an effort to report favorable statistics in a given jurisdiction.

Say it won't happen? Think again. Dishonesty frequently wins out over integrity when reputation or money is at stake, even in the noblest professions. We've seen it happen in the case of teachers caught falsifying test results and providing students with answers to tests so that their schools receive higher government rankings. Often, these rankings correlated to the receipt of personal bonuses. The same is true in other professions, where honor-based systems and self-policing just don't hold up against temptation and human frailty.

With lucrative government grants at stake, the risk of dishonesty in data reporting remains a concern. For any system to be successful, organizations must be held accountable for turning in accurate data. In order for an honest, productive evaluation to result from the data collected, checks and balances must be implemented to ensure that the data are truthful. Whether these checks and balances can be inherent in a collection system that guarantees anonymity is unclear; however, without some reliable and systematic approach, the likely result will be "garbage in, garbage out."

Regardless of these criticisms, the Traffic Stop Statistics Study Act of 1999 served as a springboard for law enforcement agencies nationwide to initiate traffic stop data collection programs that mirrored this proposed legislation and to do so voluntarily.

These early attempts at national legislation also led to other legislative proposals such as the End Racial Profiling Act of 2001, introduced to Congress on June 6,

2001,[25] and the Racial Profiling Prohibition Act of 2001.[26]

As introduced, the End Racial Profiling Act of 2001 was among the most comprehensive bills. Acknowledging racial profiling as a real and measurable phenomenon, the bill prohibited the use of racial profiling by any law enforcement agency. It provided that either the United States or a racial profiling victim may file suit in either a state or U.S. District Court against: (1) the governmental unit that employed the law enforcement agent who engaged in racial profiling, (2) any agent of such unit who engaged in racial profiling, and (3) any person with supervisory authority over such agent. The bill also mandated agencies to collect data on routine investigatory activities and report such data to the Attorney General.

The bill also sought to require agencies to implement independent procedures for receiving, investigating, and responding to complaints alleging racial profiling by law enforcement agents. Certification that such policies were in place would be required for any agency seeking grants from the government. The bill sought to establish grant money to fund: (1) officer training, (2) technology to facilitate data collection, (3) the improvement of early warning systems, (4) the development of procedures for receiving, investigating, and responding to complaints, and (5) the establishment and improvement of management systems to ensure that supervisors are held accountable for the conduct of their subordinates. Unlike its predecessor, this bill was received favorably by law enforcement and both Republican and Democratic government leaders.

The other bill, the Racial Profiling Prohibition Act of 2001, specifically sought to require states to adopt and enforce standards prohibiting the use of racial profiling when enforcing state laws regulating the use of Federal-aid highways. Specifically, the bill mandated a withholding of apportionments ranging from 5% to 10% for any states not meeting the specified requirements by a given date. These requirements included "allowing a public inspection of statistical information on each motor vehicle stop made by a law enforcement officer on a Federal-aid highway in the State."

As a natural complement to these important pieces of legislation, another bill was introduced on April 11, 2002, entitled the Racial Profiling Education and Awareness Act of 2002. Introduced in the Senate by Senators Voinovich and Dewine, the bill was read and referred to the Committee on the Judiciary. As drafted, the bill authorizes the Attorney General to carry out a racial profiling education and awareness program within the Department of Justice and to assist state and local law enforcement agencies in implementing similar programs.

If such legislation is enacted, it will in large part represent what civil rights organizations and minorities have been waiting for. Although such legislation is promising, it will be interesting to watch the progression of such proposals in the wake of future terrorist threats and see how the government will balance its "no racial profiling" policy with the need for national security.

These multiple and sometimes conflicting challenges make it even more certain that legislators and the public must tread cautiously toward legislation to address this national problem. A bad solution may be far worse than no solution at all.

(Endnotes)

1. Interview with Peter Jennings, Live With Regis and Kathy Lee (January 17, 2000).

2. Harris, David A., ACLU Special Report, "Driving While Black, Racial Profiling on Our Nation's Highways" (June 1999).

3. National Hotline Number: 1-877-6-PROFILE; California Hotline Number: 1-877-DWB-STOP.

4. National Hotline Number: 1-877-6-PROFILE

5. "ACLU to Distribute 50,000 Racial Profiling Resource Kits at Black College Super Bowl," (December 14, 1999), ACLU Press Release.

6. Harris, David A., ACLU Special Report, "Driving While Black, Racial Profiling on Our Nation's Highways" (June 1999). (Citing story reported in Rocky Mountain News.)

7. Harris, David A., ACLU Special Report, "Driving While Black, Racial Profiling on Our Nation's Highways" (June 1999). (Citing story reported in The Portland Oregonian.)

8. National Council of La Raza

9. National Association for the Advancement of Colored People. Founded in 1909, the National Association for the Advancement of Colored People is the nation's oldest and largest civil rights organization. Its half-million adult and youth members throughout the United States and the world are the premier advocates for civil rights in their communities, conducting voter registration drives and monitoring equal opportunity in the public and private sectors.

10. "ACLU Applauds Latino Partnership on Racial Profiling," (December 14, 1999), ACLU Press Release; "NAACP Calls on Congress to Enact Bill to Allow Federal Traffic Stop Statistics," (April 14, 1999).

11. "ACLU Applauds Latino Partnership on Racial Profiling," (December 14, 1999), ACLU Press Release.

12. Interview with author dated December 11, 2000.

13. "Massachusetts Police Embrace Data Collection to Fight DWB," (June 14, 2000), ACLU News.

14. *The San Francisco Chronicle*, September 16, 1999 at A18.

15. "CHP Response to Amended ACLU Lawsuit," (December 1, 1999) CHP Press Release #99-28.

16. "CHP Response to Amended ACLU Lawsuit," (December 1, 1999) CHP Press Release #99-28.

17. Letter signed by the ACLU, the Hispanic American Police Command Officers Association, the National Association for the Advancement of Colored People, the National Asian Pacific American Legal Consortium, the National Black Police Association, the National Council of La Raza, the National Latino Peace Officer's Association and the National Organization of Black Law Enforcement Executives. The full text of the letter can be found at http://www.aclu.org/congress/1011900a.html.

18. "San Francisco Is 34th California City to Collect Racial Data on Police Traffic Stops" (September 16, 1999), ACLU Press Release.

19. The entire text of the New Jersey consent decree can be found at <http://www.usdoj.gov/ crt/split/documents/jerseysa.html>.

20. Superior Court Judge Lance Ito gained his fame presiding over the O.J. Simpson trial.

21. Egelko, Bob, "$245,000 Upheld for Three Abused in Traffic Stop," *The Valley Times*, January 12, 2000 at A11.

22. Interview with Judge Greg Mathias, *Larry King Live* (January 18, 2000).

23. Hilary Shelton, Director of the NAACP Washington Bureau, observed that some Senate staff questioned the need to gather "Driving While Black" (DWB) statistics, suggesting that preliminary DWB statistics were overblown.

24. The Senate Bill was introduced by Mr. Lautenberg for himself, Mr. Feingold, Mr. Kennedy and Mr. Torricelli. The House of Representatives Bill was introduced by Mr. Conyers for himself, Mr. Menendez, Ms. Waters, Mr. Scott, Ms. Jackson-Lee, Mr. Nadler, Mr. Berman, Mr. Weiner, Mr. Cummings, Mr. Meeks, Mr. Hilliard, Mr. Farr, Mr. Lewis, Mr. Dixon, Mr. Hastings, Mr. Brady, Mr. Hinchey, Mr. Payne, Mr. Clay, Mr. Barrett, Mrs. Clayton and Mrs. Jones. The legislation is identified as H.R. 1443 and S. 821. Status of bills: H.R. 1443 was referred to House subcommittee on April 26, 1999; S. 821 was referred to Senate committee on April 15, 1999.

25. End Racial Profiling Act of 2001, S. 989; HR 2074, introduced by Representative John Conyers (Democratic-Michigan), Senator Russ Feingold (Democrat-Wisconsin),

Senator Jon Corzine (Democrat-New Jersey), Senator Hillary Rodham Clinton (Democrat-New York), Representative Christopher Shays (Republican-Connecticut), Representative David Wu (Democrat-Oregon), Mr. Kennedy, Mr. Torricelli, Mr. Schumer, Mr. Durbin, Ms. Stabenow, and Mr. Reid.

26. Racial Profiling Prohibition Act of 2001. (H.R. 1907) Ms. Norton (for herself, Mr. Acevedo-Vila, Mr. Baca, Mr. Bishop, Ms. Brown of Florida, Ms. Carson of Indiana, Mrs. Christensen, Mr. Clay, Mrs. Clayton, Mr. Clyburn, Mr. Cummings, Mr. Davis of Illinois, Mr. Fattah, Mr. Ford, Mr. Hastings of Florida, Mr. Hilliard, Mr. Jackson of Illinois, Ms. Jackson-Lee of Texas, Mr. Jefferson, Ms. Eddie Bernice Johnson of Texas, Ms. Kilpatrick, Ms. Lee, Mr. Lewis of Georgia, Ms. McKinney, Mrs. Meek of Florida, Mr. Meeks of New York, Mr. Menendez, Ms. Millender-McDonald, Mr. Owens, Mr. Payne, Mr. Rangel, Mr. Rush, Mr. Scott, Mr. Thompson of Mississippi, Mr. Towns, Mrs. Jones of Ohio, Mr. Underwood, Ms. Waters, Mr. Watt of North Carolina, and Mr. Wynn) introduced the bill, which was referred to the Committee on Transportation and Infrastructure.

PART V: We Are All Americans

CHAPTER THIRTEEN

Coming Together for a Solution

In Germany they came first for the Communists,
and I didn't speak up
because I wasn't a Communist.

Then they came for the Jews,
and I didn't speak up
because I wasn't a Jew.

Then they came for the trade
unionists, and I didn't speak up
because I wasn't a trade unionist.

Then they came for the Catholics,
and I didn't speak up
because I was a Protestant.

Then they came for me,
and by that time
no one was left to speak up.

—Martin Niemoeller (1892–1984)[1]

Varying approaches have aimed to address the issue of racial profiling, ranging from a radical revamping of the law enforcement profession to indications to do nothing. Just as there is no shortage of perspectives or recommendations about how to solve the problem, there is likewise no shortage of work that we all must do to find a solution.

When considering the feasibility of any proposal, it is important to keep in mind that success will be difficult to achieve without the commitment and cooperation of all parties: the federal government, state and local police agencies, individual officers, and persons of all colors. The plan must be comprehensive and must include changes in recruiting, training, and police discipline, along with legislation, community education, and support from elected leaders.

It is unlikely that any one solution will totally eliminate the practice of racial profiling. Racial profiling is a highly emotional and controversial issue, and as such, it presents an array of complex challenges and variables that must be addressed before any combination of solutions can be implemented on the street. It is also a product of the mind, a fact that makes it difficult to detect absent some open and notorious act of racism directed at another human being.

When looking for a solution, both sides must recognize that it is virtually impossible for any proposal to work unless there is a mutual willingness to listen and to compromise, even, and perhaps especially, when a given side's position is strong and controversial. If only one side can claim victory, the results will be fragmented and destined to fail. To achieve success, it may not be possible to adopt a singular approach nationwide. Rather, there must be a mutual recognition that the various facets of law enforcement are diverse. Not only do agencies vary in size, but they also have different overall missions and provide different services to the community. Proposals that may work for one organization may not work for another. Regardless of these variables, one thing remains certain: a mutual respect and joint effort must be the underlying basis for any solution, particularly one that will advance successfully toward the common goal of promoting civil rights integrity.

Although many problems have been identified and discussed, to find a viable solution, it is imperative to narrow the focus to address the key obstacles that continue to inhibit real progress. In order to identify the leading concerns of the public, law enforcement, and legislators, a list of these problems was compiled to ensure that each one was addressed in the context of a solution.

In this section, we will look at some of the key dynamics of the problem itself and reveal the obstacles that are hindering progress toward a workable solution. Once these areas have been identified, we will unveil a compilation of innovative, new approaches that both sides can integrate into proactive agendas, new legislation, and administrative policies.

Problem Identification

The most important recurring theme is that the practice of racial profiling is a complex problem that isn't confined to the law enforcement community. There is no law or punishment that will completely eradicate racial profiling. We will not just wake up one morning to find everyone the same skin color. But by chipping away at the discrimination and inequities piece by piece, measurable and lasting victory may not be far away. There is no better group to lead these efforts than law enforcement.

To frame effective solutions, we examined the problem from every angle. We reviewed in-depth research in the area, interviewed those on both sides of the issue, and applied nearly 50 years of combined experience in law enforcement and the legal profession. This extensive review of the problem enabled us to construct an outline representing the top concerns of those closest to the issue. It is from this outline that we began the arduous process of drafting recommendations that address the areas of contention that have hindered any unified and measurable steps toward a viable solution.

A. Racism in law enforcement. There must be a clear delineation between those in law enforcement who are deliberately engaging in biased police work that stems from prejudice and racism and those who may simply lack the training, experience, or leadership to perform their duties absent the use of ineffective racial stereotypes. Those few that use the profession to indulge their own racial agendas must be identified to prevent them from tarnishing the image of the entire profession. Others must be given the opportunity to participate in training and programs that examine race and its potential for abuse in law enforcement. Likewise, officers must be shown that race and diversity can be used as positive and powerful tools for enhancing relations with the public.

B. Officer accountability. The public would like the police to be more accountable for responding to failures within their organization. Officers who engage in biased police work should be identified and retrained, disciplined, or terminated so that the cycle of prejudice will cease. Likewise, supervisors and coworkers must be trained to identify, address, and report any violation of the policies and values of the organization.

C. Proper collection and analysis of racial profiling data. In order to derive valuable information from data collection efforts, safeguards must be put into place to ensure that data are properly collected and analyzed. Haphazard efforts at data collection are a waste of time and resources, and they perpetuate public frustration and distrust. When the data are accurate from the point of collection to the assessment, law enforcement will be provided with a powerful tool to identify specific areas of weakness and design solutions that result in real change.

D. The cost of collecting racial profiling data. The implementation of effective data collection programs must be cost effective so that organizations both large and small can take part without financial hardship. Local funds must be redirected and government grants must be secured to minimize the burden on the agency collecting data.

E. Preservation of officers' and citizens' privacy. The goal of protecting the privacy of both the officer and the citizen has significantly hindered data collection efforts. Officers fear being labeled racists despite legitimate enforcement efforts, and citizens do not want to become part of a law enforcement database just for a minor traffic stop. Both parties' concerns must be addressed and balanced with the need for accurate data collection and reporting.

F. A balance between the need for police discretion with the public's right to know. Many sensitive areas in law enforcement require confidentiality. The very nature of police work naturally prevents the public from being apprised of everything that occurs within an organization. But if the police join with the public in a valuable partnership based on the mutual exchange of information, the distrust that hinders many law enforcement efforts will be greatly diminished. Likewise, the public must have their concerns about confidentiality openly addressed so that they can understand the need for certain information to remain confidential. When law enforcement refuses to provide details to the public without valid reasons, its motives immediately and legitimately become suspect.

G. Restrictive requirements that may inhibit innovative, investigative police work. Law enforcement remains at a tremendous disadvantage in its efforts to combat crime. Not only does it fight the criminal element but also frequently the public as well because people are reluctant to come forward with information that could assist in the arrest and conviction of criminals. This frustration has often led to misguided efforts to identify would-be perpetrators by using race, a practice that is highly ineffective, outdated, and illegal. Law enforcement and the public must look to innovative approaches that have been scientifically shown to minimize the number of repeat criminal offenses. In conjunction with these new approaches, the public must be willing to help law enforcement investigate violent crimes by providing critical information in criminal investigations.

H. The difficulty in determining whether racial profiling has occurred. The line between racial profiling and legitimate police work often overlaps, even when analyzed by the experts. Absent a confession by the person engaging in such practices, many are left with a clouded view of when it may be acceptable to use race as a factor as opposed to when it is illegal. Police policies must be clear in this regard. Training in the academy and for veteran officers must be frequent and all inclusive. It must be understood that setting an officer loose on the street with insufficient training in the use of race and stereotypes is analogous to sending the officer out untrained in the use of a deadly weapon. When race and diversity in law enforcement are given the same time and attention given to the use of weapons and force, the need for stereotypes and the desire to maintain the status quo will be eliminated.

I. The effective handling of citizen complaints. The philosophy of community policing must extend to the handling of citizen complaints. Citizens must be provided a full and fair opportunity to file a complaint, whether in person or by mail, fax, telephone, or e-mail. Citizens should not be required to meet with a supervisor as a prerequisite for filing a complaint against an officer. They must trust that their complaints will be processed fairly and impartially and be assured access to a nonadversarial forum to voice concerns about their local police. Likewise, safeguards that protect law enforcement officers' privacy when complaints are retaliatory and/or without merit must be in place and followed.

J. Law enforcement initiatives to solve internal problems. Law enforcement must employ aggressive initiatives to solve internal problems that lead to public mistrust. Whether the problems are related to leadership, internal affairs, hiring and promotion, or data collection, law enforcement officers must take pride in the integrity of their organizations before they can emerge as trusted leaders within the community.

K. The Code of Silence. An organization's leaders must take a firm stand on code of silence practices. Officers must be trained early on to identify suspect practices that mandate the involvement of command staff. When an officer comes forward to report coworkers' unethical conduct, he or she must be protected from retaliation from other officers.

L. Officer training and community education. Deficiencies in both officer training and community education must be remedied. Administrators must recognize that money would be far better spent on proactive measures and prevention than on costly litigation and settlements that do incalculable damage to both the police and the community.

With these concerns at the forefront, the following solutions have been developed to address many of the issues relating to racial profiling and biased policing. Some of these initiatives are new, while others expand on systems currently in use by some agencies. If employed, these proposals will yield results that are quantifiable while representing the interests and meeting the expectations of both law enforcement and the public effectively.

The Solutions section has been divided into two parts. The solutions presented in Part A are limited to hands-on initiatives that will affect the way law enforcement and the public interact with and perceive each other. In and of themselves, these proposals yield a complete reference for those seeking solutions to the challenges presented by race and its use in law enforcement. Aside from these straightforward solutions, however, it is important to consider proposals that combine the efforts of academia, science, and philosophy. For those who are interested in a more in-depth review of

potential solutions, we have included proposals in Part B that look to restructurin
and rethinking long-held values and beliefs within the institution of law enforcemen

While we believe this section will prompt a more comprehensive look into th
vast scope of potential solutions to racial profiling, we recognize that it may not be c
interest to everyone. We would highly recommend it for those implementing extende
racial profiling training programs and for those who wish to explore innovativ
proposals for discussion and study. For those who prefer to limit the scope of the
review to the hands-on recommendations presented in Part A, we have designed Pa
B to be optional, where the reader can skip to the next chapter without disrupting th
continuity of information.

SOLUTIONS: PART A

SOLUTION I: DATA COLLECTION: A RECEIPT-BASED SYSTEM

The hottest battle raging in the war to combat racial profiling surrounds th
controversy of data collection. To collect or not to collect? That is the questio
frequently debated by law enforcement agencies, legislators, and civil rights grou
nationwide. Though legislative mandates and voluntary data collection efforts hav
perpetuated an awareness of racial profiling, its downsides cannot be overlooked.

Many collection efforts to date are substantially flawed, leading to results that d
not reflect reality. A large majority of the collection programs lack specific guidelin
and accountability measures. These random systems implemented to appease the publ
inevitably lead to data that are substantially flawed from the outset. As a result, thes
anonymous systems fail to identify those that may be engaging in suspicious practice
which results in little or no follow-up or training offered to the true offenders.

Interviews conducted within the law enforcement community and the publ
sector have revealed that most agree with data collection to some extent. Therefor
the focus must be on developing reforms to the current collection efforts in order t
provide both law enforcement and the public with an accurate measure of the proble
via standardized collection and reporting. These reforms in a reporting system are be
achieved through a receipt-based system for all citizens, regardless of color.

May I Have a Receipt, Please?

This morning Steve had some errands to run. He knew if the morning was to g
smoothly, he would have to start the day off with a doughnut and coffee. After his sto
at the doughnut shop, he went to the dry cleaners to drop off his cleaning. He realize
he was low on cash and went to the instant teller machine at his local bank to withdra
some money to go to the hardware store and buy a nifty, one-of-a-kind wrench h
needed for a special home improvement project. As it was nearing lunch, he went by

fast food hamburger stand for a $2.89 burger and fries. What do all these transactions have in common? They all produce a receipt.

As insignificant as Steve's errands were, someone would be able to take these five receipts and track Steve's activities for the entire morning and determine:

1. The businesses he patronized;
2. The time of day he went to each establishment;
3. The services rendered or merchandise purchased; and
4. The name of the cashier who conducted each transaction.

In other words, if the public is entitled to a receipt that itemizes every purchase or transaction right down to the extra onions ordered on a burger, shouldn't people be entitled to a receipt if a police officer stops and detains them? Absolutely.

One of the key goals of a receipt-based system is to restore public confidence. The public recognizes that law enforcement agencies are one of the few entities granted unbridled power to police themselves. The public does not trust this approach, and it is debatable whether they should. The system of checks and balances inherent in our government suggests that law enforcement should not be immune from oversight by regulatory agencies similar to those that oversee medical institutions, universities, corporations, and other public entities.

Just as in the private sector, violation of federal laws and regulations cannot be overlooked. As we have seen with the collapse of major corporations in the aftermath of accounting scandals, the long-term implications of serious crimes that violate federal law are astronomic. Likewise, discrimination in law enforcement is a federal crime and as such must be viewed with the same seriousness as any federal violation committed against the public. As the right to travel freely is guaranteed to each of us under the Constitution, any detention of a person—the temporary removal of that right—should be viewed as a significant event, regardless of whether the detention results in a verbal warning, a traffic ticket, or an arrest.

Under the current system, law enforcement officers are not required to generate a report or any other form of documentation when a stop is initiated that does not result in a ticket or arrest. Theoretically, if an officer wants to stop a minority citizen and engage in improper investigatory practices for two hours on the side of the road, it would be the officer's word against the citizen's as to whether the stop ever occurred. And if a citizen wants to exaggerate the details of an encounter with an officer in order to prevail in litigation, the officer may be subjected to years of costly litigation to prove that his or her motives for the stop were pure.

The following specific proposals for a receipt-based system would reform data collection efforts nationwide and provide an accurate and effective means for tracking stops and promoting a level of officer accountability that is severely lacking in current data collection programs. Unlike its numerous predecessors, this proposed system is not about race or about data collection. It's about a kind of business record keeping that would provide citizens of all races with a receipt when they are stopped and detained by the police. In fact, in states attempting to pass legislation making it illegal to collect racial data, this system could be tailored to omit race entirely as a reported item.

This color-blind, receipt-based system would be developed through the universal, mandatory implementation of a short, concise form that could be separated into three copies or integrated into a comparable computerized system. The written or electronic form would be used any time an officer detained a citizen, whether on foot or in a vehicle, in circumstances that do not immediately require the officer to issue a citation or to generate a report for the detention. In other words, there would no longer be instances in which an officer could detain a citizen without some form of documentation. The only exception to this rule would be if the officer were called to an emergency during a routine stop and did not have time to issue a receipt or if the stop took place during a call in progress. In these cases, a receipt would be generated after the fact and filed at the police station with the known information derived from dispatch records and/or the limited officer contact.

The receipts would be numbered in the same manner as the department's established system for numbering citations or other reports. The numbering would ensure that all completed receipts could be accounted for to prevent the possibility of unfavorable data being omitted.

The data on the receipts would include the following minimum criteria:

1. The name of the officer conducting the stop;
2. The age, gender, and race of the detainee (on the basis of the officer's perception) (note that race may be omitted entirely in states where the collection of racial data may someday be illegal);
3. The time and location of the stop (this may be important to put stops into context, as duty assignments, patrol areas, and time of day may affect population and roadway demographics);
4. The violation(s) and/or reason(s) for the stop or consensual encounter;
5. Whether the officer could determine the driver's race or sex prior to the stop;
6. Whether a search of a person, a person's property, or an automobile was conducted. If "yes," was it consensual? Was any contraband discovered? If the search was not consensual, what was the probable cause to justify the search?
7. The duration of the stop and/or search; and
8. Whether any warning was given and what it was for.

Although the citizen's name would be required on the form, it would be visible only on the copy retained by the citizen. In other words, the department would not be permitted to retain the identity of the person stopped. The form would take no longer than one minute to complete and would essentially be limited to checking the appropriate boxes. It may even be possible to develop a hand-held device with a touch screen that would print out a receipt for the citizen and electronically transmit and tabulate the data collected.

Copy Number One

The top copy (original) that includes the individual's name would be retained by the citizen as a receipt for the detention. In most cases, the citizen may choose to discard the receipt; however, if the stop is suspect or the citizen is the target of repeat detentions, the receipt(s) could be turned over to the agency itself to support a formal complaint. The complainant might also choose to furnish the information to an appropriate oversight organization or governmental entity that may review the documentation to determine whether further investigation or litigation is warranted. The citizen's copy would also include the officer's name.

Though there has been some debate about whether an officer should be required to identify himself or herself to the citizen, most experts agree that this is a necessary component of any successful system and is normally required by law. Moreover, an officer's identity is readily available to the detainee if a ticket is issued or by merely observing the name on an officer's badge. In some agencies, standard protocol requires an officer to provide the citizen with a business card at the conclusion of any traffic stop or detention. Therefore, providing this information to the citizen would not compromise anonymity any more than the systems already in place do.

On the back of the recipient's copy, the citizen would have the option to complete a "citizen satisfaction survey" relating to their experience with the officer. The back of the form would also have a telephone number for compliments, questions, or complaints about the stop and/or detention. This would give citizens a voice in their police agency and the opportunity to become educated in law enforcement practices if they so desire.

Copy Number Two

The second copy of the receipt would be retained by the issuing police agency. It would contain all information relating to the stop with the exception of the detainee's identity and the officer's identity. The data from these receipts would be entered into a comprehensive data tracking system that would enable supervisors and command staff to track trends within the organization.

It should be reiterated that the detainee's identity would be omitted from the receipt retained by the organization in order to protect the citizen's privacy. If the citizen chose to pursue a complaint relating to the detention, the citizen could provide a copy of the receipt to the agency voluntarily to substantiate any details about the length or reason for the detention and to establish that he or she was, in fact, the person stopped.

The officer's identity would also be omitted from the receipt retained by the organization. This would promote accuracy in the collection efforts and alleviate concerns that officers may be individually disciplined or assessed on the basis of the quality or quantity of citizen contacts. The power to initiate a complaint would remain in the hands of the citizen, who could choose to file a grievance against any officer who he or she believed engaged in inappropriate conduct. Once a grievance is filed, the department would only then become aware of the detaining officer's identity and would be able to evaluate the stop on an *individual* basis to determine whether the initiation of the stop and the officer's actions during the stop were appropriate. Citizens would also be encouraged to compliment local police for going beyond the call of duty so that positive contacts with the community are reinforced and rewarded by the organization.

A receipt-based program would deliver obvious benefits to both the citizen and law enforcement. The copy of the receipt retained by the agency would serve as an important tool for growth and development for the department as a whole. Analysts from a departmental oversight committee or academic partner could be employed to track the data collected and identify statistical trends either within the entire organization or by precinct to measure performance accurately and identify training needs. The oversight committee would include line officers and administrators, along with personnel from the internal investigation, training, and legal divisions.

Upon the quarterly review of this large body of statistics, appropriate training would be offered to cure any unfavorable trends in citizen stops and/or detentions. Some examples of unfavorable trends would be patterns of stops that are borne out of weak probable cause and detentions for minor violations that are consistently longer than average. It should be noted that the statistical studies derived from the receipts would not identify which officers were engaging in suspect practices. Instead, they would be designed as a means to track department-wide performance trends with the goal of building a comprehensive training curriculum. On the contrary, *individual* trends would be assessed through the citizen complaint process.

In addition to developing a training curriculum that specifically addresses statistical enforcement trends, internal studies could be conducted to measure the effectiveness of lesson plans and courses. When training is modified with the goal of maximizing an officer's performance, it would correlate to measurable results on the street. For example, some units may be provided with training that educates officers on statistical and demographic trends within the community. Some courses may focus on the identification of common stereotypes associated with certain groups or comparing stereotypes to facts relating to "hit rates" (searches resulting in recovery of contraband). Some courses may even challenge alcohol and drug trends that have traditionally and erroneously implicated minorities. Other units may be assigned to immersion or volunteer programs within the community. When evaluated over time, the data from these units' enforcement statistics may be compared with the data from units without such training and help to determine whether the curriculum could be implemented department-wide with beneficial results or whether revisions are needed. Undoubtedly, if data from a receipt-based system can be analyzed and linked to a comprehensive training program within the organization, officers and the public would both benefit.

Copy Number Three

Finally, a third copy of the receipt would be retained by the detaining officer as a record of the stop. The officer would be able to choose to make specific notes on his or her copy in order to recall any unusual details about the detention that may surface later. An example would be any circumstances that may have made the stop last longer than usual for the type of violation involved.

In addition to the significant record keeping and training advantages, the proposed receipt-based system would provide a consistent, accurate method for compiling data that would be the least burdensome and the most cost effective for individual departments to manage. It is the hope that a uniform system can be effectively tailored so that the data generated from the receipts will be standardized throughout the nation.

Most important, this system would be a first step in restoring the public's confidence in law enforcement agencies. The bottom line is that citizens want to know why they are being detained, what they are being detained for, and who is detaining them. If they are stopped 10 times in one month for a defective license plate light, they want 10 pieces of paper to support their complaint. In other words, they want something tangible in writing.

A receipt-based system would also address one of the most common public complaints: lack of officer accountability. It would undoubtedly alert agencies whether its officers were conducting stops based on insufficient probable cause or merely as a pretext to search for evidence of criminal activity. Even if sufficient probable cause for a stop is clearly established, the duration could be evaluated to determine whether the length of the detention was reasonable on the basis of the violation or other factors noted on the receipt. When unfavorable trends are detected within the organization, it would provide agencies with an effective early warning system to remedy associated training issues before they become legal ones. Likewise, the integrity of the written receipt would be analogous to that of a formal police report and would bear the same legal significance for truthfulness and the same ramifications for falsification.

In addition to these benefits, the receipt-based system would serve as an effective deterrent, with officers knowing that each stop would be documented and randomly audited to ensure compliance with department policies. Most important, the receipt-based system would provide citizens with a tangible form of documentation to advise them of the reason they were stopped and alleviate concerns that the detention was solely based on race or ethnicity. The public would serve as an independent oversight, of sorts, ensuring that the data on the receipt are accurate. This factor alone would go a long way to repair the relationship between the community and the police. Ultimately, citizens would be afforded a voice in their police agency and a means to measure the accountability and performance of the officers who serve their community.

This method would also serve to protect officers who may be wrongfully accused of conducting race-based stops. Many times, officers are faced with individuals who are interested only in playing the race card to get out of a traffic ticket. In more extreme cases, a citizen may initiate racial profiling accusations as a way to make a fast buck. This system would make it much more difficult for either one to occur.

For the first time, law enforcement agencies and the public would have accurate, uncompromised data to use for analysis and change. This new method of documentation would benefit and protect citizens and officers and provide those in law enforcement with valuable training and expertise to ensure that the stops they are conducting meet legal and ethical standards. When the mystery is taken out of these stops, costly lawsuits and the division they promote will most certainly decline.

The benefits of the receipt-based system would be highlighted in an aggressive public service campaign to remind citizens of their right to a receipt during a police encounter. When the public has a greater understanding of the reason behind law enforcement stops, there would be less room for assumptions that the stop was motivated by skin color or appearance. Moreover, the public and the police would recognize that if an officer intends to take away something as significant as a citizen's constitutional right to travel freely, a receipt is the least that can be offered in return.

Data Analysis Under a Receipt-Based System

If data are scientifically analyzed under a receipt-based system, the result would be information that is meaningful to both the department and the public. First, the accuracy of the data collected would be ensured by the citizen. If a citizen does not agree with the information on the receipt, he or she could opt to challenge it through appropriate channels. Next, the data collected would be subject to review by both the department and an academic partner to track trends. This nonconfrontational oversight would assist law enforcement in deriving meaning from the data and utilizing it in a way that is the most positive and beneficial for the organization and the community. Once collected, verified, and scientifically analyzed, the possibilities for these data's constructive use would be extensive.

Most important, utilizing data at the front end of the system to improve officer performance rather than at the back end of the system to establish blame marks an important shift in current data collection philosophy. When traffic stop statistics are used as a preventative tool, progress can be measured and changes implemented long before harm to the police and the public has been done.

SOLUTION II: RECRUITING AND SCREENING NEW OFFICERS

We must recruit those who come to policing in the spirit of service,
not in the spirit of adventure.

—Tom Frazier[2]

Not too long ago, Steve saw a recruiting ad for a California police agency that depicted gun-wielding officers, adorned in traditional SWAT regalia, who were breaking down a door. This image is consistent with many recruiting ads found in police oriented magazines that often portray officers with painted faces and in camouflage fatigues with high-powered rifles. These images are a far cry from an ad that shows an officer working to solve a problem with a concerned citizen. Any veteran officer will tell you that this glamorous portrayal of the law enforcement profession is far from the reality of day-to-day police work. It is only in the rarest of circumstances that police work mirrors what's portrayed in Hollywood and the media.

To successfully recruit officers interested in serving their communities, recruiting ads must be tailored to reflect the reality and goals of the profession as opposed to promoting militia-style activities that may be attracting the wrong type of candidates. The goal must be to attract racially sensitive individuals who place loyalty to principles above loyalty to personal agendas. In this vein, special emphasis must be placed upon recruiting women and minorities so that an organization's composition more closely mirrors the demographics of the community.

In addition to a change in recruitment messages, rigorous screening of a candidate's personal background and employment history will help to weed out officers who may have a history of problematic behavior. Moreover, background investigators must be held accountable for performing quality investigations and psychological evaluations on candidates. When organizations have faith in the pre-employment screening process, they will be less likely to give in to the pressures of staffing shortages by hiring candidates who may display traits that are not up to their standards. It has been proven time and again that it is better to remain understaffed than to recruit officers who are likely to violate ethical standards and practices.

SOLUTION III: TRAINING

Tell me and I will forget;
Show me and I will remember;
Involve me and I will understand.

—Chinese proverb

"The Catch"

This title probably caught the attention of every football fan. No football faithful will ever forget the winning touchdown pass thrown by San Francisco 49er quarterback Joe Montana to Dwight Clark in the last seconds of the 1981 Superbowl. Mere luck? Unlikely. Plays like that are the result of years of training, planning, and practice. Although police work is far from a football game, officers can benefit from football's basic principles: train hard, play fair, and work as a team. This simple approach will often produce a winning outcome.

Lisa will never forget her first "ride along" with a police officer. The minute she sat down in the front seat of the police car, she had to admit it was a bit surreal. After just one traffic stop into the evening, she was a changed person. There was a sudden feeling of power. She was instantly transported into a ticket-writing frenzy and pointed out every trivial violation to the officer with, "Give that person a ticket!" She even made up some violations that sounded good. Perhaps it was temporary insanity, the newfound power, or maybe subconsciously she wanted restitution for all the times she drove along helplessly while someone cut her off and she wished that there was a cop around to intervene.

Further into the evening, the officer stopped a teenager for speeding his suped-up car through a residential neighborhood at 55 mph. The young man was obviously scared. The officer came back to the car, and while he was waiting for the check on the young man's license to come back, he asked Lisa, "Would you give this guy a ticket or let him go?" Her immediate response was to give him a ticket. Once the adrenalin rush wore off, she thought about the ramifications for this young man. Higher insurance rates, a big chunk of change to pay the citation, and ultimately, the reality of facing his parents. Suddenly, she felt sympathy. At the same time, she had to balance this with the possibility that this guy would run someone down driving like this. She realized she was not ready to handle the kind of power that is given to an officer. She did not want the responsibility of making these kinds of potentially life-altering decisions. Not many of us would. But with the proper training and practice, her approach to traffic enforcement may have been different. In retrospect, this ride along experience was not unlike that of a young officer with limited training. Just about anyone can identify a traffic violation, pull someone over, and write a ticket, but without the proper training on the approach and psychology involved, "the catch" may result in a fumble. This phenomenon is particularly apparent with new officers who are eager to be productive and challenge the limits of their newfound power.

Despite the potential for overzealousness, little is done to bridle an applicant's enthusiasm for police work. Once a candidate decides to pursue a career in law enforcement, he or she can expect an initial training program that is essentially divided into three parts: (1) the police academy portion that is mandatory for all new recruits, (2) the field training program that comprises on-the-street experience under the supervision of multiple field training officers, and (3) specialized training or continuing education opportunities that may be offered intermittently throughout the officers' career, either by the department or other qualified agencies.

The training a prospective officer receives in the police academy is probably one of the ripest opportunities an organization has to develop an officer both physically and mentally. It is in this military-style environment that a recruit is trained in physical agility, integrity, and ethics, with a specific focus on the qualities an officer must possess to protect and serve the community effectively.

Once officers successfully complete the classroom portion of their training and are hired by an organization, they begin the field training program, essentially going to work as officers on the street under the supervision of field trainers. To ensure that the field training program is effective, the field training supervisor must be qualified to perform supervisory duties and given specific training materials and guidelines that incorporate ethics and reinforce topics covered in the academy. Field training programs must be tailored to teach new officers the importance of placing loyalty to principles before loyalty to fellow officers. Field trainers should represent the best of the best in an organization. They should address racial profiling, the code of silence, and integrity in the field training program.

Even the best academy instructors and field trainers recognize that the most complex areas of the police profession and the most difficult ones to "train" an officer in are the common sense, mental acuteness, and negotiation skills critical for successful interactions with the public. These skills are not easily learned and cannot be developed in a short half-day course on the subject. Surprisingly, training in this area is often insufficient, even though these skills are called upon daily when an officer makes a routine traffic stop or initiates a citizen contact. Officers who are proficient in this skill will tell you that "selling" a ticket to a citizen is better than acting like a disciplinarian who is issuing the citation as a reprimand.

This unique brand of salesmanship is not much different from that used by the door-to-door vacuum cleaner salespeople. Generally, their presence at people's front door is unexpected, unannounced, and unwanted. Despite the intrusion, the salesperson proceeds with the pitch in an attempt to sell the homeowners a product they initially do not want and cannot afford. By the end of the visit, however, the homeowners have not only purchased the product because they believe they can no longer live without it, but also they've done so at what they believe is a great price. In the course of a few minutes, the vacuum cleaner salesperson has transformed from a pushy salesperson to a friend who has knocked a couple hundred dollars off the price and thrown in a few extra attachments as a one-time goodwill gesture.

Skillful law enforcement officers can apply the same principles of salesmanship to their contacts with the public. Let's look to a traffic stop, for example. The intrusion on the driver is not unlike that of the homeowner. Not only is it usually inconvenient, but it's unwanted too. It also comes with a high price tag that the driver does not want to pay. The turning point is when the officer applies people skills to the encounter and addresses the driver courteously and offers an explanation as to the violation and the remedy. Often, the officer can actually reverse most or all of the negativity associated with the stop, with the citizen walking away thankful that the officer took the time to correct a potential safety or driving hazard.

Racial Profiling

In states such as California, mandatory racial profiling training has become the norm for new and veteran officers alike. But in states that have not mandated racial profiling's inclusion in the standard training curriculum, racial profiling is a subject rarely addressed. When it is, the course is usually limited to a few hours of overview, with little or no discussion of the cause or effects of the practice. Nor is there usually any attempt to understand the various cultural and socioeconomic dynamics within the community. When these important dynamics and their relation to proper investigatory practices are not addressed in training, an officer will rely on instinct, which may be borne from racial bias and stereotypes. But if trainers can utilize this window of opportunity to re-direct an officer's thinking in the early stages of his or her career, the potential for skilled police work is great. For example, picture a well-worn path. Walking down the path, you come to a fork. In one direction, the much-traveled path continues. In the other, a rarely used trail can be seen. Most will continue along the well-traveled path. The goal of a trainer, however, is to encourage the officer to choose the new path. After a while, the well-worn path will not be used anymore. It will become overgrown with brush and eventually disappear. In time, the new path will be the well-worn one.

An extensive review of numerous training manuals utilized in the police academy and continuing education programs for veteran officers revealed that racial profiling training curriculums were either significantly deficient or completely lacking. For example, many courses failed to cover the cause of the problem or to make a tangible distinction between *racial* profiling and *criminal* profiling. In some cases, instructors teaching the courses were not able to answer basic questions and left students with no clear direction at the conclusion of the course. When questioned, officers revealed that the problem of racial profiling is more likely to be addressed in the form of a passing comment than a comprehensive study and discussion. The result is apathy; when racial profiling is unimportant to the organization or the instructor, it is likewise unimportant to the officer on the street. But when the topic of racial profiling is incorporated in the department's training curriculum, it is firmly built into an officer's approach to the public. Moreover, when adequate training teaches integrity and proper investigatory tactics at the outset, officers no longer need to rely on race to identify suspects.

In conjunction with a specific curriculum addressing racial profiling, diversity and sensitivity training should be mandatory and provided at regular intervals for all levels of law enforcement personnel. Prejudice and prejudgment are normal human behaviors we all possess and normally learn at an early age. Unfortunately, these prejudices lead to stereotyping, which leads us to categorize an entire group or race on the basis of our beliefs, experiences, or perceptions about a few. These invalid perceptions and biases that need to be corrected though education. Mandatory training programs that explore racial stereotypes and teach officers to deal with emotions on the street are critical for ensuring that these biases are not translated into inappropriate law enforcement tactics. Moreover, biases and stereotypes should be regularly challenged and countered with statistics and facts.

Though the classroom remains an important venue for learning this type of information, it will fall short if it's not combined with hands-on experience and role-plays. Without putting this information to practical use, an officer's understanding and retention of it will quickly diminish. Though this phenomenon applies to any training topic, it is especially critical in the context of pretext traffic stops and racial profiling, mainly because of the deep-rooted and long-held beliefs associated with these practices. When organizations combine solid classroom instruction with hands-on experience, racial profiling will finally be understood and minimized.

"IS TLC"

One of the first steps toward minimizing the practice of racial profiling involves educating officers in proper enforcement tactics that are sometimes substituted with the inappropriate use of stereotypes and race. Though the laws, polices, and procedures within police jurisdictions may vary, there are five universal areas of consideration that an officer should explore in the classroom and later implement when conducting traffic stops. These considerations are key, and officers should use them as a checklist during any traffic stop. When officers follow these guidelines for good police work, stops are more likely to remain safe for all involved. But when these guidelines are not adhered to or when officers attempt to take shortcuts at any of these five areas, officer safety could be compromised, and the potential for use of illegal investigatory tactics such as racial profiling and stereotyping increases substantially. With this in mind, the following information is designed to cover both the physical components of a stop and the psychological challenges faced by an officer in an encounter with a motorist.

These five steps can be reduced to the simple acronym "IS TLC" and should serve as a guide for any motor vehicle stop:

I: INTELLIGENCE

An officer must evaluate any INTELLIGENCE that may be available relating to the vehicle or the driver prior to and at the beginning of the stop. Is the vehicle wanted? Are the people inside potentially dangerous? Is the officer responding to a specific alert relating to the vehicle, or is this a random stop for a traffic violation? Training in this area is critical, as an officer must exercise good judgment and discretion when determining who to stop for a violation. If an officer is not properly trained and retrained in the area of discretion and intelligence gathering, he or she will often rely on stereotypes and preconceived notions about certain races and may consciously or unconsciously engage in racial profiling as an alternative to good police work.

When a stop goes wrong: If an officer fabricates intelligence (or probable cause for a stop), citizens may be subjected to racially motivated stops that have no legal or factual basis. This tactic is like "shooting fish in a barrel." Although a small percentage of these random stops may lead to the discovery of criminal activity, this practice is highly ineffective, and simply put, it's bad police work. Moreover, it's illegal. If there is no legally valid probable cause for the stop, anything the officer obtains thereafter may be inadmissible.

S: SAFETY

It is critical for officers to analyze the SAFETY risk of each stop. On the basis of this initial assessment, the officer must apply appropriate safety measures that fall within the confines of the law and the public's expectations. Some of the officer's deliberations may include why and where the stop is taking place, logistics such as time of day, and a risk assessment of engaging in pursuits and vehicle stops in certain traffic conditions. For example, it may not be wise to pursue a vehicle at a high rate of speed past a busy schoolyard for a broken tail light. Nor would it be wise to pull a vehicle over across four lanes of traffic in the fog and heavy rain for a minor violation. These considerations, in conjunction with department safety directives, should guide the officer during any encounter with the public.

Although many safety tactics are learned during an officer's time on the street, it is equally important that training programs continually address safety guidelines, particularly in light of emerging technology that officers may incorporate into their routine practices. Though many equate officer safety with the use of force in high-profile encounters, safety depends more on an officer's mental processes than it does on his or her physical acts. This is especially true in the case of stereotypes and race. Often, the apprehension generated by racial stereotypes and prejudice lead to decisions that are driven by fear rather than by common sense.

When a stop goes wrong: When safety precautions are not closely followed, or when an officer's emotions are allowed to control his or her actions, officer safety and citizen safety are at risk. To be effective, the safety measures used must be balanced with the legitimate risk the officer perceives. An officer's overreaction to a situation based on preconceived notions or stereotypes about a particular race will perpetuate the public's perception that officers are targeting certain racial groups. Officers must be trained to distinguish a real threat based on articulable facts from a perceived threat based on inaccurate perceptions. When safety training is not repeated and updated regularly, officer complacency or the unilateral integration of improper safety tactics may result.

T: TACTICS

On the basis of the information gained from INTELLIGENCE, an officer must decide what TACTICS are necessary to effectuate a stop. For example, is the stop high or low profile? Are cover units required? Should the suspect be ordered out of the car? Ironically, one of the areas in which officers are most highly trained in is the use of force. These trainings focus more often on *how* to use force rather than on *when*. Without proper training, fear will often dictate police TACTICS and many times will lead to actions that are inappropriate or excessive for the circumstances at hand.

When a stop goes wrong: A review of the accounts of people who believe they have been the victim of a "black in progress" encounter with police reveals that the turning point in these encounters—the point at which the person believes he or she is being treated unfairly on the basis of race—is when officers use improper tactics during a routine stop. A common complaint among these victims is the officers' use of high-profile tactics for what should be a low-profile, routine encounter. Particularly if intelligence is fabricated or exaggerated, a victim may be forced to endure extraordinary and humiliating treatment for nothing more than a minor traffic violation.

One of the key factors in these encounters is whether the officer has been trained to handle the emotion of fear when facing a perceived threat. If an officer is well prepared mentally, he or she will not show his or her hand to a potential suspect. As in a game of poker, the officer must not let the citizen know his or her true mindset. Once the officer conveys to the citizen, however inadvertently, that he or she is fearful or anxious about the contact, he or she has essentially shown his or her hand and in all likelihood has tainted the remainder of the stop, unnecessarily turning a low-profile stop into a high-profile encounter.

L: LOGISTICS

In addition to TACTICS, the officer must consider certain LOGISTICS before engaging in high-profile stops. Evaluating the scope of resources immediately available to the officer, such as backup units and cover or drug-sniffing dogs and eyewitnesses, can mean the difference between a successful stop and one that is highly suspect in the eyes of the public.

When a stop goes wrong: An officer who misjudges logistics during a stop may subject himself or herself to allegations of racial profiling. For example, if an officer is suspicious that a vehicle is transporting drugs and makes the suspect wait on the side of the road for three hours until a drug-sniffing dog can be dispatched to the location, the officer has violated the driver's rights, whether or not drugs are apprehended. If the driver is a minority, racial profiling allegations will undoubtedly surface.

C: COMMAND and CONTROL

Who has COMMAND and CONTROL during a given stop or police encounter? The bottom line is that the officer who initiates the stop is in control of the stop and of the other officers' actions during the stop and is accountable for the outcome. The basic rule of thumb is that the officer who initiates the stop is in control of the scene until someone else arrives and expressly relieves the officer from control. This power shift may result when a senior officer or someone with senior expertise arrives at the scene, for example, a supervisor, an accident investigation expert, a narcotics expert, or the like.

Undoubtedly, the most important aspect of CONTROL is an officer's ability to control himself or herself under the pressures of the job. For example, an officer may be called to a bank robbery in progress. When the officer arrives at the bank, shots may be exchanged, followed by an hour-long, high-speed police chase through a heavily populated part of town. A human being running on fear and adrenalin would want to run up to the car once it became disabled, drag the person out, and arrest the culprit, without much concern about the injuries inflicted in the process. For an officer, these feelings of rage and emotion must be suppressed, regardless of the fact that these bank robbers tried to kill the officer only moments earlier. It is difficult to learn how to practice this kind of self-control effectively, particularly in the most volatile circumstances where a moment of complacency can mean death. Law enforcement may consider using simulators like those used for pilots so that the officer will have the opportunity to practice proper tactics in volatile situations on a regular basis.

When a stop goes wrong: When there is a lack of command and control during a stop, the likelihood of police misconduct is high. The nation has seen frightening videos that vividly illustrate extreme examples of what can result when an officer or supervisor lacks the training and integrity to take control of a situation or themselves. It is through frequent training and role-plays that officers can learn how to retain control of a scene, even in the most hostile situations. Many times officers forget that having "control of the scene" encompasses control of the suspect, the witnesses, and most important, the conduct of fellow officers. The officer or supervisor in control must be held accountable for the outcome. Absent these leadership skills, a routine stop can quickly escalate into a free-for-all. Officers must be trained to recognize when enough is enough, before personal loss of control transforms legitimate tactics into the illegal use of force. Organizations must recognize that rage and revenge are normal emotions that can arise out of these dangerous encounters and must provide officers with other outlets to release these powerful emotions.

Listening

"Watch your thoughts, for they become words.
Watch your words, for they become actions.
Watch your actions, for they become your destiny."

—Swami G. Chidvilisananda,
Siddha Guru and head of
the Siddha lineage

From a young age, we're taught the importance of listening. However, many of us have never learned *how* to listen. As toddlers, we learned to listen all too well when it served our purposes. We were proud to show off our listening skills and quick to repeat juicy tidbits at the most inopportune moments with the highest potential to embarrass the grown-ups. As teens, our listening skills evolved, and we perfected the art of making others *think* we were listening when in reality, we already had all the answers. As adults, the time we should spend listening is generally spent thinking of a good response to what a given speaker is trying to say.

The value of training and role-playing in the art of listening cannot be underestimated. Officers must listen to both suspects and witnesses. They must validate what a person is trying to convey and try to sympathize with his or her plight. Finally, they must ask the citizen follow-up questions to obtain more details about a particular situation or occurrence. These skills are particularly important when an officer is dealing with members of minority groups who may have preconceived notions about the police or who may speak English only as a second language. Moreover, an officer who develops superior listening skills has the unique advantage of being able to act as a mediator with the expertise to de-escalate dangerous situations. Officers untrained in this area will often make mistakes similar to society as a whole and will use valuable time that should be spent listening for self-serving purposes. For those officers who do not listen and instead forge ahead in volatile situations without hearing the whole side of the story, failure is almost certain and, sometimes, deadly.

Moreover, when an officer disrespects the speaker, distrust of the profession mounts, and the officer may be seen as taking sides between the victim and the suspect. By failing to listen, the officer is essentially telling the speaker that his or her message has no value and therefore disregarded as not worth listening to. Such negative encounters serve no purpose other than to taint future encounters within certain ethnic groups and perpetuate the negative profiling of police officers in the minority community. Likewise, officers may rely on stereotypes as opposed to facts, thus further widening the gap between the police and minority communities.

Although implementing listening skills may seem straightforward, those in law enforcement recognize challenging variables that make good listening difficult to practice in every encounter with the public. One factor is the incredible demands placed on an officer, who is often sent from call to call to bring quick resolution to a variety of emergencies in a very limited time. Another factor may be the very nature of the call itself. For example, when faced with an irrational suspect running high on adrenalin, an officer's life may depend on his or her ability to react quickly to the suspect to diffuse a potentially dangerous situation. In other words, there may not always be time for a counseling session prior to shots being fired.

Similarly, an encounter with a suspect who is either under the influence or mentally ill may require the use of special tactics that are more appropriately dictated by safety. This is a specialized area that will not be discussed here, as it has its own challenges that must be tailored to the specific encounter. Rather, we will look to the more common occurrence surrounding the day-to-day contact with a citizen who is angry for one reason or another.

For most of us, anger is a short-term reaction. Loosely speaking, people may express anger if they lock their keys in the car or bounce a check. The short-term reactions to these perceived "disasters," however, are very different from the stark, robust anger many officers face on the street. Many suspects are angry for a variety of reasons, none of which may be immediately apparent to the officer arriving at the scene. The suspect may not even be conscious of the cause of the anger. It may be feelings that have been bottled up without any outlet for an extended period of time. Unfortunately for the officer, the outlet or target for the suspect's anger may become either the officer or an innocent victim. When confronted with an angry suspect, an officer's first impulse may be to rush in and resolve the problem with violence. Particularly when the ratio of officers to suspects is great, the urge to bring a quick end to a volatile situation often overcomes common sense.

Officers must recognize that listening is probably the most important means of diffusing this type of anger. A person who is angry is not usually looking for a violent confrontation with police. This person is looking for someone to listen. An acronym that officers can refer to when dealing with an angry individual is "SAVE." SAVE represents the four needs of an angry person.

First, officers must step back and allow the person to have personal **Space**. It is important for the person to feel unthreatened so as not to perceive violence as imminent. Giving the person space indirectly communicates to the suspect that the officer is willing to slow down and listen to what's going on.

Second, the person may be looking for some form of **Attention**. He or she may be experiencing feelings of loss, hopelessness, fear, or guilt. This confrontation may be the only opportunity for the person to express the cause of his or her anger. Therefore, an officer's ability to give undivided attention to the individual's feelings may be the determining factor in whether the confrontation is resolved peacefully or escalates into violence.

Third, an officer must **Validate** the feelings of the suspect. Effective listening enables the officer to respond to the specific fears and concerns the suspect has expressed and to sympathize with the problem at hand. Once the problem has been put on the table and the suspect has had the opportunity to let off some steam, the suspect will become **Empowered** and **Encouraged** to cooperate and create a win-win resolution. By the time the officer has worked through this process, he or she is in a better position to evaluate and respond to the person's needs in a manner that is nonthreatening and nonconfrontational.

Some may think these mediation skills are elementary or of little importance in police work. Unfortunately, some instructors view them as so insignificant that they are not taught as part of the regular academy curriculum. Alternatively, these skills may be glossed over so much that their relevance may be overshadowed by training that instead focuses on the use of intimidation or force.

To take this concept one step further, officers must recognize that employing a cookie-cutter approach in this area is ineffective. Training must be tailored to enable officers to identify and understand better the mindset and traditions of each culture in the interest of handling confrontations and resolving problems. The goal is to give officers the requisite skills to craft an approach that will be effective for each specific set of circumstances. Particularly with respect to religious beliefs and cultural traditions, officers who arrive at a scene well educated in diversity will be armed with perhaps the most powerful weapon that will yield the greatest likelihood for success: understanding.

Diversity

It was an early Tuesday morning in a northern California city when three police officers burst into the home of a Muslim woman to arrest her on charges of child endangerment. The realization that she was being arrested for leaving her two-year-old daughter in the car momentarily while she returned library books was only half the shock. Having to endure the arrest in her bedroom by three male officers while she was clad only in a thin nightgown and underwear proved almost unbearable. As a devout Muslim, the humiliation of being seen without her traditional *hijab*, a veil worn for religious modesty, was by far more devastating than the arrest itself.

"I told them I'm Muslim," the woman cried. "I'm not dressed properly. You're not even supposed to see my hair." The officers allowed the woman to cover up after repeated protests.

Even though a few years have passed since the incident, she still has trouble shaking the experience. "This has totally affected my self-esteem," she said. "I felt they didn't respect my religious beliefs, and I had no criminal record. Why did they have to arrest me when I'm half-naked?"

Her experience is one that is played out daily as Americanized law enforcement collides with traditional beliefs within diverse U.S. cities. The influx of new cultures, languages, and religions brings with it the necessity for those in law enforcement to tailor their interactions with the public to coincide with a diverse America. Perhaps if officers had applied guidelines and conflict resolution tactics similar to that of "ISTLC" and "SAVE," they would have been better equipped to listen, identify the problem, and recognize that this was a low-profile encounter that posed little or no risk to the responding officers. Once the suspect's special needs were discovered, officers could have allowed the woman to dress appropriately before being questioned or called a female officer to the scene to handle the investigation in a less intimidating and confrontational manner.

The use of cultural information to de-escalate police encounters with the public cannot be underestimated. In light of the nation's changing demographics, the application of this information in conjunction with conflict resolution tactics would go a long way to eliminate the need for force in most police encounters. Thus, a comprehensive training program that includes hands-on interactions with different cultures within the community is one way that law enforcement can meet the challenges posed by the changing face of America.

Rather than adhering to a cookie-cutter approach throughout law enforcement, training must be specifically tailored to the needs of the community. Officers must not only learn about diversity in the classroom, but they also must actively go into the community to establish positive contacts with the public and address citizen concerns. For example, when one officer needed a Punjabi translator, he ran into a local Indian restaurant and asked the manager to interpret for him. There existed a true partnership between the police and the citizens within this community. These kinds of positive contacts will break down the distrust many of these cultures harbor toward the police. It will also serve to encourage citizens who may have avoided the police to come forward as witnesses in an effort to identify perpetrators in many unsolved crimes.

Other cities have likewise met these training and diversity challenges head on. In the northern California city of Fremont where a third of the population is Indian, Afghan, or Chinese, the police department created a 40-hour in-house panel for officers. This panel, comprised of foreign-born employees, takes time to speak with the officers about their cultures and their homelands.

Other specific programs that have been initiated include offering a 5% pay increase for officers who learn another language and establishing a program that sends local police working in a highly Asian community to visit officers in other countries such as Taiwan. In addition to these efforts, police agencies are taking part in various forms of community and cultural outreaches that give officers the opportunity to participate in cultural programs and perform volunteer work within diverse communities. In California, thousands of officers from around the state are sent to the Simon Wiesenthal Center's Museum of Tolerance in Los Angeles to learn about the Holocaust and hate crimes. Officers report that this course leaves them with valuable information that they apply in their day-to-day contacts with the public.

Though the importance of diversity training should not be underestimated, it is only a first step toward successful police and community relations. Although some organizations clearly recognize the importance of training in this area, surprisingly, many agencies overlook the use of cultural information as an important law enforcement tool.

Those closest to the issue recognize that examining the challenges posed by race solely in the context of racial profiling is far too limiting. All too often, the process of classifying an individual by his or her race is mistakenly associated with the negative form of racial profiling. When used for the purpose of *explaining* or *interpreting* another's behavior, however, this initial observation may be key to successful conflict resolution. Both science and common sense tell us that the ability for an officer to de-escalate volatile confrontations within the community or to analyze interactions in the context of cultural beliefs and traditions may be one of the most awesome crime-fighting weapons of this century.

As a first step toward this goal, officers must be taught to throw out any assumptions and stereotypes they may have about certain ethnic groups. A well-rounded training program should start in the classroom, with a significant amount of time spent exploring how individuals within a particular ethnic group handle anger and conflict. When officers feel comfortable in this new role of community outreach, training may be expanded to include learning some simple words or phrases in another language. These initial steps toward cultural understanding will help foster trust among ethnic groups who may have developed their own stereotypes about law enforcement. When officers are trained to identify and use their new understanding of cultural differences to their advantage as a way to resolve encounters on the street, the payoff can be significant.

Once the classroom portion of the training has concluded, officers can take what they have learned into the community. Officers must be encouraged to make positive contacts with minority groups; for example, they might ask community members how they can get to know residents of a certain neighborhood better. Officers might attend cultural group meetings and social events. When community members see law enforcement in these positive, social, and nonconfrontational situations and roles, they too will be able to throw away their harmful stereotypes. These positive contacts should not be limited to the adults in the neighborhood. Time spent with the community's youth is also an important investment that will pay great dividends for future generations. Officers are in a perfect position to promote a positive image by attending school functions, becoming involved in school fundraisers and sporting events, and working as mentors and role models. Work at this level may be an important deterrent to the gang affiliations, peer pressure, drug use, and violence that have become so prevalent among today's inner-city youth.

Likewise, police organizations should give the public access to their local police department, when appropriate. For example, some organizations are sponsoring open houses in which the public is invited to take tours through the police department and meet the officers and administrators that serve the community. Others are sponsoring ride-along programs and citizen police academies so that the public can experience the challenging aspects of police work and the justice system firsthand. Some have also reported positive citizen contacts through fund-raising activities, safety fairs, and car seat installations conducted in high-profile locations such as shopping malls and community centers. Agencies participating in these and similar community outreach programs report an increase in the number of their positive contacts with the public and a renewed level of cooperation within the community.

Leadership

Leadership in the context of law enforcement is not limited to those with absolute authority. Rather, leadership is a broad-based skill that must be developed within each officer from the outset. As an officer moves up the ranks, his or her role as a leader may become more visible; however, the fundamentals of leadership will not change.

Perhaps the greatest challenge of a good leader is having the courage to make unpopular decisions. Most of us would rather make decisions that leave us well liked by our peers, even though the decision may not be in the best interest of the team as a whole. Officers who come forward to report suspicious conduct by their peers must be recognized and rewarded as true leaders. Likewise, the chief of police and those in management must have the courage to bring disciplinary proceedings against any officer whose conduct does not adhere to the goals and principles of the organization. A recent study reflected the importance of this stance by leadership and noted that almost 85% of officers surveyed agreed that a police chief's strong position against abuse of authority can make a significant difference in deterring officers from abusing their authority.[3] Scholars have likewise recognized the significance a police chief's role has within an organization. "[T]he chief is the main architect of police officers' street behavior. This is so because the strength and direction of street-level police peer pressures ultimately are determined by administrative definitions of good and bad policing and by the general tone that comes down from the top."[4]

Though police chiefs and their command staff members have a substantial impact on the tone within an organization, the role of an officer's immediate supervisor is equally important. In one poll, officers themselves acknowledged overwhelmingly (almost 90%) that "good first-line supervisors can help prevent police officers from abusing their authority."

Indeed, the importance of strong leadership was underlined in an interview with Mr. Hubert Williams, president of the Police Foundation in Washington, D.C. Mr. Williams noted: "One of the most important roles of the police is to support the democratic values and ideals of this nation, not merely by enforcing laws but also through ongoing interaction with the diverse population that defines America. Written policies that are undermined at the operational level reflect weak or indifferent leadership and also suggest that an organization's culture may have more influence than its formal regulations on officers' attitudes and behavior. There is, as a consequence, great need for inspectional services supervision and monitoring to keep a chief on top of what's going on."[5]

It is important to remember that in every group, there will be those who emerge as natural leaders. Some will admirably use these leadership skills for the benefit of the group; however, there will inevitably be those who use this newfound power for personal gain. Often, training does not address the power and pitfalls inherent in leadership. It is important that leadership training not be reserved only for those who appear to show leadership potential. All officers must be trained on how to identify and strengthen leadership qualities within themselves. It's also important that those in command take an active leadership role by boosting morale and motivating officers. Command staff members that limit their involvement to making promotions and handing out assignments are missing out on the true vision of a paramilitary organization such as law enforcement.

A recent movie exemplified the traits of a true leader. In *When We Were Soldiers*, the story of one of the first significant engagements in the Vietnam War, Lt. Col. Harold Moore, played by Mel Gibson, summed up true leadership in one sentence: "I will be the first to set foot on the field [of battle], and I will be the last to step off, and I will leave no one behind."

Such a true commitment to leadership is sometimes absent among those in command. In interviews with many police officers, there is an overwhelming consensus that those in power typically prefer a "hands-off" approach and do not seek to get involved unless something goes drastically wrong. One officer from a medium-sized organization expressed the unspoken marching orders of his chief: "Make me look good. Defend me. Just fix it. Make it go away." Other officers we spoke with voiced similar sentiments and expressed the belief that the command staff has the power to improve morale within the department but sometimes opts for shifting this responsibility on to the individual. Some officers even reported frustration over their concern that fellow officers with less than stellar disciplinary records seemed more likely candidates for promotion than officers who consistently played by the rules, which sent a message that these officers' unprofessional conduct was being rewarded by those in command.

In an effort to maintain the respect and loyalty of its officers, command staff must recognize that most individuals begin a career in law enforcement with goals that are fairly simple. They want to be good police officers and be recognized for their efforts. Far too often, however, the good work is not recognized, leading to apathy and complacency. When line officers feel good about themselves and the work that they do and receive praise and recognition for their dedication, the instances of improper or illegal tactics will likely diminish. Likewise, officers will *want* to make their command staff and the organization look good by serving as proud ambassadors of the goals and values of the law enforcement profession.

In order to accomplish these objectives, efforts must be taken to bridge the growing gap between command staff and officers. Command staff must spend more time fostering relationships with its officers. For example, commanders might begin riding around in patrol cars with their officers so they can see the job the officers do firsthand. When command staff members show officers that they are willing to "step on the field of battle" with them, they will undoubtedly gain respect in the ranks. It should not be overlooked that a training curriculum that encompasses these important qualities and values may go a long way in improving the image of the police department starting from the inside out.

Ethics

On my honor
I will never betray my badge,
My integrity, my character,
Or the public trust.
I will always have
The courage to hold myself
and others accountable for our actions.

*I will always uphold the Constitution
and community I serve.*

—*Law Enforcement Oath of Honor*
as recommended by the International
Association of Chiefs of Police (IACP)

The primary duty of law enforcement is to serve the community. When ethics are compromised, officers redirect their actions toward serving themselves rather than the public. Unethical behavior is usually easy to identify. It is the headline-making misbehavior that is rooted in dishonesty, greed, and ignorance. Within the law enforcement culture, however, there seems to be a gray area that prompts some officers to go along with the program in order to get along with their peers. Analogous to the infamous title made popular by motorcycle clubs, we call this group the "1 percenters," the group that gets 99% of the press coverage. Many look upon this group as the few "bad apples" that spoil the reputation of the whole bunch.

Surprisingly, the topic of ethics is among the most deficient topics in training programs. In fact, a recent survey revealed that most departments do not conduct ethics training at all. In those departments that do, less than one third of the agencies surveyed included ethics-related categories when assessing recruits' qualifications. The survey also reported that more than a third of the agencies responding did not equip ethics instructors with planned teaching materials.[6]

With law enforcement practices coming under heightened scrutiny by the public, ethics training must become an integral part of the curriculum. Set values must be established, and supervisors must be held accountable when employees under their command deviate from these set expectations. By promoting accountability in this area, the organization will avoid setting a standard that condones or overlooks questionable practices. Those holding leadership positions must set a good example for all employees and reward those who make the right ethical choices. By offering quality training in these areas, integrity will become part of the culture, and instances of officer misconduct will be isolated and easily identified.

In addition to serving as role models for employees, those in command must show their support by participating in the organization's training program. All too often, command staff attends specialized programs designed exclusively for chiefs and commanders. Though this may be valuable, it must be balanced with participation in the department-wide training curriculum that deals with officers' day-to-day encounters on the street. Though command staff may not need this type of training in their day-to-day responsibilities per se, they should regularly sit through such programs to evaluate the quality of the information presented, the professionalism and effectiveness of the instructors, and the response of the officers attending the courses. This small step alone will help to align command staff with its officers' mental processes and aptitudes, show support for the values and goals taught, and emphasize the importance of the department's training goals.

Under the current system, ethical breaches within an organization are usually not hard to find. Even when indiscernible to supervisors, fellow officers are well aware of the unethical conduct of their peers. They know the officers who arrive late, call in sick, never leave the station, or sleep on midnights. In many organizations, this mediocrity is accepted and leads the more industrious to question why they should work so hard for the same pay and recognition. The truth is that regardless of how rigorous screening processes may be for new recruits, there will always be those who slip through the cracks. Officers may not come to police work to lie, cheat, steal, and violate the constitutional rights of others, but if the culture ignores this unethical behavior, it may evolve into the rule rather than the exception. When training programs bypass this important component of police work, officers may inevitably look to what the culture defines as ethical and may give rise to bigger problems down the road.

In order to circumvent these problems, new and veteran officers must receive ongoing training in ethics and integrity. Supervisors must raise the bar and demand high standards from all employees. The chief and upper management must reinforce the importance of ethical behavior in the execution of officers' duties. The highly ethical environment that results will serve two purposes. First, it will set goals that officers will need to achieve if they hope to be promoted or to stay on the force, and second, it will make it more difficult for officers to engage in discriminatory practices for fear that their peers will turn them in.

When officers are faced with an ethical dilemma, the following checklist should be considered:

1. Are my actions the result of anger, fear, stress, or adrenalin versus common sense and training?
2. Am I acting within the confines of the law and/or department policy?
3. If my friends and family were watching my actions, would they be proud or ashamed?
4. Will I feel good about my actions and decisions when I go home at the end of the day?
5. Would my decision be the same if I were being videotaped?
6. Would I be willing to have my friends, family, and colleagues read about my actions in the morning news?

Deficiencies in Some Training Curriculums and Their Long-Term Effects

Police academy trainers have the difficult task of teaching someone how to be a law enforcement officer in a relatively limited period of time. Unfortunately, the physical rigors of the job are assigned the most class time, as opposed to the mental challenges that are inherent in any dealings with the public. Here is a listing of some of the essential components that often are not sufficiently emphasized in police academy training programs:

- Cultural diversity training, including racism and sexism and dealing with those who may have special needs;
- Negotiation tactics, including verbal disengagement techniques;
- Psychology of effectively dealing with different cultures and personality types;
- Court respect;
- Testifying in investigations, depositions, and court;
- Consequences of perjury;
- Media and community relations;
- Morals and values including honesty and leadership;
- Corruption and gratuities;
- Code of silence education and prevention tactics;
- Abuse of force and abuse of authority;
- Work ethic and off-duty issues;
- Identifying and reporting unethical officers and behavior;
- Implementing and managing an early warning system, specifically with respect to identifying behavioral precursors to problematic behavior;
- Special projects in community policing; and
- Studies in evidence-based policing.

In addition to these frequently overlooked areas, officers and experts alike cite nonexistent or poor training programs for veteran officers as one of the key training deficiencies that leads to police misconduct. Often, the curriculum offered by police organizations is too general and merely occupies a block of time and an empty chair rather than conveying valuable information. Officers report that some programs are so elementary or watered down they do not adequately meet the needs of the officers. In many organizations, critical subject areas dealing with community demographics or specific enforcement objectives are overlooked and are replaced with a curriculum focusing on the use of weaponry or administrative tasks. Unfortunately, when developing continuing education programs, this one-size-fits-all approach is sometimes the norm.

Specific training areas for veteran officers that are generally overlooked include:

- Reiteration of police academy ethics training;
- Focus groups to discuss concerns and develop solutions specific to the community and organization;
- Teaching and leadership skills to be utilized in community policing programs;
- Updates on cutting-edge science, sociology, and technology in law enforcement;
- Advanced techniques for testifying during investigations and litigation;
- Consequences of perjury; and
- Legal updates on new case law, statutory law, and pending legislation.

Scholars are just beginning to understand the significance such specialized training curriculums can have within an organization. Though many still hold the traditional view that the most valuable lessons are learned through experience on the street rather than in the academy setting,[7] experts are now suggesting that training curriculums must evolve with the times and with the new commitments and policies held by each organization. A recent survey, for example, revealed that a majority of the officers who had received training in ethics, interpersonal skills, or cultural sensitivity believed that such training could play a role in controlling abuse of police authority. Specifically, the study reported that nearly 83% of officers who had received training in ethics either in the academy or after becoming an officer believed that the training was effective in this regard. Likewise, about 80% of those surveyed who had received training in interpersonal skills or relations believed that the training prevented this type of abuse, and 75% believed training in human diversity, cultural differences, cultural awareness, or ethnic sensitivity prevented the abuse of authority.[8]

In addition to implementing mandatory courses for veteran officers, agencies must regularly evaluate department training programs to ensure critical objectives and training needs are adequately met for every division of the force. It is advisable that frequent evaluations be conducted by an independent consulting firm or oversight committee so that department needs can be independently assessed and up-to-date research applied to develop and implement a favorable curriculum that evolves with the needs of the organization.

Implement Training Standards

Police agencies must work with state oversight committees such as Peace Officer Standards and Training (POST) to establish course standards and minimum training requirements for certain subject areas critical to law enforcement. Mandates should be set so that every officer attends a minimum amount of training annually in target subject areas including ethics, diversity, and advanced investigatory techniques as they relate to identifying potential suspects. These guidelines would be set by state oversight agencies such as POST and would be mandatory for all law enforcement organizations under its control, with any officers or administrators not meeting these guidelines pulled off the street until he or she fulfilled the training mandates.

At present, many oversight agencies provide law enforcement with limited guidelines as to the number of hours officers must attend continuing education courses. Though an officer may be required to attend a minimum amount of training annually, he or she may choose a topic that is of special personal interest in order to fulfill the requirement rather than selecting a course that would directly relate to his or her job. Often, these areas of special interest do not correlate with an officer's duties on the street. When training mandates are more structured, however, specific subject areas can be mandated for completion on an annual or biannual basis, whereas others may be elective and would educate the officers in subjects of personal interest.

SOLUTION IV: A POLICY FOR CHANGE

In light of the negative "racial profiling" publicity surfacing nationwide, law enforcement agencies have been scrambling to enact policies and procedures that send a clear message to their officers as well as to the public that racial profiling will not be tolerated in their organizations. Although many of these efforts are steps in the right direction, many of the policies and procedures enacted do not go nearly far enough. A national survey conducted by the Police Executive Research Forum (PERF)[9] indicated that in response to the high-profile events related to racial profiling, 12% of the law enforcement agencies surveyed have modified existing policies, and 19% have adopted new policies. Though most policies in place send a positive message that racial profiling will not be tolerated, few include enough details to guide the officer in his or her day-to-day enforcement practices. The result is that the officers are left to decide for themselves what constitutes racial profiling, with little or no training or guidance from either policy or practice.

When interviewed about racial profiling policies currently in place, few officers and administrators had the same interpretation of what constitutes acceptable police practices and what does not. Even within the same agencies, officers and command staff repeatedly expressed conflicting views about what would be permissible under the organization's policy. When attending a class on racial profiling, even the instructors could not seem to agree on what constituted proper police practices versus conduct that many would define as racially motivated.

Therefore, agencies must adopt policies that make the organization's position on racial profiling and biased police work clear and must provide specific guidance to the officers in their day-to-day decision-making process. Instructors in turn must truly be the experts in the field. Law enforcement personnel who are racial profiling trainers must undergo advanced courses on the subject. These courses must not only cover the fundamentals on the topic but also include the input and participation of community leaders and legal representatives with advanced training and experience in the area.

Any racial profiling policy that is implemented should contain the following minimum content elements:

1. A clear and concise statement defining racial profiling and biased policing;
2. A statement outlining the department's position on racial profiling and biased policing that reiterates that any officer or administrator engaging in either will be subject to training, discipline, or termination;
3. A brief review of the federal and state laws that make this practice illegal (i.e., Fourth Amendment, Fourteenth Amendment);
4. A guideline defining what circumstances would warrant the use of race as a factor in law enforcement practices (i.e., if a specific suspect description included race as one identification factor);
5. A provision mandating supervisors and peers to report instances of racial profiling or bias of fellow officers to ensure that peers or supervisors are not

tacitly condoning suspect practices within the organization (It should be noted here that there will be circumstances in which policy violations are deemed to be of such a serious nature that retraining would be inappropriate. The policy should maintain that any officer or supervisor who is aware of such behavior and did not report it, or alternatively, who tried to cover it up, will be subject to the same discipline and/or termination as the original perpetrator.);

6. A provision that outlines specific practices to be adopted during routine traffic stops, specifically addressing issues relating to courtesy, an explanation relating to the purpose of the stop, practices during the stop, and requests for consent to search; and

7. A mandate for annual continuing education in the areas of diversity, ethics, racial profiling, and biased policing for both line officers and administrators. These trainings should include role play, legal updates, and an opportunity for officers to volunteer time within an ethnic community in the organization's enforcement area.

Unless policies are drafted that convey the seriousness of this practice and provide specific guidelines for implementation and continuing education, officers will determine which practices are acceptable and which are not at their own risk.

SOLUTION V: COMMUNITY POLICING—FAD OR FICTION?

Community policing is often defined as a philosophy that governs how police and citizens work together to identify and address crime and disorder within their community. Whether by establishing foot and bike patrols or by organizing nighttime recreation programs and community meetings, more and more police agencies are allocating officers to community policing assignments. This trend was substantiated in a Justice Department study that reported that the number of police departments engaged in community policing nearly doubled from 1997 to 1999. Although many law enforcement agencies have initiated effective community policing programs in the past few years, other programs remain nonexistent or marginal. One of the main criticisms of some programs is the implementation of community policing as a rotational task for a few officers rather than a department-wide philosophy.

In order for community policing programs to be effective, law enforcement must involve the community in problem solving and change. When developed properly, such a program can immediately identify issues and concerns within a given locale and initiate change by creating a successful law enforcement–community partnership.

In addition to these joint intervention tactics, law enforcement must work toward becoming more visible to the public by, for example, becoming involved with schools, participating in social activities, and meeting with neighborhood groups. These efforts, along with the implementation of bike, horse, and foot patrols often work well to bring the police closer to the community. A 2000 study substantiates the importance of an effective community policing program and suggest that about 50.9% of the officers surveyed believe that community policing efforts may reduce the number of incidents involving the use of excessive force, with 41% believing that such efforts may decrease the seriousness of such incidents.[10]

When community policing programs are successful, neighborhood revitalization follows. Citizens begin to take an interest in their neighborhoods and establish a sense of pride about where they live and work. Citizens may become more self-sufficient because they know how to get things done to solve their own problems, thereby minimizing the opportunity for crime to occur. There is an instant realization even in the most troubled communities that valuable assets exist in every household upon which to build the community's future. The police and community must work together to find them.

In many cases, contacts between the police and the community remain somewhat strained and formal. In some agencies, however, law enforcement is embarking on proactive approaches to meet with community leaders on a regular basis to explore problem areas and potential solutions. In Chicago for example, the police department works closely with the public by hosting meetings where beat officers and the community engage in joint problem solving.

In addition to formal contacts between the community and the police, it is important that law enforcement not overlook extending the concept of community policing to the roadways. Since law enforcement officers make the most citizen contacts during traffic stops, this area is a fertile ground for promoting positive impressions of the police. Not surprisingly, most citizen complaints stemming from traffic stops usually involve allegations of rudeness. That is why training and role play are critical to ensure that when officers conduct vehicle stops, steps are taken to alleviate the citizen's concern that the officer may be conducting a stop motivated by bias rather than probable cause.

When an officer conducts a traffic stop, he or she must keep in mind that there are four primary reasons for the stop. First, the officer has an obligation to the public to stop ongoing violations of the law. Second, an officer who vigilantly stops traffic offenders will deter similar conduct in the future by both the individual stopped and the other would-be offenders who observe the stop. Third, if the traffic stop is a good experience for the driver, it may encourage the driver to change future driving habits to conform to traffic laws. And fourth, officers may use this citizen contact as a way of promoting a positive image for law enforcement and reinforcing the professionalism within their own department.

Even with these four motivators in mind, officers recognize that most traffic stops will have one of two outcomes. Either they will conclude with the citizen's "thank you" even in the wake of a citation, or they will escalate into a confrontation between the citizen and the officer. Regardless of the citizen's demeanor at the beginning of the stop, the quality of the officer's voice and the methods used to communicate with the driver can go a long way toward producing a successful conclusion.

It goes without saying that when dealing with the public, an officer should always be courteous and professional. Officers should begin their contact with a polite greeting such as "Good morning, sir" or "Good evening, ma'am." This often sets the tone for the entire contact. Next, the officer should introduce himself or herself to the citizen and state the name of the agency with which the officer is affiliated. Prior to asking the driver for a license and registration, the officer should state the reason for the stop. This may be helpful in those cases where the driver was not aware of the violation and immediately assumes that the reason for the stop is race based. Once the driver realizes the stop is legitimate, the officer will have a greater chance for a positive encounter than if racial profiling is suspected.

One tactic that may also diffuse hostility is the officer phrasing the violation in terms of the vehicle rather than accusing the driver. For example, "I stopped you because I saw your vehicle go through the stop sign on Elm Street without stopping" rather than "You went through a stop sign on Elm Street without stopping." If the officer still senses hostility, he or she may ask the driver politely whether there was a reason for the violation. This tactic often gives the driver a chance to vent and tell his or her side of the story. Once hostilities have been defused and there is a mutual exchange between the officer and the driver, the officer may then ask for the driver's license and registration. At this time, the officer may inform the driver about traffic citation disposition or answer any questions that the driver may have about the violation. If there is going to be a delay in issuing a ticket or checking on the driver's record, the officer should immediately explain to the driver the reason for the delay and take no longer than necessary to conclude the detention.

Once the officer issues a warning or a citation, the officer may compliment the driver on wearing a seatbelt or having a child safety seat strapped in properly. Rather than concluding the contact with a salutation such as, "Have a nice day," the officer should opt for something more appropriate, such as: "Please drive carefully. Your safety is important to us." The officer may also offer the driver advice on how best to merge back into traffic safely.

Many law enforcement organizations have already adopted specific policies and procedures for officers to adhere to during traffic stops. Others may have more general policies in place that leave the method for conducting such stops entirely to the officer's discretion. Agencies are encouraged to adopt specific policies for traffic stops and to integrate these policies into officer training, including opportunities for role play, so that traffic stops become an integral means of expanding on community policing goals.

In addition to broadening the reach of community policing to the roadways, law enforcement must encourage elected officials to become involved in the organization's community relations programs. Police agencies and community groups that hold regular meetings should invite newly elected leaders to meet with them as soon as possible so that they are aware of the problems and activities within their communities. These officials should also be invited to regular meetings in order to establish a good working relationship with the police and citizens. When these influential contacts are established early on, elected officials will be more responsive to the needs of the people and become important allies in these important partnerships.

SOLUTION VI: ACCOUNTABILITY

The lack of accountability among officers and their superiors can be very destructive to the culture of a police organization. Just as officers must be held accountable for their own actions, supervisors must take responsibility for the actions of those under their command. In the same vein, those in upper management or leadership positions must continually reinforce allegiance to the principles and values of the organization. When sworn personnel, regardless of rank, do not take responsibility for problems or incidents within the organization, the public is left to believe that moral and ethical standards within the agency are less than what is expected by society as a whole. In more extreme cases, the public may even suspect that the police consider themselves above the law.

Particularly in larger agencies, accountability becomes difficult, with officers working largely independently and supervisors overseeing a large number of individuals, some who may work conflicting shifts. In response to these challenges, many organizations opt to utilize audio or video recording devices to document police encounters with the public. Though opposed by some, these devices protect both the officer and the citizen and often serve as an important piece of evidence to exonerate an officer accused of wrongful conduct. Likewise, these tapes are used as important training tools to prevent lapses in officer safety from turning deadly in future encounters with a violent suspect.

In addition to this high-tech police oversight, many organizations are taking aggressive steps toward becoming more accountable to the public and are opting for policies designed to settle wrongs literally as they occur. For example, in instances where an officer is clearly at fault, some organizations will send a department representative out to the scene to offer the citizen an on-the-spot settlement as opposed to risking a costly lawsuit and bad publicity in the future.

Whether through high-tech devices or public relations tactics, officers and administrators must be cognizant of the link between accountability and ethics. Not only must officers remain accountable for their own behavior, but they also must play an integral role in upholding the accountability of their fellow officers. When an officer who engages in inappropriate behavior knows there is a risk of being turned in or shunned by his or her fellow officers, he or she will be less likely to engage in practices that are contrary to the standards set by the organization.

SOLUTION VII: ERADICATE THE CODE OF SILENCE

Departments are responsible to the public to cure code of silence practices within their organizations. In order to determine the existence and scope of the problem, some organizations have chosen to conduct anonymous surveys among the officers and staff, along with initiating audits of a department's internal investigation records.

This needs assessment ultimately provides leadership with a better understanding of what areas are considered the most problematic for its officers and results in goals, training, and objectives that specifically address areas considered challenging within the organization.

Once the needs assessment has been completed, all officers must take part in a comprehensive training curriculum to gain a clear understanding of what constitutes a code of silence violation. In part, this vast area of uncertainty can be simply broken down into two components: the "need to know" and the "right to know." In other words, if there is a *need* for the public to know of an officer's misconduct or if there is a *legal right* that obligates the officer to report the misconduct, it must be reported. If it is not reported, it is a code of silence violation.

Along with training and goals that are designed to identify and correct general areas of concern, internal policies must be developed that specifically address code of silence issues. In conjunction with these policies, whistleblower protection programs must be implemented to protect officers who report instances of misconduct, and employee assistance must be offered so that officers are better equipped to work through ethical choices. Some experts have suggested that police organizations implement a confidential hotline for officers to report instances of misconduct by fellow officers.

To avoid the "snowballing" of unethical conduct, intervention officers must be designated to increase the probability that someone will stop misdeeds before they escalate into serious or illegal transgressions. These officers would serve as nonsupervisory employees and would be assigned based on their ability to act as positive role models for other officers.

Even with the above systems in place, one cannot ignore the importance of fostering an overall culture that shuns the code of silence. Officers need to know that lying on the job or protecting those who engage in illegal and unethical behavior comes with serious consequences, even termination. Likewise, upper management must exhibit unwavering leadership and reinforce the premise that code of silence activities will not be tolerated within its organization.

SOLUTION VIII. OVERSIGHT BY AN INDEPENDENT POLICE AUDITOR

One of the more recent trends toward promoting accountability in law enforcement is the establishment of an independent, nonpolice city agency that is designed, in part, to provide independent review of the citizen complaint process. This form of police oversight is taking hold across the nation, with more than 100 cities initiating such programs in recent years. With several models in place, we chose to profile one highly successful program in a major California city, San José.

Since its establishment in 1993, San José's Office of the Independent Police

Auditor has been largely successful in giving the public a "watchdog" of sorts to audit the investigations of police misconduct complaints. Unlike other oversight models, the independent police auditor of San José operates on the premise of looking at the underlying cause of the complaint and making structural changes within the police organization as opposed to spending all of its time debating the merits of a particular case and using it to drive a wedge between the police and the community. This is one important distinction from other oversight programs that San José's police auditor, Teresa Guerrero-Daley, credits for its success.

From its inception, the position of independent police auditor has been held by Ms. Guerrero-Daley, a distinguished leader in the San José community. A former criminal defense attorney, private investigator, and the first female drug enforcement agent for the U.S. Department of Justice in San José, Ms. Guerrero-Daley was no stranger to the interworkings of law enforcement and the police culture when appointed to her position.

In describing her role as independent police auditor, Ms. Guerrero-Daley points to three primary functions of her office. First, the office provides an alternate location where citizens may file a complaint against the San José Police Department. Second, the office monitors and audits the investigations of citizen complaints conducted by the San José Police Department, and third, it promotes public awareness of a person's right to file a complaint against the police.

In addition to these functions, the Office of the Independent Police Auditor has been instrumental in identifying and effectuating more than 40 policy changes that have yielded positive results within the San José Police Department. Among her most significant policy recommendations has been the establishment of a review panel to examine officer-involved shootings, the designation of a medical location where blood specimens could be taken from uncooperative suspects without the use of excessive force, a mediation program to resolve complaints, and a call for new recruiting strategies designed to increase the number of female officers on the force.

In conjunction with recommending innovative changes to current policies and practices, the police auditor works closely with the San José Police Department to receive and investigate citizen complaints. The complaint system used in San José provides citizens the option of filing a misconduct complaint with the police department directly, or alternatively, at the Office of the Independent Police Auditor. Minor complaints may be resolved by a supervisor without the need for a formal investigation. Other complaints, however, must be entered into the San José Police Department's internal affairs system. This system, which is linked to the Office of the Police Auditor, ensures that any time a complaint is entered, whether by the police department or the auditor, the other is aware of it. This unique shared system enables the Office of the Police Auditor to monitor the progress of investigations once a complaint is forwarded to the Professional Standards and Conduct Unit and gives the auditor's office the opportunity to participate in the interview process of police officers and witnesses.

Once the police department has completed its investigation of a citizen complaint, the complaint is forwarded to the police auditor for review. The police auditor reviews the recommendations to determine whether the investigation was thorough and objective and to ensure that the evidence adequately supported the finding.

In addition to its success as an effective complaint auditing model, the system used in San José has multiple benefits over models used in other U.S. cities. The system is in large part a tracking program that serves as a valuable tool for anticipating potential problem areas and identifying offending officers. For example, an officer will automatically be flagged by the system if three complaints are filed against the officer within a one-year period, regardless of the outcome of the complaints. This early intervention gives the police auditor the opportunity to sit down with the officer to find out why. Although the name of the officer will be known internally as part of the early warning system, it will remain confidential to the public, as will the results of any internal investigation. This early warning system emphasizes the underlying goal that has made this program such a success: the premise of effectuating structural change rather than embarking on a witch hunt to track down offenders. The unavoidable downside inherent in such a system is that it ends up taxing the majority of the honest officers because of a few. Ms. Guerrero-Daley reports that out of the 1,400 San José Police officers, there are probably fewer than 20 who have more than three complaints per year.

When comparing this complaint tracking and early warning system to some anonymous data-collection programs in neighboring cities, it appears that this system yields a much higher success rate for identifying officers who may be engaging in biased policing or racially motivated practices. This early identification is critical, in that it gives the officer the opportunity to participate in training to correct practices or perceptions that are not consistent with quality policing. It also serves to avoid costly criminal and civil lawsuits against the department and/or the officer personally when these practices go unchecked. In other words, this system is much more effective as a long-term solution than a quick fix that may yield little or no lasting change within the organization.

More important, this auditing system instills the power of change in the public, which has the ability to pick up the phone and lodge a complaint that will be fairly and independently audited. Whenever a pattern or practice of inappropriate conduct is identified, it will be investigated. Cities that integrate similar independent oversight offices will significantly minimize the distrust the public has in systems that rely on data that are self-reported and anonymous to everyone.

One of the key components that has made this system effective are the efforts of the police auditor to ensure that all complaints are documented, regardless of how minor they are. In a recent Justice Department report, San José was reported to have received about 500 complaints per year. Ms. Guerrero-Daley notes that the underreporting of complaints is a common problem in many departments, mainly because few organizations have an effective system to document all of the contacts.

When members of the public feel that their complaints have not been documented or addressed, they are dissuaded from coming back to report problems in the future. This system is unique in that it is designed to ensure every complaint is entered in the central database that tracks allegations of police misconduct.

Even with this sophisticated system in place, it remains difficult to substantiate many citizen complaints and sometimes leaves the public with the misperception that the police department is not willing to discipline officers. The police auditor is quick to point out, however, that the outcome of the complaints represents an inability to prove whether the misconduct happened rather than the police agency's unwillingness to discipline and/or terminate offending officers.

Several factors make it difficult to substantiate misconduct allegations. One of the main challenges is that the offending officer rarely ever breaks down during the investigation to admit that he or she has acted inappropriately. In rare instances when more serious allegations surface, for example, one in which an officer was burglarizing homes, the officer is a criminal. This scenario is made even more dangerous by the fact that the offender is often a sophisticated, intelligent individual, usually working alone with total control over the environment. Many times, there are no objective, third-party witnesses to the offense, thus making it one person's word against another's. These officers choose the location and know the system, and this makes them difficult to identify and apprehend without the public's tips and intervention.

Once a complaint is lodged, the auditor classifies it into different categories depending on the allegations. In an effort to maximize the effectiveness of tracking racial profiling complaints, the auditor has switched to a more powerful means of categorizing data. One of the challenges has been categorizing cases in which a citizen had a subjective feeling that they were being stopped because of race ("You stopped me because I'm black") versus a situation in which there was a clear case of discrimination (an officer tells a citizen, "Why don't you go back to Mexico?"). With the new system, there will be a place to track any allegation of racial profiling, whether or not the allegation is corroborated by objective evidence of wrongdoing.

Despite its long-term success, this independent oversight agency has contended with numerous challenges from the outset. Upon its establishment in 1993, the office met with instant controversy, primarily among community groups who wanted a different model (mainly a civilian review board) and among the police who wanted no oversight at all. Ms. Guerrero-Daley began her tenure under a threat by San José's then-police chief to resign and under a wave of dissatisfaction voiced by community leaders and civil rights groups alike. As a further roadblock, these challenges came at a time when there were very few auditor models, many of which were unsuccessful. Regardless of the dissention, the counsel decided to give the model a try to see whether it would work. Despite the initial upheaval, 70% of San José's voters said "Yes" three years later when asked whether they wanted to have the office become permanent. The result has been a highly successful brand of oversight designed to provide an independent review of complaints against the San José Police Department. It remains an important vehicle for promoting public awareness of the citizen complaint process within San José's diverse community. As further testimony to its success, San José's unique program continues to be used as a model for other cities across the nation that are striving to increase police accountability. It has served as a reminder to any city considering implementation of a similar model that an overwhelming buy-in by the police and the public may be unlikely until the system is on its feet and success can be readily measured.

Several years later, there is still progress to be made. Perhaps the biggest challenge is letting the public know that the Office exists. Even with its small staff, the Office is committed to canvassing every neighborhood and business association making itself known. The Office has established more than 40 referral sites within the community so various social agencies can serve as a first contact with the public and ultimately refer citizens to the Office. The staff is diligent in attending community fairs and meetings and making public announcements. Brochures are available at every library and fire station as well as at the public defender's office, the jail, and the police department. Regardless of these aggressive marketing efforts, surveys indicate that 80% of the people in the community still do not know the agency exists.

Even with these challenges, Ms. Guerrero-Daley remains committed to working with the police department and the community to investigate and document citizen complaints properly. Throughout our interview, it became clear that she is highly committed to making a difference as opposed to taking an adversarial stance with the police department. She tries to identify organizations she knows are very vocal and makes sure that she meets with them and learns everything she can about this relatively new business of police oversight. Organizations she once considered adversaries are now allies that she turns to for support. She also works closely with a citizen's advisory committee comprised of a diverse sampling of the community so that she can encourage the inflow of information and feedback to her office and let those in the community know who she is and what the office does. Her dedication is a testament to any city implementing a similar model and proof that independent auditors can expect to travel an often bumpy road before a successful system is in place and making a difference.

Communities considering the establishment of an independent police oversight office should be cautioned that it may be a political "hot potato" of sorts. Inevitably, the police see this type of intervention as adversarial and generally resist efforts to have their work scrutinized. The lack of anonymity for officers is one factor that is highly unpopular with police unions. It is important that in light of these challenges, police auditors come to the position with realistic expectations so that the union between law enforcement and independent auditor can evolve into a true partnership. Ms. Guerrero-Daley's positive approach has been one factor in overcoming the initial resistance by the police. "I sincerely believe that a vast majority of the officers at the San José Police Department want to do a good job," she said. "They don't set out when they begin their shift to look at who they are going to mistreat. The reality of the job is that they're facing a lot of the worst in people. Circumstances are such that physical force is necessary. So that it's a constant monitoring to make sure that this awesome power, an authority that we as citizens vest in police, is kept in tact." While acknowledging that there is always more work to be done, Ms. Guerrero-Daley describes her relationship with the San José Police as more of a "healthy tension" that serves as a baseline for positive change.

SOLUTION IX: JUDICIAL OVERSIGHT COMMITTEE

One of the most common remedies for those who feel they have been wronged is a lawsuit against the offending agency. Though lawsuits are one avenue of attack, they do come with some downsides: they are expensive efforts that require significant resources, and they require the cooperation of a plaintiff willing to commit to a long-term and sometimes arduous legal process.

When litigation becomes inevitable, however, so does the involvement of outside parties including attorneys, judges, mediators, and experts. Law enforcement agencies must work in cooperation with these individuals and seek notification whenever a court or prosecutor believes an officer has engaged in misconduct in the course of either criminal or civil investigations or proceedings.

In addition to appropriate remedies directed at the offending officer, changes within the organization must be implemented. In civil cases where the court or court officers suspect a pattern and practice of civil rights violations or perjury, the offending officer should be turned over to an independent oversight committee at the conclusion of the litigation for further investigation. The committee should offer recommendations aimed at minimizing the possibility of future violations. When such violations are proven in a criminal case, fundamental changes within the organization should be mandated by the court, including the development of programs to detect similar conduct in the future and the establishment of mandates for officer training. When remedies that mirror those contained in consent decrees are implemented to coincide with monetary awards in civil litigation, agencies may be forced to address the larger problem rather than merely writing a check to make the problem go away.

Whatever the solution, there seems to be one common thread that suggests that to adjudicate these complaints effectively and fairly, a case-by-case analysis is necessary to determine whether accusations of civil rights violations are limited to a single incident or represent a larger problem within an organization. When those most familiar with the accused examine cases on a regular basis, repeat offenders can be identified, and changes can be recommended so that the organization can avoid similar violations in the future.

SOLUTION X: NATIONAL OVERSIGHT COMMITTEE

In order to set standards promoting ethics and integrity in law enforcement, a national ethics oversight committee must be established. This committee, which would be comprised of law enforcement leadership, government representatives, civil rights advocates, and the general public, would work to ensure that high standards in law enforcement are set forth and adhered to nationwide. More specifically, the committee would develop leadership strategies and early warning systems designed to identify employees who are not conforming to established standards.

These leadership strategies and ethical standards would be shared with law enforcement agencies through printed material, forums, and a national Web site. Law enforcement agencies would be given opportunities to test new and innovative law enforcement practices under the supervision of the oversight committee. This would enable agencies to explore the feasibility and success of new programs that could be implanted nationwide and also provide a mutual forum to share experiences through networks with other agencies. Agencies may be offered federal grants for participating in these experimental programs.

National involvement must no longer be withheld until an organization is facing major federal investigations. The government must offer law enforcement grants to develop technology, software, training, and reporting programs. This proactive approach would develop positive interactions between the Department of Justice and individual law enforcement agencies and foster cooperation to achieve common goals.

Whether implemented individually or as a comprehensive program, we believe these solutions would yield positive results for law enforcement organizations, regardless of size. More important, they would be carefully designed with the concerns and goals expressed by law enforcement, civil rights groups, and the public at the forefront. Whether these solutions are implemented from within the organization or with the assistance of an outside consultant, we recommend that the public be included in tailoring any approach to address the specific needs of the community adequately, as it is the public that will ultimately judge any program's success. Likewise, these programs must be implemented as works in progress and must enable organizations to reevaluate their success regularly and make changes so that programs reflect shifts in demographics and remain current, fresh, and relevant.

SOLUTIONS: PART B

SOLUTION XI: IMPLEMENTATION OF EARLY WARNING SYSTEMS AND INTERDEPARTMENTAL AUDITS

Early Warning Systems

The implementation of early warning systems as a means to respond to the problem police officer has grown in popularity over the years. More recently, such systems have been expanded to identify officers who may be engaging in racial profiling. It was estimated that in 1999, about 39% of all municipal and county law enforcement agencies serving populations greater than 50,000 either had an early warning system in place or had plans to implement one.[11] It is projected that the implementation of early warning systems in the law enforcement profession will increase rapidly in the coming years. This emerging trend is consistent with recommendations made by the U.S. Commission on Civil Rights as far back as 1981 and emphasizes the need for police departments to create early warning systems to identify officers "who are frequently the subject of complaints or who demonstrate identifiable patterns of inappropriate behavior."[12]

The use of early warning systems as a preventative measure to identify officers who may be engaging in racial profiling or other police misconduct cannot be underestimated. Though less than 10% of an agency's officers may be engaging in such practices, they often account for 90% of an organization's problems. Even the media recognizes departments in which as few as 2% of the officers are responsible for 50% of the citizen complaints lodged by the agency.[13] Without an effective way to identify and track the performance of officers who engage in inappropriate conduct, agencies miss a key opportunity to provide intervention and training before errant behavior escalates into actions that require formal disciplinary action.

Despite growing popularity, little has been written about the use of such systems as a management tool, particularly with respect to racial profiling. One of the most comprehensive studies addressing early warning systems as they relate to the problem police officer was published in July 2001 by the National Institute of Justice. In this study, the authors divided early warning systems into three basic phases: selection, intervention, and post-intervention monitoring. Though the study only briefly mentions the use of such systems to detect officers engaging in racial profiling, we propose that several early warning indicators be identified and expanded to identify officers who may be engaging in any form of racially biased policing. When such behavior is identified, command staff can intervene with relevant training or other appropriate intervention strategies.

The Selection Phase

The first component, the selection phase, sets forth guidelines for identifying which officers should be considered for inclusion in the early warning system. Citizen complaints, firearm discharge and use of force reports, civil suits alleging officer misconduct, resisting arrest incidents, high-speed pursuits, and vehicular damage are all factors that should be considered at this juncture. Other reports have suggested that an even more comprehensive list of performance indicators be implemented to alert an organization to problematic behavior, including search and seizure practices, reprimands, suspensions, promotions, citizen commendations, criminal charges against officers, training history, civilian arrests, on-duty preventable traffic accidents, traffic violations, traffic stops, use of sick leave, and any other misconduct or disciplinary allegations.

Despite this broad range of potential indicators, some agencies rely exclusively on citizen complaints. Among systems that use citizen complaints to select officers for intervention, 76% require three complaints in a given time frame (usually 12 months).[14] Though such a simplistic system may be better than nothing in smaller organizations with limited resources, experts caution that it would be ineffective to look exclusively at one or two indicators to predict future behavior or engage in risk assessment. Likewise, a system that relies exclusively on computer tracking may not be as effective in changing behavior since inappropriate conduct usually becomes habitual by the time it is flagged by the system. Instead, any system must factor in a wide range of variables and implement firewalls that are both computer based and human driven to predict accurately which officers might benefit from intervention and training.

In addition to the above indicators, we suggest that additional variables be researched and developed for inclusion in an early warning system. One model we found looked especially promising, though it related exclusively to personality indicators developed by police psychologists studying officers who were referred to them because of their use of excessive force.[15] Despite its limited application, we believe that similar behavior indicators may be useful in detecting officers who are engaged in racially biased policing, particularly when the use of excessive force is directed at minorities. Surprisingly, the study's findings revealed five distinct personality profiles of officers who used excessive force, only one of which supported the long held "bad apple" theory.

The first category of "at risk" officers is those coming into the profession with personality disorders. These personality disorders may be difficult to detect in pre-employment screening and will generally manifest over time in behavior or tendencies that are antisocial, narcissistic, paranoid, or abusive. Likewise, these officers will have difficultly accepting responsibility for their behavior or learning from experience, thereby leading to repeated citizen complaints and/or disciplinary action. These tendencies eventually lead to problems with judgment and personal interactions, particularly in instances where the officer's authority is challenged. Over time, the nature of police work may intensify these characteristics. Though these officers are the smallest part of the high-risk group, they are often perceived as the "bad apples," or the sole source of problems within an organization.

The second group comprises officers whose previous job experience places them at risk. These officers have often accumulated a substantial amount of "emotional baggage" from previous on-the-job incidents and are teetering on the brink of burnout. Some become isolated from their fellow officers. Often because they feel the need to conceal these feelings, these officers' emotions build, eventually manifesting in the form of one or more excessive force incidents. With an effective early warning system in place, these officers are usually amenable to early intervention via training and psychological debriefings initiated soon after stressful incidents. When early intervention is coupled with appropriate follow-up, the tendency for these officers to engage in future incidents of excessive force may be substantially minimized.

The third at-risk group includes those who exhibit problems at early stages in their police career. Experts describe these officers as "hotdogs," "badge happy," "macho," or generally immature. They are usually highly impressionable, quite impulsive, and have a low tolerance for frustration. Absent structured training and supervision by strong role models at the early stages of their careers, these officers run a high risk of conforming to negative aspects that may be present in the police culture. If such character traits are identified and addressed early on, however, these officers are likely to outgrow these tendencies and follow the positive examples of role models within the organization.

The fourth at-risk group comprises officers who develop inappropriate patrol styles. These individuals are usually sensitive to challenge and provocation, evidenced by their dominant command presence and heavy-handed policing style. They often hold rigid opinions about how police work should be conducted, sometimes using force to show that they are in charge. This group generally involves veteran officers or "dinosaurs" of the profession, who have little tolerance for new and innovative styles of policing, particularly those styles that promote accountability to the community. Often, these officers are part of special units with little supervision that operate under the erroneous belief that the command staff sanctions their behavior. Unlike other risk groups that would likely benefit from psychological intervention and counseling, experts believe that this group may be more responsive to peer or situation-based interventions that make the officer a part of the solution as opposed to part of the problem.

The last group consists of officers with personal problems, including problems at home as well as those that may be work related. Though most officers in this category do not use excessive force, the few who do may suffer from a lack of confidence, making it more challenging for them to deal with fear, animosity, and volatile enforcement situations. Because this behavior pattern usually develops over time, these officers may be one of the groups most readily identifiable by an early warning system. Supervisors who are trained to detect problematic behavior early on may be integral in preventing the behavior from escalating in the future. Key "red flags" will often include conduct that is erratic, signaling that the officer may lose control in a future confrontation. When individual counseling is implemented as an early intervention tactic, however, these officers may be in a better position to balance the challenges of their personal life with their expectations on the street.

Perhaps the most important part of any early intervention system is the ability for supervisors and command staff to identify personality traits, behavior characteristics, and other factors that may be precursors for problem behavior in an officer. When psychology plays an integral role in this equation, organizations may be in a better position to develop early warning criteria to identify officers who may be more prone to engage in civil rights violations and biased policing.

The Intervention Phase

Unlike the first phase that serves to select officers who may benefit for inclusion in an early warning system, the second phase aims to achieve the primary goal of any early warning system: to change the conduct of officers who have been identified as exhibiting unfavorable patterns of behavior. Experts recommend that this phase consist of both education and deterrence. In the education phase, the officer is offered training to provide the necessary tools to improve performance. When combined with deterrence, officers are not only empowered to change their past performance but also deterred from engaging in similar acts in the future for fear that they will face the threat of punishment. Though the deterrence phase is largely directed at officers who have been selected for participation in the early warning system, the far-reaching effect is also apparent in officers within the organization who have not been selected.

Components of the intervention phase tend to vary from one organization to another. In the report published by the National Institute of Justice, 62% of agencies surveyed reported the intervention stage as consisting of a review by the officer's immediate supervisor. Nearly half of the agencies responding indicated that other command officers participated in counseling the officer. About 45% of respondents indicated that their intervention systems included a training class for groups of officers who were selected for participation in the early warning program.

The final phase, that of monitoring the officer's subsequent performance, was an integral component in nearly all (90%) of the agencies that reported having an early warning system in place. Though most agencies limit the scope of this phase to informal monitoring by an officer's immediate supervisor, some have implemented more formal procedures, including observation, evaluation, and reporting. While the length of time most agencies continue to monitor an officer's performance may vary, nearly half do so for 36 months after the initial intervention. Others choose to monitor the officers continually or decide how long to monitor an officer on a case-by-case basis.

Though data assessing the effectiveness of early warning systems is somewhat limited, most indicators seem to project that such programs have a dramatic effect on reducing citizen complaints and improving performance indicators of officers who were selected to participate in the intervention process. In Minneapolis, the number of citizen complaints lodged against officers one year after participating in the intervention program dropped 67%. In New Orleans, that number dropped by 62% in the same time frame. In Miami-Dade, only 4% of the early warning officers had zero use of force reports prior to the intervention. Following the intervention 50% had zero use of force reports.[16]

In addition to the effect these early warning systems had on the officers directly involved, the study similarly found that the system had a significant impact on both supervisors and other officers within the department. In addition to the inclusion of supervisors as an important intervention component, supervisors were likewise reminded of their important role of closely monitoring officers who were identified by the system. Experts suggest that such involvement mandates and encourages "changes in supervisor behavior that could potentially affect the standards of supervision of all officers, not just those subject to early intervention. Furthermore, the system's database can give supervisors relevant information about officers newly assigned to them and about whom they know very little."[17]

In addition to the specific benefits for participant officers and their supervisors, experts theorize that early warning systems have a significant effect on the entire police organization. Not only do they deter errant behavior, but they also promote a positive atmosphere and a sense of accountability among officers and command staff alike. The expectation is that over time, these systems will become a more integral component in efforts to expand the level of service and accountability within the police profession. Such efforts are also seen as consistent with community-based policing goals.

Despite their obvious benefits, some have expressed concern that the compilation of such databases may produce a wealth of information for prosecutors or plaintiff's attorneys to subpoena in order to prove patterns of officer misconduct. Although this is certainly a possibility, the general consensus among legal experts is that this information may be more productively used to shield organizations from charges of negligent hiring and retention or allegations of complacency toward officer misconduct.

Before implementing an early warning program, experts caution that for a system to be effective, a considerable financial and resource commitment is necessary. In larger organizations, early warning systems often consist of sophisticated data systems as well as multiple full-time staff members assigned exclusively to enter and analyze data.

In addition to these commitments, organizations must look at such systems realistically. They will not necessarily be the ultimate solution in repairing what is badly broken; rather, they will build on the values that are already inherent within the culture of the organization.

Interdepartmental Audits

Whether or not an agency employs a comprehensive early warning system, minimum steps can be taken to identify those who may be engaging in a pattern of inappropriate conduct. It is important for any agency to perform regular and random audits, including an inspection of arrest records, detentions, enforcement actions, and radio logs. These steps will help those in command to ensure that contacts with the public are consistent with departmental policy and more important, the law and the Constitution. Though analysis and audit of such data may be performed as a part of the early warning process, it may also be accomplished independently in agencies that are not yet ready to implement such an in-depth system. These audits should be conducted under the supervision of a legal liaison who may be more adept at recognizing conduct or policies and procedures that may pose legal challenges in the future.

For the audit process to be complete, the cooperation of both the court and legal system should be encouraged. The district attorneys and judges that frequently review officers' work will, in some cases, be able to identify those officers working outside the confines of the law, both in investigations and legal proceedings.

SOLUTION XII: ACCREDITATION

The accreditation movement in this country is not new and is not limited to law enforcement. With origins that reach back to 1787, the trend began when the New York State Regents were trying to determine whether colleges in New York State met certain minimum standards.

In short, accrediting an organization is one way of ensuring that it conforms to a given body of standards within a profession. Although rooted in the education system, accreditation has begun to take hold in other sectors, as well. In the past few decades, this practice has expanded to hospitals, criminal justice agencies, and other institutions that demand accountability to the public. Unlike other professions that may have mandatory accreditation processes regulated by legislation, accreditation in law enforcement is currently limited to a voluntary, privatized process.

Recognizing the need to hold law enforcement to a higher standard, the Commission on Accreditation for Law Enforcement Agencies, Inc., was formed in 1979 as a nonprofit organization by the International Association of Chiefs of Police, the National Sheriff's Association, the National Organization of Black Law Enforcement Executives, and the Police Executive Research Forum. On the basis of several years of nationwide research, these agencies developed the *Standards for Law Enforcement Agencies*. The current publication comprises more than 400 standards that are designed, in part, to increase law enforcement agencies' ability to prevent and control crime, increase the effectiveness and efficiency of law enforcement services, and increase citizen and employee confidence in the goals, policies, and practices of a given agency. The standards address nine major law enforcement areas:

1. Role, responsibilities, and relationships with other agencies;
2. Organization, management, and administration;
3. Personnel structure;
4. Personnel process;
5. Operations;
6. Operational support;
7. Traffic operations;
8. Prisoner and court-related activities; and
9. Auxiliary and technical services.

In addition to the focus on these enforcement areas, this voluntary process raises the bar for organizations and provides benefits that strengthen crime prevention and control capabilities, control liability insurance costs, establish greater accountability for supervisory personnel, and boost support from the community and governmental officials. Moreover, the process enables state and local law enforcement agencies to demonstrate that their agency voluntarily adheres to an established set of professional standards.

The accreditation process is divided into six phases: application, self-assessment, on-site assessment, commission review, maintaining compliance, and reaccreditation.

The first phase, the application process, involves purchasing an application package. Once the agency turns in the application, the Commission will review the materials and make a preliminary determination as to the agency's eligibility to participate in the program. If eligible, the Executive Director will sign an accreditation agreement, which includes an agency profile questionnaire. The agency will then have 36 months to complete its self-assessment.

The second phase, the self-assessment, is based in part on information derived from the agency profile questionnaire. This questionnaire will trigger the delivery of the necessary materials for the accreditation manager to use in the agency's self-assessment. This process involves a thorough examination by the agency to determine whether it complies with the applicable standards.

Once the second phase is complete, the on-site assessment phase begins. The Commission selects an independent team of assessors to visit the agency. During the visit, these representatives review and verify the agency's compliance with set standards in a nonadversarial setting. The Assessors provide the agency with verbal feedback on its progress during and at the conclusion of the assessment and ultimately give the agency a written report on the findings. If there are any unresolved issues, the agency may return to the self-assessment phase, appeal the decision, or withdraw its application. After all standards have been met, a Commission review and hearing is scheduled.

At the Commission Review and Decision Phase, the final reports are reviewed, and testimony is heard from agency personnel, assessors, staff, and perhaps others. If the Commission is satisfied that the agency has met all the compliance requirements, the agency is awarded accredited status for a three-year period.

Once an agency becomes accredited, it must continue to maintain high standards pursuant to predetermined guidelines. The post-accreditation phase involves maintaining compliance and initiating the process of reaccreditation after the three-year term. The agency must submit annual reports to the Commission that evidence its continued compliance with the standards and submit information relating to any changes or difficulties experienced during the year. The Commission may opt to schedule interim hearings to consider issues of noncompliance. At the three-year mark, the agency will be given the opportunity to repeat the accreditation process in order to maintain its status as an accredited agency.

The benefits of voluntary accreditation cannot be underemphasized. It is important for every organization to have some benchmark by which to measure its performance within a profession. When an organization voluntarily embarks on this process, the result is a win-win situation for the agency and the community. When an agency willingly commits resources to undertake an in-depth review of every aspect of the organization including management, operations, and administration, potential shortfalls can be identified before they surface in either litigation or a federal investigation. Likewise, employees will recognize the commitment by the organization and remain confident that the standards imposed are fair and equitable.

Undoubtedly, accreditation is a progressive step in law enforcement. The agencies that have successfully attained accredited status boast substantial rewards, including the ability to upgrade their level of service through innovative information distributed by the commission relating to exemplary policies, procedures, and projects.

Even though voluntary accreditation among law enforcement agencies is on the rise, some propose that this process become mandatory nationwide. With such a system in place, experts project that corruption and unethical conduct within the profession would be substantially reduced.

SOLUTION XIII:
SCIENCE: A NEW WEAPON FOR LAW ENFORCEMENT

"Most of us have thought of the statistician's work as that of measuring and predicting...but few of us have thought it the statistician's duty to try to bring about changes in the things that he [or she] measures."

—W. Edwards Deming

Science may very well be one of the most valuable weapons law enforcement has to date. Surprisingly, however, it is one that remains the least used among police organizations. More specifically, the science and psychology of police work is one of the most underanalyzed and seldom-trained areas in law enforcement. Frequently, academy training focuses on the physical rigors of the job and the tactics for using force. Studies are emerging, however, that suggest it may be more important for police officers to have a keen sense and understanding of their own mental strengths and shortcomings as well as those of the citizens they encounter.

Unlike in other professions, no amount of training will adequately prepare police officers for the way in which the job will change their lives. Seeing the worst of the world on a daily basis will impact their views and their personal relationships like nothing else they will ever experience. New officers are given a daunting task from day one. They must enforce the law and, to some degree, act as psychologists in the process. This is not to suggest that after giving someone a ticket, the officer should pull out his or her notepad and inquisitively ask, "Now how does that ticket make you feel?" Studies have shown, however, that an officer's *approach* to a citizen encounter may play a key role in the outcome and often has a residual effect on the citizen and the officer.

"It was over so quickly, and the state trooper was so polite, I almost didn't resent what happened.

What had happened was that while driving from New York to Boston several years ago I was "racially profiled"—that is, stopped because I fit a law enforcement agency's 'profile' of a likely drug courier: a young black man driving a rented car. Or rather, the state trooper who stopped me thought I was young.

He had asked for my license and gone to his car; then, returning quickly and handing my license back to me, had crouched down by my door and explained:

'I'm sorry for the stop. We're on the lookout for people who're ferrying drugs from New York to Boston. So, we're looking for young black men driving rented cars with New York plates.'

Then, noting with some amazement that I was not 20-something, but in my early 40s, he added, 'You're much older than you look.' He wished me safe travel and then took off. A minor incident, you say? Absolutely. And painless too."

—Recount by Lee Daniels
Editorial Director, National Urban League

Studies have shown that the style and tone an officer brings to a citizen encounter can play a significant role in the ultimate outcome. When we speak of "outcome," we do not limit its interpretation to the immediate, measurable results of a particular stop. In fact, research suggests that an offender's response to police action varies by individual, neighborhood, and locale. These studies have led some to believe that a combination of timing, demeanor, and approach could have long-term, measurable implications for repeat violence and could potentially revolutionize the way police work is approached.

Despite its potential for success, one of the variables inherent in the profession that may make such psychological tactics challenging to implement is the unchecked discretion granted to the police. There are instances where officers do not comply with training directives or procedures when faced with an encounter on the street. Data seem to support this contention and suggest that officer compliance with mandatory arrest guidelines is poor after they are adopted.[18]

Regardless of its critics, one cannot ignore the findings of one of the most comprehensive studies documenting the potential for such an approach. The study, conducted in the Milwaukee Domestic Violence Experiment,[19] measured how variations in police practices affect the rate of repeat domestic violence offenses against the same victims and offered valuable information that could potentially be applied to all aspects of police work. More specifically, the Milwaukee study illustrated how specific components of an arrest may have a significant effect on the long-term outcome for an offender. Some remarkable differences surfaced when the following considerations were tested and analyzed: whether the defendant was treated with courtesy; whether the suspect was allowed to tell his or her version of the story; whether the suspect was handcuffed; and whether any of this occurred in front of friends, family members, or neighbors. One of the key findings revealed that out of 800 arrested offenders, those who felt they were not treated in a *procedurally* fair and polite manner by the police were 60% more likely to commit a reported act of domestic violence in the future. In summary, the data from this study revealed varying police practices often had negative, long-term implications for suspects and victims.

This theory, as it may apply to racial profiling, seemed to be consistent with opinions expressed in an interview with Teresa Guerrero-Daley, the independent police auditor for the city of San José.[20] Ms. Guerrero-Daley indicated that as police auditor, she is in a unique position to hear the different experiences people in the community relay to her pertaining to their treatment by police. She has found that for the vast majority of the people complaining of negative encounters with police, it isn't the fact that they were stopped but rather how the police treated them during the encounter. People are generally understanding when they believe they are being detained for safety or other legitimate reasons. Most can accept that the police need to be able to stop and detain citizens when the circumstances warrant. But when stories surface alleging that a citizen was just walking home and an officer initiated a stop, threw the person on the ground, cuffed the person, conducted a search, threw the person in the back of a patrol car, and then just let the person go, citizens are scared to death.

When the victim is asked how he or she would feel about the incident if he or she knew that a woman had just been raped or someone had just been killed, and the person who recorded the incident reported that the perpetrator looked just like him or her, the response immediately changed. Almost all were understanding. The problem is not always the stop itself but the lack of dignity and respect following the initial contact and a lack of communication between the officer and the citizen. Ms. Guerrero-Daley considers this a more significant factor than the actual stop and reports that she "would like to see more emphasis placed on what happens when the stop is made."

Ms. Guerrero-Daley's theory is one that has been discussed and tested among focus groups across the nation. One such focus group, facilitated by the Police Executives Research Forum in Washington, D.C., addressed citizens who had been detained because presumably, they resembled a suspect the police were looking for. The participants in the study were angered by the encounter and explained that if only the officer had communicated the circumstances to them or apologized for the inconvenience, they would have felt differently. Likewise, experts feel that offering an explanation for the stop and apologizing for any inconvenience caused has a substantial effect on minimizing the negative impacts these encounters have on the community and supports the theory that a little respect goes a long way.

In addition to the demeanor of the officer during the stop, Ms. Guerrero-Daley points to other favorable practices she has observed. In one city, when officers stop a person who they believe fits the description of a wanted suspect, and aside from this similarity, there is no probable cause, no reasonable suspicion, and no wrongdoing, the officer will advise the person to come over to the patrol car to listen to the dispatcher or to look at the computer screen to see that someone who fit his or her description was in fact reported. The result is that the citizen does not feel he or she just singled out because of skin color or some other arbitrary classification but rather that the officer had some objective criteria for pulling the person over.

This observation appears to further support the contention that the quality of the contact makes more of a difference to the person being stopped than the stop itself. Ms. Guerrero-Daley indicates that in the past couple of years, her office has been paying much closer attention to the communication and interpersonal skills that are expected of officers. She specifically looks to officers who have been on the force 20 or 30 years without a complaint. "They're doing the same job as everybody else," she said. "They're not getting complaints. There's a skill, a quality about those individuals and how they are able to interact with the public."

Despite support for this new approach to law enforcement, officers do not want to see the public led to believe that all calls should be handled in a generic, cookie-cutter fashion. Even the inexperienced officer will tell you that although police practices remain constant, a perpetrator's response to a detention or arrest may vary by offender and neighborhood. But if all these variables are studied using a scientific, statistical approach, trends can be analyzed and policies implemented to produce an optimum outcome when warranted by the individual circumstances.

In addition to studies by oversight agencies, the National Institute of Justice (NIJ) has further clarified how police departments can reduce the number of repeat misdemeanor domestic violence offenses, a theory that may well be examined in the context of other law enforcement interactions with the public. Rather than implementing a one-size-fits-all policy, experts agree that evidence should be analyzed and used to develop specific guidelines to be used by officers in appropriate conditions. Some interesting statistics lend credence to this argument:

- Offenders who are absent when police arrive (as they are in about 40% of cases) respond more effectively to arrest warrants than offenders who are arrested on the scene.[21]
- Offenders who are employed are deterred by arrest, while those who are unemployed generally exhibit an increase in offenses if they are arrested rather than handled in some other manner.[22]
- Offenders who live in urban areas of concentrated poverty commit more repeat offenses if they are arrested than if they are not, while offenders who live in more affluent areas commit fewer repeat offenses if they are arrested.[23]

Though these statistics are limited to domestic violence offenses, their implications are a virtually uncharted area of law enforcement. One cannot ignore the possibility that further investigation may reveal similar patterns in other enforcement areas, including traffic stops and the treatment of certain minority groups by the police. In light of statistics revealing that more than half of all officer line-of-duty deaths were related to traffic incidents, the possibility of utilizing such research in this regard should not be overlooked.

In addition to the specific studies related to domestic violence offenses, more general studies of this phenomenon may point to similar results. For example, a study released by the nonpartisan San Francisco–based Public Policy Institute of California revealed that minority groups are less likely to comply with law enforcement because of perceived unfairness in how they are treated.[24] The telephone study, conducted between November 1997 and July 1998, asked 1,650 blacks, whites, and Latinos in Oakland and Los Angeles to describe their recent dealings with legal authorities. These dealings included 911 calls for help, stops by police officers, and court dealings, both criminal and civil. Although all three groups had similar notions of what constituted fair treatment, most defined it as unbiased, respectful, and concerned behavior. On the basis of this definition, the resulting numbers revealed that 56% of Latinos and 61% of blacks felt they were treated fairly, compared with 72% of whites that categorized their treatment as fair. Likewise, the study found that Latinos and blacks were less willing to comply with authorities than whites. Authors of the study pointed to psychologically based reasons for the reports of unfairness and concluded that these perceptions and preconceptions of unfairness were directly correlated to these groups' compliance. They also referenced similar studies that show "that minorities receive less favorable outcomes from legal institutions than whites, including longer sentences and a higher likelihood of being questioned, arrested, and convicted." Though some may argue that this information does not provide enough evidence to connect minorities' perception of fair treatment to their compliance to law enforcement, one cannot ignore the possibility that this brand of science may play a significant future role in developing department guidelines and training programs for new recruits.

Scientific studies examining the relationship between the police and the public are far from new to law enforcement. In fact, as far back as the 1970s, the Police Foundation in Washington, D.C., published an evaluation of New Jersey's "Safe and Clean Neighborhoods Program" that was designed to improve the quality of life in 28 cities. One component of this new policy involved the implementation of a foot patrol as a way of cutting crime. Police chiefs were skeptical of the program at the outset. It would slow down response time to calls for service, they argued, and would probably not lead to any reduction in crime. Additional complaints came from police officers, who resented the potential hard work and long hours out in the cold and rain. Given all the negative commentary, it was no surprise that the foot patrol project had not reduced crime rates in large cities such as Newark, New Jersey, according to an evaluation published five years after the project began.

What did come out of the study, however, was a measurable difference in the number of citizens who had a favorable opinion of the police compared with those living in areas that did not have such a program. Moreover, residents in these neighborhoods *believed* that crime had been reduced and reported feeling safer than others similarly situated.

One might ask the burning question, was this foot patrol program ultimately deemed a "success"? The answer depends on how you look at it. Perhaps an unexpected result of the study was that the measure of success was not defined by the actual impact the program had on crime statistics. Officers who participated in walking their beats reported higher morale, greater job satisfaction, and most important, a more favorable attitude toward citizens in their neighborhoods than did the officers assigned to patrol cars.

Foot patrol officers may not have succeeded in reducing the crime rate in these areas, but citizens felt safer from confrontations with drug dealers, panhandlers, prostitutes, and the mentally disturbed. Though most of these individuals did not pose an immediate threat to the citizens in the community, they contributed to the "fear" among the residents that prevented them from going out at night or leaving their doors unlocked. Even though the neighborhoods were mainly black and the foot patrol officers were primarily white, the officers were able to establish an acceptable level of order within these communities.

Interestingly, the "rules of order" enforced by the officers could not be found in any penal code or city ordinance, but were largely defined, instead, in collaboration with the regulars on the street. For example: "Drunks and addicts could sit on the stoops, but could not lie down. People could drink on side streets, but not at the main intersection. Bottles had to be in paper bags. Talking to, bothering, or begging from people waiting at the bus stop was strictly forbidden. If a dispute erupted between a businessperson and customers, the businessperson was assumed to be right, especially if the customers were strangers. If strangers loitered, [the officer] would ask them whether they had any means of support and what their business was; if they gave unsatisfactory answers, they were sent on their way. Persons who broke the informal rules, especially those who bothered people waiting at bus stops, were arrested for vagrancy. Noisy teenagers were told to keep quiet."[25] If "strangers" or other "regulars" violated one of the rules of order, they were immediately called to the officer's attention or ridiculed by other regulars. In this unlikely collaboration, officers were no longer in a position just to drive through a community with an "us-versus-them" mentality.

Albeit for a short while, these officers became an integral part of the communities they worked in. Their presence was felt not only by those who lived there but also by those who traveled through the area to and from work, school, or play. More important, in the context of race, the community appeared to gain a new respect for working with the police. Rather than being outsiders, these officers became an integral part of the community, if only for a short while.

Though not specifically addressing the problem of racial profiling, this study serves as an important example of how coordination between the basic principles of science and police work may lead to effective solutions to the underlying problems associated with divisions between minorities and the police.

After reviewing the commentary on this study, two analogies came to mind. First, those who have been victims of racial profiling often complain about random stops of innocent people in high-crime areas, allegedly prompted by a suspect's skin color. Second, experts seem to suggest that a lack of education in diversity and cultural awareness is one deficiency that contributes to an officer's discriminatory practices.

Applying the results of the foot patrol study to the problem at hand, one could theorize that application of a similar program may work to mend the relationship between the police and the public. First, foot patrols may foster officers' familiarity with citizens on a certain beat and help them distinguish between the "regulars" and the "strangers." Armed with this information, officers would be keen to activities in their foot patrol area, and this would make them more adept at distinguishing suspicious behavior from the normal "order" in the community. Moreover, an officer's opportunity to work with different cultures firsthand is a more effective training tool than any skills training delivered in a classroom setting. This form of cultural immersion would not permit an officer the luxury of hiding in a police car to patrol the neighborhood through a glass window. Rather, such a program would force officers to initiate important contacts with business leaders, youth, and average citizens in the community and give both sides the chance to combat their fears of one another.

These few examples exploring the potential uses of science to develop more effective police practices will not unequivocally solve the problems surrounding racial profiling. But many of these theories hold promise for the development of new standards for tracking officer performance and agency-wide accountability that are *outcome* based rather than *output* based. New research suggests that listening to a suspect's side of the story prior to making arrest decisions and treating suspects with common courtesy *do* make a difference in most cases. Similar studies will undoubtedly educate police organizations to the importance of establishing and implementing scientifically based standards for determining how calls should be handled and how policies should be drafted. These studies will also provide valuable, measurable feedback that will tell police organizations what works and what doesn't. It is the hope that with deliberate, fact-based systems in place, officers will possess the tools to interact effectively with potential suspects or witnesses without having to resort to race-based or biased stereotyping.

SOLUTION XIV: REPAIR BROKEN WINDOWS

Both social psychologists and those in law enforcement tend to agree that crime and disorder are generally linked. When conducting studies based on a premise some experts refer to as the "broken window theory," a recurring trend emerged. Real-life observations have shown that when a window in a building is broken and *stays* broken, there is a high likelihood that other windows in the building will soon be broken as well. This is true whether the building is in a nice neighborhood or one that is already rundown. Experts point to the message a broken window sends to the community: no one cares, so breaking more windows costs nothing.[26]

In 1969, Philip Zimbardo, a Stanford psychologist, tested the broken window theory. His studies, conducted in Palo Alto, California, and the Bronx, New York, centered on the fate of an automobile without license plates parked on a city street with its hood up. Within 10 minutes, the car in the Bronx was attacked by vandals.

Surprisingly, the first to arrive at the "abandoned" car was a father, mother, and son who took the radiator and battery. Within 24 hours, the car had been virtually stripped of anything valuable and, shortly thereafter, subjected to random destruction and vandalism. Needless to say, most of the adults who vandalized the car were well-dressed, clean-cut whites. In contrast, the car in Palo Alto remained untouched for nearly a week. Zimbardo himself went back to the car and proceeded to smash part of it with a sledgehammer. Soon, passersby were contributing to the destruction. Within a few hours, the car was turned upside down and virtually destroyed. Again, the culprits were primarily "respectable whites."

Although many hypotheses have been developed about the cause of this phenomenon, experts suggest that in a community with a history of no one caring, vandalism begins much more quickly than it does in a community in which there is some accountability and crime does not typically run rampant. Experts suggest: "Unintended behavior also leads to the breakdown of community controls. A stable neighborhood of families who care for their homes, mind each other's children, and confidently frown on unwanted intruders can change, in a few years or even a few months, to an inhospitable and frightening jungle. A piece of property is abandoned, weeds grow up, a window is smashed. Adults stop scolding rowdy children; the children, emboldened, become more rowdy. Families move out, unattached adults move in..." The end result is that "serious street crime flourishes in areas that disorderly conduct goes unchecked."[27]

When a neighborhood is weakened to this extent, even the police are afraid to venture out to fight crime. All too often, problems are addressed through the crack of a patrol car window rather than through one-on-one contacts, which further erodes police-citizen relations. When police fear people in the community while responding to calls in neighborhoods that its own residents view as "hopeless," rights may be violated, and policies and procedures sometimes go out the window, particularly when the citizens are minorities. As Nathan Glazer wrote, "The proliferation of graffiti, even when not obscene, confronts the subway rider with the inescapable knowledge that the environment he must endure for an hour or more a day is uncontrolled and uncontrollable, and that anyone can invade it to do whatever damage and mischief the mind suggests."

To foster cooperation among police and the community, individuals on both sides must take personal ownership and realize that the solution lies in the heart of each and every person. Rather than base victimization on individual losses, law enforcement must train its officers to look to the losses of the community as a whole. Instead of taking an approach that merely treats the individual "illness," police agencies must employ preventative measures to maintain order and work with citizens to reclaim those communities with "broken windows."

Undoubtedly, the solutions presented in Part B represent a more aggressive approach for law enforcement reform and involve a commitment of dollars and other resources. Though law enforcement as an institution has traditionally resisted structural and organizational change, agencies that have been more proactive in serving the public report mostly positive results. It is recommended that any organizations considering the types of changes suggested in Part B consult with agencies and administrators who have implemented similar programs to understand fully the challenges and the commitments up front. In many cases, it is helpful to work with an independent consultant and/or liaison who can be instrumental in creating and delivering effective programs that represent the needs and desires of the community.

(Endnotes)

1. Martin Niemoeller was a Protestant pastor born January 14, 1892 in Lippstadt, Westphalia. He was a submarine commander in World War I. He was anti-communist and initially supported the Nazis until the church was made subordinate to state authority.

2. Quote of Tom Frazier by Acting Associate Attorney General Daniel Marcus. Prosecution Conference, June 1, 2000.

3. Weisburd, David, Rosann Greenspan with Edwin E. Hamilton, Hubert Williams, and Kellie A. Bryant, *National Institute of Justice Research in Brief*, May, 2000 at 6. "The Police Foundation's nationally representative telephone survey of 925 randomly selected American police officers from 121 departments explores the officers' views on the abuse of police authority. Officers also provided information on different forms of abuse they have observed, the frequency of abuse in their departments, and effective strategies for controlling abuse. General findings, as well as differing attitudes of black, white, and other minority officers, are presented and discussed in this Brief."

4. Skolnick, Jerome H., and James J. Fyfe, "Above the Law: Police and the Excessive Use of Force," at 136, (1993) The Free Press, New York, NY; see also Skolnick, Jerome H., and David H. Bayley, "The New Blue Line: Police Innovation in Six American Cities," (1986), The Free Press, New York, NY.

5. Interview with author, December 11, 2000.

6. Report published by the International Association of Chiefs of Police (IACP) entitled "Ethics Training in Law Enforcement;" see http://www.theiacp.org/publicinfo/pubs/ethictrain.htm.

7. Bayley, David H., and Egon Bittner, "Learning the Skills of Policing," *Law and Society Review* 30(3)(1984): 586-606.

8. Weisburd, David, Rosann Greenspan with Edwin E. Hamilton, Hubert Williams and Kellie A. Bryant, *National Institute of Justice Research in Brief*, May, 2000 at 6-7. "The Police Foundation's nationally representative telephone survey of 925 randomly selected American police officers from 121 departments explores the officers' views on

the abuse of police authority. Officers also provided information on different forms of abuse they have observed, the frequency of abuse in their departments, and effective strategies for controlling abuse. General findings, as well as differing attitudes of black, white, and other minority officers, are presented and discussed in this Brief."

9. Fridell, Lorie, Robert Lunney, Drew Diamond and Bruce Kubu with Michael Scott and Colleen Laing, "Racially Biased Policing: A Principled Response," (2001) Police Executive Research Forum, Washington, D.C. 20036.

10. Weisburd, David, Rosann Greenspan with Edwin E. Hamilton, Hubert Williams and Kellie A. Bryant, *National Institute of Justice Research in Brief*, May, 2000 at 7-8. "The Police Foundation's nationally representative telephone survey of 925 randomly selected American police officers from 121 departments explores the officers' views on the abuse of police authority. Officers also provided information on different forms of abuse they have observed, the frequency of abuse in their departments, and effective strategies for controlling abuse. General findings, as well as differing attitudes of black, white, and other minority officers, are presented and discussed in this Brief."

11. Walker, Samuel, Geoffrey P. Alpert, and Dennis J. Kenney, "Early Warning Systems: Responding to the Problem Police Officer," (July, 2001) National Institute of Justice.

12. "Who is Guarding the Guardians?" Washington, DC: U.S. Commission on Civil Rights, 1981: 81.

13. "Kansas City Police Go After Their 'Bad Boys,'" *New York Times*, September 10, 1991; and "Waves of Abuse Laid to a Few Officers," *Boston Globe*, October 4, 1992.

14. Walker, Samuel, Geoffrey P. Alpert, and Dennis J. Kenney, "Early Warning Systems: Responding to the Problem Police Officer," (July, 2001) National Institute of Justice.

15. Scrivner, Ellen M., Ph.D., "Controlling Police Use of Excessive Force: The Role of the Police Psychologist," (October, 1994) National Criminal Justice Reference Service (NCJRS).

16. Walker, Samuel, Geoffrey P. Alpert, and Dennis J. Kenney, "Early Warning Systems: Responding to the Problem Police Officer," (July, 2001) National Institute of Justice.

17. Walker, Samuel, Geoffrey P. Alpert, and Dennis J. Kenney, "Early Warning Systems: Responding to the Problem Police Officer," (July, 2001) National Institute of Justice.

18. Ferraro, Kathleen J., "Policing woman battering," (1989) *Social Problems* 36: 61-74.

19. Pasternoster, Ray, Bobby Brame, Ronet Bachman, and Lawrence W. Sherman, "Do fair procedures matter? Procedural justice in the Milwaukee Domestic Violence Experiment" (1977) *Law and Society Review*.

20. Interview with authors, March 27, 2002.

21. Dunford, Franklyn, "System-initiated warrants for suspects of misdemeanor domestic assault: A pilot study." (1990) *Justice Quarterly* 7: 631-53.

22. Pate, Anthony M. and Edwin E. Hamilton, "Formal and informal deterrents to domestic violence: The Dade County Spouse Assault Experiment" (1992) *American Sociological Review* 57: 691-98.; Berk, Richard A., Alec Campbell, Ruth Klap, and Bruce Western, "The deterrent effect of arrest in incidents of domestic violence: a Bayesian analysis of four field experiments." (1992) *American Sociological Review* 57: 698-708.; Sherman, Lawrence W., and Douglas A. Smith, "Crime, punishment and stake in conformity: Legal and informal control of domestic violence." (1992) *American Sociological Review* 57.

23. Marciniak, Elizabeth, "Community policing of domestic violence: Neighborhood differences in the effect of arrest." (1994) Ph.D. diss., University of Maryland.

24. Particulars of the study reported by Seyfer, Jessie, *The Times*, July 10, 2000 at B6.

25. Wilson, James Q., and George L. Kelling, "Broken Windows," (1982) *The Atlantic Online*.

26. Wilson, James Q., and George L. Kelling, "Broken Windows," (1982) *The Atlantic Online*.

27. Wilson, James Q., and George L. Kelling, "Broken Windows," (1982) *The Atlantic Online*.

CHAPTER FOURTEEN

Reflections

Look at every path closely and deliberately. Try it as many times as you think necessary. Then ask yourself and yourself alone one question. This question is one that only a very old man asks. My benefactor told me about it once when I was young and my blood was too vigorous for me to understand it. Now I do understand it. I will tell you what it is: Does this path have a heart? If it does, the path is good. If it doesn't, it is of no use.

—Carlos Castenada[1]

There will always be a blurred line between appropriate law enforcement practices and encounters motivated by racial bigotry and bias that makes it nearly impossible for the police to enforce laws effectively without occasionally intruding on individual freedoms. Society tolerates and often welcomes this invasion against those who have committed a crime, but we find it offensive and even intolerable when perpetrated against the innocent. Even the court recognizes that absent empirical studies providing guidance on the inferences for suspicious behavior, law enforcement cannot reasonably be expected to act with scientific certainty when stopping individuals they suspect are engaged in criminal activity. Thus, the reasonable suspicion determination must be based on common sense judgments and inferences about human behavior.[2] Such inferences are largely a product of the individual's mind and are influenced by stereotypes, personal experiences, and fear. When the resulting decision to detain is based on these often erroneous or tainted deductions, it becomes difficult to determine an officer's primary motivation in a given circumstance; is it good police work or racial prejudice? The stark reality is that innocent people will be detained even when an officer has the purest of motives. Errors are bound to occur. Just as one should not be suspected or detained because of race or skin color, neither should one be excluded as a potential suspect because of an officer's fear that a contact might be incorrectly construed as racially motivated.

These considerations are just a few of the major obstacles that must be overcome in the crusade to end racially motivated profiling and biased policing. Both sides must rise to the challenge of finding effective ways to deal with individual human frailties, fears, and racial bigotry while keeping at the forefront the goal of promoting effective law enforcement through investigatory contacts. History has demonstrated to date that society has been unable, through moral or legal means, to regulate individual prejudices and opinions. Outward responses and actions, on the other hand, can generally be contained and channeled through education, training, positive reinforcement, and selective hiring practices. Racial intolerance is a product of one's most inner thought process that cannot easily be changed and may be difficult to overcome in the mind of the individual. Ironically, it is the great diversity that our free society takes pride in that is the very source of so many of its challenges.

We as a society seek to protect the very essence of diversity and equality—the freedom to be different as guaranteed to us in the Constitution. We cannot doubt the fact that when the drafters began with the words "We the People," they meant each and every one of us. We all must take responsibility for ensuring that the spirit of the Constitution is upheld. "We the People" must become personally involved in our neighborhoods, schools, and government. As a basic principle of humanity, we must stand up for fellow Americans who are enduring unfair treatment because tomorrow, it may be us.

As American citizens, we must stop living under the premise that money can solve any problem. Rather than moving out of decaying cities, prosperous Americans must stay and fight for their neighborhoods. Small steps such as mowing lawns, removing graffiti, and repairing dilapidated houses can go a long way to drive out crime and improve the morale of those who live there. When public schools fail, we must get involved as opposed to sending our children to private schools. Time is our most valuable asset to invest, and it pays great dividends in future generations. When the justice system breaks down, we must come together to build it up again. A justice system that is truly color blind will be a world-class model that clearly demonstrates a democracy. Above all, when we look around at the rainbow that is America, we must let the promise of equality bring us closer together rather than draw us further apart.

Instead of each group taking sides and fortifying positions to the extreme, open dialog and compromise must be used to bridge the gap. Society does not benefit when only one side prevails. Each extreme is equally deficient: unlawful racial profiling on one hand and rampant criminality on the other.

The responsibility to ensure a fair and successful resolution falls on the shoulders of four distinct groups: the judicial system, the legislature, the police, and society itself. Each side has made recommendations that may not ultimately solve this complicated problem; however, the discussions they promote will be a key first step in bringing this issue to the forefront. There may be some initial failures, but these failures will give rise to great successes in the long term. The common theme must be mutual recognition that the crime problem cannot be solved through racial injustice.

The steps we take from this point on will be significant. In order to develop a viable solution that will prevent racially motivated profiling and pretext stops, we must recognize that as fast as solutions can be developed, dynamics of the problem are rapidly changing. The population's racial demographics continue to fluctuate, as does the racial composition of law enforcement. Law enforcement agencies around the country are encouraging minority candidates to apply for law enforcement positions so that agencies can hire officers that better represent a cross section of the communities they serve. Likewise, officers are encouraged to build one-on-one relationships with the people in the community through the practice of community policing. These challenges should not be borne completely by law enforcement. The community must become involved in these processes by reaching out to their local law enforcement to ensure that its voice is heard and that its members are represented.

Above all, we must remember that this country was built on the premise that all individuals are unique. America promotes immigration and celebrates diversity among its cultures while promising freedom and equality to each of us. Justice will be served only when all individuals, regardless of the color of their skin, the shape of their face, or the form of their spoken word, can be viewed as equally innocent. It is only when these challenges are met that the perception of inequality may end with equality.

From this moment forward, we all have important choices to make. We can choose to do nothing and accept the status quo, or we can forge ahead together to build a better place for ourselves and our children. To achieve a unified effort, all parts must be strong and supportive of the others. We must work together to fortify our own part yet be prepared to stand up for others when we see injustice occurring. Change is often a slow process and may lead us into unexpected and uncertain lands. Regardless of these detours, we cannot afford to give up or lose sight of our final destination. We may not always agree with each other on our journey, but that is okay. We must stay together and keep forging ahead. Though it may be possible to subcategorize each other by race, we must remember that 100% of us belong to the human race. We are all in this life together, and our interdependence will unite us. Our skin may be lighter or darker than another's and our words may not be the same, but that is the beauty of America.

(Endnotes)

1. Castenada, Carlos, inspired by his study of Don Juan Matus, a Mexican Yaqui Indian sorcerer. See http://www.cde.ca.gov/iasa/diversity.html for further discussion.

2. *Illinois v. Wardlow*, 120 S.Ct. 670 (2000).

APPENDIX

———·•·———

Resources

This section is designed as a reference for those who wish to obtain additional resources on racial profiling and police practices. Though we have attempted to list most of the mainstream organizations whose resources we used in our research, this list is by no means all inclusive. There are hundreds of civil rights and law enforcement organizations around the country actively involved in the fight to end racial profiling.

American Civil Liberties Union (ACLU)
125 Broad Street, 18th Floor
New York, NY 10004
212-549-2500
www.aclu.org

Amnesty International USA (National Headquarters)
322 Eighth Avenue
New York, NY 10001
212-807-8400
www.Amnesty-USA.org

Anti-Defamation League
823 United Nations Plaza
New York, NY 10017
www.adl.org

Center for Constitutional Rights
666 Broadway, 7th Floor
New York, NY 10012
212-614-6464
www.ccr-ny.org

Citizens Opposing Profiled Police Stops (COPPS)
757-624-6620
www.copps.org

The Commission on Accreditation for Law Enforcement Agencies, Inc. (CALEA)
10306 Eaton Place, Suite 100
Fairfax, VA 22030-2215
800-368-3757
www.calea.org

Federal Bureau of Investigation (FBI)
J. Edgar Hoover Building
935 Pennsylvania Avenue, NW
Washington, D.C. 20535-0001
202-324-3000
www.fbi.gov

Human Rights Watch
350 Fifth Avenue, 34th Floor
New York, NY 10118-3299
212-290-4700
www.hrw.org

International Association of Chiefs of Police (IACP)
515 North Washington Street
Alexandria, VA 22314
703-836-6767
www.theiacp.org

International Union of Police Associations (IUPA)
1421 Prince Street, Suite 400
Alexandria, VA 22314
703-549-7473
www.iupa.org

NAACP National Office
4805 Mount Hope Drive
Baltimore, MD 21215
410-358-8900
www.naacp.org

National Association for Civilian Oversight of Law Enforcement (NACOLE)
P.O. Box 19261
Denver, CO 80219
www.nacole.org

National Black Police Association (NBPA)
3251 Mt. Pleasant Street N.W., Second Floor
Washington, D.C. 20010-2103
202-986-2070
www.blackpolice.org

National Organization of Black Law Enforcement Executives (NOBLE)
4609 Pinecrest Office Park Drive, Suite F
Alexandria, VA 23312
703-658-1529
www.noblenatl.org

The National Urban League, Inc.
120 Wall Street
New York, NY 10005
212-558-5300
www.nul.org

Police Executive Research Forum (PERF)
2300 M Street, N.W.
Washington, D.C. 20037
202-466-7820
http://policeforum.mn-8.net

Police Foundation
1201 Connecticut Avenue, NW
Washington, D.C. 20036-2636
202-833-1460
www.policefoundation.org

U.S. Department of Justice
950 Pennsylvania Avenue, NW
Washington, D.C. 20530-0001
www.usdoj.gov

INDEX

—•—